"*Disbanding the Patriarchy: Sex, Policy and Power* provides a vital antidote to the regressive power of the patriarchy, super-rich and social media companies. Founded on solid research, this work is a ray of light offering practical tools for justice and equality".

Gillian Triggs, *international human rights lawyer, former United Nations Assistant Secretary-General*

Disbanding the Patriarchy

Disbanding the Patriarchy: Sex, Policy and Power presents evidence from Australia, Europe, India, the UK, and the USA, revealing the calculated efforts to impede progress, dictated by oligarchs, the media, religious dogmas, and androcentric leaders. Patriarchal forces are deliberately accelerating the regression of equality. The decline of democracy and human rights threaten health services, political frameworks, financial stability, and education systems.

Celebrating the remarkable triumphs of activists, feminists, and advocates, their strength, courage, and perseverance exemplifies how united successes are possible. The four feminist waves, along with the current tsunami, are recognised as powerful demonstrations of collective voices disrupting corruption and exposing the reality that wealth does not equate to intelligence or capacity.

Incorporating academic research, personal experiences, and a practical toolkit in every chapter, this book presents a comprehensive assessment of both contemporary and prescriptive norms that suppress autonomy, marginalise the majority, and distort reality. Readers will gain a critical, evidence-based understanding of the barriers to equality, alongside practical strategies to disband phallocentric principles and influence the implementation of sustainable, meaningful social reforms. Proportionate representation, reinforced by inclusive leadership, has been proven to deliver financial prosperity, effective governance, and social advancement, presenting a compelling case for disbanding unacceptable power structures in the pursuit of a fairer and more balanced world.

For those who wear one or many hats – feminists, policymakers, educators, caregivers, researchers, advocates, activists, journalists, students, academics, lawyers, jurists, healthcare professionals, executives, entrepreneurs, artists, NGOs, and politicians – note the United Nations calculates that at the current rate, achieving legal parity could take another 286 years. This alarming reality serves as a call to action, reminding the reader that transformative positive developments are within reach. Neutralising regression demands deliberate, sustained, and collective efforts to transform suppression into equal justice – one decisive action at a time.

Yolanda K Vega is a researcher, author, lecturer, artist, speaker, and advocate with a passion for the dynamics of sex and power imbalances and leadership. Her dynamic career has integrated journalism, entrepreneurship, policy, and research with a persevering commitment to championing justice. Vega has played a pivotal role in advancing policies and works to inspire others to take part in redesigning egalitarian systems. Vega's expertise includes international women's rights law, international affairs, diversity, equity, and inclusion. More information at: www.yolandavega.com

Disbanding the Patriarchy

Sex, Policy, and Power

Yolanda K Vega

Routledge
Taylor & Francis Group
LONDON AND NEW YORK

Designed cover image: *Power in Numbers*, by Yolanda K Vega (acrylic on canvas)

First published 2026
by Routledge
4 Park Square, Milton Park, Abingdon, Oxon OX14 4RN

and by Routledge
605 Third Avenue, New York, NY 10158

Routledge is an imprint of the Taylor & Francis Group, an informa business

British Library Cataloguing-in-Publication Data
A catalogue record for this book is available from the British Library

ISBN: 978-1-032-85040-5 (hbk)
ISBN: 978-1-032-85039-9 (pbk)
ISBN: 978-1-003-51622-4 (ebk)

DOI: 10.4324/9781003516224

Typeset in Galliard
by SPi Technologies India Pvt Ltd (Straive)

This book is dedicated to the XXs in every nation who have undertaken research to reveal truths, generously shared their time and wisdom, and shown extraordinary courage in advancing human rights and equality. It is also dedicated to those at the start of or yet to embark on their feminist journey – may you find inspiration to rise with conviction, let your voice thunder against oppression, and let your courage rattle the cages of the *status quo* as you strike at the heart of inequality.

Contents

Preface

The patriarchy consists of individuals with gynophobic tendencies, power and/or authority who intentionally marginalise, subjugate, ostracise, ignore, or devalue those with XX chromosomes.

Patriarchs control systems and structures that permeate daily life, impacting cultural norms, economic policies, education, governance, healthcare, religion, and technology. They dictate beliefs, values, wages, and laws while controlling curricula and resource distribution, further entrenching disparities.

Governments further reinforce these structures through legislation and judicial authority, while healthcare systems and religious institutions uphold androcentric biases. Meanwhile, technology – dominated by oligarchs and algorithms – amplify phallocentric narratives, embedding discrimination into digital spaces, language, and information.

The sources referenced throughout include white and grey literature: white literature is employed to provide a high standard of reliability and integrity, including scientific, scholarly research, routinely published in peer-reviewed academic journals and books. Grey literature includes reports and studies produced by organisations, both not-for-profits and businesses, traditionally not subjected to formal peer reviews. There are some marginal differences when analysing and comparing white and grey texts; the similarities and differences are presented accordingly.

The progress achieved by XXs from the 1900s to 2025 across Australia, the European Union (EU), India, the United Kingdom (UK), and the United States of America (USA) reveals their determination, perseverance, and bravery in advocating for equal rights.

Achievements include confronting, resisting, and defying patriarchal hierarchies within religious institutions, traditional media, online platforms, health, and educational institutions; expanding economic and political participation; and driving reforms in national and international laws.

The seed for this book was subconsciously sown during my time working as an executive, supporting and advocating for XX entrepreneurs, and propelled when representing my adopted country on the international stage. Researching International Women's Rights Law (IWRLs) for my PhD thesis, the irritation and frustration erupted. The thesis findings further exacerbated my exasperation and disbelief at how, in the 21st century, discrimination persists under androcentric dominance with human rights regressing globally with authoritarian leaders taking the reins.

At the start of each chapter, a *Personal Note* is included, sharing experiences relevant to each topic. Cheap therapy perhaps, but also to reveal that the studies by thousands of researchers from around the world are not just about numbers and theories, but about the universal realities lived by many.

Extraordinary, notable, and at times monumental achievements have been made by XXs, especially when considering the numerous barriers preventing progress. Together, XXs have proven they are the leaders of positive change. The fourth wave with a tsunami of voices confirming that change is imperative.

Actions are required to stop the re-emerging phallocentric norms and values that are gaining impetus and eroding freedoms and inclusivity around the world, with the potential for catastrophic and irreversible damage to all animals and Mother Earth. A fair and sustainable future is possible, irrespective of chromosomes, class, race, nationality, ability, age, socioeconomic status, gender, or sex.

The cover artwork is an acrylic on canvas I painted a few decades ago – also great therapy – which seeks to illustrate that there is power in numbers and the many hats XXs wear. At the end of each chapter, a toolkit with practical, non-strenuous recommended actions are included to assist in disbanding the patriarchy, along with a quote from a celebrated XX leader to uplift and inspire.

Remember, great successes begin as an impossibility!

Author's Note on Language

Language has the power to teach, influence, inspire, and manipulate, redefining emotions, attitudes, methods, and narratives across society, religion, the media, and the law. Words wield immense power – capable of generating discrimination or igniting empathy and understanding. Vocabulary remains one of the most formidable tools for transformation.

"Sex" and "gender" are terms often interchanged and misapplied in health, education, the economy, political, legal, and cultural narratives as being the same; however, they are different and distinct.

Sex is determined principally by chromosomes, sexual reproductive organs, and various other biological and sexual characteristics.

Gender encompasses a diverse range of elements relating to social constructs that incorporate an individual's actions, self-perceptions, identity, outward presentation, and sexual preferences, which can incite intersectional forms of discrimination.

While the systemic biases rooted in biological sex and the nuanced realities of gender are acknowledged, this book is too little to explore the vast complexities of gender. Therefore, the human chromosome identification is employed: women are referred to as XX and men as XY.

The text covering Violence Against Women (VAW) excludes the word "victim", except when referencing the proper names of reports or citing another author. Instead, "survivor" is used to honour the enduring courage of those who have faced abusive aggression, cruelty, and brutality.

When reporting currencies, the original amount is included alongside approximate converted equivalents in Australian dollars (AU$) and US dollars (US$), based on average exchange rates.

Countries are referred to as nations or member states, depending on the context. For example, UN member states and various nations within the European Union (EU).

Abbreviations

ABC	Australian Broadcasting Corporation
ABS	Australian Bureau of Statistics
ACCI	Australian Chamber of Commerce and Industry
AITC	All India Trinamool Congress
AI	Artificial Intelligence
AIED	Artificial Intelligence in Education
AIHW	Australian Institute of Health and Welfare
AHRC	Australian Human Rights Commission
AU$	Australin Dollars (currency)
AWAVA	Australian Women Against Violence Alliance
AWCCI	Australian Women Chamber of Commerce and Industry
BBC	British Broadcasting Corporation
CAWP	Center for American Women and Politics
CAT	Convention Against Torture and Other Cruel, Inhuman or Degrading Treatment or Punishment
CEDAW	Convention on the Elimination of All Forms of Discrimination Against Women
C	Century
CEO	Chief Executive Officer
CHM	Chinese Herbal Medicine
COE	Council of Europe
CSPL	Committee on Standards in Public Life
CSW	Commission on the Status of Women
CRC	Convention on the Rights of the Child
DAW	Division for the Advancement of Women
DEI	Diversity, Equity, and Inclusion
DFAT	Department of Foreign Affairs and Trade (Australia)
DPMC	Department of Prime Minister and Cabinet (Australia)
DV	Domestic Violence
ECA	Europe and Central Asia
FFP	Feminist Foreign Policy
GDP	Gross Domestic Product
GLI	Gender Legislative Index

GST	Goods and Services Tax
HEEP	Health, Education, Economic, and Political
HRT	Hormone Replacement Therapy
IC	Istanbul Convention
ICC	International Criminal Court
ICCPR	International Covenant on Civil and Political Rights
ICJ	International Court of Justice
ICT	Information and Communication Technology
ILO	International Labour Organization
IMF	International Monetary Fund
INSTRAW	International Research and Training Institute for the Advancement of Women
IPU	Inter-Parliamentary Union
IPV	Intimate Partner Violence
ISC	Independent Schools Council
IT	Information Technology
IWD	International Women's Day
IWPR	Institute for Women's Policy Research
IWRL	International Women's Rights Law
ITS	Intelligent Tutoring Systems
KPI	Key Performance Indicators
LGBTQIA+	Lesbian, gay, bisexual, transgender, queer, intersex, asexual, and plus
LVMH	Louis Vuitton Moët Hennessy
MFW	Mad Fucking Witches
ML	Machine Learning
MP	Member of Parliament
NAA	National Archives of Australia
NHS	National Health Service in the UK
NGOs	Non-Governmental Organisations
NOW	National Organization for Women (USA)
NWHS	National Women's Health Strategy
NZ	New Zealand
OCP	Oral Contraceptive Pill
OECD	Organisation for Economic Co-operation and Development
OSAGI	Office of the Special Adviser on Gender Issues and Advancement of Women
PIAFs	Political International Advocacy Forums
PM	Prime Minister
PRC	Pew Research Center
PTSD	Post-Traumatic Stress Disorder
RBG	Ruth Bader Ginsburg
ROI	Return on Investment
RSV	Respiratory Syncytial Virus
SDA	Sex Discrimination Act (Australia)

SDGs	Sustainable Development Goals
SEWA	Self-Employed Women's Association (India)
SMCs	Social Media Companies
SME	Small and Medium-sized Enterprises
SNSs	Social Networking Sites
SNDT	Shreemati Nathibai Damodar Thackersey (Women's University, India)
STEM	Science, Technology, Engineering, and Mathematics
TDV	Teacher-Directed Violence
The EU	The European Union (27 countries)
The UK	The United Kingdom
The USA	The United States of America
UDHR	Universal Declaration of Human Rights
UN	United Nations
UN Women	United Nations Entity for Gender Equality and the Empowerment of Women
UNESCO	United Nations Educational, Scientific and Cultural Organization
UNICEF	United Nations Children's Fund
UNIFEM	United Nations Development Fund for Women
UNODC	United Nations Office on Drugs and Crime
UNSC	United Nations Security Council
USAID	United States Agency for International Development
US$	United States Dollars (currency)
VAT	Value Added Tax (UK)
VAW	Violence Against Women
VAWA	Violence Against Women Act (USA)
VAWIP	Violence Against Women in Parliaments
VIP	Very Important Person
WEF	The World Economic Forum
WES	Women's Economic Summit
WGEA	Workplace Gender Equality Agency (Australia)
WHO	World Health Organization
WINGOs	Women's International Non-Governmental Organisations
WPR	World Population Review
WPS	Women, Peace and Security
www	World Wide Web

Introduction

This little book celebrates the many achievements initiated by XXs and reviews past and present discriminatory practices in Australia, the EU, India, the UK, and the USA. Each chapter stands alone but, when read in sequence, the text flows from examining who holds the majority of power to the origins of when XXs were first labelled the weaker sex.

Chromosomal differences are reviewed, along with the immoral prophets, the media, oligarchs, political powerbrokers, and organisations advocating for equal rights.

Chapter 1: In 2024, XXs illustrated their transformative economic power, contributing US$31.8 (AU$50.3) trillion globally, transforming businesses through entrepreneurial innovation and social responsibility and demanding inclusivity and sustainability. Both matriarchal systems and patriarchal principals are evaluated. The perpetual subjugation of XXs reveals how androcentric concepts and wealth manipulate individuals and governmental minds. The toolkit offers practical actionable suggestions on how XXs can increase their power, including changing shopping behaviour and asserting independence in marriage.

Chapter 2: The human animal is the only species capable of extreme sex-based inequalities. The foundational roots of sexism are traced back to Aristotle and Darwin; both continue to influence legal frameworks and religious dogmas. Areas of progress are revealed, including international women's rights laws (IWRLs), along with the barriers that remain. The toolkit recommendations emphasise championing the contributions of XXs as a means towards sustainable, inclusive growth while reminding us that embracing change opens the door to new possibilities.

Chapter 3: Feminist movements and the four waves demonstrate the intergenerational and intersectional strength of activism, revealing transformative reforms from securing the right to vote to removing tampon taxes during the fourth wave. This "tsunami" achieved significant changes through movements including #FreeTheNipple and #MeToo, exhibiting the resilience and adaptability of feminism in confronting social, cultural, and legal inequalities. The practice of *Femship* is recommended, and several advocacy tools are included.

Chapter 4: The health chapter highlights the positive changes occurring globally. The influence of chromosomes is reviewed alongside the distinction between sex and gender and the negative consequences of blending the two. Medical bias and its harmful effects on XX are exposed. The rise of ethical medical practices and the necessities, including sex-specific research and the collection of data to determine biological differences, highlights progress and what is still needed, including eliminating VAW and reinforcing the right to bodily autonomy. Global healthcare trends indicate a growing commitment to inclusive, compassionate practices and the promotion of health justice for XXs. The toolkit offers ideas to prevent VAW and suggestions for managing menopause and embracing its positives.

Chapter 5: The transformative role of education in addressing sex-based inequities, along with achievements, challenges, and potential, are reviewed. Despite progress in accessing education, significant disparities remain, particularly for XXs. Historic cultural norms continue to reinforce stereotypes, restrict opportunities, and undervalue the contributions of XXs, including discriminatory school policies, school uniforms, toxic masculine attitudes, sexual violence in schools, and the underrepresentation of XXs in science, technology, engineering, and mathematics (STEM). The complexities of single-sex versus coeducational schooling, the rise of homeschooling, and the role of AI tools are also reviewed. The historic transformations and the need for more inclusive educational systems worldwide are highlighted, with the toolkit supporting the development of effective and equitable educational frameworks.

Chapter 6: The multifaceted financial influencers contributing to XXs' economic power and participation include their global transformative spending behaviours and the historic psychology behind beauty traditions, with phenomena including the *lipstick effect*. The environmental and ethical implications of companies targeting XXs, with *femvertising* are explored, along with the income pay gap and difficulties accessing childcare. *Women's Budgets*, initiated by femocrats, illustrate how XX–led policies deliver global positive transformative solutions. The toolkit highlights how XXs can influence profits, the importance of open discussions about money, and supporting XXs in the workplace.

Chapter 7: Polity and Laws within democratic nations, together with the power of the vote, justify the equitable changes required. The rise of XXs in parliaments and their challenges highlight the critical need for greater justice and inclusivity. Quotas indicate how XX representation can contribute to nations in effective and productive ways. The urgent need to stop Violence Against Women in Politics (VAWIP) is illustrated with case studies of crimes. Practical strategies to inspire realistic actions to disband political patriarchal structures are provided in the toolkit.

Chapter 8: The Conclusion highlights the shared experiences of XX in Australia, the EU, India, the UK, and the USA, revealing systemic patriarchal suppression in every facet of life. Despite geographic differences, XXs are united in resisting further oppression, making waves to initiate changes and demanding justice.

1 The Power of Power

Personal Note

I first realised the intrinsic power of the patriarchy at the age of 18 while working as a croupier. As a young student pursuing my bachelor's degree in journalism and working night shifts at a casino, I became aware of the XYs who had the ability to control, coerce, oppress, and subjugate.

Shortly after beginning my croupier career, the casino was purchased by an English company. The new owner sought to reduce wages and benefits, claiming we were "overpaid, glorified cashiers". The staff, hearing of the proposed changes, went on strike. I was approached by the local newspaper to write a feature for the weekend edition. I interviewed various colleagues, composed the piece, with my journalism lecturer assisting with the edits.

The day after submitting it, I returned to work and was assigned to the VIP room, accessible only by invitation. The room featured a bar, a small restaurant, and a gambling area with roulette, blackjack, and baccarat. A door led to the VVIP room, frequented by the Sultan of Brunei, millionaires, and prime ministers (PMs). As I stood at my empty table, I noticed the editor of the local newspaper entering with the new casino owner. They dined, drank, and discussed various topics. I could only catch fragments of their conversation; they mentioned the article I had written. After my shift, I bought the paper, eager to see my work in print. I checked each page repeatedly, but my article had not been published. I contacted the newspaper and was informed that it would not be printed, nor would I be paid for the submission.

The surprises in the VIP room continued. I witnessed multiple extravagant displays of wealth. The junket gamblers often had young XXs under the large baccarat table while they gambled, ate, drunk and inhaled substances from small bottles. Their money afforded them every form of indulgence and excess.

DOI: 10.4324/9781003516224-1

Years later, in a different setting, the power of the patriarchy was again on full display. I submitted the necessary paperwork to establish the first chamber of commerce for XXs in Australia. The application was rejected by authorities on the grounds that it discriminated against XYs. I was advised that the Australian Chamber of Commerce and Industry (ACCI), with an all–XY executive at the time, had influenced the decision. After consulting several lawyers, I found a pro bono XX lawyer to rewrite the chamber constitution, excluding the word "woman." Following various revisions and obtaining approval from the Australian Federal Treasurer, the application was accepted, and the Australian Women Chamber of Commerce and Industry (AWCCI) became operational – with the "W" word only in the name.

My lived experiences and academic studies have brought me to this point – researching, analysing, teaching and exposing gynophobia and the obstacles enforced by patriarchal structures. By reviewing and accentuating limitations, I seek to contest power and emphasise the necessity of redesigning numerous patriarchal structures while acknowledging the encouraging progress taking place in numerous regions.

Introduction

Power is a fundamental element that influences societies, relationships, and individual experiences. It manifests in various forms, ranging from overt displays of political and financial authority to subtler dynamics of dominance and control. This chapter reviews the concept of power, with a focus on patriarchal iterations, including the state, the media, and religious frameworks and the various tools to exert power, including language.

A state refers to a democratic political organisation in power, categorised and defined by a geographic territory, a population, and an established governing body with an institutional framework and the authority to rule both within its borders and on the international stage.

Despite incremental changes around the world, sex-based discrimination persists, based on androcentric ideals, presenting XYs as strong and authoritative and XXs as incompetent, fragile, dependent, and subservient. Misogynistic attitudes also propagate misinformation and contribute to global inequalities, with traditional media and social media companies (SMCs) amplifying stereotypes.

Traditional media remains a powerful influence, shaping societal norms and public opinion, as its coverage disproportionately depicts XXs in leadership roles as less competent, even when they possess superior credentials.

The emergence of SMCs led by oligarchs through their social networking sites (SNSs) has transformed global communication systems, providing platforms for sharing content and influencing social, cultural, and political domains.

While the numerous platforms enable new narratives from voices previously unheard voices, SNSs also perpetuate harmful behaviours, including malinformation, misinformation, disinformation, and violence.

Matriarchal societies, or matricultures, once flourished across the EU, North America, and West Asia, operating as inclusive and egalitarian communities rooted in nurturing values. These societies prioritised ecological interconnectedness, social bonds, and collective well-being, offering a stark contrast to current patriarchal structures. Although patriarchies obliterated matriarchies, some matricultural practices continue, serving as models for sustainability centred on consensus and cooperation.

However, laws and various XX–led initiatives, including digital spaces and global campaigns, such as #FreeTheNipple for example, are questioning traditional power dynamics and advancing parity and independence, demonstrating the capacity and potential of XXs to reform global structures and narratives and the potential to disband patriarchs.

The Powerful

Power refers to the ability of an individual or group to influence the beliefs, outcomes, behaviours, and actions of others. It operates at all levels of society and can oppress, persuade, and control.

Power is omnipresent, embedded in everyday interactions and influencing personal freedoms, often visible only when examining relationships between individuals or organisations (Foucault, 1982). Experiencing and exerting power differ significantly, with a clear distinction between "power to" and "power over" (Fenichel Pitkin, 1967/2019; Göhler, 2009).

In this book, power is referenced as the capacity of those with the resources to manipulate conditions that dictate lives (Barnett & Duvall, 2005).

Capital Clout

In a world of more than eight billion people (UN, 2023), power remains largely concentrated among a few, primarily XYs. Their wealth enables them to shape political decisions and institutions, often impeding progress towards equality (Silve, 2015). The influence of affluent XYs across economic and political spheres further obstructs the pursuit of equal rights for XXs (Stephanopoulos, 2015), providing both power to the wealthy and power over almost everything (Göhler, 2009). The distribution of wealth "requires constant defense and enforcement" (Winters, 2017:158).

Conversely, XXs illustrated their power against bank employees in Spain when escorts, protesting the behaviour of banks, refused to provide services until they resumed lending to families and small businesses, stating that financial institutions must uphold their social responsibility. While the Spanish strategy was unique, similar anti-bank demonstrations in the USA witnessed more than 20 churches withdrawing millions from banks in protest against aggressive foreclosure practices. Both examples accentuate the power of collective action and the backlash against financial institutions prioritising profit over economic stability (HuffPost, 2012; Lewis, 2012).

The relationships between oligarchs and the state also have a substantial impact on manipulating, and at times dictating, laws that affect the majority of citizens (Foster, 2023). Although many wealthy individuals operate outside formal state frameworks, their economic power – in both developed and developing nations – provides them with considerable political influence, decentralising political power (Foster, 2023), and often to the detriment of pro–XXs agendas (Alvarez, 2006; Silve, 2015).

When it comes to influencing laws, XXs remain relatively powerless due to the overwhelming concentration of wealth among XYs, who have the power to impact individuals, governments, and businesses (Gradwohl et al., 2022; Fan et al., 2021). However, changes are happening, albeit with research often overlooking the power of wealthy XXs.

A glance at the lists of billionaires in *Forbes* or *Bloomberg* reveals a bleak reality of who holds global power, with Elon Musk, the richest person in the world as of May 2025, reportedly worth more than US$420 (AU$655) billion (Bloomberg, n.d.; Forbes, n.d.).

The Patriarchy

Patriarchal structures are characterised by rigid hierarchies that elevate XYs to positions of power, while XXs and other vulnerable groups are relegated to subordinate roles, often treated as mere resources to be exploited.

The patriarchy clutches onto discriminatory notions, including for example, "patrilineal inheritance" (Strassmann & Kurapati, 2016), where lineage – last name and property – passes exclusively through XY lines, and "patrilocal residence"' (Chapter 2), where XXs move to the XYs home after marriage (Khalil & Mookerjee, 2019). Numerous cultures continue to demand that XXs take XY's surname, thereby erasing identity.

However, this tradition is evolving. In some nations, for cultural or legal reasons, XXs retain their surnames upon marriage. Naming practices differ worldwide; for example, in Canada, Spain, France, and Greece, XXs legally keep their premarital names (Emens, 2007). Even so, most XXs voluntarily adopt XY's surname; in the USA, for example, 71% of brides take the groom's name (Hoffnung, 2006).

Patriarchal power regulates human sexuality through laws and religious doctrines designed to limit XXs' autonomy and enforce behaviours that reflect misogynistic expectations. Societies structured under patriarchy are typically organised into rigid hierarchies, ranked by class – from royals to slaves – and by sex, where XXs and non-heteronormative individuals are marginalised. Many of these practices are not merely traditions but deliberate mechanisms to sustain control. Leaders often perpetuate notions of inferiority through public remarks, some examples are listed below (Margolis, 2017), further entrenching the belief that XYs hold inherent authority over XXs and reinforcing phallocentric dominance.

Australia: Bill Heffernan, former politician (1996 to 2016): Spoke of the first female PM, Julia Gillard, saying that "I mean, anyone who chooses to remain deliberately barren… they've got no idea what life's about."
Brazil: Jair Bolsonaro, former president of Brazil (2019 to 2023): Told a female lawmaker she was "not worth raping" because she was "too ugly".
Dubai: Dahi Khalfan Tamim, a former police chief: "When a woman says no, she really means to say yes."
France: Nicolas Sarkozy, president (2007 to 2012): "Regulation in protection of XXs is all well and good in academic and government circles. If you're a small business, you'd be a lunatic to hire a woman of childbearing age."
India: Chandrakant Patil, activist and politician, said to a female politician: "If you don't understand politics, then go home and cook." Abhijit Mukherjee, the son of a former president of India and politician, referred to XXs protesting the Delhi bus gang-rape case as "dented and painted."
Poland: Janusz Korwin, Polish politician (1987 to 2022): "Women must earn less than men because they are weaker, they are smaller, they are less intelligent."
South Africa: Jacob Zuma, former president (2009 to 2018): "I wouldn't want to stay with daughters who are not getting married. Because that in itself is a problem in society. I know that people today think being single is nice. It's actually not right. That's a distortion. You've got to have kids. Kids are important to a woman because they actually give an extra training to a woman, to be a mother."
Turkey: Recep Tayyip Erdoğan, president (2014 –): Claimed XXs are not equal to XYs and described XXs who work as "half persons".
The UK: Michael Heseltine, politician and businessman: The UK PM Theresa May has "a man-size job." Dominic Raab, former Deputy PM (2021 to 2023): "Feminists are now amongst the most obnoxious bigots".
The USA: Donald Trump, president (2017 to 2021 and 2025 –): "I'm automatically attracted to beautiful — I just start kissing them. It's like a magnet. Just kiss. I don't even wait. And when you're a star, they let you do it. You can do anything. Grab 'em [XXs] by the pussy [female genitalia]. You can do anything!"

Phallocentric comments serve only the interests of XYs, to the detriment of the great majority. Power and violence reinforce the ruling class's authority, leaving the majority to bear the wounds while the elite accumulate power and wealth. Violence against women (VAW) is a global endemic (Chapter 4) (Fawole et al., 2021; Husain, 2024; Nasr Abdelhalim et al., 2024), further emphasising the devastating impact of patriarchal attitudes, systems, and their control over XXs.

The power of the patriarchy is further amplified when XXs lack equal representation in democracies (Chapter 7), and political attitudes favour masculine values (Norris & Inglehart, 2001). Conservative political narratives promoting masculine strength as necessary for national security also exacerbate toxic masculinity, often linked to xenophobic and populist parties that undermine human rights (Agius et al., 2021).

The patriarchy's dominance and its consequences over the past 5,000 to 6,000 years (Goettner-Abendroth, 2022) underscore the urgency for transformation.

Despite the many heinous crimes committed against people and Mother Earth, patriarchs continue to have the power and resources to advance XXs' status through policymaking structures (Kantola, 2006). As early as the 1980s, scholars recognised that patriarchal nations can deliver positive outcomes (Sapkota & Dahal, 2022). However, it is crucial to understand that those in power often use their positions to reinforce their own beliefs (Vega, 2023). Increasing the representation of XXs in leadership roles could drive the development of more matriarchal systems, delivering meaningful change.

The Matriarchy

In stark contrast to the patriarchy, the matriarchy, or matricultures, once dominated human history (Goettner-Abendroth, 2022; Wolfstone, 2018). Matriarchal societies flourished across the EU, North America, and West Asia (Goettner-Abendroth, 2022).

The founder of modern matriarchal studies and the revival of matricultural thought, renowned German philosopher Heide Goettner-Abendroth, has illuminated these histories by organising international conferences and publishing research to disrupt patriarchal narratives and promote matricultural philosophies, emphasising their historical prevalence and significance (Wolfstone, 2018).

Matriarchal structures were inclusive and balanced, seamlessly integrating equality into their economies and cultures. Originating in Palaeolithic societies, which spanned approximately 11 thousand to 2.5 million years ago, and continuing into Neolithic societies (10,000–3,000 BCE), these communities transitioned from hunting and gathering to agriculture. Governed by consensus and centred around XX divinities, they were matrilineal, cooperative, and peaceful. Their economies prioritised generosity, promoting social bonds and meeting the needs of the majority (Goettner-Abendroth, 2022). Grounded in maternal values, equality, and reciprocity, matricultures embraced collaboration, relational governance, and ecological interconnectedness, in stark contrast to patriarchal paradigms of dominance and greed (Harvey, 2005; Snyder, 2008).

However, patriarchies displaced matriarchies, profoundly transforming cultural, political, and economic models. The XY–controlled universal obliteration of matriarchies, often enforced through colonialism, suppressed cultural diversity and solidified their dominance (Hoskins, 1980; Gomes, 2020; Wolfstone, 2018). Nevertheless, in the 21st century, some communities preserve matricultural practices, offering models for sustainability and collective survival, albeit with XYs holding formal power and remaining central to decision-making within families and clans.

The Iroquois League – an alliance of Indigenous nations in North America, for example, established prior to European contact (Payne, 1996) – exhibits gynocratic elements, with elder XXs exerting significant influence over decision-making (Hoskins, 1980).

Derived from the Greek words "gynē" (woman) and "kratos" (rule or power), gynocracy, or gynecocracy, refers to the political supremacy of XXs. It describes systems where XXs hold dominant power and authority, governing in family, politics, or broader societal contexts (Hoskins, 1980). Gynocratic systems stand in contrast to androcracy – the "rule of men" (Remy et al., 1990:43) – characterised by the political and social dominance of XYs (Márquez et al., 2022). By opposing androcentric (Márquez Roa et al., 2022), patriarchal authority, gynocracy advocates alternative governance models grounded in the leadership and principles of XXs (Hoskins, 1980; Gomes, 2020; Wolfstone, 2018).

In Shakespearean politics, for example, gynocracy is presented as an alternative governing philosophy contrasting with androcracy, the dominant patriarchal system in Elizabethan society. Shakespeare's work reflects socio-political realities where power remained concentrated in the hands of XYs, even under Queen Elizabeth I. The XX characters, including Lady Macbeth, Queen Gertrude, and Desdemona, often illustrate the constraints of patriarchal norms, portraying XXs as tools of XYs' power or as morally complex and conflicted figures of questionable virtue when asserting authority. Shakespeare's narratives frequently highlighted societal resistance to gynocratic governance, reinforcing XY supremacy as the norm (Gomes, 2020).

Gynocracy remains a subject of academic, anthropological, and sociological exploration regarding power dynamics and sex-based roles (Hoskins, 1980). Though seldom applied to contemporary systems, it is occasionally mentioned in feminist theory and speculative discussions as a contrast to patriarchal structures.

Lexical Moderators

As clearly understood by Shakespeare – one of the greatest English writers – language is one of the most powerful, effective, and persuasive tools available.

Vocabulary influences thought, guides societies, and dictates behaviour. Laws are crafted and interpreted through parlance, with terms regulating professional norms, educational practices, and relationships. Prose shifts perceptions, moulds attitudes, and upholds social hierarchies, while expressions stimulate ideologies and perpetuate imbalances of authority, as often seen in the media. Embedded with power structures, language governs collective dynamics and plays a pivotal role in resisting or sustaining sex-based norms.

Words serve as tools to define understanding, guide movements, determine behaviours, validate identities, and act as cultural replicators (Dawkins, 2016; Eckert & McConnell-Ginet, 2003; Lakoff, 2000; Woodbridge, 2024; Young & Fitzgerald, 2006). As William S. Burroughs succinctly professed, words are a "virus" (1962).

The UN appears to be aware of the power of language; it is the "world's largest employer of language professionals" including editors and terminologists (UN, 2019). Given the inherent power and adaptability of language – the flexibility of words to evolve and their capacity to transform – have you ever paused to consider who holds the authority to dictate their use?

The masculine perspective is often promoted through language (Frimer et al., 2019; Gay et al., 2020). Often, upper-class XYs present their perspectives as "neutral" and universal (Lakoff, 2000). Biased language, such as "mankind" instead of "humankind" or "chairman" instead of "chair", positions XYs as the norm and reinforces their dominance.

The lexicon of "mateship", for example, is described as:

> a distinctively Australian cultural idiom, is a concept that traces back to convict times, equating loyalty, equality, and friendship. The term is traditionally used among men and especially to describe the bond during times of challenge or hardship. In Australia, a "mate" is more than just a friend; its usage implies a sense of shared experience, mutual respect, and unconditional assistance.
>
> (Abjorensen & Docherty, 2014)

Adopting sex-neutral language would also assist in preventing the stigmatisation and subordination of XXs (Dembroff & Wodak, 2021). Removing terms including "domestic" from domestic violence (DV), for example, could broaden its scope, reduce its impact, and aid in identifying violence beyond domestic settings. Similarly, merging honorifics like "Mrs", "Miss", and "Ms" into a single prefix, as with Mr – one of the few things XXs have more of than XYs – would help eliminate discrimination (Vega, 2023).

Research in the USA revealed a clear correlation between changes in the status of XXs and the use of XX pronouns in published books. From 1900 to 1945, XY pronouns were significantly more prevalent, appearing 3.5 times more often than XX pronouns. The trend shifted in the late 1960s, with the frequency of XX pronouns increasing and XY pronouns decreasing, suggesting pronouns align with key indicators of status, including advancements in education, increased workforce participation, and greater assertiveness – a personality trait often associated with higher social standing. These linguistic shifts reflect broader societal changes and the evolving roles of XXs in various domains (Twenge et al., 2012).

The evolution of language, often tied to social change, is ambiguous and complicated (Gay et al., 2020). Influenced by globalisation and Western culture, linguistic reforms originating in the USA, Canada, and the EU have reshaped vernaculars beyond their borders (Eckert & McConnell-Ginet, 2003). However, how language is delivered – whether through active or passive voice or sentence structure – also shapes and perpetuates power imbalances, elevating certain values while marginalising others (Woodbridge, 2024).

Words once used by previous generations to describe a person's attributes are no longer in use, with some now deemed unacceptable due to behavioural and cultural shifts. The term "gay", for example, was originally understood to describe happiness but later came to represent homosexuality – a queer person – eventually evolving into broader acronyms including LGBTIQ (lesbian, gay, bisexual, transgender, intersex, and queer/questioning), reflecting the increasing complexity and inclusivity of identities (Anderlini-D'Onofrio & Alexander, 2009). Similarly, "heterosexual" is now often replaced with "cisgender", addressing the alignment of biological sex with identity and sexual preferences (Butler, 2004). "Hermaphrodite" has been replaced with "intersex", acknowledging biological variations and atypical sex characteristics (Fausto-Sterling, 2000).

The singular use of pronouns including "they", for example, has become increasingly recognised, symbolising a shift towards greater inclusivity and the acknowledgment of individual identity (Eckert & McConnell-Ginet, 2003). However, with the US 47th president issuing executive orders declaring only two sexes are recognised (Wendling & Epstein, 2025), regression and changes in language will continue.

Under the Gavel

Laws rely on precise language and words to clearly define rights, responsibilities, and regulations, ensuring consistency, fairness, and enforceability in their application and interpretation.

Language also influences how laws and policies are written and interpreted (Hart & Gilbertson, 2018; Moore et al., 2015). Simultaneously, words can dilute, deflect, and misdirect, serving as a shield for the *status quo* as leaders and polity leverage linguistics to attain, retain, and consolidate their power, for example, by employing well-crafted language to persuade, manipulate public opinion, and legitimise authority. Euphemisms including "collateral damage", "economic adjustments", or "alternative facts" are employed to control narratives and discourage criticism (Lakoff, 2000; Young & Fitzgerald, 2006).

Historically XYs have established frameworks, including legal systems, designed to concentrate power exclusively in their hands. As a result, XYs have accumulated wealth and used laws to subordinate and marginalise XXs (MacKinnon, 2005, 2017, 2020). Political structures systematically exclude XXs from participating in politics (Chapter 7), effectively preventing them from influencing law-making processes (Sapkota & Dahal, 2022).

Although incremental changes have occurred over time, the persistent constraints from sex-based discrimination continues, rooted in ancient philosophies, including Aristotle's notion of treating "likes alike, [and] unlikes unalike"

(MacKinnon, 2017:570). Over centuries, these discriminatory principles have contributed to systemic inequalities (Hawkesworth, 2012).

Political dynamics influence the interpretation, implementation, and monitoring of laws, limiting XXs' political participation (Čickaric, 2016). Consequently, progress towards equality remains derailed. Rooted in the laws of the land, the formulas around sex-based discrimination often produce harmful effects (Neuwirth, 2005). It is inherently unjust, unbalanced, and inequitable when one sex is consistently regarded as superior or inferior to the other. As a result, there is a persistent failure to achieve parity, even with the implementation of pro–XXs laws, leaving XXs marginalised in all areas of society, with the majority of positions of power and influence still held by XYs (Eden & Wagstaff, 2020).

Despite the progress made to date, XYs continue to design systems and frameworks that preserve the distribution of power among themselves (MacKinnon, 2017). The status of XYs in society, along with their influence within cultural, political, religious, and media institutions, determines the extent of misogyny experienced by XXs across the globe.

The XYs often ignore the power dynamics that place them on top. This kind of discrimination reflects and reinforces power imbalances, making inequality appear normal rather than opposing it. Numerous and diverse feminist concepts have been developed over many decades, each driven by the pervasive influence of sexist systems (Renzetti, 2010).

The control XYs have over XXs is insidious and pervasive, enabling XYs to maintain dominance and further exert their authority through laws. If XXs are ever to be truly heard, they must reject the sexualised power that XYs hold (MacKinnon, 2013) and begin dismantling archaic power configurations.

Feminism recognises that XY perspectives are key to how they build the world to reflect their own desires, not just to control outcomes, but as the very core of their power. Feminism, in its truest form, understands truth is a construct of the powerful, those who hold the authority to define reality. This process is not only widespread but also deeply ingrained in the majority of societies around the world.

However, and crucially, power can change hands, and it is something XXs have the capacity to accomplish. For changes to occur, XXs must remain aware and alert to the reality XYs have created and recognise why it must be questioned, resisted, and transformed (Colker, 1990).

Legislations, for example, are predominantly written and passed by XYs in positions of power. Laws have the ability to influence and control all aspects of XXs' lives. Consequently, the actions of legislators dictate lived experiences, including the four determinants: health, education, economic, and political – all of which impact personal welfare, prospects, and futures, all are interrelated and define the lives of everyone.

Health, followed by education, are foundational for survival and to thrive in society. Without good health (Chapter 4), very little else is possible. Education (Chapter 5) paves the way for economic participation (Chapter 6), which, in turn, enables networks crucial for political involvement, influence, and the attainment of authority and power. The final determinant, political participation (Chapter 7), allows for authority and legislative power, ideally bringing the changes necessary for a nation to implement pro–XXs laws and comply with International Women's Rights Laws (IWRLs).

Nations striving for impartiality understand that the control and skilful use of language are indispensable for progress, including IWRLs and redefining norms (Lakoff, 2000; Vega, 2023). Simultaneously, language can mislead and consolidate power. Politicians, for example, use symbolic language to justify reforms, obscure accountability, and deflect criticism (Liguori & Steccolini, 2018).

For those who may feel detached from politics or dismiss its relevance, it is important to recognise the immense power of legislators and the imperative need for each individual opinion to be counted (Mancosu & Hopmann, 2019). To those who say they "hate politics", or believe that "all politicians are the same", or claim to "not care about politics", reconsideration is urged: every aspect of life is influenced by the decisions of those in power. Consider, for a moment, politics as a piece of art, where each vote is a brushstroke on a canvas. Sometimes, a single brushstroke can alter the entire image. Similarly, every vote contributes to the final result, just as every law determines reality.

So, whether you cast your ballot or raise your voice in protest, your participation matters to shape the course of ***herstory***. The ability to vote and have your voice heard represents the peak of empowerment (Chapter 7). It is therefore crucial for XXs to actively engage in legislative processes to ensure adequate protections across the four determinants.

Opinion Orchestrators

The media's choice of language also contributes to political outcomes and promotes archaic ideals (Hart & Gilbertson, 2018; Tidmarsh & Hamilton, 2020), perpetuating sexism. Language used by the various mediums further illustrates its power to destroy, disgrace, confuse, and increase or decrease political support (Cooperrider & Srivastva, 1987; Martyn et al., 2019), influencing how the world is perceived.

Research demonstrates that the press, television, and radio remain influential sources of information, knowledge, opinions, and attitudes for the majority of people (Ryan, 2013; Wilding et al., 2020), albeit with many now using the internet to obtain their news (Helberger et al., 2018). Nevertheless, traditional media still holds significant power to frame issues, amplify expert opinions, and present its selected narratives as "news" (Steensland, 2008).

Globally, the media's portrayal of XXs in power has been widely scrutinised, revealing that XXs face relentless abuse and denigration, although they often have greater experience and credentials compared to their XY counterparts (Hudson et al., 2015). Derogatory narratives often defend XYs and attack XXs (Ross et al., 2019).

Minimising the prevalence of rape (Rentschler, 2014) and VAW, for example, employing inflammatory language, publishing sexist images (Chapter 3), and blaming survivors instead of their attackers normalises ignorance and reinforces androcentric concepts (Hart & Gilbertson, 2018; Tidmarsh & Hamilton, 2020). Furthermore, XX survivors are portrayed with racial and socioeconomic biases, reinforcing prejudice and bigotry (Easteal et al., 2019).

Inaccurate reporting often restricts citizens from engaging in informed debate on legislation affecting public life, leaving policies unchallenged and preserving the *status quo* whilst perpetuating harmful stereotypes and negative portrayals of XXs (Steensland, 2008). For example, describing protestors as "rioters" instead of "activists" or "advocates" also has significant influence on public perception, either delegitimising or validating (Young & Fitzgerald, 2006). The deliberate use of subjective or contentious language is often employed to capture attention, provoke reactions, generate clicks, incite outrage, and perpetuate numerous forms of discrimination, including antisemitism, chauvinism, colonialism, racism, and sexism, among others.

Sensationalised reporting tends to prioritise entertainment above facts, raising division, prejudice, and hatred. Certain media moguls have even engaged in fraudulent practices to advance personal agendas, further eroding journalistic integrity (Beecher, 2024).

Unbalanced reporting further undermines efforts to hold nations accountable for failing to address inequality. Additionally, the vilification of XX journalists discourages XXs from entering political journalism, while XYs are disproportionately cited as sources in news coverage (IPU, 2022; Jia et al., 2016).

In the past, words including "suffragettes" and "ladette" were coined by the media to degrade. The British press, particularly *The Daily Mail*, coined the term "suffragette" in 1906 with the intention of belittling and mocking the suffrage movement (Holton, 1987). The use of the suffix "-ette" implied smallness and superficiality, reinforcing inferiority and unsuitability for political engagement (Tickner, 1988) and appeasing the anti-suffrage movement. However, suffragettes creatively reclaimed the term, transforming it into a symbol of resilience and strength in their fight for equality (Sawer, 2007; Sawer & Radford, 2008).

The term "ladette" was used to describe young XXs who allegedly embraced behaviours traditionally associated with "lads" (XY actions), including drinking, swearing, and disrupting societal expectations of feminine conduct. Media coverage in the 1990s reinforced a clear narrative emphasising the importance of adhering to patriarchal norms (Harris, 2010).

To further denigrate feminist efforts, the term "postfeminism" is often employed by content providers to portray feminism as outdated (Chapter 3), suggesting sex-based equality has already been achieved (Faludi, 1992; Lister, 2013; Silve, 2015; Hawkesworth, 2012; Vega, 2023). Moreover, media discussions of postfeminism frequently target a white, middle-class demographic, effectively marginalising and overshadowing the diverse experiences of XXs from different racial, ethnic, and socioeconomic backgrounds (Tasker & Negra, 2005).

The various persuasive messages also typically reinforce traditional ideals of femininity, beauty standards, and domesticity, while failing to acknowledge the ongoing discrimination and systemic constraints that continue to impede justice.

In many countries, technology has empowered the public to actively participate in changing language. One example is by voting to include new words in a dictionary. This democratic approach to language evolution reflects the increasing interplay between cultural shifts and technological innovation. For example, in 2024, Macquarie Dictionary's Word of the Year was voted to be "enshittification", a term capturing societal frustration with declining quality or degradation in various contexts (Macquarie Dictionary, 2024). The inclusion of the new word, influenced by thousands of voters, highlights how language can serve as a mirror to collective sentiment and contemporary limitations.

Using erroneous language leads to actions that have detrimental consequences on XXs worldwide. Nevertheless, employing specific language to perpetuate marginalisation is a subtle process, making it challenging to recognise and resist (Lakoff, 2000; Young & Fitzgerald, 2006).

Sexist language enables patriarchal systems to oppress XXs, defining them as unequal and inferior within cultural, political, and social realms. Revising grammatical structures to support cultural shifts is essential for dismantling sex-based discrimination (Gay et al., 2020; Lakoff, 2000; Steels, 2011).

Research indicates that XXs must advocate for themselves to dismantle sexualised masculine power structures (MacKinnon, 2017). Transforming masculine language is achievable, particularly through the efforts of the media, religion, politics, educators, scientists, and activists (Eckert & McConnell-Ginet, 2003).

The Pious

Globally, religious institutions are intertwined with the media, distributing messages through the press, television, radio, and the internet, perpetuating dogmas and archaic notions (Naas, 2016). This relationship has "globalatinized" religious messages (coined by Derrida in 1998), making them widespread. Their continuous spread of dogma and archaic notions (Naas, 2016) aids the patriarchy in maintaining its dominance over XXs.

Language wars, often evident in religious contexts, extend far beyond simple debates; they correspond to divisions over identity, power, and inclusion. The capacity to control dialogue can dictate who is acknowledged, whose voices are amplified, whose contributions are valued, and who dictates behaviour (Lakoff, 2000). Terms classified as either compliant or taboo are often weaponised to deepen divisions and reinforce outdated norms associated with prescribed sex-based expectations and phallocentric interpretations of morality.

Sexist commentary and visuals disseminated by religious organisations often perpetuate confusion among followers, reinforcing outdated principles that vilify XXs (Bailliet, 2016; Foucault, 1999; Reid, 2013).

The masculine deities, ranging from God to Allah and other XY figures, are exalted by the majority of religions, often placed above any XX divine representations. Disinformation, malinformation, and misinformation are propagated to polarise, further enabling the patriarchy to maintain authority and dominance. Furthermore, religious devotees often project their biases against XXs, constructing barriers that disrupt and prevent the eradication of sex-based discrimination (Raday, 2018).

The rationale presented by religious leaders and their followers raises critical concerns about why those at the helm of religious institutions fail to promote and uphold fundamental human rights laws without reprisal (UN, 2020) – perhaps their financial power allows them to evade accountability?

The great majority of nations allow religious institutions to operate tax-free. The oldest documented example of these tax exemptions is traced back to ancient Egypt, around 2600 BCE (Garay, 2010; Newman, 2019; Wood Daly, 2021).

It is impossible to ascertain the global income of religious institutions; however, in the USA, one national study revealed an annual income of more than US$378 (AU$601) billion, as a conservative estimate (Grim & Grim, 2016).

Taxation laws are complex and vary globally; nevertheless, all governments have the power and authority to tax citizens, including religious institutions (Garay, 2010). Additionally, the Declaration of Human Rights states that "Universal taxation is indispensable; it must be equally shared by all citizens according to their resources" (Garay, 2010:49). The religious, however, have successfully avoided taxation to a significant extent (Garay, 2010; Grim & Grim, 2016; Wood Daly, 2021).

Unregulated Power Brokers

Similar to religious organisations, SMCs evade taxation; however, some governments have attempted to implement strategies to generate revenue, for example, by requiring payments for hosting news content on their platforms (Enache, 2024; Evans, 2024), efforts that have largely been ineffective or unsuccessful to date.

The owners of SMCs have been progressively exhibiting their enormous power and wealth (Smith & Niker, 2021), with a concerning lack of accountability and significantly more influence than can be effectively identified or continuously monitored. "Moreover, oligarchs alone are able to use wealth for wealth's defense" (Winters, 2017:163).

The new oligarchy comprises the owners of platforms used as the "primary source of news for many Internet users" (Helberger et al., 2018:2). Among the most popular SNSs are Facebook and Instagram, both under Meta Platforms, owned by Mark Zuckerberg; Twitter, now X, owned by Elon Musk, originally co-founded by Jack Dorsey, Biz Stone, and Evan Williams; TikTok, developed by Zhang Yiming; and LinkedIn, founded by Reid Hoffman and Eric Ly, now owned by Microsoft – a company started by Bill Gates and Paul Allen and led (since 2014) by XY CEO Satya Nadella.

The rise of oligarchs controlling SNSs, predominantly XYs holding unprecedented power, further complicates the dynamics of reliable, impartial information and corrodes societal standards with minimal accountability (Helberger et al., 2018; Rozgonyi, 2023).

The dissemination of "fake news" instead of reality, exacerbates discrimination and entrenches existing power dynamics as they exercise immense influence. SMC owners are the new oligarchs: self-serving, privileged, and affluent individuals who utilise their immense financial resources to gain power. By marginalising the less affluent, they secure their personal wealth, uphold their societal status, and shape political outcomes to their advantage (Foster, 2023; Jordan & Gray, 2019; Pleines, 2009).

The influence of these oligarchs and their SMCs is unprecedented, and their full impact is highly concerning, exceeding the power of all previous media moguls (Beecher, 2024). For example, the online sharing of videos depicting the executions of reporters to align with terrorist groups highlights how extremists increasingly employ social media platforms to publish their views and attract followers. This trend is escalating rapidly in both scope and intensity across the globe.

Regulations have the potential to not only save lives but also stop the transmission of malicious, corrosive information; however, globally governing these SMCs presents complex resistance that even the UN has struggled to address (Wu, 2015).

The exploitative power of SMCs continues to grow as they collect personal data, often without consent, using sophisticated algorithms to commoditise (Corcos & Hodara, 2023; Valeriani, 2023).

Algorithms also reinforce the SMC oligarchs' ability to control what is seen, read, heard, and purchased, developing and designing the ultimate formula for managing systems, including content delivery methods. The structure and growth of communities are designed to keep users engaged and dependent (Corcos & Hodara, 2023). With vast resources at their disposal, SMC oligarchs can easily obtain or control anything they desire, including political power, as money is no object (Jordan & Gray, 2019).

For example, Musk, the richest XY in the world as of May 2025 (Bloomberg, n.d.; Forbes, n.d.), exemplifies this dynamic (Khan, 2021; Phillips, 2024) – shifting from maverick to media mogul (Ricketson & Dodd, 2024). Musk, the owner of X, obtained an office in the White House in 2025 and was reported to be "one of the most influential and controversial powerbrokers in the new

Trump administration", expending more than US$277 (AU$360) million aiding Trump's re-election (Maher, 2025).

In August 2024, Brazil's Supreme Court ordered the suspension of X after Musk was accused of disseminating misinformation about the 2022 Brazilian presidential election and failing to appoint a legal representative in the country, a requirement under Brazilian law. X's non-compliance with previous court orders to block accounts spreading disinformation further exacerbated the situation (Choucair, 2024; Derico & Wells, 2024).

Musk argued that the decision posed a threat to free speech. The ban ignited debate over whether other nations might adopt similar measures to enforce compliance with national laws by SMCs (Choucair, 2024). However, shortly after the suspension, the same court lifted the ban after the company paid a fine of 28 million Brazilian Reals (AU$7.5 / US$4.7) million and agreed to appoint a local representative (Derico & Wells, 2024).

In January 2025, the owner of Facebook, Instagram, and Threads, Zuckerberg, revealed plans to eliminate fact-checkers, significantly decreasing censorship and promoting an increased volume of political content (Booth, 2025).

In 2018, Zuckerberg explained Meta's data privacy practices to the US Senate. Although evidence indicated that his platform was distributing false information and influencing elections, it remains largely unregulated (The New York Times, 2018). Similarly, in December 2018, Sundar Pichai, CEO of Google, was questioned about user data privacy and allegations of political bias in search engine results, but no legal penalties followed (Romm & Timberg, 2018).

Two years later, in November 2020, Zuckerberg and Jack Dorsey, then CEO of Twitter, defended their platforms in front of the US Senate Judiciary Committee, claiming mechanisms were in place to reduce misinformation while maintaining free speech. Again, no legal consequences followed (BBC News, 2020).

In March 2023, TikTok CEO, Shou Zi Chew, appeared before the US Congress to address data privacy and security concerns. Similarly, in January 2024, executives from TikTok, Meta, X, Snapchat, and other SMCs were summoned before Congress. Despite strong expressions of outrage from lawmakers and the public, no legal actions were taken, and operations continued unchanged (Fung & Duffy, 2024).

In 2024, Zuckerberg and other SMC leaders were questioned about the harm their platforms caused to young people during the "Big Tech and the Online Child Sexual Exploitation Crisis" hearing. While Meta apologised to affected parents, no legal ramifications followed, leaving predators to roam free and lawmakers frustrated (ABC News, 2024).

The power exhibited by these oligarchs and their SMCs significantly undermines free speech and democracy, as they remain unaccountable in most democratic nations, manipulating their influence to divide communities and consolidate power. Their capacity to dominate and disseminate ideologies presents a grave threat, with misinformation, malinformation, and disinformation often masquerading as a pretence of communal good and freedom of expression. The primary objective of these SMCs is to maintain power within an elite, extraordinarily wealthy, male-dominated ruling class.

The laws required to regulate SMCs could have been implemented decades ago. Today, managing these oligarchs, their wealth, and their power raises significant opposition, even for established legal systems. Nonetheless, "Internet, social media, and app shutdowns have become frequent, not only in authoritarian states but also in emerging and fragile democracies" (Santos et al., 2024:131).

For example, Pavel Durov, co-founder of Telegram, was arrested in Paris on August 24, 2024, accused of supporting criminal conduct and distributing illegal content, an event that could change the future of SMCs (Koskie, 2024; Meaker, 2024; Rankin, 2024). Durov, dubbed the "Russian Zuckerberg", went into exile in the United Arab Emirates a decade earlier (2014) after refusing to comply with Russian government demands for user data from VKontakte, aka VK – a Russian SNS launched in 2006, similar to Facebook (Santos et al., 2024).

Telegram, a messaging platform chosen by users pursuing confidentiality, with built-in proxies and robust encryption, allows users to bypass government censorship, making it a tool for political mobilisation and secure communication, particularly in authoritarian regimes (Akbari & Gabdulhakov, 2019; Santos et al., 2024). As the EU evaluates its response to Telegram following Durov's arrest, the platform continues to spark critical debates about privacy, freedom of expression, and the future of digital independence (Rankin, 2024). Durov was released on €5 million bail (AU$8.3 / US$5.2 million) and legal proceedings were ongoing at the time of publication (France 24, 2024).

Global Facilitators

SNSs and social media platforms have revolutionised modern communication, providing unparalleled opportunities to share and exchange diverse content, including text, images, videos, and audio (Lam, 2016).

Digital spaces have become integral to global connectivity, facilitating discussions and interactions that shape social, cultural, economic, and political landscapes (Cassidy, 2016).

However, both traditional and social media remain largely biased against XXs, as they are predominantly owned and controlled by XYs with significant economic power. This dominance allows them to shape societal conversations, frame perspectives, define social constructs, and influence what is read, seen, and heard. Their control extends to policymaking, where media narratives often reinforce patriarchal norms (Jaworska & Larrivée, 2011; Ross et al., 2019).

As of October 2024, almost 70% of the global population, or 5.52 billion out of 8.05 billion people, have access (Statista, n.d.) to the internet. On average, users spend 145 minutes daily on mobile devices and laptops, totalling more than 36 days per year. Activities include exchanging messages, seeking entertainment, obtaining information, liking posts, and sharing recommended content (Corcos & Hodara, 2023).

While SNSs offer tools for empowerment and societal transformation, they also present adversities, including misinformation and harassment, raising concerns about their impact on democratic systems and public trust.

SNSs have emerged as influential entities, akin to traditional media but with added unique complexities. They empower individuals and communities to amplify their voices and address critical societal issues. However, unlike traditional media, SNSs operate with minimal oversight, embracing unregulated environments where harmful behaviours thrive (Douglass et al., 2018). These platforms often act as damaging influencers, with negative voices distorting information quality and enabling the global dissemination of content in ways unprecedented in traditional media.

In recent years, significant transformations have occurred within the largely unregulated digital landscape. While most major platforms remain XY–dominated, owned by SMCs, exceptions now exist where XXs are founding, building, and controlling platforms, creating inclusive online communities and redistributing wealth. These changes are particularly notable given the rapid growth of the digital advertising market.

The negative power of SNSs and other digital tools has unsettled many, raising concerns about the blurred line between fact and fiction. Misinformation and fake news are often presented as legitimate, undermining democratic principles and eroding societal trust (Thornthwaite et al., 2018; Lam, 2016). Additionally, harmful actions by SNS users, regardless of their impact, are frequently not deemed unlawful. The viral nature of misinformation poses significant threats, enabling the rapid spread of distorted narratives that influence public opinion, laws, and societal trust while normalising bigotry and sexism (Cassidy, 2016).

The decline of objective journalism, exacerbated by the spread of misinformation and fake news, further undermines democratic processes, leaving voters uninformed or manipulated (Wilding et al., 2020). The future of democracy is increasingly questioned as SNSs blur the lines between facts, fiction, and fake news, empowering some users while harming others (Thornthwaite et al., 2018; Lam, 2016).

A significant concern on SNSs is the prevalence of sexual harassment, disproportionately affecting XXs and non-heterosexual groups. Researchers describe this as an "emerging phenomenon", often perpetuated by individuals practising rape culture (Douglass et al., 2018; Sills et al., 2016). The lack of robust legislative frameworks exacerbates these issues, leaving survivors without adequate recourse and allowing perpetrators to exploit digital anonymity. Studies reveal that such behaviours are culturally tolerated, perpetuating sex-based inequality and reinforcing harmful norms (Cassidy, 2016; Sia et al., 2021).

Despite the drawbacks, online XX campaigns have achieved remarkable success. For example, the #MeToo movement obtained global attention, surpassing the reach of traditional media efforts.

In Australia, for example, Mad Fucking Witches (MFW n.d.), an activist group founded by Jennie Hill, opposes systemic misogyny in the media, government, and society. MFW's campaigns have successfully pressured companies to withdraw advertising that promote and/or tolerate VAW and misogyny (Dent, 2019; Martin, 2024).

Hill said: "We've been using the #StatusBro hashtag and the reason for that is most of the world is controlled by old white men and they're not doing a very good job of it. ... Women are being silenced for talking about a man calling for a woman to be silenced. Isn't it ironic, don't you think?" (Dent, 2019). For example, one comment on radio advised listeners on how to hold a "woman's arms from behind like a wheelbarrow, and then 'you go to town and just butcher the pussy'" (Martin, 2024). MFW's efforts highlight the collective power of its 55,000 members, who demand balanced reporting (Dent, 2019; Martin, 2024).

Similarly, global campaigns including #LahuKaLagaan, #Delhibraveheart, and #FreeTheNipple (Chapter 3) demonstrate the transformative potential of SNSs in amplifying previously silenced narratives and confronting sex-based violence (Fileborn & Loney-Howes, 2019). The #AskThicke campaign critiqued Robin Thicke's controversial song *Blurred Lines*, further illustrating how digital tools oppose misogyny (Turley & Fisher, 2018).

The global digital advertising market is projected to grow at a compound annual growth rate of 15.5%, reaching around US$796 (AU$1,264) billion by 2030 (Grand View Research, n.d.).

Several XX entrepreneurs worldwide, from Australia (WeAre8) to India (SHEROES) and the USA (Spill n.d.), are securing a share of the advertising revenue, creating inclusive online ecosystems, securing funding, and disrupting SMCs (Onmanorama, 2022).

WeAre8's approach centres advertising around people, enabling users to drive positive change by watching advertisements. Advertisers allocate half (50%) of their spend to users, 5% to a charity selected by the brand, and 1% to reduce carbon. The platform features a self-serve ad-buying engine comparable to Facebook's Ads Manager. The platform's model seeks to revolutionise traditional advertising by developing a socially responsible and engaged user base that contributes to meaningful societal and environmental impact (B & T Weekly, 2022; WeAre8, 2022). In April 2022, the company announced an AU$15 (US$9.3) million investment (Lomas, 2022).

SHEROES, founded by Sairee Chahal, provides a supportive social network for XXs in India, offering resources, a marketplace for entrepreneurs, and a free counselling helpline (SHEROES, n.d.). In 2015, US$5.98 (AU$9.5) million worth of investments was obtained over six rounds (Tracxn, n.d.). SHEROES also features a marketplace that supports XX entrepreneurs by enabling them to buy and sell products, promoting economic growth. Additionally, users can access job listings and mentorship programmes (SHEROES, n.d.).

Spill, launched by former Twitter employees Alphonzo Terrell and DeVaris Brown, emphasises safety for marginalised communities, using Artificial Intelligence (AI) to monitor and mitigate abuse (Dunn, 2023). It also prioritises safety for diverse communities, addressing concerns prevalent on other online platforms including X. This initiative comes amid a notable decline in X's user engagement and advertising revenue, highlighting a user shift towards alternative platforms (Dunn, 2023).

The XX–led enterprises highlight the potential of SNSs to deliver transformative changes, constrain entrenched inequalities, and develop inclusive digital spaces, especially where wealth is concentrated in the hands of a few XYs. Additionally, XXs now possess mammoth spending power, influencing markets and steering economic changes. Their spending power was estimated at US$32 (AU$51) trillion globally (Chapter 6) and XXs are expected to control 75% of discretionary spending within five years; XXs also influence between 70% and 80% of household purchases (NielsenIQ, 2024).

Conclusion

The power of power, historically monopolised by patriarchs, is experiencing an inspiring change as XXs reclaim and redefine norms. The accomplishments of XXs in dismantling obstacles, disrupting stereotypes, and building equitable paths mark a pivotal moment in the ongoing quest for balance. While the process to disband the patriarchy remains complex, the triumphs of XXs highlight the transformative potential of resilience, collaboration, and innovative action.

Power, while often concentrated among a privileged few XYs, also presents opportunities for change as awareness grows and societal structures evolve. Recognising the capacity of individuals and groups to influence outcomes is key to advancing progress. As global political shifts occur, the potential for equitable power distribution offers hope, in some regions, for a more balanced future.

The entrenched dominance of the patriarchy highlights the need for systemic transformation. While the impacts of current systems are profound, progress is possible through increased XX representation in leadership roles. Such advancements can interrupt longstanding inequalities, promote fairness, and encourage the development of more inclusive, balanced societal structures, ensuring meaningful change for future generations.

For example, matriarchal societies, rooted in equality, cooperation, and ecological interconnectedness, present an inspiring contrast to patriarchal systems of dominance. Although displaced, some matricultural practices persist, offering models for sustainability and collective well-being. Exploring gynocracy further accentuates the potential of XX–led governance to constrain existing androcentric hierarchies, supporting a vision for inclusive and balanced societies.

Language is a powerful tool to influence thought, guiding societies with the potential to increase equity. As societies evolve, linguistic reforms reflect change, empowering and validating diverse identities. By adopting inclusive terms and questioning biased expressions, language can remove barriers and promote justice. Despite resistance, the adaptability of language also offers optimism in creating balanced narratives across cultures, including *herstory*.

Legislative language remains a critical tool for addressing systemic legal imbalances. While XYs have historically dominated legal frameworks to consolidate power, XXs possess the capacity to disrupt these structures. By actively engaging in legislative processes and harnessing the transformative power of language and technology, XXs can drive powerful change across health, education, economic, and political areas. Empowerment through participation, whether by voting or advocacy, is vital to disbanding entrenched patriarchal practices and redesigning an equitable future.

The media's language choices are instrumental in defining narratives and societal perceptions, often reinforcing negative stereotypes and influencing political outcomes. Despite the prevalence of biased reporting and systemic barriers, change is possible. Calling out bigotry, XXs are limiting patriarchal norms and advancing progress. Public participation in language evolution demonstrates a collective drive, highlighting the potential for transformation. With collaborative efforts across media, politics, education, and activism, eradicating discriminatory narratives and achieving justice and fairness for all remains an attainable goal.

Media and religion remain deeply interconnected, reinforcing outdated patriarchal ideologies that systematically marginalise and vilify XXs. While these institutions have extraordinary power and influence, often evading accountability through financial power and tax exemptions, opportunities for change remain. Advocating for their taxation and application of human rights laws is crucial to rectifying systemic imbalances and to deliver justice.

The unregulated power of SMCs and their oligarchs continues to challenge democracies, free speech, and societal cohesion. Despite their immense influence and the dissemination of distorted narratives and images, opportunities for reform are available; legal regulatory implementations need to be globally executed immediately. Strengthening regulations and holding these oligarchs accountable can ensure fairer practices, greater transparency, and adequate taxes. Collaborative efforts among governments and institutions are essential to mitigating the risks posed by these monopolies while encouraging a digital landscape prioritising truth, privacy, and equity. Authoritative efforts are required to balance technological tools to provide educational empowerment rather than control and distribution of disinformation.

SNSs offer a powerful duality – enabling societal transformation while presenting significant dangers. Although SMCs have historically perpetuated inequalities, recent XX–led initiatives in Australia, the EU, India, and the USA exemplify the potential for innovation, empowerment, and collaboration.

By leveraging globally growing markets, XXs are creating opportunities and advancing equality. These developments emphasise the transformative potential of SNSs to drive progress, amplify voices, and promote equitable digital ecosystems, embracing and advancing digital innovation to create fairer economies and political systems.

This chapter celebrates the progress made by XXs while acknowledging the quantity of work that remains to be done to disband the patriarchy and democratically regulate oligarchs. It calls upon individuals, institutions, and governments to commit to building a world where power is not confined to the hands of a few but is democratically distributed. The path to disbanding the patriarchy is neither linear nor simple, but with continued collective efforts and determination, it is a quest, a mission well worth continuing.

"The enemy of feminism isn't men. It's patriarchy, and patriarchy is not men. It is a system, and women can support the system of patriarchy just as men can support the fight for gender equality".

Jennifer Justine née Wilson, Canadian author
(AzQuotes, n.d.; Wikipedia, n.d.)

Toolkit

Challenge the Patriarchs' Controlling Norms

To confront patriarchal expectations involves asserting autonomy, making independent decisions, and rejecting traditional sex-based roles; for example, questioning traditional standards that dictate how XXs should behave, dress, and desire.

Double-check all information, and do not simply accept what you see, read, or hear; remain informed and aware of misinformation, malinformation, and disinformation.

Consider using XX–owned platforms instead of those controlled by XY oligarchs. Avoid consuming traditional media that promotes misogyny and bigotry; remember that audiences influence advertisers, and without income, businesses cannot exist.

As individuals and as a collective, XXs can denounce sexism ingrained in religious dogmas and the media. Calling out misogynistic content that promotes VAW or pursuing opportunities typically dominated by XYs reflects this power. Ultimately, you hold the ability to reshape narratives and societal perceptions, creating a more equitable power dynamic between XXs and XYs, one action at a time.

Set Boundaries to Obtain Equal Respect

Consider rejecting the convention of surrendering family names, a symbolic yet powerful assertion of autonomy. In doing so, the preservation of identity can be retained, resisting the embedded expectation of phallocentrism. This seemingly small act is, in fact, a profound statement – one that can disrupt the notion that XXs are extensions or possessions of XYs. Retaining a name after marriage reinforces the reality that identity is self-determined, not defined by others.

Confronting misogynistic language can influence behaviours and attitudes. For example, the word "cunt" is often used to describe a reprehensible, objectionable, or undesirable individual. Why not choose a term that does not perpetuate derogatory connotations towards XXs instead? Demonstrating the impact of linguistic shifts is crucial in supporting campaigns that call out androcentric behaviours.

2 Countering Patriarchs

Personal Note

My name was not a parental decision; it was partly dictated by the Spanish Catholic Church. Back then, parents did not have the luxury of choosing a name. Instead, every newborn had to be christened with a traditional Catholic name to qualify for baptism. Baptism was not optional – under the rule of the fascist dictator General Francisco Franco (1939–1975), it was mandatory. No baptism meant no school. I changed part of my name as an adult to delete all enforced traces. The religious dogma's control over names was only one part of its grip on my mother's life – her name was Sagrario, meaning tabernacle.

Sagrario was placed in a convent aged two. My grandmother, a single parent, was intent on keeping her only daughter safe from the crimes of war and starvation. At the age of 22, although she had informed the nuns that she wanted to stay, the church ordered her to leave. Her birth certificate excluded her father's signature and children born out of wedlock were not accepted. No one ever found my grandfather during or after the Spanish Civil War; consequently my mother's dream career was out of reach, hence she pleaded with me to be a nun.

My experiences with the Sacred Heart of Jesus were eye-opening. I learned that hypocrisy ruled and that the brothers and priests who had sex with my teenage friends received no castigation; the treatment and repercussions for the young XXs were far different. Several were also taken out of school and subjected to child marriage against their will, yet the clergy failed to intervene. I left as soon as I could and did not graduate from high school.

Filled with fear from her many traumas, my mother told me that as an XX migrant, no university would ever accept me. My father persuaded me to ignore her; he often reminded me that if I could see it in my mind's eye and feel it, I would live it. And so, I applied as a mature-age student and graduated with a BA in journalism, majoring in communications and sociology.

DOI: 10.4324/9781003516224-2

As a journalist, I worked for various publishers, including newspapers owned by the Murdoch empire. On one occasion, the face of a far-right politician aspirant was published on the front page of a newspaper with a readership of close to one million. I approached the picture editor and asked why she had been on the front page for a week. His response still resounds in my mind: "Because she is better looking than all the other blokes." He was serious. He did not have the awareness nor the capacity to understand the power of the media. Allegedly, he was just doing his job.

A few years later, in my first job as a public relations officer, I received a 200-page document outlining my duties and key performance indicators (KPIs) on my first day at the office. I was stunned, to say the least, when I read that there was to be no "cuntism" in the office. When I asked my boss to explain, he advised that he knew "women were bitchy" when they had their menstrual period.

Several careers later, at the inaugural Asia-Pacific Economic Cooperation (APEC) *Women and the Economy Summit* (WES), I was pleasantly surprised to witness the remarkable policy and advocacy efforts of XXs from around the world working together tirelessly, many without pay. However, despite the historic significance (Clinton, 2011), I was disheartened and somewhat distressed by the lack of acknowledgment of the landmark event by the government and the media.

Countering Patriarchs reviews the dangerous and pervasive influence of religious dogmas and the international laws advocating for and instigating positive changes.

Introduction

Sex-based inequalities, rooted in biological disparities, were originally shaped by Aristotle's and Charles Darwin's theories, which have often been misused to justify XY dominance. Religious doctrines have historically perpetuated these inequalities and continue to suppress and control XXs, frequently reinforcing strict sexual behavioural codes.

The systemic phallocentrisms embedded in most religions, including Christianity, Hinduism, Islam, and Judaism, propagate patriarchal values with teachings that marginalise XXs and suppress autonomy and sexuality.

Despite various progressive legislations around the globe, religious leaders resist change, citing threats to traditional norms. Additionally, religious practices, including clerical celibacy, are misused to justify or conceal abuse. While secularisation challenges religious dominance in governance and societies, the clergy continues exerting significant influence, often opposing diversity, equality, and inclusion (DEI) and ignoring human rights laws.

The hypocrisy of some religious leaders, prioritising reputation over justice, aggravates the oppression of XXs, children, and non-heteronormative individuals. The intersection of religious doctrines, patriarchal traditions, and their enduring impact on XXs' rights and roles across societies are alarming. For example, the teachings and promotion of XY being superior to XXs continue to confine XXs to subservient roles, perpetuating androcentric principles and limiting human rights.

Hinduism, for example, intertwines spirituality and culture, often portraying XXs as symbols of purity and devotion. Fasting for a husband and practical restrictions during menstruation are demanded. *Sati* – when a widow sacrifices herself on the husband's funeral pyre – though outlawed, continues. Despite these constraints, XXs find ways to challenge inequalities through domestic rituals, balancing cultural expectations and autonomy.

Islam, like most other religions, strictly prohibits sexual relations outside marriage, categorising them as illicit acts with severe consequences. Its teachings on modesty and chastity significantly impact XXs' roles in familial, societal, and legal contexts. While some interpretations of Islamic principles advocate for equality, traditional readings reinforce patriarchal expectations, imposing restrictive dress codes and severe punishments.

Judaism also prescribes modesty and behavioural regulations, with practices including hair covering for XXs. They are also traditionally encouraged to assume roles as caregivers and homemakers and are often excluded from leadership roles and specific rituals. Jewish feminists are demanding equity, resulting in incremental changes in some synagogues. Religious laws, including prohibiting menstruating XXs from sexual and religious practices until purification, continue to restrict autonomy.

Religious doctrines, though not explicitly mandating child marriage, continue to contribute to the act through interpretations that justify or excuse the practice, disproportionately impacting XXs. Despite laws and numerous international efforts to eliminate child marriage, deeply ingrained cultural, social, and religious norms continue to delay progress, partly due to legal loopholes.

IWRLs, including the Convention on the Elimination of All Forms of Discrimination Against Women (CEDAW) and the UN's Sustainable Development Goals (SDGs), form the backbone of global efforts to address sex-based inequality and promote human rights. However, persistent gaps between the creation and implementation of national and international laws, coupled with discriminatory practices and policy inconsistencies, are delaying progress. Strengthening laws, advocating for the ratification of IWRLs, and punishing perpetrators are essential to advance human rights. These changes are possible when XXs lobby for compliance.

For example, Women's International Non-Governmental Organisations (WINGOs) have been instrumental in advocating the rights of XXs, leveraging research and global networks to instigate transformative changes in laws and societal norms. By nurturing international collaboration, challenging patriarchal structures, and implementing innovative strategies, these XX–led organisations have achieved significant milestones, from legal reforms to increased political representation, paving the way for a more inclusive and equitable future.

Blame it on the Animal

The human animal is the only species that "possesses the capacity to carry out sexual inequality to its greatest known extremes" (Shlain, 2003:335). But why?

To understand the origins of sex-based injustices and bigotry, the roots of phallocentric notions are traced back to Aristotle (322 BCE) and Charles Darwin (19th c.).

As a zoology student, Lucy Cooke, author, believed she was a "loser" because she was an XX (Cooke, 2023:xiii). The origins of the exploitation of XXs, Cooke blames on Aristotle and Darwin, pointing out that Darwin:

> … gave a handful, of notably male, devotees of the new science of evolutionary psychology the ideological authority to claim that a host of grim male behaviours – from rape to compulsive skirt chasing to male supremacy – were 'only natural' for humans, because Darwin said so.
> (Cooke, 2023:xxii)

The evolutionary disparity between eggs and sperm, positioning XXs as biologically disadvantaged, forms the basis for all subsequent sex-based inequalities, as stated by Richard Dawkins in his book *The Selfish Gene*, originally published in 1976, on genetic interactions and evolution (Cooke, 2023; Dawkins, 2016).

These disadvantages were originally highlighted by Aristotle (*On the Generation of Animals*), written around the fourth century BCE, and later by Darwin (*On the Origin of Species by Means of Natural Selection*), originally published in 1859. However, Darwin's additional research on sexual selection was unattractive to the scientific patriarchy (Cooke, 2023) of the time, which allowed erroneous androcentric interpretations of human and animal behaviour to persist and define patriarchal regimes, including laws and legal interpretations.

International Law

Providing legal solutions to issues that negatively affect large groups of people is a crucial aspect of global governance (Sauer & Wöhl, 2011; United Nations Committee for Development Policy, 2014). International laws are not merely a collection of rules but serve as foundations for coexistence and collaboration between nations. Human rights laws, in particular, act as protectors, defending the dignity and freedom of individuals globally.

The Universal Declaration of Human Rights (UDHR), for example, was initiated after the atrocities of World War II and adopted in December 1948, with 48 countries voting in favour, eight abstaining, and two failing to vote (General Assembly Resolution 217 A). The declaration was designed to ensure freedom for all people (UN General Assembly, 1948) and continues to influence national constitutions, laws, and judicial decisions worldwide. UN member states are legally obligated to uphold the international contracts signed (Henkin, 1990, 1995), including IWRLs (Basu, 2016; Vijeyarasa, 2021d). However, ratification and enforcement of these laws remain inconsistent across nations (UN, 2021).

Despite their importance, the general public remain generally unaware (Broinowski & Wilkinson, 2005). Some scholars argue these laws are enigmatic, frequently disregarded, or perceived as superfluous due to their selective ratification (Crawford et al., 2017; Woodiwiss, 2006). Greater public awareness could encourage states to ratify and implement IWRLs, reinforcing accountability and further promoting equality initiatives.

The Role of Politics

"Law is made by political actors, not by lawyers, throughout political procedures, for political ends. The law that emerges is the result of political forces as are the influences of law on state behaviour" (Henkin, 1990:183). Political forces often determine the success or failure of international initiatives aimed at progressing the rights of XXs (Barnett & Duvall, 2005).

Real change requires sustained scrutiny and gradual modifications, as policies alone are often discretionary, with their success dependent on ratification, adaptation, and reform (Merry, 2009). However, "law as a means of pursuing or securing rights for XXs is far from straightforward" (Grabham & Hunter, 2008:2). Since laws embody values, ideologies, and mechanisms intended to deliver justice, the failure to implement international commitments exposes deficiencies in those very principles (O'Toole, 2000).

Laws and treaties are managed by a variety of stakeholders, including governments, intergovernmental organisations, NGOs, private entities, and other actors (Weiss, 2016). Effective policy implementation requires an examination of both internal and external actors within policy structures to determine why failures persist, including those with the power to provide political backing and financial benefits (O'Toole, 2000; O'Toole and Montjoy, 1984). However, "… law is gendered, being a manifestation of power that often works to the detriment of women. This need not be the case" (Vijeyarasa, 2024:115).

International laws have historically prioritised state sovereignty and security over social and cultural rights, disproportionately impacting XXs. A feminist reimagining of international laws seeks to expose these oversights and reconfigure the law as a tool for equality and justice. Incorporating diverse perspectives that intertwine human rights with feminism, and includes femocrats, are essential to challenging entrenched patriarchal paradigms and advancing inclusive global legal systems (Vega, 2023).

Legal Mechanisms and IWRLs

IWRLs addressing inequality have been enacted to promote equal rights (Aeberhard-Hodges & McFerran, 2018; Edgar & Thwaites, 2018). IWRLs include various agreements, mandates, and conventions signed by UN member states, creating binding international obligations for more than seven decades (CSW, 2019; Nawaz & Deegan, 2018; Vijeyarasa, 2021d).

CEDAW supports policies aimed at eliminating sex-based discrimination (Baldez, 2011; CEDAW, 1979; Vijeyarasa, 2021c). Since 1945, states, advocates, and XXs have invested significant resources in implementing global mandates against sex-based discrimination (CSW, 2019; UN General Assembly, 1948). However, the "wicked problem" (O'Brien et al., 2017); is described as "wicked" because it cannot be resolved independently of social, political, and economic contexts (Grint, 2010). Despite the longstanding commitments to IWRLs and the SDG targets and deadline, significant implementation gaps remain (Heideman et al., 2014; United Nations, 2018), particularly as the 2030 deadline approaches and time is running out.

Political International Advocacy Forums (PIAFs), including the UN and its numerous agencies (Vega, 2023), play a crucial role in addressing sex-based discrimination. Research suggests businesses and XX–led organisations can influence legislators to prioritise sex-based initiatives, including Goal 5 of the SDGs (Bailliet, 2016; Basu, 2016; UN, 1995; WHO, 2019).

Accountability

The persistence of discriminatory laws reflects the failure of governments to prioritise XXs, further entrenching patriarchal norms (McConnell, 2016; Watt, 2013). Many XXs remain marginalised in education, healthcare, economic participation, and political representation, often due to laws that perpetuate exclusion (Hudson et al., 2015; MacKinnon, 2005; WEF, 2020a).

Legal mechanisms are frequently obstructed at the implementation stage, where political complexities and competing interests prevent progress (McConnell, 2016). Accountability is therefore essential to close the gap between international and national laws. Nations must face consequences when promoting discrimination or failing to act on their international obligations (Neuwirth, 2005). The International Court of Justice (ICJ) and the International Criminal Court (ICC) play a critical role, as they contribute to interpreting agreements, setting legal precedents, and influencing the evolution of international laws.

Despite legislative advancements, discriminatory laws continue to violate international commitments, including those under CEDAW, the International Labour Organization (ILO), and other PIAFs (Thomas & Turnbull, 2021; Vijeyarasa, 2020). The interpretation and implementation of international laws remain highly inconsistent across nations, weakening their impact (Vega, 2023). The nations that promote themselves as "good international citizens" actively "encourage and develop the spread of international law, principally through their foreign ministers" (Rothwell & Crawford, 2017:1).

However, both national and international laws have achieved measurable progress in advancing rights for XXs and can, in part, act as agents for change (O'Toole, 2000; Sotarauta & Srinivas, 2015).

For example, in 2008, the UN recognised rape as a war crime and prosecuted it accordingly (UN Chronicle, 2008; Wood, 2018), marking a pivotal moment in addressing VAW. "It was the very first time in human history that sexual VAW during war was viewed as anything other than a natural consequence and entitlement of soldiers who encountered civilians" (Hudson et al., 2015:23).

In essence, international laws and treaties serve as essential instruments for dismantling patriarchal systems and addressing sex-based inequality. Yet, the persistent gap between agreements and their ratification and enforcement underscores the need for accountability. By understanding IWRLs, XXs can campaign, advocate, and demand governments ratify, enforce, and fulfil their legal obligations to deliver justice for all XXs worldwide. The most relevant PIAFs are outlined in this chapter.

The United Nations

The UN, as an international system, holds authority and should be held accountable for its failure to prevent inequality (von Bogdandy & Steinbrück Platise, 2012) and for misconduct at an international level (Spinedi, 2002). While the UN declares its greatest achievement to be the establishment of inclusive human rights laws, scholars argue that substantial improvements within the UN itself are urgently required (Hanhimaki, 2008).

Since its inception in 1945, the UN, one of the numerous PIAFs, has been a committed advocate for XXs' rights (Reilly, 2019; UN General Assembly, 1948). The 193 member states (UN, 2025) are legally bound to strive towards the full realisation of all human rights and fundamental freedoms (UNSC, 2024).

Despite the UN's intentions and laws, no nation has fully provided XXs with equal rights compared to XYs (IWPR, 2015; WEF, 2020a; UN Women, 2015). Furthermore, many targets and policies proposed by the UN and other PIAFs are yet to be achieved (APEC, 2011; Vega, 2023; WEF, 2020a) – equal pay for equal work, for example.

The agenda to advance XXs' rights remains challenging (Băluță, 2015; Fleming, 2007; Stephanopoulos, 2015). Criticism often centres on the UN's inability to effectively hold perpetrators accountable, including religious institutions and nations in the UN Security Council (UNSC) (Basu, 2016; Cornwall & Rivas, 2015). The Russian Federation is a prime example (UNSC, 2024; UNSC, n.d.).

A long-standing debate persists regarding the UN's capacity to influence member states to implement meaningful change. Some argue that the UN lacks sufficient power, while others claim it can influence its members through intricate networks developed over decades (Wiseman, 2015). Hence, the UN has the potential to instigate, promote, and adopt standards that could provide XXs with the same rights as XYs (Miéville, 2005; Moxon, 2007).

It is also argued that the UN should investigate violations when member states neglect their obligations under international law (Bailliet, 2016; Thomson, 2017). However, few nations have been held accountable or castigated for failing to deliver the required outcomes (Baldez, 2013; Bailliet, 2016; Thomson, 2017).

Nevertheless, the UN continues to achieve valuable outcomes, albeit with other PIAFs often reinforcing blockades and obstructing the public disclosure of policy conflicts (Basu, 2016; von Bogdandy & Steinbrück Platise, 2012; Thomson, 2017).

However, critics also highlight that UN laws fail to address power imbalances and inadequacies in measuring progress. As a result, the UN continues to fall short in securing sex-based equity, particularly without empowering the majority of XXs within complex global power systems (Arat, 2015).

Diplomacy often involves strategic negotiations to secure influence and opportunities. Effective diplomats employ considerable power, advocating for critical issues, including sexual and reproductive health rights (Vega, 2023), the elimination of child marriage, and VAW (UN Women, 2020). Addressing these issues is vital for advancing global equality.

Rape, for example, is frequently employed as a military strategy or tactical practice during armed conflicts to instil terror and enforce ethnic cleansing as a means to control. XXs account for the great majority (95%) of those subjected to conflict-related sexual violence (UN, 2020; Wood, 2018). The UN's *Action Against Sexual Violence in Conflict* initiative unites 14 UN entities to coordinate efforts, strengthen accountability, and deliver comprehensive support to survivors.

Additionally, in 2016, the ILO acknowledged the impact of VAW in the workplace and aligned its efforts with Goal 5 of the SDGs (Aeberhard-Hodges & McFerran, 2018). Although debates persist regarding the UN's efficacy, it remains clear that the UN has the power to influence, advocate, and monitor progress for the rights of XXs. However, the sovereignty to ratify or disregard international laws on sex-based discrimination ultimately resides with member nations. The actions of individual nations determine whether sex-based discrimination should be eliminated by the 2030 deadline established under the SDGs.

Introduced in 2016, the 17 SDGs were designed with the overarching aim of transforming global economic progress while protecting the planet's sustainability (UN, 2017). Goal 5 specifically seeks to achieve equal participation for XXs alongside XYs in political, economic, and public life (DPMC, 2022; Kusuma & Babu, 2017; UN, 2018). However, the SDGs face considerable challenges. For example, data from the World Economic Forum (WEF) and the UN indicate that progress toward the 17 goals has been slow, often characterised by stagnation and, at times, regression (Krook & Restrepo Sanín, 2020; Vijeyarasa, 2021b; WEF, 2020b; WHO, 2019).

As the 2030 deadline looms, the elimination of sex-based discrimination remains unfulfilled in all nations (Bailliet, 2016; Vijeyarasa, 2021a; WEF, 2020a; World Bank Group, 2020).

UN Women

The UN's entity, UN Women, was created in 2010 to increase its impact. The formation was completed through the amalgamation of four other UN agencies – the Division for the Advancement of Women (DAW), the International Research and Training Institute for the Advancement of Women (INSTRAW), the Office of the Special Adviser on Gender Issues and Advancement of Women (OSAGI), and the UN's Development Fund for Women (UNIFEM) – to create a single agency intended to enhance human rights for XXs globally. The changes provided UN Women with a higher status than its predecessors, including the ability to allocate specific budgets and collaborate with other agencies, including the Commission on the Status of Women (CSW) and CEDAW (Boyne, 2011).

UN Women supports UN members, designs "laws, policies, [and] programmes," and promotes, coordinates, and advances the economic empowerment of XXs, including planning, budgeting, and development (Ban, 2014:277). Moreover, UN Women appeals to its members to advance XXs into leadership positions to achieve a 50/50 ratio between XXs and XYs (UN Women, 2015). There are 41 executives on the UN Women board, representing the great majority of nations (UN Women, n.d.).

UN Women also advocates for the celebration of International Women's Day (IWD) on March 8, with a distinct theme designated by the UN each year. Originally recognised in 1977 (UN, n.d.-c), the day is promoted to recognise and celebrate the achievements of XX "… without regard to divisions, whether national, ethnic, linguistic, cultural, economic or political" (UN Women, 2024).

Although the exact date marking the origin of IWD remains contested, some records indicate it commenced in the 19th century, with XXs protesting poor working conditions between 1848 (UN, n.d.-c) and 1857 (Kaplan, 1985). In New York City, for example, XX garment and textile workers protested 12-hour shifts. Law enforcement ended the protests, but their battles continued (Kaplan, 1985). Others argue it began in 1908 or 1919 in the USA and in 1910 in several EU countries (Wøjdemann et al., 2017). Where there is consensus is that March 8 was designated based on the 1917 Russian Revolution (Chatterjee, 2002).

In contemporary times, IWD is mainly celebrated by the privileged, businesses and corporations that promote success, opulence, and cupcakes. Critics argue that the commercialisation now overshadows the origins of the working-class XXs' resistance to capitalism. The shift over the centuries reflects a market-driven culture where gifts are exchanged (Søland, 2019; Chaudhuri, 2022). The media talk about XXs more on IWD than any other day of the year; with food, alcohol, and good times replacing the original fight, while many around the world are still struggling for basic human rights.

CEDAW

Often referred to as the "international bill of women's human rights," CEDAW is recognised as a pivotal instrument within the international human rights system, addressing equal rights for XXs and contributing positively to global efforts for equality (Englehart & Miller, 2014; Raday, 2018; Htun & Weldon, 2010; UN Women, 1981).

Established by the CSW, CEDAW was adopted by the UN General Assembly in 1979 to tackle all areas where XXs experience discrimination (DFAT, 2020; Raday, 2018). CEDAW actively advocates for member states to amend domestic laws to eliminate sex-based prejudices and ensure the protection of their human rights (Thornton, 2010).

Despite these obligations, nations ignore the rights of XXs. Critics argue that CEDAW sometimes lacks the clarity and strength needed to influence IWRLs effectively and is susceptible to cultural and religious pretexts that denigrate XXs (Nussbaum, 2016; Raday, 2018; Rosenblum, 2011). The Convention and its Committee work to eliminate sex-based discrimination, guarantee access to human rights for XXs, and monitor compliance among its 189 signatory nations, making it the leading legally binding international convention promoting equality for XXs (Vijeyarasa, 2021c).

The CEDAW Committee, in made up of 23 independent experts, meets three times a year (AHRC, 2022) to monitor implementation, provide recommendations, identify intolerances, and advise member states to act on its recommendations and obligations under international law (Arat, 2015; Nussbaum, 2016).

Member states are required to submit reports every four years, detailing how they fulfil their commitments under the Convention. However, the Committee lacks enforcement capacity and prosecutorial powers, as CEDAW operates without regulatory enforcement. Its limitations allow states to avoid penalties for failing to meet obligations or for submitting late reports (Australian NGO Coalition, 2018; Merry, 2003, 2009). Additionally, states may comply with reporting requirements while omitting unfavourable evidence, further weakening CEDAW's impact (Nussbaum, 2016).

NGOs play a vital role in supporting the CEDAW Committee by submitting shadow reports and participating in informal consultations (UN Women, 2022). NGOs are also given opportunities to engage directly with the Committee during prearranged public meetings and country-specific briefings (International Women's Rights Action Watch Asia-Pacific, 2022). However, critics highlight that the Committee's complacency has restricted NGO efforts creating uncertainty among governments and policymakers (Thomson, 2017).

Despite its wide adoption the effectiveness of CEDAW remains uneven, with patchy successes. Many states struggle to understand and implement their provisions due to differences in legal and judicial systems (McCrudden, 2015). Moreover, the perception of XXs as a homogeneous entity further complicates efforts to achieve meaningful progress (Arat, 2015).

Although most UN member states have endorsed CEDAW – with the notable exception of the USA, which signed it in 1980, but has yet to ratify the Convention (de Alwis & Verveer, 2021) – many nations disregard its provisions, allowing patriarchal norms to persist and continue obstructing advancements for equality. This highlights the urgent need for enforceable laws to enhance opportunities for XXs worldwide and dismantle entrenched inequalities (Basu, 2016; Mackay, 2008; Shaw et al., 2013).

Commission on the Status of Women (CSW)

Established in 1946, the CSW advocates for the rights of XXs across political, economic, civil, social, and educational domains globally (UN Women, 2019; CSW, 2019). In 1996, its mandate was expanded to include monitoring and reviewing progress on the implementation of the Beijing Declaration and Platform for Action, aligning its efforts with broader UN goals (UN Women, 2019). At the Beijing Declaration and Platform for Action in 1995, it was recognised that inequalities between the sexes had persisted and that significant obstacles remained. Governments acknowledged the urgency of prioritising actions for the empowerment and advancement of XXs (Basu, 2016; Ban, 2014; UN, 1995).

However, critics argue that CSW, as a state-centric organisation, often fails to reflect the priorities of XXs, claiming that: (i) CSW resolutions are incomplete; and (ii) broad policies are often amalgamated into one resolution, which constrains NGOs from challenging nations on individual components of wider policy areas (Rincker et al., 2019).

Although CSW provides platforms for NGOs to raise concerns internationally, like other UN entities, the CSW lacks the authority to enforce compliance. Reports indicate that global progress remains insufficient to achieve Goal 5 of the SDGs (UN Women, 2019). Additionally, with the majority of attendees being XXs, annual meetings often amount to preaching to the converted.

The International Labour Organization (ILO)

A specialised agency within the UN, the ILO is recognised as the world's largest "tripartite" organisation, comprising employers, unions, and states, and remains the only entity focused exclusively on work-related issues (Hodges, 2014:566).

Since its establishment in 1919, the ILO has aimed to recommend better working conditions, achieving notable successes despite occasional disagreements among its 187 member states, as of May 2025 (Haworth & Hughes,

2010; ILO, n.d.; Thomas & Turnbull, 2021). Key achievements include strategies to maintain autonomy, ensure relevance, promote leadership, and engage externally (Thomas & Turnbull, 2021:16).

The ILO has also addressed workplace sex-based violence through several established treaties, including the Discrimination (Employment and Occupation) Convention, 1958 (No. 111), the Workers with Family Responsibilities Convention, 1981 (No. 156), and the Maternity Protection Convention, 2000 (No. 183) (Aeberhard-Hodges & McFerran, 2018:251). As previously mentioned, in 2016, the ILO also recognised the impact of VAW in the workplace, aligning its support with Goal 5 of the SDGs (UN Women, 2020).

However, the ILO's influence and effectiveness remain subjects of debate. Critics note its lack of "power of enforcement," likening it to other UN entities (Thomas & Turnbull, 2021:874). Nonetheless, others argue the ILO has maintained relevance and achieved significant progress in improving working conditions since its inception (Haworth & Hughes, 2010). To ensure its future impact, the ILO must develop strategies to hold violators of international contracts accountable (Ryder, 2015).

Despite the ILO's advocacy, many nations continue to disregard international laws, thereby perpetuating systemic inequality. The global income pay gap, for example, remains an alarming concern driven by a narrow androcentric agenda. Among the 146 nations measured in the *Global Gender Gap Report*, a 31.5% gap remains, reflecting only minimal progress over the years (WEF, 2024).

Other reports indicate that the gap between the sexes "will take 131 years to reach full parity" (WEF, 2023:5). However, at the current rate of progress, the UN estimates it will take an additional 286 years to eliminate discriminatory laws and address gaps in legal protections for XXs (UN, n.d.-b).

The persistent discrimination, evidenced by issues including VAW (Chapter 4) and the enduring income pay gap (Chapter 6), accentuates the failures of XY leaders. While the impediments present a bleak outlook, advocates for equality persist in their efforts to achieve justice within and beyond the framework of laws.

Visionary Forces

WINGOs and NGOs vigorously campaign for the rights of XXs around the globe. Over the decades, global networks have ignited political pressure and demand to initiate pro–XX institutions and policies (Caglar et al., 2013; Reza, 2022). As a result, a number of legislative measures have been obtained, including various anti-discrimination legislations in the great majority nations.

Research highlights the importance of a focused approach for XXs to achieve further success. NGOs engaging with authorities and using data to convey the realities and struggles of sex-based discrimination need to continue (Jansen et al., 2010; Rincker et al., 2019).

The International Monetary Fund (IMF, 2018), for example, concluded that NGOs play a crucial role in enhancing a nation's understanding of the issues impacting XXs, echoing the message delivered in 1975 by the UN:

> The World Conference of the International Women's Year, [is] aware that the problems of women, who constitute half of the world's population, are the problems of society as a whole, and that changes in the present economic, political and social situation of women must become an integral part of efforts to transform the structures and attitudes that hinder the genuine satisfaction of their needs.
>
> (UN, 1975:2)

WINGOs and NGOs have encouraged and enabled activists to demand equal justice and opportunities, exemplified when the UN proclaimed the "Decade for Women". This period (1976–1985) inspired international feminist advocacy but did not achieve all the intended objectives. Nevertheless, numerous feminists became experts and, with their qualifications and knowledge, were able to strategically identify the underlying causes of ongoing sex-based inequality and unequal power dynamics. They also explored strategies to further the objectives of feminism, including addressing the impact of VAW (Caglar et al., 2013).

Over the years, WINGOs and NGOs have played a pivotal role, engaging in constructive actions with states and effectively influencing leaders by sharing well-researched strategies, robust data, and relevant information (Sauer & Wöhl, 2011). These efforts have led to transformative changes in local, national, and international laws, evidenced by significant milestones and achievements (Chapter 7).

Reforms led by numerous XXs, united to address the pervasive issues of sex-based discrimination, leverage national and international platforms to expose injustices (Reza, 2022). Additionally, feminist movements have further amplified their influence through active engagement in international systems (Sauer & Wöhl, 2011).

Before the UN's formation, XX groups were instrumental in shaping agendas. In 1946, for example, WINGOs endorsed the General Assembly's resolution granting XXs equal political rights (UN General Assembly, 1948).

Although nations leverage formal agreements including CEDAW, smaller NGOs often adopt alternative tactics, including distributing knowledge. The XX–led NGOs have contributed to positive narratives at the UN, highlighting their achievements and resilience (Alger, 2013; Caglar et al., 2013). Persistent advocacy has amplified diverse viewpoints within UN deliberations, enhancing the authority and efficiency of international laws (Reza, 2022).

Resistance from those exercising androcentric power at various stages of policy development, however, continues to delay progress. Nevertheless, NGOs and WINGOs exert significant influence on parliamentary representation. Patriarchal traditions, nonetheless, persist as a recurring barrier, frequently preventing advancements.

To overcome obstacles, XX–led organisations often leverage the "boomerang principle" (Keck & Sikkink, 1998:12), also referred to as the "boomerang effect" (Casas et al., 2023), a strategy through which NGOs in one country activate transnational networks to exert pressure elsewhere (Chapter 3). These strategies have proven effective in amplifying advocacy efforts and securing changes. Nations that align with international systems tend to achieve greater success, particularly when other tactical considerations are in place (Casas et al., 2023; Thomson, 2017).

Progress has been achieved, albeit slowly, including an increase in XX leaders (Colley & van Acker, 2021; IPU, 2024). Other landmark achievements include the Equality for Men and Women at Work Act in Sweden (Swedish Parliament, 2000); the implementation of quotas in various regions (Bush, 2011), including in Indian local elections; the abolition of the tampon tax in numerous countries; and several other milestones, some of which have been partly driven by online campaigns (Barclay et al., 2024; James, 2022), further reviewed in Chapter 3.

As awareness of the pervasive issue of sex-based discrimination increases, XXs continue building and cultivating partnerships to combat all forms of subjugation (UN, 1975). The advocacy efforts of XX–led organisations remain not only fully justified, but essential, as heinous crimes against XXs continue to occur. The ongoing violations necessitate ongoing collaboration in the pursuit for equality, including efforts to challenge harmful phallocentric practices within religious institutions.

Immoral Prophets

Religious institutions and their doctrines have further propagated the belief that XXs are inferior and must be controlled (MacCulloch, 2024; Reid, 2013; Walker, 2011). For example, religious doctrines often impose strict regulations on sexual behaviour: XXs are expected to remain virgins, with their hymen intact until marriage, while no equivalent expectations exist for XYs. Through such controls, religions have consistently dominated and inhibited human sexuality, oppressing individuals and their actions.

Determining the exact number of religions worldwide is challenging due to the difficulty in distinguishing distinct faiths from their myriad denominations. This section, nonetheless, focuses on the most widely practised religions – Christianity, Hinduism, and Islam – along with Judaism, which holds significant historical connections to various religious traditions. The systemic oppression of XXs through religious doctrines is a recurring theme across the great majority of faiths.

Christianity, the world's largest religion, has around 2.6 billion believers, accounting for three in ten (31%) of the global population. Islam, the second largest, has around 1.9 billion followers, representing a quarter (25%) of all people. Hinduism, the oldest major religion, claims 1.2 billion adherents, or three out of 20 (15%) of the global population (Statistics & Data, 2023; World Population Review, 2024).

In contrast, Judaism, though practised by more than 14 million people (less than 0.19% of the global population), holds significant cultural and historical influence (MacCulloch, 2024; Padoux, 1984; Statista, 2022; World Population Review, 2024).

The historical foundations of these religions reveal deeply entrenched and persistent misogyny (Shlain, 2003). Interestingly, global data from 192 nations indicate that XXs are more likely than XYs to affiliate with religious communities: more than 83% of XXs compared to around 79% of XYs (PRC, 2016a, 2016b).

The level of misogyny inherent in archaic religious constructs cannot be fully evaluated, analysed, or accurately quantified (Priest & Biddle, 2017), as XXs have been largely excluded from writing history, omitted from historical records, and their contributions distorted or ignored (Dowse, 2014; Hawkesworth, 2012). Teachings from influential religious leaders – the vast majority of whom are XYs – infiltrate the minds of followers globally, perpetuating and reinforcing discrimination (Hunsberger & Jackson, 2005).

Canon law and other faith-based rules position religious institutions as the ultimate arbiters of morality, extending their influence beyond spiritual practices to regulate personal behaviour, social norms, laws, and political institutions.

Religious doctrines often demonise sexual acts deemed "unnatural" – including adultery, fornication, homosexuality, and masturbation – thereby promoting and intensifying shame and repression while granting religious leaders the ability to impose orders and reinforce authority (Haliczer, 1996; MacCulloch, 2024; Nelson, 1983; Padoux, 1984; Sipe, 1995). Such ritualistic suppression deprives individuals of the understanding of intimacy and pleasure as natural and sacrosanct aspects of life.

Feminist assessments of canon law's impact on XXs are not new, novel, or unwarranted. Historically, religious institutions have positioned the family as the moral cornerstone, relegating XXs to roles as mothers, wives, and moral guardians, thereby excluding them from spiritual, public, and political domains.

Many, however, have fought back and continue to do so. For example, in 19th c. France, rationalists and republicans asserted that XXs' allegiance to religious establishments represented a barrier to societal advancement and posed a significant challenge to the development of a secular state (Chavura et al., 2019). Those who rejected motherhood as the "natural vocation" and sole acceptable career path for an XX, were labelled as "anti-patriotic" (Boxer, 1982:551).

In the 21st century, growing numbers of worshippers are questioning religious dogmas, and others are disengaging. Whilst diversity and pluralism flourish, sexual activity outside of marriage continues to be labelled sinful, viewed as a deviation from divine intentions.

Christianity, Hinduism, Islam, and Judaism continue condemning homosexuality among XYs as sacrilege, depraved, and perverse boundaries – standards constructed and enforced by XYs. These perspectives, rooted in archaic theologies, reinforce heteronormative values (Hunt, 2013; MacCulloch, 2024; Ratcliff & Haltom, 2023).

Historically, marriage has functioned less as a romantic union and more as a contractual arrangement between a deity, a bride's father, and the husband. These patriarchal constructs, deeply entwined with religious traditions, continue to suppress XXs' independence and reinforce their subjugation (MacCulloch, 2024; Winkler, 1998).

Religious leaders also exert considerable influence over laws and governance, frequently deepening divisions and fuelling resistance to change (Hunt, 2013; MacCulloch, 2024; Ratcliff & Haltom, 2023). Conflicts between faith-based institutions and governments over legislative initiatives, particularly concerning XXs' rights, have long existed and still prevail.

For example, the UK Equality Act 2010 (UK Parliament, 2010) – partly influenced by a 2008 directive from the European Commission for equal treatment regardless of sex, sexual orientation, age, religion, or belief (Hand et al., 2012) – faced resistance from religious groups claiming it infringed upon their liberties.

Similar debates were witnessed with Australia's 1984 Sex Discrimination Act (SDA) (Hunt, 2013; Commonwealth of Australia, 1984), with critics arguing that the legislation threatened to dismantle long-standing family norms and traditions, framing it as a disruptive force against established values.

The pious' resistance to equity remains primarily focused on sexual rights and civil partnerships, signalling a pivotal moment in the evolving role of religious institutions within secular and pluralistic societies.

As religious influence declined with the growth of secularisation in UK society, for example, the Church was compelled to adapt its rhetoric from moral absolutism to rights and freedoms (Hunt, 2013). A broader institutional struggle to reconcile entrenched religious teachings on sexuality with contemporary expectations of DEI (Bull et al., 2022; Colgan & Colgan, 2011) became evident as tensions between the old guard and a more secular nation emerged.

Despite opposition, both Acts in Australia and the UK were passed, and no significant adverse effects have been observed. On the contrary, the SDA in Australia has facilitated numerous progressive legislative developments, contributing positively to legal, cultural, and social reforms (Commonwealth of Australia, 1984; Vega, 2023). Religious leaders have partly justified suppression by asserting that XXs are irrational, with XYs claiming that "women lack logic", "cannot learn scientific procedures", and that their intellect is inferior to XYs (Walker, 1994:511).

Religious leaders continue to authorise the suppression and abuse of XXs based on fictitious and anachronistic assumptions (Gudorf, 2011; Hunsberger & Jackson, 2005; Reid, 2013), depicting them as the "devil's gateway" (Walker, 2011:1), thereby justifying and forcing XXs to live under a cloud of purported disrepute.

Throughout history, "religion continues to be used as a shield" to violate human rights, despite declarations by the UN that there is "no justification for such violations" (Farrior, 2009:84). While religious leaders do not always achieve their objectives, religious institutions directly influence how the world is governed, including the rule of law, international relations, diplomacy, foreign policy, and numerous other legislative considerations (Henne, 2018; Johnson & Grim, 2013; Mansouri et al., 2015; Miéville, 2005; Moxon, 2007). Religious institutions are also exempt (Chapter 1) from various income and property taxes, thereby enabling and reinforcing their economic power and institutional privilege (Bengtsson, 2023; Blaney, 2022; Newman, 2019; Torrance, 2021).

Despite secular frameworks in democratic nations, starting with a prayer, for example, has been customary in numerous Australian parliaments and councils since 1901 and continues (Parliament of Australia, 2022). This tradition is increasingly facing criticism and protests, with opponents arguing that it is unlawful (Beck, 2021, 2023; Sanders, 2024; Sapkota & Dahal, 2022).

Prayer positions religion as a source of cultural values, norms, and symbols, offering principles that guide actions and behaviours (Gregg, 2016). Those who fail to comply with imposed rules – accused of moral transgressions, heresy, or committing sins against God – have historically faced severe punishments, including banishment, expulsion, ostracism, burning, drowning, stoning, or beheading. For example, Jeanne d'Arc (aka Joan of Arc) was burnt at the stake in 1431 in France, after being accused by a bishop of heresy and witchcraft (Grigat & Carrier, 2007; Hobbins, 2005; Kolbaba, 2003; Noor, 2010).

Although individuals are no longer executed for defying orthodoxy in contemporary contexts, severe forms of punishments persist in different forms, with equally devastating consequences. For example, the criminalisation of non-heterosexual partnerships, and various depraved practices including *sati* and child marriage. Numerous religious sects also exert extraordinary control over XXs, with authorities often unable or failing to intervene and protect.

Several major reasons for the continuation of illegal practices include the influence of patriarchs who prioritise XYs. Whether consciously or unconsciously, the devotees' mindset sustains and reinforces the subservience of XXs, both historically and in contemporary societies (Jaworska & Larrivée, 2011; Reid, 2013).

Devout leaders also continue exhibiting hypocritical behaviours, prioritising status over justice. Clerical celibacy, for example, has often been exploited to commit acts of abuse within the sanctum of confessionals, including misconduct with married XXs and the sexual abuse of children. These actions exploit, oppress, and persecute communities, inflicting profound psychological, social, and spiritual harm on individuals and societies (Frawley-O'Dea, 2007; Haliczer, 1996; MacCulloch, 2024; Sipe, 1995).

Prioritising status over equity, justice, and morality – principles many religious actors endorse and claim to uphold but often ignore – remains their primary focus. By promoting heterosexual expectations, they also often provoke atrocities against the innocent (Frawley-O'Dea, 2007; Haliczer, 1996; Nelson, 1983; Sipe, 1995).

Numerous religious institutions continue to evade accountability, shielding their misconduct from scrutiny and disregarding secular norms (Frawley-O'Dea, 2007; Haliczer, 1996; MacCulloch, 2024; Nelson, 1983; Sipe, 1995). To date, few of these criminals have faced consequences proportionate to their crimes, let alone punishment as severe as being burnt at the stake!

Christianity

The Virgin Mary, sanctified in Christianity as the embodiment of virginity and celibacy, serves as a powerful symbol reinforcing sexual restraint as the moral ideal of XX purity. This model is further sustained by the framing of marriage as a remedy for sexual sin – a patriarchal construct to dominate, subjugate, subordinate, and control XXs (MacCulloch, 2024; Nelson, 1983; Sipe, 1995).

Theologians have long positioned XXs as inherently inferior to XYs, both physically and morally, to justify their exclusion from clergy leadership, pious authority, and sacred power.

Originally, Christianity absorbed and reinterpreted Judaic dogmas on sexuality and sexual acts, advocating celibacy and chastity as virtues based on the belief that sexual desire detracts from spiritual commitment. XXs were regarded as sources of temptation and moral frailty, necessitating divine supervision to uphold order, morality, sacred integrity, and communal purity (MacCulloch, 2024; Nelson, 1983; Padoux, 1984; Winkler, 1998).

In Catholicism, celibacy remains central to those devoted to God's work. While sex is deemed good, it is strictly confined to marriage. Sex outside of marriage, referred to as fornication or adultery, is regarded as a sin that separates individuals from God, carrying significant consequences, including divine judgment. Within marriage, sexual relations are primarily intended for procreation, ensuring the continuation of a bloodline and fulfilling divine commandments, as expressed in the Bible: "Be fruitful and multiply" (Ademiluka, 2020; Crowther-Heyck, 2002; MacCulloch, 2024).

Polygyny – one XY with multiple XXs – has been practised throughout history, often for sexual selection and to ensure reproductive efficiency and success (Choi & Park, 2023; Low, 1988). In theory, all wives were to be treated equally. Within Christianity, polygyny was historically regulated to ensure fairness – examples are included in the Old Testament, with Abraham, David, and Solomon indicated as having multiple wives. Over time, monogamy became the norm, influenced by social and fiscal factors. However, numerous Christian denominations, particularly in Africa, continue to practise polygyny (Allen, 2014; MacCulloch, 2024; Rompis et al., 2020).

Although marital norms have evolved, XXs continue facing exclusion from leadership roles. For example, while some Christian denominations ordain XXs as priests or ministers, the majority of Christian practitioners maintain traditional XY–only priesthoods.

To further confirm the ostracisation of XXs from top ranks, in 2016, Pope Francis said: "the Catholic Church's ban on women becoming priests is forever and will never be changed" (Kirchgaessner, 2016). These messages, together with the accompanying narratives of religious views (Foucault, 1982), reinforce archaic phallocentric faith-based principles that perpetuate the alleged inferiority of XXs, legitimise XY dominance, and promote patriarchal authority (Reid, 2013).

In early Christianity, however, XXs held significant leadership roles. Additionally, the rumoured Pope Joan was believed to have been a "hermaphrodite"; their intersex was allegedly revealed when they gave birth. Still, Pope Joan's existence is consistently denied by most religious authorities (Gengler & Lee, 2002; Homolka & Schöttler, 2013; Macy, 2008; Rustici, 2006; Urbaniak & Willman, 2023).

Hinduism

Sexuality transcends physical expression, encompassing metaphysical and symbolic significance intertwined with culture and spirituality in Hindu philosophy. The merging of an XX and an XY symbolises the balance and interconnectedness of opposites within the universe.

The *Kama Sutra* highlights the art of love and sexuality within defined boundaries, but societal norms impose limitations, to allegedly uphold social order and purity, whilst portraying XXs as both tempting and potentially dangerous. These contradictions underscore Hinduism's complex perspective, where sexuality is both fulfilling and a pathway to enlightenment, while constraining XXs' autonomy (Padoux, 1984; Suri, 2017).

Hinduism, like most other religions, is rooted in patriarchal foundations that historically govern, oppress, and subordinate XXs. Hindu law imposes rigid responsibilities, positioning XXs as perpetual dependents on their fathers, husbands, and sons. Chastity, obedience, and self-sacrifice are promoted as virtues, reinforcing XY dominance and entrenching sex-based inequality (Muller & Bühler, 2001; Narayan & Gurung, 2016).

Directives on chastity and purity are cornerstones for XXs, irrespective of their roles as "mother, virgin, or goddess" (Banerjee, 2010:271). For example, XXs are prohibited from participating in religious rituals or entering temples during menstruation, perpetuating exclusion and impurity perceptions. Matrimonial traditions like *Karva Chauth*, where XXs fast for their husbands' strength and longevity, further highlight their dependence on XYs, often at the expense of their health and autonomy (Ram, 2021; Suri, 2017).

Despite these constraints, XXs assert influence in specific ritualistic practices within the home, challenging inequalities and the pursuit of personal independence (Narayan & Gurung, 2016; Pintchman, 2007).

Hinduism's repression of XXs' sexuality and autonomy is exemplified by the outlawed practice of *sati*, reflecting deeply ingrained beliefs wives are extensions of husbands. Although illegal, isolated cases persist, driven by cultural and religious injustice that continues to devalue XXs' rights, particularly among upper caste. Widowhood imposes rigid orthodox practices, minimising sovereignty and subjecting widows to lifelong exploitation and marginalisation (Harlan, 1992; Hawley, 2023; Lekha & Kumar, 2025; Misra, 2020; Sarkar, 2014). Emerging around 500 CE, *sati*, depicted as an act of self-sacrifice, is linked to the village goddess *Sati*, admired for her devotion through self-immolation (Hawley, 2023; Sarkar, 2014).

A widely publicised case in 1987 brought global attention when Roop Kanwar, an 18-year-old XX widow, reportedly leapt onto her husband's funeral pyre. The incident sparked condemnation from feminists and human rights activists, prompting the Commission of Sati (Prevention) Bill in 1988. The Bill prohibited monuments honouring *sati* but faced resistance from local protesters and religious groups defending cultural traditions (Banerjee, 2010; Misra, 2020; Padoux, 1984; Sarkar, 2014).

The true motivations behind *sati* remain elusive, as those who practice it vanish alongside their husbands, making the triggers for this act difficult to research and understand (Hawley, 2023; Sarkar, 2014).

Islam

The Qur'an strictly prohibits all sexual relations outside of marriage, categorising them as illicit sexual intercourse (*zina*), encompassing both fornication and adultery. Modesty and chastity are mandatory, with severe consequences prescribed for premarital and extramarital sexual acts (El-Ali, 2021). Venerated as the literal word of God, the Qur'an originates within a narrative involving a father and his son and serves as the primary source of spiritual, legal, moral, and sexual guidance in Islam.

As one of the world's most widely practised religions, Islam's theological doctrines, social norms, and cultural customs significantly structure the lives of XXs. Practices, both traditional and contemporary, vary widely, with diverse interpretations of Islamic law observed across Southeast Asia, the Middle East, and North Africa. While some nations adopt more inclusive and egalitarian readings of Islamic principles, the intersection of Islamic traditions frequently reinforces patriarchal constructs (Arosoaie & Osman, 2018; Gross-Wyrtzen, 2023; Hessini, 2007). Interpretations of texts often serve to dominate, subjugate, and subordinate XXs, exerting control over their roles and rights within familial, societal, and legal frameworks.

Historically, the interpretation of Islamic texts has been dominated by XY scholars. These interpretations confine XXs to roles as caregivers, mothers, and wives, while granting XYs authority over them. Critics argue that such readings reflect cultural biases rather than the Qur'an's inherent egalitarian ethos, asserting that Islam provides XXs with the same rights and privileges as given to XYs (Ahmed, 1992; El-Ali & El Fadl, 2022; Esposito, 2011; Mernissi, 1991).

However, laws prescribing severe punishments, including stoning for adultery or sexual misconduct, disproportionately target XXs, placing the burden of upholding family honour on them. Notably, stoning is not explicitly mentioned in the Qur'an, yet its continued practice demonstrates the influence of interpretative traditions. The abolition of stoning remains a contentious issue globally, with growing calls for alignment with contemporary human rights (Korbatieh, 2018; Cope et al., 2019; Noor, 2010; UN, n.d.-a).

Legal dress codes mandating garments, including the hijab, niqab, or burqa, continue in countries including Iran and Afghanistan. These dress codes, at times voluntary, are often justified as protective measures, citing their role in reducing objectification and providing a deeper connection to religious and cultural heritage. However, mandatory veiling laws raise significant ethical and legal concerns, as they function both as tools of liberation and mechanisms of control. Courts frequently confront the challenge of balancing the right to religious freedom against competing interests, including equality, public safety, and national security (Esposito, 2011; Gibson, 2007; La Fornara, 2018; Poulos, 2019).

Judaism

One of the oldest monotheistic faiths, Judaism has profoundly influenced the roles, rights, and experiences of XXs and influenced other religions throughout history. The Hebrew Scriptures, particularly the *Song of Songs*, poetically depict acts including kissing and crying, symbolising deep emotional and spiritual connections. These gestures portray intimate expressions of love and devotion (MacCulloch, 2024).

Jewish jurisprudence imposes strict guidelines for sexual conduct. For example, menstruating XXs are deemed impure, prohibiting them from engaging in sexual relations and from participating in religious practices until completing a purification ritual (*mikveh*) following their menstrual cycle. While these laws are deeply rooted in religious tradition, they significantly restrict the autonomy and freedoms of XXs (Hauptman & Greenspahn, 2009; Holub, 2012).

Additionally, dress codes and religious practices regulating behaviour and public appearance are integral to Judaism. For example, Orthodox XXs are required to adhere to principles of modesty in their attire and cover their hair, which is considered alluring, particularly among married XXs. The use of wigs enables XXs to honour their faith while adapting to changing contexts (Bronner, 1993; Fader, 2009).

As in many other religions, XXs in Judaism are encouraged to assume roles as caregivers and homemakers and are excluded from positions of leadership and certain ritual practices. In Orthodox Judaism, for example, XXs are barred from becoming rabbis and are often segregated during synagogue services. Deeply entrenched androcentric values permeate Judaism, much like the great majority of religions. Consequently, Jewish feminists continue to challenge traditional norms, advocating for equitable treatment within their faith and legal philosophy. While progress has been slow, some synagogues now permit XXs to hold leadership roles and contribute to decision-making processes, reflecting incremental change. Nevertheless, the presence of an XX is still considered by some to be a distraction to XYs' spiritual experiences (Adler, 1998; Gordan et al., 2020; Green, 1999; Hauptman & Greenspahn, 2009).

Religious patriarchal institutions continue to exert control over XXs globally and remain among the most sexist misogynistic establishments on earth. Their resistance to progress and equality, as well as their culpable avoidance of laws designed to protect the rights of XXs, must be addressed through prosecution. These institutions dictate beliefs and behaviours that create dire obstructions to human rights, including the perpetuation of child marriages.

Child Marriage

Globally, an estimated 720 million XXs were married as children, with more than 250 million married before the age of 15 – amounting to one in five XXs married as minors. The prevalence of child marriage is six times higher among XXs compared to XYs. South Asia has the highest rates, where one in two XXs are married under the age of 18, followed by sub-Saharan Africa, the Middle East, North Africa, and parts of Latin America. Child brides face higher risks of DV, frequently experience adolescent pregnancies, and are less likely to obtain an education. Although the legal minimum age for marriage is generally 18 years, discriminatory legislations allow minors to marry in various democratic regions (Arthur et al., 2018; UNICEF, 2014, 2023).

For example, in the USA, child marriage persists under inconsistent legal frameworks, with some states permitting minors to marry with parental consent or judicial approval. One study estimated that one in every 161 children aged 15 to 17 is married in the USA.

Child marriage is not explicitly mandated by religious teachings; however, various ideologies often contribute to its prevalence (Wilkinson et al., 2024). In many cases, certain religious interpretations are used to justify or excuse this universally condemned practice. Child marriage is also heavily influenced by cultural, social, and economic factors, as well as legal loopholes (Arthur et al., 2018; Fan & Koski, 2022).

Efforts to restrict child marriage have faced limited success due to deeply ingrained cultural and religious practices. Despite international commitments, including the SDGs, to eliminate child marriage by 2030, enforcement measures have shown minimal progress (Koski & Heymann, 2018; UNICEF, 2023).

The UN, alongside states and advocacy groups, continues working to eradicate child marriage by addressing fundamental contributors including sex-based discrimination, poverty, and a lack of education (Efevbera & Bhabha, 2020). Longitudinal studies reveal persistent gaps in eliminating legal loopholes, creating significant constraints to achieving global reforms and improving the lives of young XXs (Fan & Koski, 2022; Rafferty, 2013; Siddiqi & Greene, 2022).

A brighter future requires empowering faith-based custodians and mandating XY leaders and devotees to embrace equitable and inclusive principles, regardless of political rhetoric or religious beliefs.

Conclusion

This chapter reviews the hindrances faced by XXs globally, as mandated by religious and legal institutions. However, the actions of many XXs also illustrate significant achievements.

The resilience and determination of XXs in their advocacy work at national and international levels have driven changes towards greater equity and justice. Their collective efforts have not only challenged entrenched patriarchal norms but also laid the groundwork for transformative change, inspiring hope and motivation. By exposing discriminatory practices and lobbying for reform, XX–led organisations can influence governments and leaders.

While patriarchal values are deeply embedded in religious doctrines and laws, XXs have consistently fought against these constraints. Within Christianity, Hinduism, Islam, and Judaism, feminist scholars and activists work to reinterpret sacred texts, challenge discriminatory practices, and demand recognition and inclusion in leadership roles.

The incremental changes achieved – including permitting XXs to hold leadership positions in some synagogues or challenging dress codes and behavioural restrictions – highlight the power of sustained activism and leadership.

In Hinduism, the challenge to traditions, including *sati*, demonstrates how cultural expectations can be confronted and reformed. Meanwhile, XXs across religions have leveraged their roles in domestic rituals to challenge inequalities and assert autonomy, showcasing the creative ways they navigate phallocentric obstacles.

International legal frameworks, including CEDAW and the SDGs, have been instrumental in addressing sex-based discrimination and promoting the rights of XXs. These international contracts, treaties, and conventions provide a platform for global reform, compelling member nations to ratify laws that promote equality. While gaps persist between the creation and implementation, the contributions of WINGOs and NGOs have significantly advanced the conversation and, at times, increased governmental accountability and ignited positive changes.

Beyond formal legal and institutional frameworks, XXs continue to challenge patriarchal structures. The role of international advocacy in supporting XXs cannot be overstated, as justice-based laws, including IWRLs, have played a pivotal role in educating societies about the realities of sex-based discrimination and in leveraging data and research to inform policy discussions. By nurturing collaborations across borders, WINGOs sustain a collective commitment to challenging patriarchal systems and advancing human rights.

While progress has been made, significant challenges remain. Androcentric resistance continues to obstruct advancements in many areas, and inequalities persist within religious and legal frameworks. However, the achievements of XXs – both at grassroots and institutional levels – demonstrate the potential for transformative change. By continuing to advocate for equitable solutions, challenge discriminatory practices, and leverage international collaboration, individuals and NGOs must persist in their efforts to create a more just and equitable world.

"Freedom and justice cannot be parcelled out in pieces to suit political convenience, I don't believe you can stand for freedom for one group of people and deny it to others".

Coretta Scott King, American civil rights leader, activist, author, and founder of the Martin Luther King Jr. Center for Nonviolent Social Change, 1927–2006. (King, 2000)

Toolkit

Question Traditions

Challenge religious dogmas and expectations by rejecting stereotypes that dictate how you should act, look, sound, reproduce, or live. Marriage, at its core, remains an outdated institution that reinforces patriarchal ideologies, sex-based hierarchies, and sexual inequalities.

If marriage is what you wish for, prior to committing, discuss your shared goals and expected responsibilities. Redefine marriage as a partnership rather than a traditional act. Discuss consent, equity, and the autonomy of each person within the marriage, including equal participation in major decisions, from family planning to finances. Discuss economic independence to ensure your autonomy and a balanced relationship.

Promote Justice

Promote social justice by challenging legislations that exclude marginalised voices or perpetuate inequities, specifically laws discriminating against XXs. Remember, politicians make laws, and your vote counts!

Campaign and advocate for the introduction of pro–XX laws. Voice your concerns. Ask politicians to use the *Gender Legislative Index* (GLI) when introducing bills to amend legislations – the great majority of politicians have a presence on social media. Potential new policies and programs, or changes to existing laws, can be replicated or adapted to assist in meeting the UN's 2030 SDGs deadline.

The GLI interface (Vijeyarasa, 2019) offers a method to measure new bills and existing national laws against international standards and expectations without expending time and resources on additional data collection. The GLI provides a means to gather information based on international XX's rights norms, helping to prevent the introduction of discriminatory legislation. The GLI technology can support future anti-discrimination policies.

It is important for all, including the polity, to understand that IWRLs and pro–XX legislation need to be ratified and monitored to ensure that:

(i) all Members of Parliament (MPs) and policymakers consult the GLI prior to proposing or amending laws to prevent negative impacts on XXs; and
(ii) there is further accountability in policy change and policy ratification.

Share knowledge and help educate other XXs about their legal rights and the support available to counsel them in making informed decisions when facing legal obstacles.

Build and/or encourage support for organisations that offer XXs legal, emotional, and financial assistance to counteract legal intimidation and help XXs navigate systemic barriers with confidence (Robinson & Yoshida, 2024).

Change the Lens

Advocate for and/or implement workplace policies that enhance organisational practices to strengthen equity and encourage inclusive attitudes and programmes. Persuade decision-makers to incorporate diverse perspectives, particularly for XXs, to create productive, safe, and inclusive environments. Promote and exercise justice in all roles, not just leadership positions, to ensure representation and diversity at every level.

Identifying and championing the contributions of XXs can challenge "mateship" culture and androcentric exclusionary procedures. It is imperative to remember that diversity is essential for growth; change paves the way for new possibilities.

3 Liberation Legacies

Personal Note

As one of many from my generation, I too was indoctrinated to believe that "feminist" was a dirty word; that the war between the sexes had ended. However, dealing with the powerful in politics and corporations made me realise how naive I had been. Nevertheless, I persevered and embraced the opportunities that came my way.

In San Francisco, at the APEC annual WES, XXs from 21 nations gathered in large rooms – Hillary Rodham Clinton, Michelle Bachelet, Madeleine Albright, Indra Nooyi, and Cherie Blair, to name a few. It was then that I learnt about Madeleine Albright's ethos: "There is a special place in hell for women who don't help other women".

My work as the chief executive officer (CEO) of the AWCCI from 2009 to 2017 (Wikipedia, n.d.-a) was relentless. Although I sat on various federal government advisory boards and regularly met with MPs, the XYs in power seldom listened to the facts; their assumptions were deeply ingrained, and little could be done to alter their androcentric beliefs.

It took me years to understand that their actions – both right- and left-wing parliamentarians – were mostly about ticking boxes. Real change was not their goal and the needs of XXs were often consigned to the "too hard" basket. The corporate leaders I engaged with, all XYs at the time, were of a similar ilk. Fortunately, changes are taking place. I also realised that policies and programmes have the potential to transform lives, including those of the self-employed XXs.

To my surprise, a decade later, I encountered a former AWCCI member who thanked me for the advice I had provided – a recommended investment in a start-up had paid off, enabling her to attain financial security and retire early. Her gratitude reminded me of a piece I wrote in 2013 on the concept

DOI: 10.4324/9781003516224-3

of "femship" – how it should function for XXs much like "mateship" does for XYs. Femship describes the deep connections between XXs as being more than mere friendships. Femship should evoke a sense of shared experiences, mutual respect, and support – practices I had not previously conceived possible.

I wish I had begun my feminist journey much earlier, as there is so much to be done.

During the past decade, researching this book and listening to the harrowing, gut-wrenching experiences of numerous international students, my understanding of the brutal realities has significantly increased. I now better appreciate the urgency and why new generations refuse to follow in the footsteps of their mothers and grandmothers. Instead, they are speaking up, shouting out, and demanding change – dismantling oppressive cultural traditions and refusing to remain silent in the face of injustice.

Yet, I, too, remained silent for years. As a survivor of intimate partner violence (IPV), I internalised the stigma, convinced myself it was my fault – that I had failed to protect myself, or worse, that I had somehow deserved the abuse. At the time, these crimes were not discussed, and I was naive to believe silence would protect me.

Throughout this little book, I extend my gratitude to all those who have shared their stories with me and to those who have advocated for XXs. "Liberation Legacies" reaffirms the tenacity and collaboration of feminism, and the many battles won; the book celebrates persistence, leadership and the numerous XX achievements.

Introduction

Characterised by four metaphorical feminism waves, "Liberation Legacies" provides an overview of feminists' movements and the victories obtained through their advocacy and activism in Australia, the EU, India, the UK, and the USA.

According to the Cambridge Dictionary, a "wave" is defined as "to make a movement with your hand that tells someone or something to move in a particular direction" (Cambridge University Press, n.d.).

Throughout the tides, feminists and advocates have consistently exposed the patriarchy's resistance to change, maintaining that progress depends on consciously embedding inclusivity and egalitarianism – not as abstract ideals, but as guiding principles for how societies organise, lead, and live.

The four waves reveal a stream of forces dissolving patriarchal systemic inequalities one wave at a time. Their trajectories provide an appreciation for the many XXs who have demonstrated adaptability and employed diverse tools to turn the tides for positive changes. From community-led actions to legislative reforms, educational initiatives, and digital activism exposing predators and misogynistic leaders, the four waves capture their resilience and innovative efforts.

From the first to the fourth, each wave builds upon the previous one, navigating ongoing discriminatory practices while expanding feminist channels to advance parity. Each wave is founded on the same principles: securing equal human rights and justice for XXs, just as these were bestowed upon XYs – an idea first championed by Mary Wollstonecraft before the first feminist wave was recognised.

Focusing on suffrage and property ownership, the first wave planted the seed that continued to be watered and cultivated throughout the second and third waves, providing education and information to address labour rights, reproductive autonomy, intersectionality, and the unremitting fight to end VAW.

The momentum of previous waves led to the tsunami currently underway (Varela, 2020), drenching the patriarchy and creating ripple effects for wider societal reforms around the globe, leveraging digital technology to challenge phallocentric toxic attitudes eroding the rights of XXs. Achieving equality across race, class, and sex is not an easy feat; however, exposing androcentrism and resisting subjugation continues, one groundswell at a time.

By reviewing the roots and the rise of feminism, this chapter focuses on the enduring significance and reflective capacity of the movement's meaningful changes – impacting and changing behaviours, laws, and values across societies. The effectiveness of XXs is energising, supporting, and inspiring others to take proactive steps and serve as role models is highlighted throughout this chapter.

Some argue that feminism is no longer necessary – a claim that has been repeatedly made since the first wave – insisting the fundamental goals towards equity have already been achieved. If only!

A closer examination of feminist heritage reveals that the movement's goals remain as relevant today as they were at the start, with ongoing efforts and achievements continuing to redesign our world for the better.

The proficiency and leadership of XXs are not only essential and impactful, but also warrant greater recognition. Despite the many meaningful ripple effects caused by the various waves, obstacles persist, including the income wage gap and VAW, for example, highlighting the ongoing need for further action and sustained global vigilance.

The Phases of Feminism

Critics of the wave analogy argue the concept oversimplifies the continuous and interconnected nature of feminist activism (Evans & Chamberlain, 2014), claiming "waves" fail to identify and emphasise the continuity of activists and their ongoing appeals (Nicholson, 2010). Nevertheless, the term "wave" is employed in this book for consistency with the research, albeit with the wave metaphor

(Nicholson, 2010) failing to fully capture the complexities and multiplicities of the pain endured, the work completed, and the achievements accomplished – efforts that continue to this day (Kakroda & Sole, 2023; Rome et al., 2019).

The wave metaphor provides a valuable framework for understanding cultural, economic, social, and political settings through the evolution of the movements, the legacies of struggle, and our feminist heritage. Each wave continues to provide answers to the question: *How did we get here?*

Feminist movements have been a continual force in resisting and confronting injustice entrenched in patriarchal rule, advocating for equal rights in health, economic, educational, and political participation, irrespective of biological or sexual-social identifiers. At its core, feminism advocates for parity and a balanced distribution of power.

Starting predominantly in Western Europe and the USA (Malinowska, 2020), suffrage extended its reach globally (Malinowska, 2020). Since then, the results of the first wave have continued to erode the *status quo*. For example, in 1893, New Zealand (NZ) was the first self-governing country to grant XXs the right to vote, followed by Australia granting XXs the right to vote and stand for parliament in 1902 (Edwards & Roces, 2004; Grimshaw, 2000; Wright, 2018). Finland, in the EU, was the first in the world to elect XXs into a national parliament in 1906 (Haavio-Mannila, 1979).

From the second wave, where the liberation movements of the 1960s demanded legal rights and social equality, to the third wave, which recognised individuality, diversity, and the repercussions of rejecting the demands of the fashion industry (Gillis et al., 2007), sexual hierarchies have remained on the global agenda.

Feminist movements are not a concept of the past but dynamic, evolving initiatives motivating and mobilising to obtain equal human rights – a movement that continues to inspire change, improve the lives of XXs, and ensure its relevance in addressing both old and emerging misogynistic institutionalised sexism. Each wave, including the recent tsunami, defines the objectives of feminism: "the belief that women should be allowed the same rights, power, and opportunities as men and be treated in the same way, or the set of activities intended to achieve this state" (Cambridge University Press, n.d.). Both XXs and XYs can be feminists if they believe in equal rights.

The principles of equality are reflected in legal and social practices, including, for example, XXs adopting the XY's surname (Goldin & Shim, 2004) – a requirement in some regions and illegal in others. One study revealed that one in ten (10%) XXs opted for a hyphenated surname, while almost one in four (20%) retained their maiden names. Geography, traditional beliefs, career aspirations, and education all influenced their decision. Changing surnames upon marriage has significant implications; it can result in the loss of identity and further reinforce the perception of XXs as property to be controlled, first by their fathers and then by their husbands. Those who preserved their maiden name are often evaluated as being professionally ambitious (Gibbs Knotts et al., 2018; Miller & Willis, 2015; Noordewier et al., 2010).

Although some opponents argue that the liberation of XXs has faded (Rampton, 2015), claiming the waves were irrelevant or that equal rights have been attained, the fourth wave has proven many critics wrong, with global campaigns continuing to expose sexism and misogyny. These exposures have led to positive legal outcomes (Barclay et al., 2024) that better protect XXs from dangerous phallocentric expectations and discriminatory laws. Yet sex-based prejudices remain rampant. As a result, global feminist movements continue exposing sex-based prejudices, demanding reform with the tsunami shifting attitudes towards justice.

The First Wave: 1800s–1920s

Before the first wave began, Mary Wollstonecraft's work in the 18th century – often regarded as the foundational text of feminism – sought social, political, and educational equality for XXs (Wollstonecraft, 1792). Her intellectual brilliance and logical reasoning laid the groundwork for feminist thought (Volkova, 2014), contending that for truth to be truly transformative, both sexes should have equal opportunity in order to develop their intellectual and moral capacities and be equipped to better please their lover; additionally, without truth, collective behaviour would remain superficial and ineffective (Volkova, 2014; Wollstonecraft & Blick, 2024).

Although the patriarchy regarded Wollstonecraft's, *A Vindication of the Rights of Woman* (1792), published in London, as "radical" at the time, the text did receive one favourable evaluation in a Spanish publication (Kitts, 1994). Wollstonecraft's powerful critique of the patriarchy and her vision for equality continues to resonate in contemporary debates on social and sexual justice, centuries after the text was published.

The timeline for suffrage varied across nations, with some countries reforming their voting laws well into the 20th century. The first wave focused primarily on addressing legal inequalities, including suffrage and the right to own property (Malinowska, 2020; Nicholson, 2010; Rome et al., 2019). Historic accounts attribute the origins of the first wave to the EU, the UK, and the USA. However, exclusion prevailed in various regions. For example, Indigenous people, both XXs and XYs, were denied the right to vote *en masse* until 1962 in Australia (Grimshaw, 2000).

The first wave of feminism also focused on education, with activists advocating for reforms to address systemic restrictions (Malinowska, 2020; Wright, 2009). Educational reforms were seen as crucial for empowering XXs to participate more fully in both the workforce and civic life (Ginzberg, 2002), laying the foundation for broader social and economic transformations. The industrial era provided new opportunities for XXs' economic participation but also introduced significant pitfalls, inspiring debates about the rights and involvement of XXs in civic and public dialogue and initiatives.

In Paris in 1878, for example, the first international feminist congress took place during the *Exposition Universelle* (World Fair), assembling XXs from 11 countries representing 16 organisations. The congress centred on the quest for equal rights; however, suffrage was excluded from the agenda to maintain unity (Weiss, 2018). Furthermore, activists sought to diminish the Catholic Church's influence over the roles and expectations assigned to XXs (Chapter 2), recognising its significant impact on shaping societal norms (Boxer, 1982).

Despite the differences, dominant patriarchal structures, alongside the universal needs for equality, identity, and belonging, create common ground for XXs who continue to adapt to evolving societal pressures (Caughie, 2010; Faupel & Werum, 2011; Rajgopal, 2022).

Deeply troubling, however, are the racial injustices, from Australia to India, the USA, and beyond, where XXs of colour are at times marginalised by other feminists, who neglect to recognise intersectional nuance, ultimately perpetuating further injustices (Ginzberg, 2002).

In non-Western countries, the first wave of advocates and activists demanded labour rights, education, anti-racism measures, and legal reforms, building upon the demands of Western feminism. For example, in India, activists called for significant changes to address systemic injustices rooted in race, class, and the pervasive colonial inequalities and biases of the time (Caughie, 2010).

In India, intertwined caste and sex-based oppressions remain central since the anti-colonial movement began. Efforts to address and transform these deeply embedded discriminatory practices within cultural, economic, and religious structures (Caughie, 2010; Puri, 2015; Rajgopal, 2022) have led to several notable successes. For example, the Hindu Succession Act of 1956 granted XXs equal rights to inherit property (Pande, 2018), and the Hindu Marriage Act of 1955 prohibited polygamy and bigamy, permitted inter-caste and inter-religious marriages, and established a minimum marriageable age – 18 years for XXs and 21 for XYs.

In the UK, as in Australia, the EU, and the USA, feminists were striving to dismantle entrenched patriarchal norms that marginalised and excluded XXs from voting as well as historic and cultural narratives (Heilmann, 2005).

In the USA, the first wave of feminism developed between 1910 and 1930, with activists focusing on both national and state-based projects. While the movement reached its peak with the national suffrage victory in 1920, following earlier successes in granting voting rights to XXs in various US states, progress was met with backlash and fading momentum. For example, the Supreme Court overturned key feminist-supported legislation, including child labour protections in 1922 and minimum wage laws in 1923, significantly stalling progress (Faupel & Werum, 2011).

Although activists campaigned for suffrage during the first wave in various countries, the outcomes were asynchronous. Multiple and layered injustices further highlight that, while humans share universal needs, feminist movements vary across cultures and contexts. Nevertheless, the efforts of the first wave were instrumental for XXs, demonstrating that when they advocate for change collectively, laws can shift like powerful tides, surging forward, and redesigning societies on a global scale.

Although 40 years passed before the emergence of the second wave, many continued to engage in local advocacy and activism, laying the groundwork and creating further ripples that flowed over into the second wave (Legge, 2017).

The Second Wave: 1960s–1980s

The phrase "Sisterhood Is Powerful" became a prominent slogan of the era, inspired by *Sisterhood Is Powerful: An Anthology of Writings from the Women's Liberation Movement*, edited by Robin Morgan (1970). Among the major achievements of the movement were the introduction of anti-discrimination legislation and the establishment of XXs' study programmes in academia (Nicholson, 2010).

The second wave also saw the creation of counter-histories that centred on the voices and perspectives of XXs, the coining of *herstory*, a term intended to challenge traditionally androcentric narratives by offering alternatives and aiming to highlight the systemic oppression embedded within them (Heilmann, 2005:1; Kakroda & Sole, 2023; Ng & McGowan, 2023).

Another key outcome was the introduction of legislation addressing sex-based disparities in the labour market. Legal reforms sought to rectify imbalances and grant XXs opportunities and economic rights equivalent to those enjoyed by XYs (Eveline, 1994; Kakroda & Sole, 2023).

Before, during, and after the legal reforms, feminism employed various methods to challenge patriarchal narratives and improve the status, independence, and dignity of XXs with *herstory*. These efforts included the publication of new ideas aimed at countering and rectifying misogynistic rhetoric and prejudices (Heilmann, 2005).

Australia

Born in Melbourne, Germaine Greer became a defining voice of the second feminist wave with her influential work *The Female Eunuch* (1971). Greer explained to publishers that the book would articulate the experiences of XX, similarly to how Black XYs had published their struggles. At 31, Greer was a household name (Finlayson, 2018; Lake, 2016).

The book received polarised opinions and feedback. The narrative on the roles of wives and mothers led some to dismiss Greer's expectations for XXs, whilst for others, it changed their views, their lives, and their sexual conduct and experiences. *The Female Eunuch* was a blend of academic analysis, free-flowing introspection, and provocative rhetoric inspired by Greer's studies of Shakespeare during her time at Cambridge and the Black movement in the USA – it has since been translated into numerous languages (Buchanan, 2016; Cosic, 2016; Taylor, 2020; Finlayson, 2018).

One of the most renowned and influential feminists at the time (Finlayson, 2018), Greer sold the collection, including numerous archival boxes filled with personal notes and letters from the public, for AU$3 (US$2.2 / £1.8) million; the collection now resides at the University of Melbourne (Lake, 2016; Taylor, 2020; Simons, 2013).

Australia became the first Western democracy to appoint an XX to the "Women's Affairs" section within a federal government in 1973. "Ms Elizabeth Reid was employed to conduct research and advise the Prime Minister (PM) [the Whitlam Government] on a range of domestic issues, especially those bearing on the welfare of women" (NAA, 1973), representing a major breakthrough in acknowledging XXs and an innovative step in public policy (Dowse, 2014; Johnson, 2024).

Although affirmative action in Australia – designed to increase opportunities for XXs in employment and education – aimed to boost their participation in traditionally XY–dominated industries, including mining for example, the purported tokenism adopted in some sectors often reinforced patriarchal attitudes. As a result, XXs were further marginalised, subjected to harassment, and faced persistent misogynistic adversities at work (Eveline, 1994).

In 1984, the SDA was introduced, influenced by the principles outlined in CEDAW (Vega, 2023), with the aim of eliminating obstacles preventing XXs from achieving economic and social parity with XYs.

The EU

Feminist achievements and areas of focus varied significantly throughout this region. For example, in Sweden, affirmative action initiatives adopted neutral approaches, exemplified by the Equality for Men and Women at Work Act. The "Free Men" campaign encouraged XYs to take parental leave, challenging traditional expectations and emphasising shared parental responsibilities. As with similar programmes worldwide, outcomes were mixed. While the visibility of XXs in XY–dominated industries increased, the dismantling of patriarchal power structures was stalled by cultural resistance and systemic biases (Eveline, 1994).

The Swedish example also unintentionally reinforced workplace constraints, similar to those experienced in Australia. For example, the "Leading Lady" programme emphasised stereotypically "feminine characteristics" (Eveline, 1994:163–164), which pigeonholed and perpetuated limited perceptions of XXs professional capabilities, particularly in managerial roles (Eveline, 1994).

In Spain, the oppressive censorship and conservative ideals imposed by Franco's dictatorship (Chapter 2) resulted in feminist thought being influenced by narratives from democratic countries, including *The Second Sex* (de Beauvoir, 1953) and *The Feminine Mystique* (Friedan, 1963).

Following Franco's death, Spanish feminists began challenging entrenched androcentric norms, marking a pivotal shift as the nation transitioned towards democracy. Campaigns called for transformative reforms, including the legalisation of contraceptives, reproductive rights, the decriminalisation of adultery, and a suite of legal measures to advance equity (Godayol, 2022). Momentum grew, amplified by media coverage and the landmark *Conference on Women's Liberation* held in Madrid in 1975 (Larrondo Ureta, 2020).

Under a democratic government, significant progress followed, with the abolition of adultery as a crime in 1978, the passing of the Divorce Act in 1981, and the partial legalisation of abortion in 1985. These milestones signalled the beginning of a new era of political and cultural freedom for XXs in Spain (Godayol, 2022).

India

The formation of democratic governance in 1947, following independence from British rule, stimulated activists to address human rights through grassroots movements. Alongside the adoption of a new Indian constitution, XXs presented compelling arguments for equality, despite concurrently confronting entrenched phallocentric cultural norms and identity (Pande, 2018; Misra, 1997).

The second wave of feminism in India focused on education, economic independence, political representation, and the pursuit of social equity (John, 2005; Pande, 2018). The prohibition of polygamy, the legalisation of inter-caste and inter-religious marriages, equal divorce rights for both sexes, legal action against dowry-related violence, and land rights for XXs were among their pressing concerns (Misra, 1997; Pande, 2018).

In 1973, the Shreemati Nathibai Damodar Thackersey (SNDT Women's University) in Bombay formally incorporated the lived experiences and perspectives of XXs into academic research, aiming to address the gaps in traditional scholarship (John, 2005). In 1981 the first *National Convention on Women's Studies* had more than 400 participants. The convention emphasised XX studies as a critical perspective rather than a standalone discipline (John, 2005). The SNDT continues to educate and is recognised as the first XXs' university established in India and Southeast Asia (SNDT, n.d.).

In 1974, the *Towards Equality* report provided further momentum to the second wave when it revealed the socio-economic and political disadvantages faced by XXs despite the protections enshrined in the new constitution. The formation of feminist groups and grassroots organisations advocating for legal reforms across both rural and urban India impacted legal reforms (Pande, 2018; Misra, 1997) that rippled for decades thereafter.

The UK

In 1975, Laura Mulvey, a feminist and film theorist, authored a highly influential anti-patriarchal essay examining perpetuating forms of misogynistic control (Malinowska, 2020; Rome et al., 2019). *Visual Pleasure and Narrative Cinema* focused on the concept of the "male gaze", illustrating how films were constructed through a phallocentric lens. Mulvey argued that XXs on screen were frequently depicted as mere sexual objects, serving solely to fulfil the desires of XYs (Mulvey, 1975).

Addressing issues arising from the sexual revolution, the second wave in the UK also played a crucial role in challenging systemic inequalities in healthcare. Activists and advocates demanded reproductive rights while critiquing outdated medical systems and practices that had seen minimal advancement for XXs since the 19th c., perpetuating patriarchal control and dominance, denying autonomy, and limiting access to essential knowledge about their health (Arnold-Forster, 2021; Rome et al., 2019).

Numerous other impediments in the corporate and public sectors were also conquered as XXs undertook leadership positions and advanced their careers (Ng & McGowan, 2023). The pioneering efforts affirmed their expertise, capabilities, and skills in executive roles, with the majority being the first to climb the corporate ladder within their respective industries and organisations.

The USA

As in other regions, the second wave in the USA also centred on reproductive rights and workplace equity. Affirmative action strategies and legislations were introduced, including the Equal Pay Act and the Violence Against Women Act, aimed at protecting XXs from systemic inequalities and racial discrimination, influenced by the civil rights movement (Kakroda & Sole, 2023; Pant & Sharma, 2024).

Affirmative action measures were anticipated to reduce the long-standing effects of centuries of systemic racism and discrimination. The strategy, however, faced considerable backlash, with critics arguing that reverse discrimination would undermine the principles of meritocracy (Elisburg, 1978). The meritocracy argument – a hierarchy where people are compensated, promoted, or provided with positive prospects based on their abilities, skills, and accomplishments rather than their affluence, networks, or heritage. The ideal of a social order based on merit, however, fails to acknowledge that meritocracy is frequently an illusion that disintegrates within a practical reality (Daniels, 1978; Rhode, 2021).

Despite ongoing criticisms, affirmative action measures play a crucial role in addressing discrimination and inequality. Although at times constrained by legal restrictions and enduring racist and androcentric resistance, hurdles can be removed. For example, the National Organization for Women (NOW) represented Maria Pepe, a 12-year-old who was removed from her local Little League team in 1972 because she was an XX. The league's XY–only policy justified her exclusion. However, in 1973, the courts ruled in her favour, paving the way for XXs across the country to participate in Little League sports (Abrams, 2012; Colley, 2019). The landmark case of *NOW v. Little League Baseball Inc.* set a precedent for sex-based inclusion in youth sports.

The many other cases not included in this book also significantly influenced and instigated legal and cultural changes across the USA, with two publications having significant repercussions.

The Feminine Mystique (Friedan, 1963) highlighted the pervasive dissatisfaction of suburban housewives. Despite their access to domestic luxuries, XXs found themselves confined to their home as their primary source of fulfilment, famously referred to by Friedan as "the problem that has no name" – the title of the book's first chapter (Friedan, 1963). Friedan's work directly challenged the post–World War II societal ideals that demoted XXs to the sole role of homemaker.

Our Bodies, Ourselves (Boston Women's Health Book Collective, 1968), celebrated as a landmark feminist narrative, addressed menstruation, pregnancy, and menopause, which had historically been misdiagnosed and treated as illnesses requiring the intervention of XYs. Enhancing XXs' health education with self-help practices and patient-centred care, it inspired XXs to understand and take control of their health (Arnold-Forster, 2021), encouraging greater well-being and autonomy.

Throughout the second wave, new narratives amplified *herstory* and the ideas and authority of XXs, flowing into the tide of greater independence, dignity, and representation, whilst reconstructing the health and legal rights of XXs in the USA and beyond.

The Third Wave: 1990s–2010

The previous waves did not achieve all they set out to accomplish, resulting in overlaps and continuities that challenge the perceived exclusivity and limitation of previous feminist narratives (Gillis, et al., 2007; Mahoney, 2016).

Since the 1990s, researchers have observed a revival of interest in feminist movements, stemming partly from regressive legislative and societal shifts, as well as the aggression presented by neoconservatives and neoliberals, deliberately attempting to erode global hard-won XX advancements (Evans, 2015; Kelly, 2005; Walby, 2011).

The backlash against feminism has received significant global media attention, resulting partly from the rise of VAW, the blatant sexual objectification of XXs across all ages, persistent assaults on bodily autonomy, and ongoing financial inequalities.

Although the timeline of the third wave varies, this movement had undeniably profound and transformative, vibrationally momentous global impacts, encouraging a plurality of views, addressing transnational issues, and emphasising the shared yet distinct experiences of XXs across cultures and societies. A renewed focus on fluid identities and the significance of personal experiences was introduced and surged globally with technological advancements, recognising the complexity of contemporary identities and lived experiences (Kinser, 2004; Evans, 2015).

The third wave also generated confusion. For example, terms including "postfeminism" and "post-modern feminism" were often used interchangeably without clear definitions or explanations of the purported decline in feminist principles. The contradictory language and interpretations, exacerbated by the diversity of national and transnational contexts, intensified important debates and led to feminist misunderstandings (Lotz, 2003).

"Postfeminism" is a contested term that suggests feminism is over, rendering movements unnecessary and outdated or failed while maintaining a complex relationship with its principles. Promoters of postfeminism, often visible in the traditional media (Chapter 2), challenge feminism's relevance, arguing that its goals have been fulfilled. However, critics of postfeminism reject this notion, emphasising that systemic sex-based inequalities persist.

Historically, postfeminism dates back to the 1920s, when the term was first used to describe resistance and backlash against feminists movements (Chidgey, 2020; Lister, 2005; Tasker & Negra, 2008).

What is free of confusion and undisputed is that the penultimate recorded wave emphasised intersectionality – a term coined by Kimberlé Crenshaw in her essay *Demarginalizing the Intersection of Race and Sex* (Crenshaw, 1989). Crenshaw addressed overlapping forms of oppression, arguing that identities do not exist in isolation but intersect, creating unique experiences of both oppression and privilege (Crenshaw et al., 1997; Carbado et al., 2013).

The third movement was partially inspired by hope, driven by the desire for inclusivity, and motivated by the ambition to challenge the perceived exclusivity of earlier feminist movements – particularly the tendency to marginalised XXs who were not white and middle-class. This wave addressed issues of class, cultural representation, race, and sexuality (Kelly, 2005; Rome et al., 2019), emphasising individualism and cultural representation, and thereby contributing to and enriching feminist narratives and dialogues (Kakroda & Sole, 2023; Snyder, 2008).

This movement also critiqued culture (Snyder, 2008) while reclaiming pop culture (Kinser, 2004). For example, "womanhood" was challenged as a singular, universal concept that reduced the political significance of feminism (Mahoney, 2016:1007). With negative representations of XXs in the media (Kinser, 2004; Kelly, 2005), technology and globalisation were also critiqued. New communication platforms created during the third wave provided spaces for intersectional voices, capturing international attention and amplifying the perspectives of non-white XXs, who had been excluded in previous movements (Kelly, 2005).

New concepts including "cyberfeminism" and "ecofeminism" – further reviewed in the fourth wave – also emerged (Gillis et al., 2007; Sabherwal et al., 2021; Wrye, 2009). Growing awareness of the many androcentric practices and legal discriminations inspired and strengthened the efforts of advocates and activists worldwide, redefining feminism across borders (Evans, 2015; Kelly, 2005; Mahoney, 2016; Snyder, 2008).

Australia

The 1990s were shaped by both international influences and the country's unique context. Australian feminists focused on intersectionality, highlighting the diverse issues faced by XXs of different ethnicities, social classes, and sexual orientations in urban, regional, and rural areas.

New generations challenged previous movements for their exclusionary focus, advancing and elevating the voices and experiences of Indigenous XXs and other underrepresented groups (Ang, 2001; Bulbeck, 1997; Ichitani, 2007).

Emerging within a neoliberal and postfeminist cultural environment, young XXs engaged with diverse feminist principles in multifaceted ways, including consumer culture, personal sexual freedoms, and self-determination (Harris, 2010).

Characterised by grassroots activism, the use of digital media, and cultural critique, activists focused on changing reproductive rights, confronting the lack of DV protection, and addressing workplace inequalities. The Australian labour market exhibited a relatively high level of sex-based segregation based on OECD standards – while challenging media and societal patriarchs (Henderson & Taylor, 2020).

However, this wave also faced criticism for its emphasis on individualism and the influence of neoliberal ideals, which at times weakened collective feminist action, a pattern also observed in various other nations (Aune & Holyoak, 2018; Bulbeck, 1997; Lister, 2005).

Despite the substantial impact of previous movements, many whose lives had benefited from the achievements of prior activists began to distance themselves from the term "feminist", often perceiving it as irrelevant and assuming that the war between the sexes had already been resolved. Many were unaware of the intergenerational dialogues required and the necessity of evolving strategies to align with shifting social and cultural issues (Bulbeck, 1997; Harris, 2010).

The value of equality was widely expressed, yet XXs who distanced themselves from feminism contributed to the fragmentation of feminist activism, prioritising personal empowerment through individual action rather than advocating for structural patriarchal transformations. Constrained by conventional views around sex and sexuality, feminist achievements were often reduced to narratives indifferent or blind to class and race, with the motto "girls can do anything" (Henderson & Taylor, 2020:2). The divisions of unpaid labour and the income pay gap (Chapter 6), however, remained unabated.

A transition from unified movements and collective activism occurred, leading to more fragmented actions during the third wave, with decentralised and individualised forms of engagement taking place in Australia (Harris, 2010) and other regions. For example, cyberfeminism, combining feminism with digital technology, challenged patriarchal systems, first emerging in art collectives in the 1990s, where it has remained most influential. For example, *VNS Matrix*, are recognised for establishing cyberfeminism, displayed their "Cyberfeminist Manifesto" on a billboard in Sydney in 1991, declaring in part that:

> We are the virus of the new world disorder, … saboteurs of big daddy mainframe, the clitoris is a direct line to the matrix… infiltrating, disrupting, disseminating, corrupting the discourse, we are the future cunt.
>
> (VNS Matrix, n.d.)

The group maintained a website that frequently changed servers, and their specific cyber activities were ambiguous at the time (Gillis et al., 2007:170–171). Since then – the original members Virginia Barratt, Francesca da Rimini, Julianne Pierce, and Josephine Starrs – have continued exhibiting their work. In 2024, at the *Biennale of Sydney* – an annual event exhibiting artists from more than 130 countries (Biennale of Sydney, 2024; VNS Matrix, n.d.) – *VNS Matrix* affirmed their continued influence on cyberfeminism and digital art.

The EU

Bodily autonomy was a significant issue for many in the EU. For example, to retain and protect abortion rights from neoliberal conservatives, the right-wing government proposed legislative changes to allow doctors to refuse abortion requests and protect their moral autonomy based on conscientious objections – a position supported by many Christian general practitioners (Nordberg et al., 2014). However, the proposed legal changes neglected XXs' right to safe and accessible healthcare, prompting public resistance in Norway during the early 2010s (Sümer & Eslen-Ziya, 2017).

The public backlash included widespread protests across Norway. Pressure from local and international feminist organisations, including the European Women's Lobby, incorporated digital technologies – particularly leveraging IWD – gaining widespread collective unified support. The combined efforts of physical and online activism compelled the government to abandon the conscientious objection proposal, marking a significant victory for the reproductive autonomy of XXs in Norway (Sümer & Eslen-Ziya, 2017) and delivering a clear message to other conservative governments.

The Norwegian example reinforces and validates the power of feminism and the power of united collective action, also serving as a reminder of the fragility of democracy and demonstrating the potential ability of governments to reverse hard-won feminist victories. This example, along with many others not included in this book, serves as a call to action for all XXs to remain vigilant and to persist in challenging patriarchs to protect legacy achievements and continue progressing towards a more egalitarian world.

The Eurocentric nature of the third wave also observed feminists arguing about the neglected perspectives and previously unacknowledged experiences of intersectional discrimination encountered by non-white XXs. However, understanding local historical forces influencing feminism in different regions extend beyond Western hegemonic perspectives, with feminists in India, for example, focusing on grassroots movements to disband patriarchal structures and streamline social and political systems (Mahoney, 2016).

India

As in many other nations, in India the third wave was partly influenced by Western feminist concepts, while also addressing the unique cultural, historic, and societal dynamics that had evolved in response to various limitations encountered during the second wave – with particular consideration placed on intersectionality.

Acknowledging the interconnected nature of various forms of subjugation, ranging from colonial-era social reforms to intersectionality and ecofeminist activism, with caste, class, and sex oppression being central to the Indian agenda, reflecting diverse and complex wicked problems, the efforts of numerous activists, too many to name, continue to impact reforms (Phillips & Cree, 2014).

For example, ecofeminism focused on interconnected methods of domination, including capitalism that exploits both XXs and Mother Earth, clearly exposing and linking patriarchy with ecological destruction. With its deeply rooted environmentalist principles, ecofeminists demanded justice whilst addressing the intersection of race, class, and sex in ecological issues. Advocating for inclusive approaches to sustainable development, they emphasised ethical care, biodiversity, and the rights of marginalised communities to resist extractive industries, calling for urgent action to promote ecological preservation with unity and diversity (Lamas et al., 2021; Sabherwal et al., 2021; Singer, 2020).

To prevent deforestation in the Himalayan regions, XX activists used their bodies to form barriers in the *Chipko* movement, preventing axes from destroying forests. Their non-violent resistance aimed to protect natural resources, identified as fundamental to the survival of their communities. Additionally, the environmental degradation caused by exploitative development projects were brought into focus (Mack-Canty, 2004; Sahu, 2023).

The *Chipko* movement, despite beginning in the 1970s, became a fundamental element of ecofeminist activism. Vandana Shiva was central in linking environmental justice with the oppression of XXs in the Himalayan region, opposing the exploitative practices of globalisation (John, 2005; Sahu, 2023) and identifying and connecting local injustices with global movements.

Distinct injustices were also highlighted, with lower-caste groups asserting their experiences previously ignored or overlooked. The *Dalit* movement, for example, strengthened the voices of marginalised XXs by addressing the intersection of caste-based and sex-based discrimination. *Dalit* efforts contributed to the establishment of organisations including the Self-Employed Women's Association (SEWA), which campaigned for economic justice and advocated for the dismantling of caste-based and patriarchal oppression, representing a vital strand of Indian feminism that emphasised inclusivity and intersectionality (Sahu, 2023).

Additionally, raising awareness about VAW, reproductive rights, and political representation was achieved by Indian feminists. Policy advancements, including reserved quotas for XXs in local elections, were instrumental in enhancing political participation.

The Constitution of India, however, continues to regard XXs as a weaker section of society, recognising the need to address their social and economic disadvantages (Thaker, 2023). Nevertheless, the third wave clearly illustrates the ability of XXs to influence discussions including ecofeminism, demonstrating the power of local activism in influencing global movements that persevere.

The UK

Since 2000, a new generation of XXs and XYs emerged in the UK, confronting entrenched sex-based inequalities influenced by unique socio-political contexts. This included neoliberalism and a heightened focus on class struggles, further prompted by the globalisation of ideas and responses to post-feminism during the third wave.

Once hailed as the "can-do" generation of the late 1990s and early 2000s, young XXs embodied an individualised, neoliberal culture that was both empowering and precarious. They excelled academically and challenged workplace obstacles with sex-positivity, ambition and aligned with luxury brands. Yes this cohort was also depicted as "at risk" associated with binge drinking, teenage pregnancy, and youth unemployment (Aune & Holyoak, 2018; Bradford & Cullen, 2014; Harris, 2004; Lotz, 2003).

Stressing intersectionality and collective action, feminists in the third wave questioned the views of white feminists' perspective and questioned the lack of attention to diversity, equity, and inclusion (DEI). Central concerns included street harassment, negative media representation, cultural stereotypes, economic inequalities, systemic injustice, and sexual violence (Aune & Holyoak, 2018; Gillis et al., 2007; Herr, 2014).

However, some critics raised concerns about their focus on consumerism and hyper-femininity, arguing that it shifted attention away from systemic inequalities towards individualistic self-expression. For example, feminist scholars contend that adopting a generational lens to examine feminist differences risked triggering division rather than encouraging meaningful dialogue for universal understanding (Gillis et al., 2007; Pedwell, 2006). This wave has also been accused of fragmenting previous movements due to a lack of a unifying collective identity (Lister, 2005).

Despite the criticisms, meaningful progress in amplifying *herstories* added new cultural and political narratives. By recognising the multifaceted progressive influences of political feminist history, UK movements avoided oversimplified stereotypes, rejecting attempts to dismiss XXs' ongoing political and social progress (Aune & Holyoak, 2018; Gillis et al., 2007; Pedwell, 2006).

Young XXs also actively rejected notions of disengagement, instead embracing narratives that highlighted their contributions and directly opposed paternalistic practices. However, the significant reliance on digital platforms, though innovative and timely, have also been criticised for potentially excluding those without access to technology – a vital reminder that inclusion must also address digital divides (Aune & Holyoak, 2018).

Although SNSs were regularly employed to mobilise support throughout this movement, UK activists also organised public events, including *Feminist Fightback* and *Ladyfest* (Aune & Holyoak, 2018). Predominantly directed by local volunteers, feminist events demonstrated a strong commitment to grass-roots activism, emphasising the universal resonance of feminism and the power of global solidarity (Lelea & Voiculescu, 2017).

The not-for-profit phenomenon *Ladyfest*, which began in 2000 in the USA, quickly grew. By 2017, festivals were held worldwide, including in China, Germany, Mexico, NZ, Norway, Ukraine, and the UK, to name a few (Lelea & Voiculescu, 2017).

Initiated by the *Riot Grrrl* movement in the USA, *Ladyfest* created new spaces for feminist gatherings that encouraged and promoted inclusivity. The *Riot Grrrl* ethos – Do-It-Yourself – highlighted how feminist initiatives could build communities and provoke cultural change, featuring art, film, and music (Aune & Holyoak, 2018; Lelea & Voiculescu, 2017; Snyder, 2008).

The *Feminist Fightback* conferences, launched in 2006, for example, became powerful symbols of resistance against androcentric conventions. They revolutionised feminist heritage, redirecting and advancing coordinated community responses to austerity, reproductive justice, and employment rights. Actively opposing neoliberalism's relentless prioritisation of profit over equity (Aune & Holyoak, 2018), grassroots organisations, including the Fawcett Society, alongside UK activists and media platforms including *f word*, played a crucial role in strengthening acceptance and promoting inclusive feminist spaces (Herr, 2014).

the f word, established by Catherine Redfern in 2001, publishes articles, blogs, and reviews with relevant narratives, supporting new voices, inspiring critical reflection, and developing dialogues centred on sex-based issues (the f word, n.d.). While *the f word* and other digital platforms focused on facilitating discussions about body positivity, legal reforms, and intersectionality, they also helped raise awareness about workplace inequalities, sex-based pay disparities, and the need for legislative reforms (Dean, 2009; Herr, 2014).

Traditional derogatory labels, including "slut," "bitch," and "cunt," were redefined to reclaim femininity, embracing and appropriating these terms in opposition to patriarchal Western contexts, reframing them as symbols of strength, power, and self-determination (Snyder, 2008:179). Although the language was similar in numerous English-speaking societies, an important difference between the UK and the USA was the focus and consequences of pop culture, also accused of promoting chauvinism and marginalising new XX generations.

Pop culture in the UK was further criticised for placing less emphasis on addressing systemic sex-based inequalities and for encouraging the "I'm not a feminist but …" attitude (Aune & Holyoak, 2018:187). *The Spice Girls* phenomenon, for example, was argued to promote a form of individualistic empowerment that departed from collective feminism, ultimately contributing to the commodification and exploitation of XXs (Whelehan, 2000).

Additionally, makeover television shows often portrayed personal transformation as confidence-building while manipulating perceptions of success and identity (Tasker & Negra, 2008; Whelehan, 2000).

The UK's shared objectives and aspirations are argued to have been more structured and critical of neoliberalism compared to the USA, where the wave was more decentralised and individualistic (Aune & Holyoak, 2018). Nevertheless, feminists in the UK, the USA, and other regions shared allegiances in opposing patriarchal structures, albeit through distinct methods and by rejecting the ideals of their predecessors – "feminist mothers" (Snyder, 2008:175).

The USA

Emerging in the early 1990s – nearly a decade before the UK – the third wave began responding to the backlash against the second wave, starting with a big splash in 1991 (Evans, 2015).

Anita Hill, an African American attorney and academic, engulfed national conversations on sexual harassment. During a US Senate confirmation hearing, Hill accused Clarence Thomas – her former colleague and a Supreme Court nominee – of sexual harassment. Thomas denied the allegations, describing the proceedings as a "high-tech lynching." Despite the controversy, Thomas secured confirmation, albeit with a narrow vote. Hill did not press charges, but her testimony placed workplace sexual harassment at the forefront of public consciousness, resulting in increased awareness and legal reforms (Cushman, 2012; Dean, 2009; Hartman, 1992).

A year later, *Backlash*, Faludi's book (1992) explored the pervasive opposition to feminism, revealing how media, political structures, and cultural narratives deliberately blocked XX's advancement and equality. In the same year, Rebecca Walker's essay *Becoming the Third Wave*, published in *Ms. Magazine*, exemplified several key issues, including the "assault of the human spirit ..." and "women's credibility and power." This passage is an excerpt from the essay:

> I acknowledge the fact that we live under siege. I intend to fight back. I have uncovered and unleashed more repressed anger than I thought possible. For the umpteenth time in my 22 years, I have been radicalized, politicized, shaken awake. I have come to voice again, and this time my voice is not conciliatory. ... I am sick of the way women are negated, violated, devalued, ignored. I am livid, unrelenting in my anger at those who invade my space, who wish to take away my rights, who refuse to hear my voice. ... To be a feminist is to integrate an ideology of equality and female empowerment into the very fiber of my life. It is to search for personal clarity in the midst of systemic destruction, to join in sisterhood with women when often we are divided, to understand power structures with the intention of challenging them. ... Turn that outrage into

> political power. Do not vote for them unless they work for us. Do not have sex with them, do not break bread with them, do not nurture them if they don't prioritize our freedom to control our bodies and our lives. I am not a postfeminism feminist. I am the Third Wave.
>
> (Walker, 1992)

Content providers in both traditional and online mediums (Chapters 1 & 2) have contributed and remain integral to feminist movements, serving both as platforms for activism and sources of phallocentric critique. Significant popular cultural and technological shifts gave rise to digital platforms, transforming activism, democratising feminism, enabling XXs to disseminate ideas at the click of a button and mobilise support within seconds – an unprecedented technique in human history.

Technological advancements, for the first time, provided the tools to bypass traditional media control and, at times, rendered media moguls and their gatekeepers obsolete. Communication systems expanded with blogs, online forums, and eventually SNSs, where personal storytelling became central, linking individual experiences to systemic issues (Kinser, 2004). For example, the #MeToo movement, further examined in the fourth wave, exemplifies the power of grassroots digital activism, demonstrating its ability to spark action (Evans, 2015; Kelly, 2005; Kinser, 2004; Mahoney, 2016).

Pop culture was also a key focus in the USA, as third-wave feminism critiqued and deconstructed conventional sex-based assumptions continuously perpetuated through traditional media channels. Misogynistic depictions of XXs through various mediums further illustrated and reinforced the cultural expectations that commodify and objectify XXs, giving rise to protests using creative forms.

Music, as a communication tool, also drew attention to oppressive systemic patriarchal inequalities, heightening visibility among new generations, particularly regarding sex-based violence and the fight for bodily autonomy.

Riot Grrrl, a countercultural movement merging feminist ideology, and punk music – directly reproaching the XY–controlled punk scene – with political activism, also initiated *Ladyfest* (Riot Grrrl, n.d.). *Bikini Kill*, pioneers of the *Riot Grrrl* movement, boldly confronted patriarchal narratives that perpetuate the dangerous myth of XXs "asking for it" with their raw lyrics promoting resistance that resonates strongly with audiences around the world (Hart & May, 2018; Snyder, 2008).

The unfiltered phallocentric vernacular used by certain XYs is included in the band's lyrics, exposing prevailing toxic attitudes and the dehumanising language that reduces XXs to mere objects. Their unapologetic sincerity provokes listeners to reflect on the uncomfortable realities, sharpening critical consciousness of the pervasive harm caused by VAW.

"White Boy", a song released in 2014, for example, powerfully decries dominance by entitled white XYs that dehumanise and objectify XXs. The vivid and unsettling imagery in the lyrics emphasises the brutal realities of violence, control, and silencing, while the direct call for accountability attacks their gratification, demanding recognition of the pain inflicted on XXs and revealing androcentricity with unambiguous precision. *The Riot Grrrl* movement endures as a powerful symbol of resistance, accentuating the power of culture to alter attitudes (Hart & May, 2018; Snyder, 2008; Rolling Stone, 2001).

Additionally, The *Guerrilla Girls*, an anonymous feminist art collective started in 1985 – wearing gorilla masks and adopting deceased female artists' pseudonyms – exposed and challenged sexism and racism in the art world (Malinowska, 2020). Their art continues to be exhibited around the globe in 2025 (Guerrilla Girls, n.d.).

Various online spaces were also created by XXs throughout the third wave to reconstruct perspectives, redefine oppressions, introducing emerging priorities and broadening feminist narratives.

Elevating cultural critique was a key strategy to expand discussions on misogynistic subordination, offering alternative perspectives. The efforts of feminists and advocates ranged from addressing VAW to supporting ecofeminist activism and prioritising numerous paternalistic threats. By revolutionising individual storytelling, third-wave feminists reframed past emergencies while addressing pressing issues that embraced diverse, multifaceted expressions of femininity, whilst further submerging patriarchal norms worldwide.

Fourth Wave: 2010–

Beginning in the early 21st c., somewhere between 2007 and 2012 with its endpoint yet to be determined, the fourth wave appears to be the longest-lasting to date.

This wave is not rehashing the ideals held by the "mothers" of previous waves, but represents a significant evolution, facilitated by technological advancements (Barclay et al., 2024; Snyder, 2008). Originating primarily in the USA and Western Europe, this wave rapidly expanded globally, gaining international traction through the internet (Munro, 2013; Wrye, 2009).

Functioning as a central element, the internet and SNSs are bridging the third and fourth waves and substantially increasing the "call-out" culture that promotes truth-telling and challenging sexism and misogyny (Munro, 2013:23).

Partly due to technology, feminism has evolved into a multifaceted concept encompassing diverse ideological perspectives and a range of socio-political movements seeking transformative changes and further disbanding the patriarchy. It has been developing on public stages, with three principal characteristics: the interplay between individual and collective feminist consciousness, the formation of communal storytelling, and the transnational spread of activism and advocacy (Garrido Ortolá, 2022).

Digital technologies and SNSs are enabling the creation and retention of universal communities, amplifying diverse voices, and strengthening and unifying ideological perspectives in efforts to challenge patriarchal concepts ingrained in culturally oppressive androcentric structures (Barclay et al., 2024; Lam, 2016). Consequently, SNSs are key components regularly consumed globally (Cassidy, 2016).

An excerpt from *Nueva Sociedad* (*New Society*) highlights the profound ripples the fourth wave is creating, its reach and potential impacts described as a "tsunami" with far-reaching swells.

"To the girls, the teenagers, the young women — those who will undoubtedly witness the fall of the patriarchy. Feminism is polyphonic, its multitude of voices resounding simultaneously in every corner of the world, in diverse tones and registers. A melody with different lyrics but with the same music, a song with a collective project, emancipatory, with nothing human being foreign to it.

A tsunami is a complex event involving a series of high-energy waves of varying sizes, caused by an extraordinary phenomenon that shifts a massive vertical volume of water. In much the same way, feminism has emerged in the early decades of the 21st century like a tsunami. The extraordinary phenomenon is the frustration of millions of women around the world who have reacted in an impressive way, confronting violence, oppression, and discrimination. Geophysics states that this type of wave moves a much greater amount of water, far superior to the waves produced by wind and tides. Hence, the fourth feminism wave, fuelled by the three previous waves, social media, and the growing consciousness of younger generations, is agitating the foundations of the patriarchy like never before ..." (Varela, 2019, 2020).

The number of people connecting with digital technologies is remarkable. As of May 2025, close to seven out of ten (70%) of the global population (5.6 billion out of around 8 billion) were accessing the internet (Roser et al., 2023; Statista, 2024); local, national, and global issues are discussed with SNS providing users more power than ever before to influence. Their impact is evident across social, cultural, economic, and political domains (Korn & Kneese, 2015).

The #MeToo movement, which exposed widespread workplace sexual harassment and the deep-rooted trauma inflicted by powerful patriarch, is one notable example. Initiated by Tarana Burke in 2006, the #MeToo went viral globally in 2017 (Drewett et al., 2021) following a flood of allegations against film producer Harvey Weinstein revealing the predatory behaviour of powerful XYs.

Survivors were inspired to end their silence, aiming at supporting other survivors of sexual harassment and assault. The #MeToo movement generated currents of solidarity and a universal demand for accountability (Malinowska, 2020; Chawla et al., 2021), illustrating the tsunami's emphasis on culpability and the power of XXs when unified.

The full impact of the #MeToo movement has yet to be clearly and comprehensively assessed with longitudinal data. However, the movement ignited significant changes in consciousness, bringing widespread attention to the sexual violence that has long been silenced (Fileborn & Loney-Howes, 2019) and inspiring a new generation of feminists to be active and alert.

One of the many reasons for the developing ripples in the fourth wave is that the word "feminist" has shifted from being a "dirty word" and a publicly abandoned ideology to becoming a topic of renewed interest (Chidgey, 2020:1055), pouring out both curiosity and criticism. Additionally, an ever-growing list of prominent A-list celebrities are openly identifying as feminists (Chidgey, 2020), helping to sustain the momentum of this tsunami.

"Dirty" has also long been linked with menstruation, a fundamental biological function essential to the survival of XX mammals (Catalini & Fedder, 2020). This archaic perception continues to cast menstruation as taboo, reinforcing stigma and imposing restrictions (Chapter 2) including financial burdens from sales taxes on menstrual hygiene products, discussed in this chapter.

As a testament to the power of this tsunami, numerous countries are now eliminating or reducing the "tampon tax" (Baptista, 2023), signalling a positive global shift towards understanding menstruation.

Digital activism, a defining feature of the fourth wave, distinguishes it from its predecessors with a unique emphasis on spirituality, community participation, and global activism (Wrye, 2009). The tsunami, using SNSs as powerful tools, is demanding public accountability and building on the achievements of earlier movements (Munro, 2013), further exposing entrenched androcentric unacceptable behaviours and extending the reach and relevance of feminism in contemporary societies (Phillips & Cree, 2014).

Building on the third wave's emphasis on inclusivity – streaming in from previous waves – feminists are addressing the intersections of sex, class, and race (Phillips & Cree, 2014; Rampton, 2015), further recognising and confronting the global oppression of XXs and other marginalised groups and preventing access to health, economic opportunities, education, and political participation.

Understanding the intersection between the personal and the political, the current movement is, in part, driven by environmental crises, pervasive and endemic disparities, and sustained patriarchal dominance. The fourth wave also distinguishes itself from earlier waves by integrating spirituality and community involvement into its mission, with evolutionary awareness addressing trauma to heal individuals and Mother Earth. Additionally, it is advancing issues around social justice and human rights and promoting peace and community well-being, working towards global evolutionary awareness and transformations (Wrye, 2009).

As a case in point, Greta Thunberg's global rise to prominence in 2019. As one of the most renowned and youngest ecofeminists, Sweden-based Thunberg has had significant impacts worldwide (Bowie, 2024; Haugseth & Smeplass, 2023). Often referred to as the "Greta Thunberg Effect", her influence illustrates how grassroots campaigns can motivate, lead, and inspire global climate action among her generation and beyond (Sabherwal et al., 2021:323).

Thunberg's language, exemplified by the phrase "I want you to act as if our house is on fire. Because it is" (Sabherwal et al., 2021:321), and her *Fridays for Future* campaigns highlight intergenerational justice, resonating with politically engaged youth. The "Thunberg Effect" appears to resonate more strongly with liberals than conservatives; nevertheless, the connection between environmental degradation and patriarchal oppression is evidently exhibited (Haugseth & Smeplass, 2023; Sabherwal et al., 2021) to advance environmental and social justice through ecofeminist principles.

As illustrated by the Thunberg Effect and the #MeToo movement, this tsunami is flooding with information and amplifying the voices of young XXs with effective tools to broadcast information while challenging power structures.

Whilst raising awareness, XXs are confronting and opposing androcentric prejudices, misogynistic behaviour, and sexual harassment, while drawing renewed focus to ecofeminism (Phillips & Cree, 2014), sexual violence, and online harassment (Munro, 2013); these injustices remain despite the existence of pro–XX laws, prompting the critical question: "Why do such structural discriminatory injustices and power imbalances continue?"

The answer can partly be attributed to the continued dominance of XYs legislating at both national and international levels and their phallocentric ideologies steering the global order, including the UN – a direct manifestation of the persistent underrepresentation of XXs in leadership roles (Brooks, 2002).

In a deeply interconnected world, however, isolationism is now obsolete; global partnerships are pivotal to enhancing international cooperation and increasing human rights (Chapter 2). The power dynamics that prioritise collaboration and community service over dominance are being contested, along with cultural narratives and the media, which continue harmful portrayals throughout editorials and advertising (Munro, 2013; Phillips & Cree, 2014), further alarming and mobilising the masses.

The Women's March, initiated by Melissa Miotke in 2016, for example, inspired thousands to take action in Washington, marking the beginning of another movement that quickly went viral globally (Women's March, n.d.; Wikipedia, n.d.-b). The inauguration of a bigoted and misogynistic president in the USA further intensified the global tsunami effect (Crozier-De Rosa & Mackie, 2018).

The marches extended into 81 countries, and in January 2017, demonstrators crowded their local streets to protest the world's opposition to the newly elected president and his administration, which was criticised for discriminatory behaviours toward XXs and various other groups (Ward, 2017). Local issues were also on display, with many holding placards delivering various messages highlighting the need for human and XX rights. The events were widely covered by the traditional media (Ward, 2017).

Time magazine, for example, featured an image of a "pussy hat" – a pink knitted hat with ears worn by the marchers – on its February 2017 cover

(Gökarıksel & Smith, 2017; Alter, 2017). The international coverage contributed to magnifying public opinion, including feminist opponents.

Earlier-wave feminists often critique the tsunami for prioritising individuality and digital activism over traditional methods, framing it as a generational divide between grassroots and online activists. For example, "clicktivism" and "slacktivism" are claimed to create the illusion of progress without disbanding androcentric discriminatory practices, thereby weakening the movement's efforts. These new "isms" refer to the practice of engaging with online activism with minimal effort – liking, reposting, or signing online petitions, for example – without substantive participation, which critics argue diminishes the impact of feminist campaign strategies. Additionally, recording acts of resistance is criticised for taking precedence over resistance itself, as the boundaries between online and offline identities often blur (Karpf, 2010; Koerber, 2001; Phillips & Cree, 2014; Munro, 2013; Rome et al., 2019).

Others argue that the so-called division signals the adaptability of feminism, demonstrating how each generation resists and contests patriarchal oppression within diverse socio-political contexts (Munro, 2013; Wrye, 2009). The tsunami phenomenon accentuates the transformative potential of technology in disbanding the permeating and drenched androcentric ideals, even as concerns about "clicktivism" and "slacktivism" persist (Munro, 2013; Phillips & Cree, 2014). Irrespective of the criticisms, the achievements obtained in the 21st century indicate progress, and the undercurrent is expected to continue.

Additionally, the voices advocating for equality are placing increasing pressure on employers to be aware and act. The rising financial costs of sexual harassment litigation, for example – often reaching millions of dollars – are becoming a major global concern for employers across all industries (Chawla et al., 2021; Phillips & Cree, 2014; Willness et al., 2007; Wrye, 2009).

Australia

Throughout the fourth wave, feminists in Australia are focusing on intersectionality, acknowledging the heightened discrimination faced by XXs from diverse backgrounds, particularly Indigenous XXs. Initiatives, including the *National Indigenous Women's Gathering*, are amplifying their voices, focusing on their unique challenges and emphasising the importance of inclusivity (Clark et al., 2021; Moreton-Robinson, 2020). Nevertheless, much remains to be improved.

Often referred to as the "lucky country", an ironic term describing Australia as reliant, narrow-minded, and culturally insular (Horne, 1964), the big island remains a patriarchal state where the practice of "mateship" continues to define its national values (Simic, 2016).

Mateship is deeply embedded in Australian culture (Historical Dictionary of Australia, 2014) and has been a dominant force in perpetuating toxic behaviours as well as maintaining and reinforcing negative and hostile attitudes towards XXs. Mateship practices continue defining Australian nationalism

(Chapter 1) and remains central to the countries identity (Simic, 2016), incorporating "misogynistic" (Dyrenfurth, 2007:231) and homophobic elements (Payne, 2019).

If the dream of equality is to be realised, the Western ideals of mateship and "manliness" (Runyan & Peterson, 2014:4), which perpetuate phallocentrism and androcentrism, must be eradicated. To illustrate the misogynistic Australian culture and how XXs are fighting back, six epoch-defining events reported by XX journalists are reviewed (Gorman, 2021; Milligan, 2021; Murphy, 2021).

The first incident: In November 2020, the Australian Broadcasting Corporation (ABC), Australia's public broadcaster, aired the television documentary *Inside the Canberra Bubble* (Cronau & Milligan, 2020). This investigative programme exposed the misconduct of several senior XY political leaders.

One former Liberal Party (conservative) staffer stated on camera: "The behaviour [of XYs in parliament] is not okay, and the culture is not okay. And there should be something done about it" (Cronau & Milligan, 2020). Sexual harassment in the workplace is ingrained in Australian working culture and regularly overlooked by politicians. Consequently, activists and advocates during the fourth wave are striving for substantial constructive changes.

The second incident: In January 2021, Grace Tame, from Tasmania, was named Australian of the Year (National Australia Day Council, 2021). Tame's campaign, #LetHerSpeak, advocated for sexual assault survivors to be given the freedom to speak out. The gag law, under Section 194K of the Evidence Act 2001, prohibited survivors of sexual abuse from publishing their experiences, purportedly to protect them from being identified without consent (Department of Justice, 2001).

Tame's advocacy efforts succeeded, resulting in legislative reforms that enable sexual abuse survivors in Tasmania to speak publicly about their experiences. Tame continues to advocate for policy reforms to prevent sexual abuse (Humphries, 2020) and launched *The Grace Tame Foundation*, which engages political and societal leaders while providing financial support to peak organisations advocating for significant change (The Grace Tame Foundation, n.d.).

The third incident: In February 2021, Brittany Higgins, a 24-year-old Liberal Party political staffer, alleged on national television that she had been raped inside a ministerial office by a colleague, Bruce Lehrmann (ABC News, 2021). When questioned by the media, the PM stated that his chief of staff would investigate the matter. Higgins met with the PM in April 2021; according to media reports, the conversation was described as "difficult" (Murphy, 2021).

Following the trial, a federal inquiry exposed damning admissions from media executives across television and the press regarding their role in sensationalising the coverage and supporting the accused rapist. They admitted to ethical breaches, including paying the alleged rapist for exclusive, unethical interviews that jeopardised due process and amplified prejudicial narratives.

Shocking revelations detailed that media payments covered the alleged rapist's interviews, purchases of illicit drugs, sex workers, restaurant meals, rent, golf outings, and flight expenses (Saeed, 2024; Meade & Cassidy, 2024). Additionally, prosecutors were found to have withheld vital evidence and police displayed prejudice, with some officers questioning the complainant's credibility (McCulloch, 2023). These actions obliterated ethical boundaries, further eroding public trust and highlighting the alarming influence of media moguls, mateship, and the justice system working against XXs.

Higgins is reported to have reached a confidential settlement with the government (ABC/AAP, 2022). As of August 2025, Lehrmann continues to defend himself against two other rape accusations, allegedly committed in Queensland, and has requested a judge-only trial (McCray, 2025; Wockner, 2024).

The fourth incident: Following high-profile cases exposing misogynistic laws and sexual misconduct by XYs within the Australian Parliament and beyond, nationwide outrage erupted. In response to continued sexual VAW, more than 200 *March4Justice* rallies were staged in March 2021 around the country. Demonstrators demanded justice with placards stating that "enough is enough" (Gorman, 2021; March4Justice, 2021).

The outrage was based on: a. Sexual harassment in the workplace; b. The requirement for survivors to testify while alleged rapists have the legal right to remain silent during a trial (Saunders, 2024); and c. The conduct of media moguls suppressing survivors and supporting perpetrators (Gorman, 2021).

Further infuriating the population, the conservative PM at the time, Morrison, admitted he did not want to address the crowd (Gorman, 2021). Later that day, in parliament, he said:

> Today here, and in many cities across our country, women and men are gathering together in rallies, both large and small, to call for change and to act against violence directed towards women … . This [Australia] is a vibrant liberal democracy. Not far from here, such marches, even now, are being met with bullets – but not here in this country. It is a triumph of democracy when we see these things take place.
>
> (Parliamentary Debates, 2021:2195)

The message from the former Australian PM clearly illustrated his definition of "democracy" reflects patriarchal systems that excludes XXs (McBride & Mazur, 2010), a concern also denounced by ecofeminists.

The fifth incident: In September 2019, Niamh and Harriet, high school students, launched *School Strike 4 Climate*, demanding climate justice and policy reforms that exposed political failures (Petray, et al., 2022). Previous protests had taken place in various cities, with students as young as 11 skipping school (Cox, 2018; White et al., 2022). This reaffirmed Thunberg's belief that collective action drives change, amplifying youth voices and promoting grassroots, intersectional activism to shift concerns from awareness to action (Haugseth & Smeplass, 2023; Sabherwal et al., 2021).

The sixth incident: After decades of advocacy to remove the "luxury tax" on tampons and menstrual pads – hygiene products had been excluded from classification as essential medical items or basic necessities (Fox, 2020:5) – the Australian federal government reviewed the tax in 2019, removing the 10% Goods and Services Tax (GST) on tampons and pads (Davidson, 2018; Crawford & Spivack, 2019).

Prior to the removal of the luxury tax, menstrual hygiene products cost XXs between AU$30 (US$18.5) million and AU$48 (US$30) million collectively each year. While the removal of the luxury tax was acknowledged as a positive economic and pro–XX policy, it failed to address broader sex-based inequities, including menstrual stigma and economic subordination (James, 2022). Concerns remain, including the stigma surrounding bleeding, and excessive pricing by manufacturers and retailers on hygiene products.

The EU

There are many great accomplishments obtained by XXs throughout the EU – too many for this little book to include. Nevertheless, the many activists, irrespective of language, culture, and geography, are fighting the same enemy: patriarchs.

Across the 27 EU member states (Countries of the World, n.d.), the tsunami is characterised by transnationalisation, a means of protest that also brought the #MeToo movement to both European screens and streets. Tagged as "one of the most powerful moments in modern history" (Garrido Ortolá, 2022; Varela, 2020), the movement continues resonating across the EU.

Drawing inspiration from the UK's successful #NoMorePage3, the movement exposed the broader issue of sexist media representation and gained momentum as part of the surging tsunami (Barclay et al., 2024; Dore, 2016; Varela, 2019).

The "*Stop Bild Sexism*" campaign, for example, launched in Germany, by Kristina Lunz, an Oxford University student, targeted *Bild-Zeitung*, Europe's largest-selling newspaper, with an annual circulation of 2.2 million. Notably, *Bild-Zeitung* had featured a photograph of a topless XX on its front page every day for 28 years.

The campaign successfully eliminated the newspaper's long-standing practice of publishing topless images and derogatory depictions of XXs bodies (Dore, 2016). The newspaper announced the end of topless pictures on International Women's Day (IWD) in 2012 (Greenslade, 2012), a year after the centennial of IWD (Ruthchild, 2012).

In Sweden, the impact of the #MeToo movement contributed to the introduction of legislation criminalising sex without consent, enacted in 2018 (Pollack, 2019). The movement also increased visibility of sex-based discrimination in sports, prompting greater openness in discussing the experiences of those subjected to abuse (Abrams & Bartlett, 2019). Sexual misconduct is present across all types of sports, though it is particularly prevalent in those traditionally associated with masculinity (Fasting 2015). Spain's national women's football team, *La Roja*, which won the 2023 FIFA Women's World Cup, is a case in point, having sparked global outrage about abuse and power in sport.

India

Movements have increasingly focused on addressing unique and deeply entrenched forms of sexism. As in many other nations, the tsunami in India is characterised by intersectionality and political mechanisms, reinforced by technological advancements that influence narratives within the world's most populous country (Crossley, 2015; Jain, 2020; Worldometers, n.d.).

Activists are reorienting and reengineering initiatives and strategies, realigning priorities, and intertwining global feminist philosophies with local realities (Barclay et al., 2024). Digital advocacy for social and political change, which has emerged as a key strategy for XXs across the country, is often cited as an example of successful activism.

Local realities are prompting activists and advocates to initiate and launch numerous campaigns to address sexual abuse, VAW, workplace harassment, and the prevalent rape culture, including gang rapes and femicides. The numerous abhorrent acts against XXs are provoking national and international outrage, distress, disgust, and indignation (Barclay et al., 2024) calling for action and accountability.

These movements have achieved meaningful change and increased awareness, targeting sexism, racism, casteism, and religious discrimination (Chapter 2). The #MeToo movement also strengthened workplace harassment laws and forced resignations from high-profile figures. Several important movements include the *Pink Chaddi Campaign*, #DelhiBraveheart, #LahuKaLagaan, and #IWillGoOut campaigns, to name a few.

The *Pink Chaddi Campaign* dissented the moral policing of a Hindu right-wing group. After members of the *Sri Ram Sene* (Army of Lord Ram) attacked XXs in a pub in 2009, Nisha Susan used an SNS to organise the campaign. Within a week, 30,000 people mobilised, opposing misogyny, the patriarchy, and Pramod Muthalik, an Indian right-wing (conservative) politician. Part of the campaign included sending 3,000 pairs of pink underwear to the leader of *Sri Ram Sene* (Barclay et al., 2024; Subramanian, 2015).

The #LahuKaLagaan (Blood Tax) campaign successfully led to the elimination of the "tampon tax" in July 2018 (Crawford & Spivack, 2019; Gupta & Trehan, 2021). The removal of the 12% Goods and Services Tax on feminine hygiene products was instigated by activists and public figures challenging India's "… indiscriminate tax policy on menstrual hygiene" (Gupta & Trehan, 2021:292).

The policy change made menstrual products more accessible for some individuals. However, research on the impact of the tax removal on affordability and consumer prices has been inconsistent and lacks detailed analysis (Fox, 2020). Nevertheless, the removal of the tampon tax represents a step towards improving menstrual hygiene and addressing period poverty, particularly among low-income XXs (Crawford & Spivack, 2019). However, sex-based injustices remain overshadowed by brutal acts of VAW in India.

The #DelhiBraveheart case gained national and international attention, exposing systemic failures in India. A profoundly disturbing and harrowing gang rape occurred in Delhi in December 2012, igniting widespread horror and outrage. The case shocked consciences, evoked sadness, and unleashed a torrent of fury and anguish, sparking numerous hashtags and drawing global attention to the monstrous crimes (Jain, 2020). Numerous SNSs became powerful platforms for collective condemnation, activism, and expressions of despair. Prominent feminists and activists also led mass public demonstrations, demanding urgent legal reforms and justice in a system that has long failed to protect XXs (Titus, 2018).

The *Nirbhaya* case – the fatal assault of a 22-year-old XX who was gang-raped, tortured, and thrown off a bus after being gutted by six XYs, including a minor and the bus driver – was a barbaric, inhumane sexual assault and murder proving the pervasive power of patriarchal violence. The term *Nirbhaya*, meaning "fearless", was adopted by the media to reference the case, adhering to Indian laws that prohibit identification – her name was Jyoti Singh Pandey (Nieder et al., 2019). One of the nurses who cared for Jyoti had herself been a survivor of gang rape (Kaur, 2017; Rana, 2020).

The *Nirbhaya* attack was described by the Indian legal system as the "rarest of the rare" due to its "sheer barbarity and viciousness" (Rana, 2020:141). Four adults were executed by hanging in 2020; the juvenile was convicted of rape and murder, receiving the maximum sentence of three years' imprisonment in a reform facility (Baghel, 2022).

In 2013, President Pranab Mukherjee promulgated the Criminal Law (Amendment) Act, implementing a series of new laws and establishing courts dedicated to adjudicating rape cases. However, even with the implementation of new laws, critics argue that the Indian androcentric legal system remains apathetic in judging and prosecuting. Although severe punishments were introduced and were symbolically significant, sexual violence, including rape, continues to rise, indicating that punitive measures alone fail to address the underlying causes of VAW (Baghel, 2022).

A few years after the 2013 legislative changes, a series of sexual assaults occurred in Bangalore during a New Year's Eve celebration attended by over 60,000 people. In response, the #IWillGoOut hashtag emerged, sparking a collective movement that organised marches and events across more than 30 locations in India. Further outrage followed when an Indian minister blamed XXs' Western attire for the sexual assaults, leading to the #MassMolestation campaign (BBC News, 2017; Diwanji et al., 2021).

Numerous feminist movements in India have played pivotal roles in challenging traditional phallocentrism and weakening hostile influences in certain regions. Without widespread protests, meaningful change would have been improbable. Various legal amendments exposed government and police failings as root causes of VAW in India. Once again, the law demonstrating how XXs' rights are disregarded, leaving them disadvantaged by legislation generated by patriarchal cultural beliefs (Dey, 2020). Human rights and freedoms are severely restricted, enabling exploitation, domination, oppression, and humiliation (Sah, 2022).

Regardless of some legal reforms, sexism remains deeply entrenched. Patriarchs in government, religion, and culture (Lekha & Kumar, 2025) continue to perpetuate discrimination through subtle means (Chapters 2 & 4). The legislative changes, nonetheless, provide some optimism for XXs living in India. Additionally, the various movements – irrespective of legal frameworks – continue to encourage online solidarity into strategic offline action using SNSs (Titus, 2018).

To fully grasp the evolving nature of these feminist movements and the intricate resistance efforts of XXs in India, further research is needed to fully understand unique complexities and the shifting power dynamics. The numerous movements are also signalling the rise of another feminist groundswell that may soon be recognised as the fifth wave (Barclay et al., 2024; Chiu, 2020).

The UK

Similar to India and Australia, the UK also eliminated the value-added tax (VAT) on menstrual hygiene products, albeit later than other nations. The tampon tax was abolished in January 2021. Initially, menstrual products were taxed at the standard VAT rate of 17.5%, reduced to 5% in 2001, complying with EU regulations that restricted further reductions (Flinders & Lowery, 2023). In 2021, after Brexit, the UK gained full regulatory autonomy and eliminated VAT on menstrual products entirely (Crawford & Spivack, 2019).

This long-overdue achievement was advanced through years of activist campaigning to remove the tax. However, critics noted that while the tax removal reduced costs, it did not resolve deeper challenges, including affordability for low-income XXs and the broader issue of period poverty (Flinders & Lowery, 2023). Despite these concerns, the legislative reform represents a step forward towards sex-based equality, reinforcing the recognition that menstrual hygiene products are essential necessities, not luxuries.

The tsunami in the UK has also been characterised by numerous digital campaigns. Although too many to detail in this book, two significant movements illustrate how feminists continue to resist XY–supremacist practices: 1. the #NoMorePage3 campaign and 2. the #FreeTheNipple movement, which also addresses the stigma surrounding public breastfeeding.

The first: the #NoMorePage3 campaign targeted *The Sun* newspaper's practice of featuring topless XXs on page three – a practice normalising everyday sexism for decades. Feminists highlighted how media perpetually portrays entrenched misogynistic androcentric cultural biases, demanding accountability and rejecting the casual objectification of XXs' bodies.

The movement leveraged SNSs, blogs, and online petitions to amplify its message and sustain momentum.

Public pressure ultimately compelled *The Sun* to stop publishing the images in 2015, after nearly 45 years of exposing XXs' breasts, including nipples. By challenging this cultural artefact, the #NoMorePage3 campaign achieved its immediate goal, again demonstrating the power of collective action and strategic digital advocacy (Barclay et al., 2024; Munro, 2013).

The outrage and exasperation on overt sexism by the media and the double standards regarding the XX body had begun long before the #NoMorePage3 started. Although tabloids featured topless images, laws prohibited XXs from appearing topless in public. The legal repercussions for exposing breasts, including nipples, differed significantly for XYs and XXs in many Western societies, exposing sexist injustice in how public decency laws are enforced (Harbke & Lindemann, 2023) and further emphasising the patriarchy's desire to control the XX body.

The second: the #FreeTheNipple movement employed diverse imagery, including XXs breastfeeding and post-surgery photos to challenge oppressive phallocentric constructs gaining international recognition and inspired a documentary (Free the Nipple, 2015; Matich et al., 2018).

Activists decried oppression, demanding an end to legal and social double standards and petitioned for their desexualisation. Employing digital engagement and public demonstrations with high-profile celebrities, including Keira Knightley (English actor) and Naomi Campbell (English fashion model), the campaigners further amplified its international impact (Matich et al., 2018).

The focus on the nipple is significant as the patriarchy has historically fetishised the XX breasts, framing them as a sexual object. However, XXs' breasts symbolise nurturing, subverting traditional constructs that separate "mother" from "sexual being" (Young, 1992).

The #FreeTheNipple movement directly confronted this fetishisation by advocating for body autonomy and freedom of expression. Global discussions expanded the urgent need to eradicate entrenched phallocentric demands of the XX body. By defying oppressive views, roles, and patriarchal expectations, the campaign and the film further accentuated global glaring legal double standards (Matich et al., 2018).

Despite legal protections under the UK Equality Act 2010 (UK Government, 2010), public breastfeeding remains stigmatised. Archaic cultural attitudes continue to undermine legal rights, leading to negative consequences for XXs and their infants (Grant, et al., 2018). The critical health benefits of lactation, for example, provide unique immunological and nutritional advantages for both infants and mother (Boyer, 2011). To further counteract objectification and judgment, "lactivism" emerged as a national movement. Public "nurse-ins" and breastfeeding picnics were designed to contest misogynistic expectations and normalise breastfeeding (Boyer, 2011:431).

However, many breastfeeding parents in the UK feel scrutinised and judged, with some delaying feeds in public due to intimidation and fear of being objectified (Grant, 2016). This judgment often stems from perceptions of exhibitionism rather than recognising breastfeeding as a natural and essential act of care. One activist expressed her frustration:

> The suggestion to breastfeed in a toilet is disgusting! Would you eat your meal in a public toilet? Apparently, breasts are only acceptable if they're on page three of a tabloid, but not when feeding a baby. The way some of you have spoken about these mothers is appalling.
>
> (Grant, 2016:56)

Although these events sparked both support and criticism, promoting positive representations of breastfeeding remains crucial to eliminating sexist attitudes (Grant, 2016; Boyer, 2011). Naturalising and normalising breastfeeding in all public areas is essential for strengthening equal standing and challenging the harmful perception that breastfeeding parents invite inappropriate attention. This shift requires reframing societal views of the XX body as nurturing rather than inherently sexual (Gallagher et al., 2023; Grant, 2016).

These UK campaigns, along with many others not mentioned, illustrate the core of the tsunami, where digital and physical platforms contested transnational XY hegemony and androcentric laws.

The USA

Regrettably, laws, including pro–XX legislation, can be reversed or overturned. Two such cases include 1. *Fisher v. University of Texas* in 2013 and 2. *Roe v. Wade* in 2022.

The first: The University of Texas included race as one factor in its undergraduate admissions process, which led to a legal challenge in the Supreme Court case *Grutter v. Bollinger* (2003) ruling. A white applicant that was denied admission, filed a lawsuit claiming the practice violated the Equal Protection Clause. Although the district court upheld the university's policy, the Supreme Court later overturned the ruling, stating that the university had failed to meet the strict scrutiny standard, emphasising that institutions must demonstrate a compelling and legitimate interest for using race-based classifications and prove such measures are essential to achieving their goals. The decision, imposing stricter scrutiny on affirmative action programmes, was argued to significantly limit the legal scope to address racial inequalities effectively (Casebriefs, n.d.; *Fisher v. University of Texas*, 2013; Pant & Sharma, 2024).

The second: The landmark 1973 case, *Roe v. Wade*, legalised abortion by establishing a constitutional right to terminate a pregnancy under the right to privacy. The ruling permitted XXs to access abortion by choice, during the first trimester, and struck down restrictive state laws in the USA. However, in 2022, the Supreme Court overturned 50 years of legal precedent (Murray, 2021; Reingold & Gostin, 2023; Watkins-Hayes & Adams-Santos, 2023), resulting in profound and far-reaching negative consequences for XXs in the USA and instigating global reverberations.

The courts decision ended federal protections for abortion, granting individual states the authority to regulate access as they see fit. As a result, the legal risks for XXs and medical professionals have increased significantly, further marginalising communities already facing systemic barriers to healthcare. This legal change has disproportionately impacted poor, migrant, and racially marginalised XXs, for whom essential healthcare has become both inaccessible and prohibitively expensive (Watkins-Hayes & Adams-Santos, 2023).

Following the overturning of *Roe v. Wade*, several US states secured abortion rights within their constitutions through democratic efforts, while others implemented highly restrictive, androcentric regulations (Reingold & Gostin, 2023).

President Biden, in office from 2021 to January 2025, supported changes permitting the mailing of abortion medications aimed at reducing risks for both patients and providers (Reingold & Gostin, 2023). Nevertheless, the end of national reproductive rights provoked international debates surrounding law, morality, and religion, with pro-life groups advocating for restrictions and deepening inequalities in abortion access (Murray, 2021). The restrictive measures are projected to prevail and increase under the Republican leadership of the 47th presidency, which commenced in January 2025.

Activists are leveraging support and building global solidarity campaigns through grassroots protests and digital movements. #MeToo, the most notable example, originated in the USA and transformed the fourth wave into a powerful global tsunami.

Much like in the UK, toplessness in the USA remains illegal for XXs in many jurisdictions while being widely accepted for XYs. The sexist regulations of nudity reveal systemic discrimination, with both legal and social condemnations. Although certain regions in the USA have progressed towards toplessness equality, the pervasive moral policing of the XX body continues, reinforcing outdated patriarchal norms and the Madonna-whore dichotomy (Harbke & Lindemann, 2023:104; Munford et al., 2007), which reduces XXs to polarised roles of either purity or promiscuity.

Menstrual hygiene products, as in other countries, are classified under the tampon tax as "luxury items" in the USA instead of being treated as tax-exempt essentials like medical supplies or groceries (Fox, 2020:12). Inconsistencies between states call for policy reform, with the "No Tax on Tampons" campaigns unmasking the alarming oppression of institutionalised misogyny. Some jurisdictions have implemented local reforms, and half of the US states have abolished the tax in response to public outrage.

A pioneering initiative in New York City, for example, provides free menstrual products in schools, jails, and shelters, reflecting broader efforts towards menstrual equity by recognising that bleeding is anything but a luxury (Office of the Mayor, New York City, 2016; Ooi, 2018). Eliminating the luxury tax signifies progress in recognising menstrual hygiene as a basic human right, reducing inequality, and improving the dignity of XXs. This progress is a testament to the advocacy of both past and present feminists (Crawford & Spivack, 2019; Ooi, 2018).

Further evidence of XXs' advocacy is reflected in the heartfelt public outcries of Caroline Kennedy and Mary L. Trump, who made determined efforts to prevent their relatives from attaining power in hopes of averting catastrophic consequences. Despite their conviction and courage, their efforts were unsuccessful, and both men obtained positions of power.

In 2025, Caroline Kennedy, a former US ambassador, sent a letter to senators, and posted her appeal online, requesting that her cousin Robert F. Kennedy Jr.'s nomination for Secretary of Health and Human Services be rejected. She accused him of being an exploitative predator who secures personal wealth through manipulation. The divisive Jr. is also known for spreading vaccine-related conspiracy theories (Al Jazeera, 2025).

American psychologist Mary L. Trump warned the American public not to vote for the Republican nominee during his first presidential campaign. Her published memoirs (Trump, 2020) revealed that her uncle is narcissistic and dangerous; a weak, inept bully, and that she wanted to "take him down." The president's attempts to block the book from being published were unsuccessful (BBC News, 2020). However, two of his three presidential campaigns resulted in electoral victory and his subsequent occupation of the White House are having negative global effects.

Conclusion

The feminist movements, aka waves, with unified collective tides, have founded powerful legacies of resilience and progress, transcending geographical, political, and cultural boundaries, pursuing justice across race, class, and sex.

The four waves of feminism have demonstrated the ability to unite in solidarity, redefining and reforming social paradigms, and disbanding various oppressive models. By building on the legacies of predecessors and leveraging innovative strategies, feminism continues to inspire change, ensuring that the human rights of XXs remain an enduring and dynamic force in the 21st century.

From Wollstonecraft's 1792 publication, planting a seed, to the first wave, where suffrage opened the channels for global legal reforms, resistance has continued to pull apart patriarchal assumptions that XXs are subservient. Although shaped by regional contexts with varying priorities, feminism's primary objectives – political representation, property rights, and access to proportionate education and healthcare – remain on agendas in every country.

The second wave expanded feminist advocacy by focusing on workplace discrimination, reproductive rights and VAW. Legislative reforms, including Australia's SDA and the USA's Equal Pay Act, encapsulated the movement's ability to influence legal reforms. This wave also extended cultural analysis, introducing new terms including *herstory*, disputing androcentric narratives and elevating academic fields that legitimise the voices and experiences of XXs. Numerous feminists published books that both shocked and inspired.

However, the limitations of this wave were evident in its exclusivity, with critics denouncing the marginalisation of non-white XXs and those from lower socioeconomic backgrounds.

The third wave, emerging in the 1990s, amplified intersectionality, defining the interconnected forms of oppression experienced by individuals based on race, sex, and class. It was also marked by the rise of grassroots activism, digital communication, and pop culture. These reclamations aimed at challenging traditional representations of femininity. The *Riot Grrrl* movement and global *Ladyfests* reimagined XX spaces by blending art, music, and activism to promote inclusivity and celebrate diverse identities. These XX-led initiatives were highly successful.

The tsunami embodies the peak of combined past waves while powerfully integrating online tools for activism and "call-out" culture, exemplifying global solidarity. Additionally, the rise of ecofeminism gained traction, emphasising the interconnectedness of environmental injustice, linking environmental degradation to patriarchal exploitation, as seen in India with the *Chipko* movement and the global *Thunberg Effect*; both reinforcing the urgent need for collective action against phallocentric systems that fuel, escalate, and perpetuate destruction.

The current wave, the tsunami, insistently alerts both old and new wicked forms of sex-based suppression that persist. The enduring sex-based pay gap, reproductive restrictions, and sexual violence, for example, reaffirm the imperative for mobilisation, vigilance, and continued resistance.

The resilience of feminism and activists epitomises their unwavering ability to sustain, adapt, and commit in solidarity across generations and borders. The legacy of numerous local and global movements is defined by their power to inspire, mobilise, endure and instigate pro-XX laws.

The ongoing battle against the patriarchy to improve the lives of XXs is no easy feat, yet the sisterhood has continually proven it is possible. From securing the right to vote and advancing labour and civil rights, to abolishing the luxury tampon, feminist movements have driven transformative change while embracing intersectionality.

In a nutshell: Herstories are celebrating, and will continue to celebrate, numerous critical breakthroughs, from the revival of feminism and the rise of SNS activism and ecofeminism to the disbanding of outdated patriarchal laws and cultural practices. The waves opened the floodgates for greater XX representation in leadership – one drop at a time. This chapter reaffirms that feminism remains both relevant and essential.

"Activists see themselves as amplifiers of the voices of people and advocates of civil, democratic and human rights, and, therefore, willing to take adversarial positions against injustice in any form".

Aruna Roy, Indian social activist, professor, former Sub-Divisional Magistrate, and former president of the National Federation of Indian Women (Roy, 2024; Wikipedia, n.d.-c)

Toolkit

Drawing directly from the evolution of feminism, each recommendation listed aims to inspire and prompt readers to engage, re-engage, and take steps to achieve at least the minimum: ensuring that the progress obtained to date is preserved and that we can coexist regardless of sex.

Participation Avenues:

- Leverage digital platforms to challenge sexism and promote equality. Inspire others to drive change – albeit sometimes requiring a step backwards before moving forward – similar to a tsunami's ebb and flow before a significant surge.
- Ignore critics of "slacktivism". If clicktivism is all you can do, thank you! There is undeniable power in numbers.
- Make use of policy advocacy tools. Visit websites, for example Change.org and Avaaz.org, which allow individuals to create or support petitions aimed at driving legislative reforms.
- Amplify the stories of others to emphasise the shared efforts of those marginalised and the bravery of many.
- Encourage dialogue on topics including inequality and the patriarchy in the workplace to create a wave of resistance among your colleagues.
- Attend rallies if you are able. You may meet new people to collaborate, advocate, or learn from.
- Mentor and support the next generation. Offer guidance and create opportunities for younger XXs, ensuring the continuity and growth of movements, which require momentum and solidarity to achieve positive changes.
- Keep learning. TEDx programmes, feminist podcasts, and books can deepen your understanding. Remember: information is power.

4 Health Practice and Control

Personal Note

My journey through the healthcare system has left me with a sense of gratitude, albeit at times fraught with frustration and at times compounded by a sense of neglect that many XXs also experience globally.

As a teenager, I endured debilitating menstrual pain and persistent acne. Hoping for a comprehensive evaluation, my mother and I were shocked when the doctor's treatment consisted solely of prescribing the contraceptive pill and antibiotics. There were no blood tests or dietary inquiries. Looking back, the sheer volume of milk I consumed daily likely contributed to both my pain and skin issues – a simple dietary adjustment and an exercise regime might have better addressed the symptoms.

In my early 20s, I was trapped in an abusive relationship – my brain still developing – that escalated into IPV, resulting in physical and mental trauma, and a miscarriage caused by physical violence. The untreated symptoms, including post-traumatic stress disorder (PTSD) and the implications of the violence, induced serious ramifications for several decades.

Despite eventually reporting the abuse, the system's indifference was dehumanising. When I finally found the courage to leave and attempted to press charges, the perpetrator's false counterclaims were prioritised; he had reported the violence in reverse, leaving me legally silenced. He was 15 years older than me and had a hidden history of IPV. At that time, the law made no concessions for my unrecorded experiences. Without reports, I had no case – a clear example of the numerous legal and medical complexities survivors continue to encounter.

Traversing through the various menopausal phases was also painful. However, the metamorphosis was exceptional. From the onset of perimenopause to the moment I finally began to feel like myself again, a decade passed; but I was eventually transformed for the better.

DOI: 10.4324/9781003516224-4

From the start of menopause, I received multiple diagnoses, including a brain tumour and bipolar disorder. The following years involved exploring various treatments – antidepressants, sleeping aids, herbal remedies, and different forms of hormone replacement therapy (HRT), including patches, pills, and gels. While some treatments led to negative side effects, contributing to suicidal thoughts, cognitive fog, and physical impairment, I remained committed to finding respite. With each new prescription, I persisted in trying to alleviate the symptoms and regain my health.

My new postmenopausal chapter was energising, fulfilling, and rejuvenating. The suffering and anguish of perimenopause and menopause have almost been forgotten, especially as my sexual energy and libido are reminiscent of those enjoyed throughout my 30s. I am experiencing a new, sexually liberated existence that allows me to pursue my true desires, free from the without societal expectations that previously confined me to act like a "lady".

Nevertheless, like Jane Fonda (Brizendine, n.d.) – American Academy Award-winning actor, fitness icon, and activist – I too wish I had read *The Upgrade: How the Female Brain Gets Stronger and Better in Midlife and Beyond* (Brizendine, 2022) before or during my hormonal transition. In this new episode of my existence, I am far more resilient and self-aware, with higher emotional intelligence and a more realistic sense of self-confidence. I completed my PhD, exhibited my artwork twice, researched and wrote this little book

My lived experience and the personal stories revealed by my students, friends, colleagues, and family members are among many that encapsulate the systemic failings of cultural, legal, and healthcare systems around the world. Their stories and experiences illustrate how medical biases, the lack of medical research into the XX body, and entrenched androcentric power dynamics combine to undermine the health needs of XXs.

The academic research and international reports included in this chapter highlight experiential truths, drawing attention to the urgent need for sex-specific research, healthcare reforms, and the recognition of XXs' unique health needs.

Introduction

Health is the foundational determinant among the four key pillars – health, economic, education, and political (HEEP) – which dictates the overall well-being of individuals. Without equitable access to both mental and physical healthcare, progress in other areas is profoundly constrained.

The incorrect interchangeable use of "gender" and "sex", for example, has significant negative consequences. Health research relying on binary categories indicates that both sexes have the same hormones, though in different quantities. Entrenched heteronormative ideals are inextricably linked to sex-based prejudice in healthcare (Rollins, 2011), systematically marginalising XXs' health needs.

Studies around the globe confirm that prejudices – once a quiet undercurrent – have become visible and critical issues within healthcare systems, highlighting the urgent need for reform (Gebhard, 2017; Moore et al., 2015; Perry & Albee, 1998; Werbinski, 2008). Treatments are often based on sex-based assumptions and regulated by deep-rooted universal prejudices. These biases limit sex-specific research and lead to the disproportionate distribution of resources while designing systems and policies that fail to promote equitable care, regularly favouring the XY demographic.

Encouragingly, scholars and policymakers are increasingly recognising the profound impact of sex-based discrimination on health outcomes, and meaningful changes have begun. Some XXs have benefited from medical progress; however, deeply entrenched systems of power in various regions continue to restrict autonomy and well-being. These imbalances are what IWRLs aim to address.

The CEDAW, for example, adopted by the UN General Assembly in 1979 (Chapter 2), is commonly referred to as the "international bill of rights for women." Article 12 of the Convention mandates that XXs have "access to health care services" (UN, 1979).

Although international laws (Chapter 2) prohibit both direct and indirect discrimination on the grounds of sex (Fredman, 2022), XY dominance persists and is often obscured by political decisions framed as responses to perceived difficulties or risks (Dockray-Miller, 2008).

Additionally, the failure of some medical practitioners to adhere to national or international laws – compounded by structural, biological, and societal factors – continues to undermine the well-being of XXs and perpetuate healthcare discrimination across Australia, the EU, India, the UK, and the USA.

The absence of robust sex-disaggregated data further exacerbates inequities, restricting the potential for effective medical analyses and treatments. Historically, medical research has prioritised XYs, resulting in distorted interpretations that have caused adverse reactions and misdiagnoses for XX patients. Structural inequalities necessitate reforms through data-driven policies that prioritise sex-specific research and integrate survivor-centred approaches into medical practice.

Additionally, VAW remains a global public health crisis with severe physical and psychological impacts. Many XXs experiencing trauma from DV and IPV are often ignored or dismissed. Systemic failures in treating survivors contribute to traumatic brain injuries and chronic pain – with adverse health effects extending across socioeconomic and cultural divides. These outcomes are compounded by persistent misconceptions that attribute violence to biology, despite evidence showing that aggression is driven by environmental factors more than by sex, genetics, or hormones alone.

While some nations have implemented progressive policies to address VAW, others continue to uphold androcentric norms that delay survivor support and enable their persecution, including coercive control – often leading to disastrous consequences including unwanted pregnancy or femicide.

The reproductive freedoms of XXs are also increasingly under threat, with some nations implementing primitive legislation that limits access to contraception, abortion, and maternal healthcare, the USA for example. Restrictions on reproductive rights and bodily autonomy, coupled with medical ignorance, including menopause, highlight the broader systemic disregard for the holistic health needs of XXs throughout their lives.

The prolonged underrepresentation of XXs in drug efficacy studies has also contributed to adverse reactions and misdiagnoses. With an increasing ageing global population, research into the menopausal transition is expanding to explore more effective treatment options. Notably, recent studies show promising progress in addressing the physical, emotional, and psychological challenges of perimenopause and menopause.

The toolkit in this chapter provides practical recommendations for navigating menopause more effectively, outlines potential interventions, and suggests measures for preventing VAW.

The Chromosome Factor

The presence or absence of a Y chromosome determines an animal's sex (Ainsworth, 2015). In humans the practical implications of chromosomal sex differentiation have reinforced mechanism and structural systems that marginalise XXs in comparison to XYs. Differential treatment based on biological sex constitutes "sex-based discrimination" (Hrdy, 1999; Jackson, 2010). Moreover, stereotypical behaviours are influenced by chromosomes – the cellular sturctures that carry genetic information in the form of DNA (Beecher-Monas & Garcia-Rill, 2006) – and are further influenced by cultural traditions that reflect societal expectations regarding the roles of XXs and XYs.

There are no hormones exclusive to either sex, despite the widespread misconception that XXs and XYs are hormonally district. Both sexes have the same hormones: "The only differences between males and females [hormones] lie in the varying levels of enzymes that convert sex steroids and the differences in receptor distribution and sensitivity" (Cooke, 2023:9).

The fundamental disparity between individuals bearing XX and XY chromosomes resides in their genetic composition, dictating biological sex. This chromosomal variance produces distinction in the formation of reproductive organs, secondary sexual traits, and hormonal profiles (Madsen et al., 2017). For example, XXs typically have ovaries, produce eggs, and exhibit secondary sexual characteristics including breasts and broader hips. Conversely, XYs typically grow testes, produce sperm, and have facial hair and deeper vocal tones (Madsen et al., 2017).

The usage of the terms "sex" and "gender" require a clear distinction as both terms are often inaccurately used interchangeably; for example, "sex-based discrimination" and "gender inequality" (Madsen et al., 2017; Samango-Sprouse et al., 2021).

Sex verses Gender

Despite the etymological differences, "sex" and "gender" are frequently combined in political, legal, cultural, and health contexts (Fleming, 2007; Samango-Sprouse et al. 2021). The concepts of sex and gender are inherently complex and are further compounded when intersecting identities – including religion, class, and sex – are incorporated within a framework (Sapkota & Dahal, 2022).

Simone de Beauvoir's seminal work, *The Second Sex* (1949), declared that the subordination of XXs is rooted in divisions based on a person's sex (Changfoot, 2009). Additionally, "sexism" is founded on the notion that one sex should be evaluated and treated differently from the other (Little, 2023).

The introduction of the term "gender" stems from its perceived neutrality and objectivity compared to the term "women" (Muehlenhard & Peterson, 2011; Saunders, 1990). The departure from "women's issues" to "gender equality" emerged when XYs began taking an interest in the discrimination faced by XXs and started contributing in the 1950s (Palmieri, 2013:69; Söderlund & Madison, 2017).

For example, when Ruth Bader Ginsburg (RBG), American lawyer, jurist, was advocating for equal rights – prior to becoming a Justice of the US Supreme Court – RBG presented cases that signalled the unconstitutionality of "gender discrimination," working to improve legal equity for both sexes (Resnik, 2013; Turk, 2023).

The evolving nature of gender identity, influenced by shifting societal norms, adds complexity to both terminology (Wood & Eagly, 2015) and healthcare delivery. Global discrimination against other groups, including LGBTQIA+ people, encompasses intricate, diverse, and interwoven complexities that extend beyond the capacity of this little book; however, other researchers have focused on their discriminatory experiences.

Exposing Medical Bias

Across the globe, XXs' experiences of health-related prejudices and bias are interwoven with systemic discrimination, inadequate government funding, economic disparities, and broader injustices – factors that collectively result in devastating health and social consequences (Gebhard, 2017; Moore et al., 2015; Perry & Albee, 1998; Werbinski, 2008).

Researchers have examined the complex layers of unjust treatment preventing XXs from receiving the medical care they require and deserve. Medical treatments differ based on a person's sex, influenced by practitioners, government budgets, political philosophy, education levels, and economic power.

Conditions uniquely affecting XXs, long ignored and under-researched, are now receiving some attention. These acknowledgements are not merely progress; they represent a long-overdue correction, reinforcing that healthcare must account for the needs of everyone – especially XXs, whose complex bodies have the power to give birth.

Inadequate diagnosis results in severe adverse ramifications for XXs, sustaining scholarly and medical concerns about their well-being (Moore et al., 2015). The failure to account for sex throughout the research lifecycle – from research grant submissions to clinical implementation and diagnosis – compromises scientific accuracy, resulting in adverse health outcomes and escalating healthcare costs, that have far-reaching consequences for social services and elder care delivery (Wainer et al., 2020).

A persistent pattern of XX exclusion is evident in clinical research, medical trials (Cullen et al., 2019; Price et al., 2022), and diagnostic practices (Costello & Greenwald, 2022), with omissions obscuring critical insights, weakening the reliability of therapeutic interventions, and sustaining a cycle of inadequate medical care for XXs. The ramifications of neglecting biological distinctions and sidelining XXs' health are profoundly grave (Calderone, 1990; Gebhard, 2017; Healy, 1991).

For example, a significant issue in medical research is the long-standing bias against XXs, who experience pain differently. Yet these biological differences have been neglected in medical trials. Integrating biological considerations into medical practice would assist patients in receiving tailored and effective treatment plans (Calderone, 1990; Gebhard, 2017; Healy, 1991). A convergence of minds among medical experts and health policymakers would further strengthen collective resolve (Madsen et al., 2017) and prevent the recurrence of past failures.

For example, aspirin, sold worldwide since 1904, caused adverse reactions in XXs, yet these effects were not considered until a hundred years later, revealing major failures in medical research and triggering legislative actions, including the establishment of the *National Institutes of Health* in the USA (Tannenbaum et al., 2016), for example. However, the adjustments to the aspirin again failed to fully consider those with XX chromosomes: "In 2017, further evidence also accrued on the value of its [aspirin] use in women at high risk for preterm preeclampsia" (Montinari et al., 2019:7), a condition affecting the arteries carrying blood to the placenta.

Coronary heart disease research has historically focused almost exclusively on the XY body, resulting in the undertreatment of XXs and contributing to higher mortality rates (López Ferreruela et al., 2024; Hamoda & Sharma, 2024; Healy, 1991). Despite the medical neglect, XXs continue to outlive XYs globally. However, their life expectancy has declined in recent years compared to XYs. According to a WHO report (2019), at the age of 80, XXs still hold a longevity advantage, living around 11 years (14%) longer than XYs. Nonetheless, cardiovascular disease remains a significant concern, with research reinforcing power structures are at the centre of discrimination (Dockray-Miller, 2008).

One option, to initiate necessary changes, is through policies that consider and respect the unique needs of individuals with XX chromosomes – not only with a biological lens, but also through a more comprehensive, holistic approach. International fears have been published by the WHO (2019), identifying the lack of access to medical care.

In sex-specific medical research, for example, significant deficiencies due to a lack of knowledge are common (Wainer et al., 2020). Medical trials often exclude sex-disaggregated testing and neglect treating XXs as "persons" (Young et al., 2019:51). Researchers aware of these exclusions have been advocating for change.

Amidst these bleak medical realities, there are glimmers of optimism with progress in various parts of the world. The recognition of disparities is an initial step, leading some to review the realities faced by XXs and investigate discriminatory healthcare practices.

In Australia, in 2020, the University of New South Wales, for example, released a communiqué advising that new research programmes should aim to remove sex and gender bias from medical research, including examining how and why diseases differ between XXs and XYs, recommending appropriate allocations of medical research funds, laboratory research procedures, and methods of circulating research findings (Dunlevy, 2020).

To address sex and gender differences, disaggregated research data was proposed to be included in medical peer-reviewed journals (Wainer et al., 2020), pointing out how medical inexperience – a lack of understanding of sex and gender differences – and financial limitations continue to prevent progress.

In the state of Victoria, in Australia, an *Inquiry into Women's Pain* found that chronic pain disproportionately affects XXs, yet they often face medical prejudice, bias, and discrimination, resulting in inadequate treatment and pain relief for numerous conditions, including cardiovascular, reproductive, and autoimmune diseases. Thousands of community members, clinicians, and healthcare workers contributed to the consultation, providing strategies to promote equitable pain management outcomes, recognising diverse identities, and emphasising the necessity of adopting inclusive language (Victorian Government, Department of Health, n.d.).

In the UK, the *Women's Health Strategy for England* outlined a plan to address sex-based disparities in healthcare and improve health outcomes for XXs. The strategy identified significant disparities in access to healthcare services, delays in diagnosis, and the underrepresentation of XXs in medical research and clinical trials. Additionally, XXs often reported feeling dismissed or treated as insignificant by healthcare providers, particularly for conditions such as endometriosis, menopause, and cardiovascular disease. Mental health, reproductive health, and VAW were also highlighted as priority areas for improvement (Young, et al., 2019).

Plans to introduce specialised health hubs for holistic care, improve access to menopause support, and launch public awareness campaigns to address health misinformation were included. The strategy emphasised a whole-system approach, recognising the importance of inclusive language and culturally sensitive services across the UK. Collaboration between the government, the National Health Service (NHS), and healthcare professionals was undertaken to increase funding for XX health research, increase the collection of sex-disaggregated data, and improve health education on XXs in medical training (Department of Health and Social Care, 2022). Longitudinal results from the 2022 strategy were yet to be published in May 2025.

In the USA, as in other nations, there is a critical gap in healthcare for DV and IPV survivors, who often suffer head trauma and/or strangulation. These afflictions are frequently ignored by medical professionals. Around a quarter (25%) of traumatic brain injuries are violence-related; however, medical professionals often classify DV–related injuries as mild in the USA. Alarmingly, only one in ten (10%) physicians routinely screen DV survivors for traumatic brain injuries, despite the long-term psychophysical health risks. The lack of screening is highly concerning, as brain injuries from IPV and DV occur around 12 times more frequently than those experienced by military personnel or athletes, combined (Costello & Greenwald, 2022).

Reproductive Freedoms

Freedom of choice can be a matter of life and death. The brutal assault on XXs' bodies is no longer a silent obliteration – it is a catastrophic cataclysm. Reproductive autonomy is under siege, crushed by draconian phallocentric laws imposed by suffocating conservative powers that govern, dictate, and control XXs, stripping autonomy from their womb to their wealth.

Some countries present a disturbing lack of reproductive rights, drawing unsettling parallels with *The Handmaid's Tale* (Atwood, 1987), where body autonomy is revoked. In both fiction and reality, the reproductive capabilities of XXs are regulated by phallocentric attitudes through the enactment of patriarchal laws that control the XX body. The alarming themes of the *The Handmaid's Tale*, the book and television series (Der-Ohannesian, 2021) resonate with certain contemporary legislation that increasingly restricts access to reproductive healthcare. This distressing reality illustrates how, when individual rights are compromised for religious or political purposes, XXs are further propelled into the dystopia that Atwood profoundly warned against.

The far-reaching implications of the 2022 Supreme Court decision in *Dobbs v. Jackson Women's Health Organization*, for example, are not just fragmenting abortion laws and transforming access across all 50 states in the USA (Cohen et al., 2023; Kaufman & Mayall, 2023; Nolen et al., 2024; Strasser et al., 2024), but are also triggering irreversible chaos, inflicting catastrophic consequences on legal and healthcare systems around the world.

Self-determination is a human right. Becoming pregnant, however, is not always a matter of choice, as indicated by coercive control. Unintended pregnancies accounted for one in nine (11.2%) cases between 2015 and 2019, with obvious regional differences. In Western EU nations, for example, the rate of unintended pregnancies was as low as one in 29 (3.5%), while Eastern EU nations saw a two-thirds reduction, continuing a long-term decline since the 1990s. These improvements are largely driven by international family planning initiatives that have strengthened reproductive autonomy. However, persistently high unintended pregnancy rates in lower-income regions emphasise the urgent need for sustained investment in comprehensive sexual and reproductive health services (Bearak et al., 2023).

To save the life of an XX, abortion is permitted in 81 out of 153 countries, with additional allowances for health risks, rape, or severe foetal anomalies. A study on abortion, contraception, and post-abortion care further reveals that third-party authorisations and age-related restrictions are impediments to accessing sexual and reproductive health services. Despite international human rights mandates requiring post-abortion care, only 28 of the 153 countries examined provide legal guarantees for post-abortion care (Ferguson et al., 2024).

Post-abortion care remains critical even in countries with progressive abortion laws. Yet, another study, examining 53 nations, revealed that the great majority (94%) of countries continue to impose criminal penalties for abortions. In almost half (43%) of cases, only those assisting face legal repercussions, while almost two of five (38%) countries penalise both the pregnant individual and those assisting. Notably, countries in the Americas enforce harsher punishments for those seeking abortions compared to nations in Asia and the EU (Skuster et al., 2022).

Despite global advocacy for equal access to healthcare services, numerous XXs continue to face unjust discrimination in their sexual and reproductive rights. The complex interplay between human rights, laws, policies, and their practical implementation governs and constrains the lives of XXs (Tahmindjis, 2005).

Androcentric concepts persist in structuring restrictive laws and obstructing the full realisation of health rights and autonomy for XXs. While some laws provide essential protections and frameworks, others impose boundaries that limit access to care and fundamental freedoms on a global scale (Ferguson et al., 2024).

The gap between global health systems and the realities of sexual and reproductive health indicates that traditional biomedical approaches, narrowly focused on health outcomes, fail to address the underlying power structures and social conditions that perpetuate health inequalities for XXs (Coates & Allotey, 2023).

Policy surveillance enables the systematic collection and analysis of legislation related to public health, including abortion regulations. Even in countries with progressive abortion policies, many impose unnecessary restrictions that fail to align with contemporary evidence on safe, self-managed abortions. In nations where abortion is legally supported, access continues to be limited due to requirements that the procedure be performed in specific settings, further restricting availability and accessibility (Coates & Allotey, 2023).

For example, two key UN agreements, the Millennium Development Goals (UN, 2010) and the SDGs (Kusuma & Babu, 2017; UN, 2018), set measurable targets to improve health outcomes for XXs. However, both initiatives often prioritise quantifiable results, with countries aiming for high scores (Vega, 2023) while neglecting the broader health needs of XXs and failing to ensure equitable access to essential medical treatments and procedures.

Policies and programmes require the prioritisation of XXs' autonomy in decision-making, empowering them to make informed reproductive choices rather than being dictated to (Coates & Allotey, 2023). For genuine equality, reproductive health policies need to address the unique physical needs of XXs and ensure that these needs are met irrespective of race, class, or geography.

Australia

Changes to decriminalise abortion have been evolving since the 1930s in the land down-under; however, draconian laws inherited from the UK remain evident (Morgan, 2012; Rankin, 2018).

Each of the six Australian states and two territories has its own abortion laws. For example, New South Wales decriminalised abortion in 2019, permitting the procedure up to 22 weeks' gestation. Thereafter, two doctors are required to approve the abortion (NSW Government, 2019). However, XXs living in rural and remote areas face limited access to healthcare, with private providers dominating the market.

In Western Australia, abortion is legal but regulated under the Health Act 1911, permitting abortion up to 20 weeks. Beyond this period, a panel of six doctors must approve the procedure. In Tasmania, where abortion was decriminalised in 2013, abortions are permitted up to 16 weeks of pregnancy; two doctors must approve the procedure (Baird, 2017).

Similar to other countries, Australia's reforms to reproductive freedom laws are often influenced by the ideologies of political parties. Despite local legislation and international law, some medical practitioners continue to refuse to perform safe medical procedures, citing religious beliefs and/or moral objections (Keogh et al., 2019).

The refusal by medical (un)professionals to provide treatment to XXs on conscientious grounds became a significant concern when the Australian government attempted to introduce the Religious Discrimination Bill (Commonwealth of Australia, 2020) in 2022. Although the Bill was not passed, its introduction raised fears that, had it been enacted, it would have granted medical staff the legal right to refuse services if they had a conflict of convictions, leading to the possibility of both "direct" and "indirect" discrimination against XXs (Schofield-Georgeson & Rawling, 2020:435).

The EU

Liberalising abortion access has been a progressive measure for several EU countries, while others enforce strict regulations, deepening the complexities of reproductive rights across the continent.

Some legislative measures are creating inequalities and heightening risks, particularly affecting XXs' ability to make autonomous healthcare decisions. Recent changes to abortion laws in some countries impose restrictions that prevent XXs from accessing the healthcare required (Cioffi et al., 2022).

Legal gestational limits for abortion vary significantly across the EU. As in many other regions, healthcare providers also refuse treatment on moral or religious grounds. These conscientious objectors generate resistance and impose severe constraints for XXs, often resulting in delays that cause them to exceed the legally allowed gestational limits (De Zordo et al., 2020).

Limitations imposed by gestational timelines have led to more than four out of every five individuals (79%) seeking abortions to travel abroad, due to restrictive legal time limits typically set at 12 or 14 weeks of gestation. After these time limits, abortions are prohibited unless there are specific circumstances, including significant medical risks or severe foetal anomalies (De Zordo et al., 2020). Additionally, reflection periods are mandated before the medical procedure is conducted. The lack of clear information about abortion services in many EU countries adds further impediments.

In Belgium, for example, legal abortions are permitted up to 12 weeks without substantive conditions. However, abortion is not fully decriminalised, as it remains restricted to specific cases, including threats to the life or health of XXs and severe foetal abnormalities (De Meyer, 2020a). In contrast, Iceland's legislation, updated in 2019, permits abortions up to 22 weeks of gestation (Cioffi et al., 2022).

In Italy, abortion is permitted within the first 90 days of pregnancy, but beyond that period, it is allowed only if an XX's life is at risk. Italy also has a notably high rate of conscientious objectors, which complicates access to safe and legal abortions despite laws intended to support XXs' autonomy and health.

In the Netherlands, abortion is allowed until 24 weeks of gestation; however, numerous clinics apply a limit of 22 weeks. In Spain, abortion is permitted up to 14 weeks, increasing to 22 weeks for serious health risks or foetal anomalies (Cioffi et al., 2022).

Extremely stringent abortion restrictions remain in place in several EU countries, including Poland and Malta, severely limiting access to safe and legal procedures. In 2020, Poland enforced near-total prohibitions, allowing abortion only in cases of rape, incest, or life-threatening conditions, despite widespread protests and public opposition to its restrictive reproductive policies (Cioffi et al., 2022; Dyer, 2021).

Malta enforces some of the world's harshest abortion regulations, imposing strict prohibitions and prison sentences for individuals acquiring or facilitating an abortion. The absence of comprehensive family planning services further weakens autonomy, leading to unintended pregnancies. However, the organisation *Women on Web*, led by XXs, is instrumental in reducing the dangers associated with self-managed abortions by offering online access to abortion pills and other services. According to their website, *Women on Web* provided support to XXs across 171 countries in 2024 (Cioffi et al., 2022; Dibben et al., 2023; Women on Web, n.d.).

The restrictive gestational limits and legal constraints on abortion in countries including the Netherlands, Spain, and the UK compel XXs to search for care abroad, often creating financial, emotional, and logistical dilemmas (Cioffi et al., 2022).

Following the overturning of *Roe v. Wade* in the USA (Chapter 3), Finland introduced legal reforms allowing abortion on request up to 12 weeks of pregnancy, removing the previous requirement for approval from two doctors and streamlining access to care (Kaufman & Mayall, 2023).

In Finland, abortion was criminalised until the 1950s. By the 1970s, advocacy from feminist movements led to the passage of the broader 1970 Abortion Act, which allowed social and economic reasons to be considered, but retained the requirement for physician consent (Takala & Häyry, 2023).

Today in Finland, individuals seeking a termination are required to undergo contraceptive and psychosocial counselling, which reflects lingering paternalistic attitudes and continues to limit personal autonomy. After the first trimester, terminations are permitted in cases of medical necessity or other serious reasons, and at times the XY of the foetus can be consulted (Takala & Häyry, 2023).

Across the EU, younger XXs face additional socioeconomic constraints when accessing abortion services, often intensified by not realising they are pregnant. Research reveals that more than one in two (56%) XXs become aware of their pregnancy only after 14 weeks, which disqualifies them from obtaining a legal abortion in their home country. This situation forces many to travel to foreign countries, encountering significant emotional and practical difficulties, including financial strain, time off work, organising care for their families, and cross-border travel arrangements (De Zordo et al., 2020).

Geographical disparities continue to create difficulties in accessing legal abortions (Kaufman & Mayall, 2023). Even in relatively progressive countries, XXs often need to travel within the EU to receive abortion care, contributing to a rise in telehealth services.

Inconsistencies in health legislation across the EU highlight the obstacles in reconciling reproductive rights with deeply rooted cultural and religious values, resulting in significant variances in access to safe and legal abortion services depending on their location (Cioffi et al., 2022; De Zordo et al., 2020; Takala & Häyry, 2023).

India

The extreme "sex bias in relative care" and neglectful healthcare services (Sen, 2003:1297), combined with social and religious practices, present enduring injustices leading to sex imbalances and XX foeticide, which have significant impacts on sex-based justice and human rights in India.

The "missing women" phenomenon was coined by Sen (2003) in the early 1990s to highlight the sex-selective practices in Asia and North Africa. The 1993 Nobel Prize winner (Encyclopaedia Britannica, n.d.) revealed that 100 million XXs were missing worldwide – more than 44 million in China and 37 million missing in India.

Since then, the numbers have not improved, with the ratio of XXs to XYs remaining largely unchanged. Additionally, both pre-natal and post-natal elimination of XXs continue to distort India's sex ratio (Kumar, 2022; Narayan, 2018), which has remained unbalanced since the 1970s (Chao et al., 2020).

Around 500,000 XXs are aborted annually, an average of 2,000 XXs each day (Jha et al., 2006). Research estimates that by 2030 there will be a 2-million demographic imbalance of XX births in India (Chao et al., 2020).

Sex-selective abortions, facilitated in part by ultrasound technology, allow for early sex determination, significantly contributing to the sex imbalances. Additionally, in many communities, religious influences also contribute to disparities in sex ratios (Narayan, 2018).

Historically, from the Female Infanticide (Prevention) Act of 1870 – and despite contemporary legal interventions, including the Pre-Natal Diagnostic Techniques Act of 1994, later altered to the Pre-Conception and Pre-Natal Diagnostic Techniques Act banning sex-selective abortions (Grey, 2021; Kumar et al., 2014) – sex-selective terminations continue to contribute to the elimination of XX foetuses.

Irrespective of legislation, these practices persist as the Acts fail to address the societal preference for XY children. Affluent and educated families, particularly in northern and western Indian states, continue to disproportionately contribute to the population imbalances with increased accessibility to diagnostic technologies (Narayan, 2018).

The restrictions under the various Acts have inadvertently impacted XXs' access to safe abortions, forcing many to pursue unsafe procedures and face significant health risks. A lack of enforcement and deficiencies in the legal systems have resulted in very few violators being convicted of illegal sex determination practices. This trend, together with sex-based discrimination in healthcare, reveals a distinct intersection between socioeconomic privilege and sex-based bias, further compounding the "missing women" phenomenon in India (Kumar, 2022; Narayan, 2018; Sen, 2003).

In 2022, the Supreme Court of India made a ruling that expanded abortion rights, marking a significant development in reproductive freedom and justice. The judgment recognised abortion as a fundamental right, regardless of marital status, reflecting a progressive shift towards greater autonomy for the unmarried. The Supreme Court emphasised that reproductive choices are not merely biological decisions but are influenced by social, economic, and political factors. The ruling contrasted with previous restrictions under the Medical Termination of Pregnancy Act of 1971, which permitted abortions primarily in cases of rape or foetal abnormalities, with a gestational limit of 24 weeks. The 2022 judgment broadens the legal framework, ensuring more comprehensive access to abortion services, subsequently addressing a critical gap in reproductive rights (Jain, 2023).

The Supreme Court also acknowledged the structural restrictions that limit access to safe abortions for marginalised groups – including caste discrimination, poverty, and inadequate healthcare access – and directed the government to implement measures to ensure all individuals have access to safe abortion services, contraceptives, and reproductive health education. This directive and ruling have set an important precedent for reproductive rights in India (Jain, 2023).

The UK

Access to abortion healthcare has improved in the UK. Further decriminalisation and supportive legislation have been essential to ensure that those requesting abortion care receive the necessary support and that their medical necessities are identified, acknowledged, accepted, and consistently treated as a routine part of healthcare. These practices are expected to further contribute to eliminating stigma and removing unnecessary legal obstructions, making abortion care more accessible and compassionate (Footman et al., 2024; Romanis, 2023).

In the UK, terminations are allowed up to 24 weeks, with concessions for cases involving severe foetal conditions and/or risks to life (Cioffi et al., 2022; De Zordo et al., 2020; Footman et al., 2024). Legalised through the Abortion Act of 1967, abortion is permitted in England, Scotland, Wales, and Northern Ireland under specific conditions. For example, Northern Ireland decriminalised abortion in 2019. Nonetheless, XXs continue to travel to England for care, as access remains limited in Northern Ireland, further impacted by economic and/or social circumstances (Cioffi et al., 2022; Romanis, 2023).

The relationship between abortion laws and access to care is complex in the UK, as abortion remains criminalised under certain circumstances, perpetuating stigma for both providers and patients. Despite the limitations, positive legal developments have occurred in the 21st c., including, for example, the legalisation of home-use termination medication and the introduction of telemedical termination services during the COVID-19 pandemic, which improved access, particularly for marginalised XXs, who face additional difficulties with clinic-based care. These changes have reduced some of the previous difficulties experienced by individuals in obtaining safe abortions without in-person visits.

While the UK's legal system is generally permissive and facilitates access to termination services, it fails to meet expectations in providing long-term protections and comprehensive support for patients, leaving deficiencies in reproductive healthcare (Romanis, 2023). For example, provider preferences revealed that healthcare professionals tend to favour offering either medication or surgical terminations, with a significant inclination towards medication options. More than half (52%) of providers exclusively offered medication terminations, while slightly less than half (43%) provided both medication and surgical methods. Approximately two in three (62%) providers expressed a preference for offering both options (Footman et al., 2024).

The growing reliance on medication terminations is largely driven by systemic constraints, including restrictive laws and policies that limit access to other options. Since 2021, around nine in ten (88%) terminations were administered using medication, a notable increase of almost half (47%) over a decade (Footman et al., 2024). Systemic stigma, along with medical gatekeeping and topographical disparities, continue to delay access to necessary healthcare, despite the UK's jurisdictional framework (Romanis, 2023).

The USA

The availability of termination medications via virtual healthcare, enabled by XXs' digital innovations is expanding access to safe reproductive care, providing agency and supporting independence through private and convenient options while reinforcing personal autonomy. However, severe setbacks are intensifying hardships and endangering the stability of the healthcare system across the USA (SteelFisher et al., 2019).

The decision to overturn *Roe v. Wade* (1973), which had established a federal constitutional right to abortion, was a landmark case where a Texas resident successfully contested the state's criminalisation of abortion, arguing that it violated her right to privacy under the *Due Process Clause of the Fourteenth Amendment*, serving as a global precedent for reproductive rights (Cohen et al., 2023; Kaufman & Mayall, 2023).

The 2022 *Dobbs* ruling dismantled nearly 50 years of precedent, allowing states across the USA to mandate and enforce strict abortion prohibitions and restrictions (Kaufman & Mayall, 2023). The regression that transformed the federal constitutional rights into state-determined abortion laws has created a convoluted legal landscape. Rather than streamlining abortion regulations, the decision has intensified interjurisdictional conflicts, contributing to confusion in healthcare, particularly in obstetric services, and delaying critical treatments, thereby increasing health risks for patients. Additionally, it has exacerbated complications for federal and state legal systems and further strained healthcare systems (Cohen et al., 2023; Kaufman & Mayall, 2023).

Maternal death rates are escalating across numerous US states following the removal of federal abortion protections and the implementation of restrictive termination laws. Additionally, legal restrictions are forcing many to travel long distances or resort to unlawful methods to obtain reproductive healthcare (Cohen et al., 2023; Kaufman & Mayall, 2023).

The *Dobbs* ruling has also led to a decline in medical education, as fewer providers are choosing to train or practice in regions with restricted abortion access (Strasser et al., 2024). Additionally, the spread of misinformation, both domestically and internationally, is deterring patients from seeking terminations.

Vulnerable populations, including racial and ethnic minorities, low-income individuals, and rural residents, are also disproportionately affected, as the new restrictions further marginalise these groups and exacerbate existing healthcare disparities (Nolen et al., 2024; Strasser et al., 2024).

Additionally, there are complex legal and ethical impediments for healthcare providers, exacerbating workforce shortages, particularly in states with the most restrictive abortion laws, where clinics are closing or relocating, forcing patients to seek unsafe procedures. States with anti-abortion laws have increased the surveillance of terminations, contributing to fear and confusion (Nolen et al., 2024).

On a positive note, proponents argue that the ruling enhances state autonomy, allowing laws to reflect local values. Several states have used the ruling to strengthen abortion protections, with California, Connecticut, Illinois, New York, Oregon, and Washington, for example, expanding services for out-of-state patients and advancing reproductive rights (Cohen et al., 2023; Kaufman & Mayall, 2023).

Conservative efforts to resist pro-choice advancements are further contributing to delays in medical care, reinforcing abortion stigma, and negatively affecting patients, healthcare providers, and their carers. On a global scale, millions are perturbed, discontented, and exasperated with the regression in the USA, which is affecting more than just reproductive freedoms. Internationally, the ruling has drawn criticism from global human rights advocates, who warn it could embolden anti-abortion movements worldwide.

For example, some conservative governments view the decision as validation for restrictive abortion policies, a perspective reinforced by conservative groups' US$28 (AU$44.9) million expenditure between 2016 and 2019 to support anti-abortion movements across Africa, the EU, India, and Latin America, further igniting global conversations about reproductive rights and healthcare (Cohen et al., 2023; Kaufman & Mayall, 2023; Nolen et al., 2024; Arguedas-Ramírez & Wenner, 2023; Strasser et al., 2024).

El Salvador, Nicaragua, Poland, and the USA are the only countries that have imposed increasingly restrictive termination regulations (Strasser et al., 2024). The USA's decision to overturn *Roe v. Wade* (1973) exposes how a single ruling can transform the lives of millions globally.

Despite the numerous significant setbacks, optimism prevails. Over the past 30 years, more than 60 countries have expanded abortion access. Between 2000 and 2020, 50 nations, including Argentina, Mexico, and Finland, have strengthened abortion rights (Kaufman & Mayall, 2023). The WHO's abortion care guidelines continue to promote global deregulation (De Meyer, 2020b).

The high digital accessibility in the USA, and globally, reflects the growing involvement of international entities in abortion care, with some nations influencing cross-border healthcare options (Cohen et al., 2023). Telemedicine and remote abortion services, including mail-order abortion pills, have expanded access in restrictive regions, avoiding bans through international networks (Nolen et al., 2024). *Women on Web*, for example, supply medication and support to individuals in more than 171 countries (Women on Web, n.d.).

The Monthly

The human animal physiological process of a menstrual cycle prepares the XX body for pregnancy. Each cycle, also known as a period, is monthly and typically repeats every 25 to 30 days on average.

From the Latin word *menstruus*, meaning "monthly" (Etymonline, n.d.), "Menstruation can serve as a barometer for the health of a young woman" (Beharry, 2015:371).

Throughout menstruation, physiological and psychological attributes can vary depending on hormonal changes, including mood swings, energy levels, and brain function. Understanding the menstrual cycle's intricacies is crucial for recognising normal reproductive health and identifying potential disorders. Digital technologies are assisting many in tracking their menstrual cycle and symptoms to improve management (Critchley et al., 2020).

The menstrual cycle progresses through a sequence of hormonal changes that regulate ovulation and fertility. Ovulation occurs when luteinising hormone levels rise – hormones produced in the pituitary gland that control the reproductive function of XX and XYs – and triggers the release of a mature egg around the middle of the cycle. The egg then travels into the fallopian tube, where it remains capable of fertilisation for 12 to 24 hours. Fertility attains its apex during this phase, priming the body for pregnancy (Reed & Carr, 2018).

The health impacts of menstruation are diverse; some experience almost no symptoms, whilst others are highly impacted. For example, periods that occur less than 21 days apart are classified as polymenorrhea – a disorder that triggers short cycles. On average, the amount of blood flow during menstruation is typically around 30 millilitres; excessive bleeding over 80 millilitres is classified as "abnormal" (Reed & Carr, 2018).

As with other health-related issues, the biological process of menstruation and reproductive health have been underrepresented in scientific research. Integrating patient experiences into diagnostics and treatments globally would enhance menstrual health research, with further interdisciplinary collaboration required among scientists (Critchley et al., 2020).

Menstrual disorders also require healthcare providers to improve knowledge, including adolescent health, in order to be competent and provide accurate information and appropriate care, including alternative hormonal treatment options, to eliminate or reduce menstrual bleeding (Beharry, 2015).

Adolescents' management of menstruation is often difficult and can present a diverse range of menstrual disorders, including abnormal uterine bleeding and polycystic ovarian syndrome, among others (Beharry, 2015). Around one in three (30%) experience abnormal uterine bleeding; others experience fibroids and adenomyosis – endometrial tissue growth in the uterus – these and other conditions can have negative economic and social impacts, which are further amplified by poverty and menstrual stigma (Critchley et al., 2020).

One of the most common medications used to manage menstrual cycles and for birth control is the oral contraceptive pill (OCP).

Sexual Health Freedoms

The sexual liberation movement began at the start of the second wave in the 20th century (Chapter 3), influenced by the introduction of the OCP, also known as "the pill", which enabled reproductive autonomy for XXs (Lake, 2013). The medication marked the beginning of the sexual revolution and generated concerns about global population transformations while questioning the boundaries of pharmaceuticals and governance on a global scale (Marks, 2010).

The introduction of the OCP was met with resistance from various religious institutions, while some medical practitioners refused to prescribe the pill or assist patients with reproductive health concerns, citing ethical or personal objections. In some countries, including Australia, unmarried XXs were ineligible (Kirby, 2016; Lake, 2013; Rushton, 2019). Its availability across most regions significantly impacted on reproductive health, family planning, and XX's sexual and reproductive autonomy.

Studies indicate that the OCP has various functions, including decreasing pain associated with ovarian endometriomas – ovarian cysts, for example. However, the OCP also has adverse effects, including headaches, back pain, nausea, and irregular uterine bleeding (Harada et al., 2008; Kotb et al., 2022). One study examining the use of OCP as a treatment for anxiety disorders indicated that since OCP lowers oestrogen levels, the OCP also facilitated anxiety reduction to alleviate fear (Raeder et al., 2019).

Hormonal changes, including oestrogen levels, contribute to corporeal and cognitive variations, including excessive bleeding, anxiety, and depression. Excessive bleeding can also occur during hormonal transitions, including the transition to peri- and menopause (Reed & Carr, 2018; Shaw & Pettinger, 2024).

Mēn-Pausis

The term "menopause" originates from the Greek words *mēn*, meaning "month", and *pausis*, meaning "cessation" or "pause", referring to the monthly menstrual cycle (Etymonline, n.d.; Oxford English Dictionary, n.d.; MenoLabs, n.d.) and marking the final menstrual period.

The study of menopause in medical research was introduced in 1821, by the French physician Charles Pierre Louis De Gardanne, who examined the biological and psychological impacts of menopause in those aged 40 and above (MenoLabs, n.d.). Two hundred years later, however, research requires further advancement to understand the profound natural transition experienced by half of the global population.

As many as eight in ten women (80%) encounter various symptoms related to menopause (The Menopause Society, 2023). Menopause also refers to the transition phase, which begins with menstrual changes and concludes one year after the last cycle (Hickey et al., 2022). Menopause is a result of declining ovarian function and reduced oestrogen production – oestrogen is a hormone essential for regulating reproductive processes (Brizendine, 2022; Gholamrezayi et al., 2019).

Hormonal changes occur throughout the premenopausal, perimenopausal, and postmenopausal stages, influencing emotional processing, mood, metabolism, and cognition. The repercussions of menopause, however, extend beyond the physical symptoms, including psychological and social aspects.

Research

Despite being a universal experience, the health impacts of midlife changes remain insufficiently investigated and inadequately documented. However, new research initiated by XXs in numerous countries and World Menopause Day aims to encourage research and increase knowledge (Baber, 2023).

The lack of research, other than knowing why human animals change, prevents exactitude in determining how and who will be impacted by what, contributing to the uncertainties of the life-changing process, including depleting sex hormone levels and gastrointestinal complications that few can explain or understand (Shaw & Pettinger, 2024). The average age of menopause onset in Western societies varies, with some sources reporting 48 years (Beck et al., 2018) and others indicating around 51 years (Riach & Jack, 2021), with menopause confirmed after 12 consecutive months without a period.

Menopause experiences differ for each individual, and most XXs do not use medication unless their symptoms are significantly debilitating (Hickey et al., 2022). Even with scientific findings and healthcare advancements, including alternative and pharmaceutical treatments, scientific comprehension and awareness of menopause are not yet comprehensive.

While there is a pressing need for more in-depth research to fully understand the complexities of menopause – including metabolic and cognitive shifts, muscle weakness, and impaired balance – there have been some advancements in understanding and managing the changes during the transition (Hickey et al., 2022; Johnson et al., 2019; Macêdo et al., 2023).

The Changes

The adversities before, during, and after menopause include addressing physiological symptoms holistically by considering social, psychological, and lifestyle factors alongside biological changes. Recognition of the need to address all symptoms, including cardiovascular and musculoskeletal health issues, is increasing. Raising awareness about the health disruptions XXs endure is essential, along with new research, treatment, education, and policies regarding menopausal healthcare (Baber, 2023).

Symptoms may include anxiety, weight gain, and memory issues, highlighting the complex impact of hormonal fluctuations on emotional regulations and metabolic markers. Glycated haemoglobin (HbA1c) levels – a form of haemoglobin chemically linked to glucose (sugar) molecules in the blood – were nearly 6% higher during perimenopause, correlating with neural activity in cognitive association regions, including the temporal-parietal-occipital junction – an area of the brain where the temporal, parietal, and occipital lobes intersect (Berent-Spillson et al., 2017).

Menopausal status also impacts physical function, with reductions in muscle strength and mobility rates. Approximately 70% of research in the Americas and the EU suggests poorer physical outcomes compared to premenopausal counterparts. Socioeconomic factors, including income and access to healthcare, also significantly influence outcomes (Macêdo et al., 2023).

Menopause can also be medically or surgically induced due to health conditions, including endometriosis, premenstrual dysphoric disorder, or cancer treatments. However, the sudden hormonal changes associated with induced menopause can significantly affect cardiovascular health, bone density, cognition, and overall quality of life, increasing the risks of long-term health issues. Moreover, counselling before undergoing such medical or surgical procedures is often inadequate. Those advised to undergo these procedures need to be informed about the consequences, including fertility preservation methods and the long list of issues that accompany the menopausal transition (Hamoda & Sharma, 2024).

Efforts to raise awareness of menopause-related symptoms across countries, and to ensure that healthcare systems address the growing need for better services, require acceleration. Evidence-based menopausal advice, rather than being prescribed medication without comprehensive support, is essential. This requires prioritising education and promoting fact-based support to enable individuals to make informed decisions about their health without over-reliance on pharmaceutical interventions.

Medication

Research indicates that hormonal shifts characteristic of menopause, particularly the decline in oestrogen levels, play a significant role in physical changes and can be treated with HRT to help stabilise physiological changes, including maintaining musculoskeletal strength and bone density (Macêdo et al., 2023).

Critical examinations of healthcare for menopause reveal that, in Western countries including Australia, the UK, and the USA, menopause has become increasingly medicalised, with a predominant focus on pharmaceutical treatments, including HRT. This trend is driven by the assumption that menopause requires medical intervention rather than being treated as a natural biological transition (Beck et al., 2018; Hickey et al., 2022).

Whilst HRT is promoted as a treatment, research into its risks, benefits, and assumptions magnifies the implications and broader issue (Hickey et al., 2022): the lack of cohesive and well-supported systems for effectively understanding and managing menopause effectively.

The necessity of HRT to manage menopause is also a divisive topic. Some researchers argue that menopause should be treated with pharmaceutical drugs, while others believe the evidence on HRT's effectiveness is inconclusive and view menopause as a natural process that should not be medicalised (Hickey et al., 2022).

Some researchers have questioned the assumption that declining oestrogen levels automatically lead to increased health risks, criticising the limited and often inconclusive evidence used to promote HRT as a preventive measure. Studies also indicate discrepancies in health outcomes and hormone usage across different regions, particularly between Western countries and nations including Japan and China, where lower rates of HRT usage are accompanied by lower incidents of heart disease and osteoporosis.

Despite the widespread promotion of HRT, large-scale clinical trials have not demonstrated significant benefits in preventing heart disease. Additionally, viewing menopause as a deficiency condition is largely a Western phenomenon, where HRT is heavily marketed and prescribed (Meyer, 2001).

Most individuals avoid medications unless their symptoms are severe. Several factors – including socioeconomic status, education, cultural attitudes, and biological influences, such as "smoking, diet, and body mass index" – affect both the type and severity of symptoms (Hickey et al., 2022:1).

The promotion of HRT by conservative media outlets in the UK, for example, has led to a significant rise in prescriptions. Between 2021 and 2022, HRT prescriptions increased by 50%, with 520,000 issued in January 2022 alone – more than double the figures reported in 2017 (Orgad & Rottenberg, 2024). This surge reflects the growing acceptance of HRT as a standard treatment for menopause symptoms, despite ongoing debates about its safety and effectiveness. Further scientific research is necessary, with caution against the increased involvement of pharmaceutical companies promoting potentially unnecessary medications.

In the UK, a study critically analysed the medicalisation of menopause, arguing that it is often framed as a condition requiring treatment, particularly through HRT. The study revealed that this medicalisation is driven by a biomedical model that views menopause primarily as a deficiency state characterised by declining oestrogen levels rather than as a natural life transition (Beck et al., 2018).

Alternative medicine indicates potential for some of the 30 symptoms associated with menopause (Smith, 2020). For example, "hot flushes, sleep problems, mood disorders, sexual dysfunction, weight gain, declines in cognitive functioning", and fatigue can be managed with aromatherapy, while hypnosis has been shown to reduce the frequency of hot flushes for some (Johnson et al., 2019:1; Smith, 2020). The evidence supporting the effectiveness of interventions and therapies, however, remains inconclusive. Exercise, including yoga, demonstrates promise but also lacks strong scientific validation, accentuating the need for further research and for those experiencing debilitating symptoms to be better informed in order to manage related symptoms

The effectiveness of Chinese herbal medicines (CHM) compared to HRT treatments has revealed that CHM reduced hot flush frequency by 29% compared to the placebo, while HRT showed a higher reduction rate of nearly

50%. Although CHM demonstrated a statistically significant improvement in managing some symptoms, its effects were less pronounced than those of HRT. However, participants reported minimal adverse effects, indicating that CHM may offer a safer alternative for those seeking non-hormonal treatments. However, although CHM has potential, larger-scale trials are required to confirm efficacy and better understand its mechanisms compared to standard HRT (Kwee et al., 2007).

The complex interplay of social, environmental, behavioural, and biological factors that contribute to health disparities throughout the menopausal transition includes experiences of "racism, discrimination, chronic stress, and trauma" all of which have been linked to heightened symptom severity and an increased risk of cardiovascular disease during the menopause transition (Cortés & Marginean, 2022:1). Chronic stress and trauma further increase the burden of menopause symptoms linked to cardiovascular risks. Additionally, individuals with low socioeconomic status, limited access to healthcare, and language barriers are more likely to experience adverse physiological changes and poorer health outcomes during the menopausal transition (Cortés & Marginean, 2022).

Advocacy

In some countries, the concerns of XXs are beginning to be acknowledged. To address the numerous issues highlighted worldwide, World Menopause Day, established in 1984 and celebrated annually on October 18, aims to raise awareness, increase research, stimulate open conversations, change the stigma around menopause, and enhance understanding and management of menopausal symptoms (Baber, 2023; National Today, n.d.).

Current laws in most nations fail to protect XXs in the workplace, where menopausal discrimination remains prevalent. In the UK, for example – despite growing attention to menopause – the Equality Act 2010 does not provide adequate safeguards against discrimination: menopause is not explicitly recognised as a protected characteristic, and the law does not fully address intersectional claims related to age and other factors. Although the UK Parliament's Women and Equalities Committee recommended reforms to support XXs experiencing menopause, the government rejected these recommendations, arguing that existing laws were sufficient. Despite the laws, many continue to face workplace discrimination due to the lack of appropriate policies and legal protections (Westwood, 2024).

Pause at Work

Persistent sex-based stereotypes are also contributing to performance pressures, with menopausal symptoms significantly affecting work performance. Support remains insufficient as menopause remains a taboo topic across many professional and social contexts, perpetuating misconceptions and preventing the development of supportive policies. This leaves many individuals without adequate resources to address menopause-related symptoms (Beck et al., 2021).

One study reveals that among 2,000 participants, the majority (77%) experienced significant symptoms, yet less than half (44%) reported that their work was affected. In 2022 alone, nearly one million XXs left their UK jobs due to menopausal symptoms, highlighting the scale of the issue and the urgent need for workplace support (Westwood, 2024), which is also required to prevent a brain drain and increase the number of XXs in leadership (Chapters 5).

Additionally, those aged 45–60 faced adversities in XY-dominated workplaces, including stigma, embarrassment, and fear of discrimination. However, workplaces with open cultures, supportive managers, and friendly environments enabled more comfortable discussions (Hardy et al., 2019).

Legal cases involving menopause-related discrimination rose from five in 2017 to 23 in 2021 in the UK alone, partly because many small businesses often lack policies to support individuals through this transition, leaving many without adequate assistance (Westwood, 2024).

Menopause also disrupts caregiving responsibilities, adding to stress. Conversations about menopausal health with managers are often avoided due to fears of age-related discrimination (Smith, 2020), and employees endure overlapping burdens, including a lack of workplace support and persistent sex-based stereotypes. These issues are compounded by workplace inequalities, including inflexible policies (Riach & Jack, 2021).

After the Pause

There is some positive news: the reduction in fertility hormones has been linked to increased assertiveness and a renewed sense of purpose, enabling menopausal survivors to prioritise their own emotions and needs as they transition into post-menopause.

Studies focusing on the relationship between XXs' hormones and emotional well-being are limited. However, Brizendine (2022) emphasises that to better manage menopausal symptoms and improve well-being, it is important to consider lifestyle, such as a protein-rich diet and pelvic floor exercises, for example (Brizendine, 2022; Wikipedia, n.d.).

Notably, the decline in oestrogen leads to a recalibration of the brain, allowing for greater focus, enhanced personal growth, and a sense of inner fulfilment rather than being influenced by reproductive-driven impulses after menopause. Brizendine's research, along with her personal experiences and those of her patients, highlights how this phase presents new opportunities (Brizendine, 2022).

Free from the hormonal fluctuations that characterised earlier stages of life, midlife is described as a period of opportunity where the brain's evolution leads to increased strength, confidence, and a deeper sense of purpose; a time of self-empowerment and renewed autonomy, characterised by cognitive enhancement, reduced anxiety levels, and the freedom to engage in activities aligned with their true desires, free from the constraints of societal expectations (Brizendine, 2022).

Unfortunately, however, freedom from societal constraints does not extend to all XXs – even after menopause, many remain at risk of experiencing violence identified as a "health epidemic" (Cullen et al., 2019; WHO, 2024).

The Biology of Violence

Before reviewing the phenomenon of VAW in Australia, the EU, India, the UK and the USA, it is essential to first question the idea that biology explains or excuses violence by those with XY chromosomes. The age-old expression of "boys will be boys" is not only regressive but unacceptable – it perpetuates harmful behaviours, which must be denounced and eliminated.

Human behaviour is often misinterpreted as entirely biologically determined, leading to the assumption that violence is an unavoidable aspect of human nature. However, this perspective oversimplifies the nuanced and multifaceted reality.

Recognised as a public health crisis, the "shadow pandemic" of VAW (Sedman, 2024) demands immediate, urgent, and strategic intervention. To eliminate violence, a holistic approach that combines biological insights – how hormones and external influences interact to produce varying behavioural trajectories – with targeted social policies is crucial. Research into violent behaviour reinforces that biological factors cannot be viewed independently (Beecher-Monas & Garcia-Rill, 2006; Berenbaum & Beltz, 2016; Lee, 2019; Meurer, 2021). Violence arises from psychological, social, environmental, and biological factors.

Rather than acting as an isolated determinant, biology provides a crucial framework for understanding the interaction between "nature" and "nurture", offering valuable insights into the mechanisms that regulate aggression and behavioural responses (Lee, 2019). Biological influences, including genetics, hormones, and external factors including culture and environmental stressors, are contributors; dominant cultural codes should not be presumed to predetermine violent behaviour.

Hormonal imbalances, including testosterone and androstenedione – an anabolic steroid converted to other sex hormones – have been linked with increased aggression. Low serotonin levels have also been linked to impulsive and violent behaviours, with genes increasing susceptibility rather than guaranteeing violent behaviours (Beecher-Monas & Garcia-Rill, 2006; Berenbaum & Beltz, 2016; Stevens, 1994).

Epigenetics – the study of how environments and experiences can affect the way genes work – provides insights that can strengthen prevention initiatives if implemented with ethical oversight, community participation, and systemic justice (Meurer, 2021). Caution is also advised in the use of genetic and hormonal research in medical, legal, and societal approaches for violence prevention.

Addressing environmental stressors and improving standards for evidence-based assessments can help reduce violence while upholding ethical considerations (Beecher-Monas & Garcia-Rill, 2006).

However, researchers warn against shifting the burden of responsibility onto individuals, as this may exacerbate inequities. Instead, governments need to create safe environments that support health and prevent violence while being held accountable for their failures to eliminate VAW (Beecher-Monas & Garcia-Rill, 2006; Meurer, 2021).

To identify violence-related risk factors and prevent the shadow pandemic from further escalating, intervention programmes should be introduced; modelled, for example, on smoking cessation and/or road safety initiatives (Stevens, 1994). Data-driven interventions targeting structural issues are required without stigmatising vulnerable populations (Meurer, 2021).

A nuanced and ethically responsible approach is essential to ensure that biological research informs violence prevention efforts without perpetuating harmful stereotypes or systemic inequalities. Predictions of violent behaviour based on genetic predispositions, including gene mutations, must be critically assessed to prevent the reinforcement of outdated and discriminatory practices (Beecher-Monas & Garcia-Rill, 2006). However, further research is also required to increase knowledge of the mechanisms through which hormones influence violent behaviour, as their effects are neither uniform nor consistent.

Violence Against Women (VAW)

Every ten minutes, an XX is killed by a partner or relative somewhere in the world (UNODC, 2024). VAW and femicide violate all human rights laws; yet these crimes are preventable (Cullen et al., 2019). Barbaric injustices and atrocities against XXs are intensifying (Tidmarsh & Hamilton, 2020), with around 852 million XXs subjected to physical and/or sexual violence globally (Decker et al., 2014; UNODC, 2024; WHO, 2024).

Although both XXs and XYs experience violence (Basile et al., 2006), the data is clear – XXs are disproportionately impacted and are three times more likely than XYs to be killed in their home. Half of all femicides are committed by an intimate XY partner (Cullen et al., 2019; Price, 2017).

VAW transcends geographical, socioeconomic, educational, racial, and cultural boundaries, with factors including poverty, isolation, and conflict further increasing the risks. Countless studies and reports affirm the devastating impact of VAW, including its most extreme outcome – femicide (Moulding et al., 2021).

Sexual violence encompasses a range of behaviours, from the most severe forms, including femicide, genital mutilation, human trafficking, non-consensual sexual acts, and rape – during both peace and war (Wood, 2018) – to forced marriage, sexual abuse, and assault. VAW also includes abusive contact, such as unwanted touching, as well as non-physical forms including emotional abuse, financial control, coercion, threats, and/or verbal harassment (Krook & Restrepo Sanín, 2020; Moulding et al., 2021; Price et al., 2022; UNODC, 2024).

Although the Vienna Declaration (1993) reaffirmed the importance of legal protections for XXs, and despite national and international laws, VAW remains pervasive (UN Women, 2020) and reveals disturbing truths about the violation of fundamental human rights, which impact the physical and mental health of XXs around the globe (Campbell, 2002; Krahé et al., 2014). The longstanding prevalence of VAW has afflicted societies for centuries, significantly compromising the health and well-being of XXs. However, its escalation is extremely alarming.

The WHO has classified VAW, including DV, IPV, and non-partner sexual violence, as a "health epidemic", revealing severe, escalating, and pervasive global human rights deteriorations (Cullen et al., 2019; WHO, 2024). The definitions of what jurisprudence classifies as violence and "victims" adds further complexities to measuring VAW crimes.

For example, sexual harassment, both at home and at work, can have detrimental physical and psychological effects. Words can have powerful consequences (Chapter 1). Not adhering to a traditional feminine role – whether by exhibiting traits typically associated with masculinity or by working in XY–dominated professions – intensifies the likelihood of XXs experiencing sexual harassment. Additionally, XXs from ethnic minority groups are more frequently harassed and pursued. While XXs remain the primary recipients of harassment, there is also some evidence of sexual harassment directed toward XYs (Chawla et al., 2021).

Consequences, causes, and VAW patterns are measured at psychological, social, and physical levels. Data collection seeks to inform policies designed to suppress VAW. However, the exact number of crimes exceeds the recorded figures. The reported numbers are alarming, but reality is worse; many survivors do not report crimes, choose not to pursue perpetrators, and often refrain from obtaining help due to social stigma, fear of retaliation, or dependency on their abusers, particularly older XXs who are reliant on caregivers (Meyer et al., 2020). The data and the lived experiences expose the severity of the VAW global emergency.

Additionally, people with hearing or vision impairments are at a significantly higher risk of experiencing violence and abuse. Those with cognitive impairments are also increasingly susceptible to sexual violence (Kudon et al., 2024). Sexual exploitation can also lead to increased risks of sexual and reproductive health issues (Burke et al., 2024), as well as mental disorders, including depression and suicidality (Basile et al., 2006; Kaniuka et al., 2024). VAW at a young age further increases health threats.

The development of the human brain, for example, occurs between the ages of ten and 24 years. Until the age of 25, the brain is still maturing, with the prefrontal cortex – responsible for decision-making, impulse control, and emotional regulation – being one of the last areas to fully develop

(Johnson et al., 2009). Puberty also triggers significant hormonal shifts that affect emotions and motivation, contributing to increased risk-taking and impulsive behaviours often observed during adolescence (Arain et al., 2013).

Ongoing brain development partly explains why young XX adults exhibit heightened emotional responses, engage in risk-taking behaviours, and struggle with planning and impulse control. Recognising this developmental trajectory has critical implications for healthcare policies (Johnson et al., 2009). Understanding brain function is crucial for developing effective interventions for IPV and DV.

Understanding the distinction between DV and IPV is essential for recognising the complexities of violent crimes. Although IPV is a subset of DV, the terms are often used interchangeably, which distorts the distinct characteristics and consequences of each form of violence. Both could involve physical and sexual aggression – including hitting, kicking, or beatings – intimidation, financial control, and isolation tactics aimed at severing survivors from their support networks, among others. Both IPV and DV represent severe forms of VAW that commonly occur within the home (Walker-Descartes et al., 2021).

Domestic Violence (DV)

On average, one XX is murdered every 10 minutes somewhere in the world from DV. The incidences of femicide are rising globally, and there is #NoExcuse (UN Women, 2024).

DV encompasses a broader range of violence within a household, involving family members: parents, children, siblings, or others sharing the same living space (Walker-Descartes et al., 2021).

Torture is a term used to describe the multifaceted nature of DV, which spans emotional, physical, sexual, verbal, and economic dimensions, making it a global concern of paramount significance. The UN defines DV as a "pattern of behaviour in any relationship that is used to gain or maintain power and control over any intimate partner." This includes "behaviours that frighten, intimidate, terrorise, manipulate, hurt, humiliate, blame, injure, or wound someone" (UN, n.d., para. 1). DV also causes reproductive health complications and restricts economic autonomy, whilst coercive control also causes torment (Singhal, 2015). Hence, XX survivors find themselves marginalised while their perpetrators appear to hold all the power (UN Women, 2020).

In past years, there was a prevailing belief that DV was confined to low socioeconomic areas – a notion that was called into question in 1983 (Scutt, 1983). Reinforcing this mistaken assumption was the disturbing global surge in VAW recorded during the COVID-19 pandemic, particularly throughout 2020 and 2021 (Fitz-Gibbon et al., 2021). Additionally, the closure of schools and childcare facilities resulted in an increase of child abuse (Evans et al., 2020).

These conditions further enabled perpetrators, leading to the escalation of violence and leaving survivors even more vulnerable, as many were deprived of access to support and/or safety. Tragically, improvements after the pandemic are yet to be recorded. The ongoing murder of mid-life XXs by family members continues. In Australia, for example, around 200 XXs aged 55 and over have allegedly been killed in the past decade, with their sons making up the vast majority of suspected perpetrators (Lyons, 2025). Global numbers, however, remain obscured.

Without realistic numbers, budgets, policymakers, and healthcare authorities are unable to provide precise insights, facilitate meaningful health improvements, or ensure that interventions effectively address the complex realities survivors confront (Spigelman & Rendalls, 2015; Victorian Government, Department of Health, n.d.).

Improving accountability and encouraging survivors to report DV crimes must be a priority for every government. Moreover, legal systems ought to guarantee survivors are not retraumatised during judicial processes – including removing misogynist judges from the bench (Stavrou, 2024). All perpetrators must be held accountable, exposed, subjected to strict penalties, disciplined, and, where necessary, prosecuted and/or confined.

Efforts to prevent VAW must extend beyond legislation to challenge and change cultural norms, toxic masculinity, and phallocentric laws. Supporting DV survivors is paramount; training for professionals working with XXs and children must be improved, and rehabilitation and well-being programmes need to be integrated into policies to assist survivors.

Intimate Partner Violence (IPV)

IPV involves coercive control, emotional manipulation, and/or sexual, psychological, and physical abuse inflicted by a current or former intimate partner. Three in ten XXs (30%) report experiencing physical and/or sexual IPV at some point in their lives, revealing the pervasive, widespread, and insidious nature of this global plague.

Four out of every ten (38%) XXs are killed by their current or former romantic partner globally (Abrunhosa et al., 2021; WHO, 2024), with one in seven murders (13.5%) being a result of IPV. The deadly consequences of abuse reveal that XXs are six times more vulnerable to predatory dangers than XYs.

When exposed to IPV during pregnancy, XXs face a significantly higher risk of severe health complications, including miscarriage – affecting one in six (16%) – and preterm birth, which occurs in four out of ten (41%) pregnancies. Additionally, XXs are one and a half times more likely to contract sexually transmitted infections and twice as likely to undergo abortions as a direct result of IPV (Vicard-Olagnea et al., 2021; WHO, 2024).

Both young people and the elderly face additional obstacles in attaining a healthy life, free of VAW. Notably, approximately five in seven (71%) XXs who experience IPV report their first incident before the age of 25 (Walker-Descartes et al., 2021).

Globally, XXs aged 50 and above report experiencing IPV at alarming rates, with nearly six out of ten (59%) affected in high-income countries, including the USA and Israel, for example, with psychological abuse being the most frequently reported violence (Meyer et al., 2020). Survivors face additional obstacles when seeking community support due to limited mobility, stigma, and a lack of age-sensitive healthcare resources.

Additionally, cultural expectations and social norms further define how this collective is perceived, reported, and responded to, leading to underreporting and, in some cases, acceptance of abusive behaviour (Meyer et al., 2020). Systemic biases, including police blaming survivors, medical personnel, and social workers, further obstruct justice and access to essential support services (Sereno et al., 2024).

In Australia, one in ten (10%) to nearly one in two (47%) XXs reports experiencing IPV. In the EU, one in five XXs reports experiencing IPV; however, this rate varies significantly from country to country, ranging from one in 20 (5.5%) to two in three (66%) (Abrunhosa et al., 2021). In the USA, IPV prevalence spans from one in ten (9.6%) to more than one in two (54%), with the highest incidence detected in low-income populations (Vicard-Olagnea et al., 2021).

When an XX aged 15 or older seeks primary care services in Australia, the EU, or the USA, for example, the clinical signs associated with IPV often manifest as depression, anxiety, PTSD, addiction, and other psychological issues, including panic attacks or persistent worry. Physical symptoms frequently include chronic pain, headaches, and an increased reliance on painkillers. Additionally, IPV survivors are at heightened risk of sexually transmitted infections and unwanted pregnancies, and they report medical consultations more frequent compared to those not affected by IPV (Vicard-Olagnea et al., 2021).

Professionals working with IPV survivors also encounter substantial risks, with bias exhibited by police, medical personnel, social workers, and legal professionals.

For example, a two-decade study in the USA, between 2000 and 2020, revealed the effects of bias training. While interventions showed some positive impacts, the study found no consistent relationship between the type of training delivered and a measurable reduction in prejudice. The inconsistencies emphasise the need for improved, standardised training and further learning to ensure those working with survivors receive effective support, adequate guidance, and appropriate preparation (Sereno et al., 2024).

Next, the status of VAW in Australia, the EU, India, the UK, and the USA are reviewed.

VAW in Australia

Sex-based discrimination is deeply ingrained in Australian health systems (Department of Health and Aged Care, 2018; Wainer et al., 2020), with varying policies across the eight jurisdictions making healthcare harmonisation increasing constrained.

As in most other parts of the world, the majority of casualties from VAW in Australia continue to be XXs and children (Aeberhard-Hodges & McFerran, 2018; Tidmarsh & Hamilton, 2020). On average, two XXs are killed by IPV each week; police attend a VAW callout every two minutes nationally (ABS, 2022b; Our Watch, 2018). Concerningly, almost nine in ten (87%) XXs who have been sexually assaulted never report the crime (Khadem, 2022).

In 2021, Australia saw an alarming rise in reported sexual assaults, reaching the highest levels since 1993, with rates escalating from 69 to 121 survivors per 100,000 individuals (ABS, 2022a).

Around two-thirds of sexual assaults occurred in a residential location from 2010 to 2019 (67%, n=17,395 survivors); suicide rates for XXs increased from 5.0% to 6.3%; and mental health issues were frequently attributed to intimate relationships – the third most common cause of XXs' mental health issues (Moulding et al., 2021). Sorrowfully, one in six young XXs (17%, n=1.6 million) experienced partner violence after the age of 15 (ABS, Recorded Crime–Victims 2021).

The ongoing epidemic of VAW contributes significantly to the deaths of XXs aged 15 to 44 and is projected to worsen, as young people aged 13 to 16 are more prone to hold beliefs that justify and tolerate VAW (Dawson et al., 2020).

Reports also reveal that Australia's inherently XY–dominated society, for example, continues to blame survivors, despite the fact that half of all femicides are committed by an XY intimate partner (Cullen et al., 2019; Price, 2017). Additionally, coercive control involves manipulative actions by perpetrators aimed at conditioning survivors to believe they are responsible for the abuse (Tidmarsh & Hamilton, 2020). The undermining of contraceptive methods, for instance, is a form of reproductive coercion, whereby XXs are pressured into making pregnancy-related decisions that are not their choice, but are instead dictated by a partner and/or healthcare provider (Cullen et al., 2019; Price et al., 2022).

Jurisdictions acknowledge that changes are required; for example, the *National Women's Health Strategy* (NWHS) 2020–2030 recognised that improvements are necessary to enhance XXs' health and well-being. The strategy includes five priorities:

1. Maternal, sexual and reproductive health;
2. Healthy ageing;
3. Chronic conditions and preventive health;
4. Mental health;
5. Health impacts of violence against women and girls.

(Department of Health and Aged Care, 2018:21)

The flawed management and reporting of healthcare data specific to XXs remains a significant issue. Quality and safety data is often aggregated for both sexes, providing inadequate insight into patient-specific outcomes, thereby obscuring important variations in care and weakening efforts to address the unique health requirements of XXs. Policymakers and healthcare providers need to collect precise data to deliver meaningful healthcare improvements (Spigelman & Rendalls, 2015; Victorian Government, Department of Health, n.d.).

VAW has profoundly negative ramifications for XXs' health and well-being (Australian Institute of Health and Welfare, 2019; Dunlevy, 2020; Wainer et al., 2020), which also limits their potential to access education (Chapter 5) and participate in the economy and politics (Chapters 6 & 7). Yet, funding for essential services is continually being cut by various governments, signalling apathy and indifference to the endemic scale of the epidemic, and intensifying the "horror and fury" of what has been describes as a "national emergency" (Lyons, 2024; Price, 2017).

Although Medicare in Australia is the publicly funded universal healthcare system, it faces difficulties, as noted in the *Inquiry into Women's Pain* (Victorian Government, Department of Health, n.d.). Additionally, "out-of-pocket charges in Australia are higher than the OECD average" (Callander & Fox, 2018; Law et al., 2022).

On a more optimistic note, policies in Australia aimed at improving XXs' health have produced positive outcomes over the decades, including the legal sale of the contraceptive pill in 1961 and the elimination of luxury taxes on menstrual hygiene products (Chapter 3), which also led to improvements (Krusz et al., 2019).

Accessing inclusive reproductive health services, including abortion, contraception, and maternal healthcare, remains complicated for XXs across Australia. Those in lower socioeconomic communities, and those living in rural and remote areas, often face additional constraints due to geographic isolation and underdeveloped healthcare infrastructure, with distances making it difficult to receive timely and appropriate care. Bridging this gap is crucial to ensuring that all XXs, regardless of their location or economic status, can access the healthcare required (Spigelman & Rendalls, 2015).

VAW in the EU

One in three XXs has reported facing violence since the age of 15 in the EU, a pattern consistent with this global crisis (Humbert et al., 2021).

The Council of Europe (CoE) introduced the Istanbul Convention (IC), as a comprehensive framework aimed at preventing and combating VAW (CoE, 2011). The policy objective is to eradicate IPV and DV across the EU, through measures promoting sex-based equality, protecting the rights of XXs, and ensuring accountability for perpetrators while eliminating discrimination and violence. As of 2024, the IC had been ratified by "37 states" (Baumeister, 2024:497).

Despite the IC and its claim to combat VAW (CoE, 2011), in 2024, VAW across the EU remained pervasive. One in two (50%) XXs experience DV, while almost one in two (44%) report psychological IPV, and at least two XXs are killed every day by DV or IPV. Additionally, half of the EU XX population (50%) has reported sexual harassment (Baumeister, 2024).

Following the ratification of the IC, some EU nations broadened policies to address various forms of VAW, including stalking, forced marriage, and female genital mutilation (Chen et al., 2020). Despite these advancements, obstacles persist, including underreporting and low conviction rates. For example, in Portugal, DV remains one of the most frequently reported crimes, constituting approximately one in 12 (8%) criminal offences (Capinha et al., 2022). The number of reported cases of VAW is particularly alarming, given Portugal's relatively small population of just 10.2 million – 5.3 million XXs and 4.9 million XYs (World Population Review, 2024).

Some positive results include raising awareness and shifting public perceptions. For example, the proportion of DV incidents reported increased significantly before and after policy implementation, from 76.2% to 90.5%, indicating a greater willingness among survivors to report their abusers. The acceptance of violent behaviour also saw a significant decline, dropping from 9.5% to 1.6%, demonstrating a shift in societal attitudes towards DV (Alves et al., 2019) and illustrating that awareness campaigns can have meaningful and positive impact.

In the Nordic countries – often regarded as some of the most egalitarian – there exists a paradox where higher rates of VAW are reported compared to other EU member states. The reported prevalence of VAW in these regions is influenced by cultural norms, an emphasis on personal independence and autonomy, and robust practices that encourage XXs to report crimes. Nearly half of survivors (47%) reported abuse in this region. In Finland and Denmark, for example, more than half reported abuse (52%), and almost half (46%) did so in Sweden (Humbert et al., 2021). These figures indicate that while sex-based equality initiatives are robust, other societal factors contribute to the visibility of VAW.

For example, the prevalence of IPV reporting in Sweden compared to Spain differs significantly. In Sweden, around one in four (28%) XXs has reported experiencing IPV, compared to around one in seven (13%) in Spain. The breakdown between physical and sexual IPV also varies: Sweden recorded more than one in four (28%) cases of physical IPV, whereas Spain recorded around one in eight (12.5%) cases (Gracia et al., 2019).

Overall, research identified an 80% probability that a randomly selected Swedish XX will report experiencing physical IPV compared to a Spanish XX. For sexual IPV, this probability rises to more than 96%, with nearly all Swedish XXs reporting the crime (Gracia et al., 2019). These findings highlight significant disparities in IPV prevalence between the two countries, likely shaped by differences in cultural norms, reporting practices, and societal attitudes towards IPV (Gracia et al., 2019).

Another study conducted in Spain explored the gap between bystanders' intentions and their actual behaviour when witnessing VAW. While many claimed they would intervene, their actions often diverged from their stated intentions. Bystander responses indicated that approximately three out of five (60%) adults would call the police if they witnessed IPV; XXs were more likely to encourage the survivor to report the violence, whereas XYs tended to favour more direct, aggressive intervention (Sánchez-Prada et al., 2022).

Notably, around one in four (23%) Spanish adults acknowledged knowing an XX in their social circle who had been a survivor of IPV, with XXs more inclined to urge survivors to leave the abusive relationship, while XYs were more prone to direct confrontation (Sánchez-Prada et al., 2022).

Those aged 16 to 29 in Spain were more likely to intervene directly, whereas older adults, tended to prefer indirect forms of action. Younger XXs reported higher rates of IPV compared to older age groups, particularly those aged 30 to 50 and above. Approximately one in three (36%) adolescents were aware of couples where the XY abused the XX. Additionally, three in five (62%) university students reported either experiencing or knowing someone who experienced VAW (Sánchez-Prada et al., 2022).

As observed in other countries, higher education levels among XXs in Spain are associated with a reduced likelihood of experiencing IPV, regardless of age. In contrast, unemployed XXs face a greater risk of IPV, emphasising the link between economic vulnerability and exposure to violence (Sanz-Barbero et al., 2019).

VAW in India

With a population of 1.45 billion, India is projected to become the most populous country in the world by 2030, with XXs accounting for approximately half (49%) of the total population – 698.3 million (The Global Statistics, 2024) – a figure that must be interpreted in the context of sex-selective foeticides.

In recent years, international attention has focused on the issue of sexual VAW in India, sparked by several tragic gang rapes of enormous proportion (Chapter 3). In a world influenced by patriarchal values (Sah, 2022), sexual VAW by XYs has become normalised in India and subtly accepted by both XXs and XYs as a routine aspect of their everyday lives and relationships (Kimuna et al., 2012), with patriarchal, misogynistic, phallocentric ideologies asserting ownership over XXs' bodies, freedom, autonomy, and sexuality.

Sexual VAW is often normalised and condoned as a facet of family dynamics. The tolerance of VAW is perpetuated through socialisation, which causes XXs to adopt and internalise societal expectations and attitudes tied to their sex, often absorbing attitudes of reliance and submission (Saravanan, 2000).

The societal pressure to maintain a facade of familial stability and happiness leads many survivors to underreport VAW. The prevalence of DV across India ranges from one in six (18%) to three in four (75%) (Kalokhe et al., 2017). Indian cultural values and the perception of DV as a private family matter – reinforced by biases within the legal system – fail to provide adequate protection for XXs (Nigam, 2020). Additionally, practices including honour killings, unwarranted dowry demands, and DV (Bhandari & Hughes, 2017) leave behind a trail of devastation across the country.

A review of 137 quantitative studies revealed that around two in five (41%) XXs in India endure DV at some point in their lives, encompassing physical, psychological, and sexual abuse (Kalokhe et al., 2017). In densely populated urban slums, XXs face additional impediments and restrictions, including limited access to vital resources and increased exposure to violence from both partners and extended family. These adversities are exacerbated by socioeconomic hardships, cultural stigmas, and inadequate legal and healthcare services (Sabri & Campbell, 2015).

Furthermore, those who give birth to an XX baby are disproportionately targeted and subjected to violence (Mahapatro et al., 2011). The fear of tainting the family's reputation and facing potential reprisals from abusers discourages survivors from reporting crimes (Abeyratne & Jain, 2012).

The psychological scars from traumatic experiences alter survivors' emotional states and disrupt their sense of self and overall well-being. Additionally, survivors of sexual VAW face a higher probability of developing mental health conditions, including depression, which at times leads to suicide (Nieder et al., 2019).

As seen in the EU, initiatives promoting bystander intervention could serve as crucial catalysts in motivating individuals in India to assist survivors during moments of vulnerability and provide a critical lifeline when official channels fail (La Ferle et al., 2019; Sánchez-Prada et al., 2022).

University students report that street harassment is exceedingly widespread, with XXs experiencing public sexual harassment between half (50%) and all of the time (100%) in certain areas (Dhillon & Bakaya, 2014). A vast number of XXs experience sexual harassment in broad daylight, with a significant portion of these incidents occurring in public settings (Akhtar, 2013; Jagori, 2011).

Committing sexual VAW in public settings serves as a tool for XYs to exert control over XXs, thereby reinforcing their confinement to private spaces (Gangoli, 2007). This deeply entrenched androcentric dynamic dissuades XXs from venturing outside their homes under the guise of protection, perpetuating the notion that public spaces pose inherent risks.

Governments at all levels must prioritise preventive strategies, enact educational initiatives, and cultivate meaningful cultural transformation that addresses the root causes of VAW and reconstruct androcentric mindsets and behaviours towards XXs. For the many who have experienced or will experience VAW, the preservation of phallocentric dominance within Indian society remains a contributing factor to the prevalence of sexual VAW (Kalra & Bhugra, 2013).

The gap in mental and sexual education within Indian society further prevents XXs from envisioning a life without sexual violence. Education (Chapter 5) is paramount, as it can serve as a protective factor. When XXs have access to education and employment, they are more likely to feel empowered and less vulnerable to assaults and aggression – not only in India, but worldwide (Dhiman, 2023; Jain & Mathur, 2024; Riaz & Pervaiz, 2018; Shastri, 2022; Stromquist, 2015).

VAW in the UK

In the UK, unlike in India and the USA, XXs constitute a slightly higher proportion of the population, accounting for 51.4% of the 69.1 million (World Population Review, 2024). Despite XXs outnumbering XYs, VAW remains as prevalent as in many other countries, indicating that a higher XX population does not correlate with improved safety or reduce levels of VAW. As in many parts of the world, XXs in the UK continue to face severe and often life-threatening violence perpetrated by XYs.

In 2024, DV accounted for more than one in six (15.8%) of all violations documented by police (Oxley & Lipscombe, 2025). Between 2010 and 2020, an average of 80 XXs per year were murdered in England and Wales, reinforcing the persistent and deadly nature of IPV (Dheensa et al., 2024).

The number of DV cases surged significantly during the COVID-19 pandemic, mirroring the global proliferation of VAW. Femicides reached their highest level in 2019, further highlighting the persistent and escalating severity of this global epidemic (Aldridge, 2020). The Crime Survey for England and Wales revealed that 1.9 million adults aged between 16 and 59 reported experiencing DV in the UK, with XXs accounting for the majority – 1.2 million of these cases (Pell et al., 2024).

Policy measures aimed at improving the health system's response to DV have expanded to incorporate mental health and primary care services for those who have experienced violence since the age of 16 (Office for National Statistics, 2022). These interventions specifically target the vast majority (80%) of survivors who seek help through health services but do not report their abuse to the police.

The integration of DV advisors within healthcare settings has proven effective, leading to the increased identification of "hidden" survivors, many of whom face complex and pervasive complications, including severe anxiety and depression. These policy measures have facilitated earlier identification and support for survivors, enabling more timely interventions (Pell et al., 2024:2).

Part of the challenge, however, lies in the need for significant improvements in social work practices, which have remained stagnant over the past decade. For example, XXs are still frequently held accountable for failing to protect their children from abuse, a stance that not only overlooks the complexity of their circumstances but also contributes to further mistreatment and trauma (Stewart & Arnull, 2023).

Seven out of ten (70%) XXs, in the UK, expressed fear of losing their children due to coercive practices by social workers. This fear is compounded by the lack of transparency regarding the information collected and how it is used, demonstrating that UK child protection practices continue to be heavily influenced by patriarchal norms (Stewart & Arnull, 2023).

XY perpetrators are often disengaged and invisible during intervention processes, reinforcing androcentric norms that unfairly place the burden of protection solely on XX parents. Child protection services commonly present XX parents with an ultimatum: either leave the abuser or risk losing custody of their children. This approach fails to consider the serious risks associated with leaving an abusive relationship, including an increased threat of severe harm or even death.

Around one in two (45%) DV survivors report their abuse to healthcare professionals in the UK. Emotional hurdles, including fear, embarrassment, and self-blame, were reported by approximately seven out of ten (69%) survivors as reasons for withholding information. Additionally, three in eight (38%) reported other obstacles, including the partner's physical presence during appointments, controlling behaviour, manipulation of healthcare professionals, unsuitable environments, and insufficient time for disclosure. The acknowledgment and validation of abuse by healthcare professionals, particularly the recognition of emotional abuse as legitimate, were critical in helping survivors feel safe enough to confide and disclose (Heron et al., 2022).

Healthcare workers, researchers, and advocates also face significant challenges in addressing DV. One key issue in data collection is the difficulty researchers face when interviewing XY perpetrators of DV and IPV. Impediments include navigating complex power dynamics during interviews, managing the emotional labour involved, and striking a delicate balance between building rapport and avoiding confrontations with perpetrators (Dheensa et al., 2024).

Often employing tactics to portray themselves positively, XYs' behaviour complicates the data collection process. Additionally, their attempts to intimidate or flirt with XX researchers, breaching professional boundaries, create difficulties as researchers work to maintain neutrality without interruption or judgment. These behaviours lead to internal conflict and frustration among researchers (Dheensa et al., 2024).

Additionally, XYs also often minimise, justify, or deny their abusive actions, making it difficult for researchers to build rapport without inadvertently validating their behaviour, especially when XYs make offensive, threatening, or sexist remarks. Their inappropriate misogynistic comments leave many researchers feeling vulnerable, particularly in confined spaces where XYs' aggression poses a threat. The fear of potential violence compelled researchers to prioritise their safety over collecting comprehensive data, limiting the depth of exploration possible during interviews (Dheensa et al., 2024).

A comparative analysis of various surveys on sexual VAW in the UK – including the Crime Survey for England and Wales, the EU VAW survey, the Scottish Crime and Justice Survey, and the National Survey of Sexual Attitudes and Lifestyles – revealed significant discrepancies in reported prevalence rates. For example, one report indicated that one in 20 (5%) had experienced a serious sexual assault since the age of 16, while another found that approximately one in ten (9.8%) XXs reported non-consensual sex since the age of 13 (Brunton-Smith et al., 2020).

Another survey revealed that more than one in ten (11%) of XXs had experienced sexual violence from the age of 15. Despite the variations, surveys consistently show that XXs experience significantly higher rates of both attempted and completed sexual violence compared to XYs. For example, approximately one in six (17.6%) XXs in England and Wales reported experiencing attempted sexual violence, compared to approximately one in 24 (4.2%) XYs (Brunton-Smith et al., 2020).

Efforts to engage XYs in the prevention of VAW often encounter significant obstacles, as activists and practitioners struggle to mobilise this group amidst decreasing funding for VAW services (Burrell, 2018). Additionally, the rise of "gender-neutral" policies has also had adverse effects, as they have diluted the focus on VAW, impairing efforts to hold XYs accountable, support XX–specific services (Aldridge, 2020:825), and recognise the distinct experiences and needs of XXs.

As in other countries, the COVID-19 pandemic had profound effects on XXs, with abusers intensifying their control. In the UK, police-recorded DV crimes rose by 7% between March 2019 and March 2020. Additionally, one charity reported a "150% increase" in calls from teenagers regarding forced marriages during the lockdown, whilst a specialist children's hospital recorded a "1,493%" increase in new child abuse injury cases compared to previous years (Proudman & Lloyd, 2023:236).

Additionally, "the Ministry of Justice showed that between April and June 2021, there were 66,357 new cases in the family courts" representing a "14%" increase compared to the same period in 2020; the average waiting time for Children Act cases extending "from a waiting time to 41 weeks" (Proudman & Lloyd, 2023:237). These figures demonstrate how the pandemic exacerbated DV, IPV, and child abuse, disproportionately affecting XXs and their children.

VAW in the USA

During the COVID-19 pandemic, the use of strangulation and weapons by perpetrators in the USA increased nearly two and a half times. Physical IPV cases were significantly higher in 2020, with white XX survivors making up the great majority (65%) of cases, compared to one in four (26%) in previous years. Although fewer survivors sought care during the pandemic, those who did presented with more severe injuries (Gosangi et al., 2021). Cohabitation illustrating that it can further jeopardise XXs facing lethal threats behind closed doors.

With an estimated 346 million people, approximately 172 million (48.5%) are XXs (World Population Review, 2024). One in three (31.5%) report experiencing IPV in the USA. Specifically, one in six (15.4%) XXs report being slammed against something, and more than one in seven (13%) report being hit with a fist or a hard object by a partner. One in two (47%) XXs experience psychological aggression from an intimate partner (Aldridge, 2020).

An encouraging development indicates that when the number of XX police officers rises, the number of DV killings decline by approximately 16% in the USA. The increase in XX police officers – tripling from "3.4% to 10.1%" – has significantly increased crime reporting, particularly for violent crimes against XXs and DV (Miller & Segal, 2019:2221).

The presence of XX police officers is also linked to a decline in IPV femicides and repeated incidents of non-fatal DV. Overall, as the number of XX officers increases, more XXs report assaults: for every one-percentage-point rise in XX officer representation, there is a corresponding one-percentage-point increase in reporting by XX survivors. This illustrates that XXs helping survivors incentivises and encourages the violated to seek help and report the criminals (Miller & Segal, 2019).

Nonetheless, less than one in four (23%) rape incidents and less than one in two (49%) DV cases are reported to police in the USA (Franklin et al., 2020). These numbers indicate a critical gap between the realities of trauma survivors and the assumptions within justice systems, accentuating the need for more trauma-informed approaches in law enforcement.

Police officers handling DV crimes exercise considerable discretion in the USA, often opting against arresting individuals perceived as less likely to commit violence. Arrest decisions are heavily influenced by physical injury and the survivor's readiness to cooperate; psychological or verbal abuse is less likely to lead to arrests. Consequently, in three of four (75%) DV incidents, no arrests are made when there is no clear evidence of physical violence (Myhill, 2019). Survivors, however, often exhibit symptoms, including diminished emotional expressions, disjointed memories, and emotional numbing, which do not always align with the stereotypical behaviour expected by law enforcement (Miller & Segal, 2019).

Different types of warrantless DV arrest laws in the USA – discretionary, preferred, and mandatory – also indicate significant reductions in intimate partner killings, particularly among current and former spouses.

Warrantless arrest laws were associated with a 43% decrease in homicides involving current spouses, and an estimated 107% decrease in killings involving former spouses between 1976 and 2016 (Chin & Cunningham, 2019). Although the reduction in IPV homicides is positive, extensive analyses found no substantial evidence that mandatory or preferred arrest laws directly contributed to declines. Moreover, the research suggests that while arrest laws are generally effective in reducing IPV–related deaths, the specific type of law may not be the decisive factor in decreasing femicides (Chin & Cunningham, 2019).

Additionally, survivors of DV in the USA often encounter significant prejudices when requesting civil protection orders, also known as restraining orders or orders of protection. Around one in two ("40%") individuals seeking legal protection are unable to secure it, leaving them vulnerable and exposing critical gaps in the implementation of the Violence Against Women Act (VAWA) (Stoever, 2019:333).

For example, one-third of DV-related civil protection orders are dismissed or discontinued due to the inability to locate the perpetrator – a critical procedural step. Flaws in the system prevent meeting the expected implementations, with inefficiencies emphasising the urgent need to reform and streamline legal processes to prevent further suffering and ensure that protective mechanisms are accessible and effective (Stoever, 2019).

The toll of violent crimes extend beyond immediate harm, deeply affecting XXs and children across the USA. Both physical and psychological abuse have extensive consequences, resulting in physical injuries, mental health disorders, and, in severe cases, death. Alarmingly, approximately one in three (30%) to two in three (60%) of American households that experience IPV also report child abuse. During pandemics, these incidents escalate as isolation and stress increase the risk and severity of violence. IPV is linked to between two in five (40%) and half (50%) of XX deaths, with most survivors experiencing physical abuse from their partner prior to being killed – the vast majority ("83.3%") of cases involved XX survivors (Walker-Descartes et al., 2021:456).

In rural America IPV survivors face additional violence and policy gaps that impede access to adequate healthcare services. Geographic isolation, limited transportation options, and a scarcity of healthcare providers, particularly for mental health support, exacerbate their vulnerabilities. Policies that require documentation to prove abuse before receiving support also create additional constraints to accessing the help XXs need, further marginalising survivors (Mantler et al., 2022).

Studies conducted between 2013 and 2020, primarily in the USA, across various disciplines – including medicine, psychology, social work, and nursing – identified the promising potential of neuroscientific approaches in IPV interventions. Techniques including cognitive trauma therapy, neurofeedback, mindfulness-based stress reduction, and trauma-sensitive yoga have shown potential benefits for survivors (Baird et al., 2022).

The integration of neuroscience into IPV interventions remains inconsistent, pointing to a lack of standardisation in how these mitigating approaches are applied. The scarcity of research in this area should serve as an impetus for greater incorporation of neuroscience into social work practice and IPV research (Baird et al., 2022) to improve the health and recovery of survivors.

An examination of premature mortality data, from 2006 to 2015, across 16 states in the USA revealed that XXs represented the majority of partner fatalities – approximately three of every five ("59%") (Graham et al., 2021:18). Further research is urgently needed to address this epidemic by examining the number of IPV–related murders and their profound impact on secondary survivors – especially children who, although not always the primary targets, are deeply traumatised by witnessing IPV

Additionally, XX survivors, on average, lost five years of life due to IPV; however, the impact was even more severe for Hispanic XXs, who lost more than 16 years of life from IPV-related killings, emphasising a stark racial disparity. Black, American Indian, and Alaskan Native XXs lost nine or more years compared to white IPV survivors (Graham et al., 2021).

Research on American Indian survivors further reveals that financial obstacles and the lack of culturally relevant services significantly deter them from seeking help. Approximately three in every four (68%) acknowledged financial constraints, housing instability, and transportation restraints as major obstacles. Fear of homelessness or insecure housing was a key reason many chose to remain in abusive situations. Distrust in mainstream healthcare and law enforcement – driven by experiences of racism and the absence of culturally sensitive support – prevented many XXs from accessing services. Only one in four ("24%") XXs received medical care, often only when a bystander called 911 (Luebke et al., 2023:2088).

Overall, VAW in the USA and globally represents a complex and deeply societal crisis, characterised by systemic barriers to justice, racial and geographic disparities, and heightened risks during periods of crisis – highlighting the pressing need for intersectional, trauma-informed, and survivor-centred responses.

Conclusion

Meaningful change is possible when efforts are united to disband systemic patriarchal obstacles, biases, and phallocentric discriminatory practices; prioritising the health and well-being of all equally is a future we must demand.

Despite the persistent challenges in healthcare, there have been significant improvements towards achieving practical and equitable medical management for many. In recent years, increased advocacy, research, and policy reform have begun to reshape healthcare systems to better respond to the specific needs of diverse XXs populations.

For example, the global medical community is increasingly recognising the need to collect sex-disaggregated data to ensure that medical interventions account for biological differences rather than defaulting to XY–centric models. This is a key development, with several countries mandating the inclusion of XX participants in clinical trials, leading to more accurate and effective medical practices.

Efforts to address VAW have also gained traction in recent years. International campaigns have heightened awareness and collaboration, prompting governments to improve reporting methods – including increasing the representation of XX police officers in several countries, strengthening legal protections, and funding survivor support programmes.

Various countries – including Australia, several within the EU, and the UK – have implemented comprehensive frameworks that integrate healthcare, legal services, and social support to assist survivors of violence. These measures focus on trauma-informed care, ensuring survivors receive compassionate and holistic support.

Access to contraception and safe abortion services is expanding in several regions, reflecting growing recognition of reproductive autonomy as a fundamental human right. In contract, others, including the USA, have taken regressive steps that undermining the human rights of XXs globally. Nevertheless, telehealth services and other XX–led online initiatives are providing effective alternatives. Grassroots movements and international advocacy groups continue to be instrumental in ensuring that reproductive healthcare policies remain inclusive and equitable.

Healthcare providers, alongside researchers and advocacy groups, are working to reduce the stigma around menopause. There is now greater attention aimed at improving quality of life and workplace well-being for XXs globally. Increased public discussions have led to increased awareness and, to some extent, the removal of the taboo topic, with various national health strategies providing some relief during the hormonal transition.

World Menopause Day, for example, is promoting awareness and inclusive research initiatives. Traditional and alternative treatments, although both require further research, can assist individuals manage the menopausal transition. These positive developments signal a global shift towards more equitable healthcare practices.

By enhancing collaboration between policymakers, medical practitioners, and advocacy groups, and amplifying the voices of those affected, the future promises a healthcare system that upholds dignity, respect, and justice.

Amid the numerous obstacles within global health systems, there are opportunities to redefine the narrative, break down existing barriers, and create pathways towards a future where the health of XXs is not an afterthought but a key component of medical systems. Additionally, understanding legal protections, healthcare structures, and practices enables XXs to more effectively address and prevent issues that impact their well-being.

"The best thing about self-defense is knowing there is a self, worth defending".

Gloria Steinem, acclaimed journalist, grassroots activist, vanguard feminist. (Michals, 2017; Steinem, n.d)

Toolkit

Medical

Remember, you only have one body, and it cannot be replaced!

Before attending a medical consultation, it is advisable to conduct your own research and prepare a list of questions to ensure your concerns are fully addressed. Be as clear as possible when describing your symptoms and repeat them if the doctor is not listening.

During the appointment, ask detailed questions, seeking clarity on the doctor's assessments. If informed that nothing is wrong, ask for an explanation of how this conclusion was reached and request tests. Should you be advised to simply take an aspirin or another type of medication and be sent home, do not hesitate to get a second opinion. Trust your instincts – your feelings are valid, and the healthcare system must understand your concerns and pain in detail.

Have open discussions with family members; remember, DNA carries genetic information that can help identify potential health risks, allowing you to take preventive measures and improve your overall well-being.

VAW Prevention

Before entering into an intimate relationship or moving in with someone, make sure to obtain any information that could be important in the future. If possible, seek feedback from past partners and do not disregard their experiences simply because they are a former partner.

Be a mentor and/or have open conversations with children and young people about what healthy sexual behaviour looks like and what is unacceptable. Explain how real-life sexual experiences and relationships can differ significantly from what is available online.

Access to NGOs and technologies that support and enhance healthcare services is available. Take the time to research and understand your options before experiencing potential violence, coercion, or harassment – remember being informed can significantly strengthen your ability to seek help and make empowered decisions. For example, mobile applications designed to address VAW offer a range of support; some focus on emergency responses, while others provide preventive strategies.

Having a range of applications readily accessible can be highly valuable should the need arise for yourself or others; statistics indicate that there is a high probability that you know someone enduring IPV and/or DV.

There are numerous vital initiatives to encourage individuals to step forward and support survivors during moments of vulnerability. Bystander intervention can also be an effective approach – do not fear asking for help, irrespective of who you are or where you are.

Remember, it is NEVER your fault, and the perpetrator must be held accountable. You have every right and deserve to live free from violence.

Share your experiences, tell your stories, and ask for help from reliable people. VAW experiences should not be silenced.

When confronted with legal obstacles, double-check your rights; do not assume one person has all the information. Ensure you get several perspectives before you make any legal decisions. Help to educate other XXs on their legal rights and the advice and resources available to assist in making informed decisions.

Self-Defence

When individuals feel equipped to defend themselves, the fear of vulnerability decreases, transforming into a greater sense of autonomy and freedom.

Learn self-defence and encourage young XXs to take classes at the start of primary school (Vega, 2023). The psychological benefits are equally significant: self-defence builds resilience, instils confidence, and dismantles the paralysing effects of fear. The ability to resist and counteract an attacker goes beyond physical protection – it reshapes how threats are perceived, encouraging heightened situational awareness and assertive decision-making.

Self-defence also provides key preventive strategies for XXs, providing educational techniques that develop both physical and mental skills, fundamentally altering psychological states and promoting a sense of control in the face of unpredictability.

Importantly, self-defence techniques function as a societal deterrent, as potential perpetrators are less likely to target individuals perceived as capable of resisting. On a broader scale, self-defence education promotes a culture of self-reliance and empowerment, challenging norms that perpetuate passivity and compliance. In a world where systemic protections often fail, self-defence serves as both a pragmatic solution and a powerful assertion of personal agency. Additionally, it contributes to overall physical fitness and well-being!

Public Safety

Advocate for public spaces to adopt inclusive approaches that address infrastructure and social attitudes. Contacting local, regional, or national political representatives ahead of elections is often the most effective time to influence change. Improvements like clear signage, ample lighting, and accessible pathways not only enhance both actual and perceived safety but also attract more visitors and help deter violence. Raising awareness of safety issues and demanding equitable, accessible environments can help transform public spaces into supportive settings where XXs can fully participate in civic life.

Promoting sex-based equity in leadership positions within urban design teams could also provide more diverse perspectives at all stages of planning. Public art and symbolic representation also play an important role in addressing safety. Featuring artworks created by or depicting XXs creates a sense of belonging and changes traditional narratives that have historically excluded XXs.

Collaborative efforts between governments, communities, and organisations are essential for building inclusive spaces. Addressing safety concerns through effective partnerships reinforces and supports a sense of security for XXs to remain actively engaged in communities (Women's Health East, 2020/2021).

Call for the implementation of crowd-mapping tools to enable real-time feedback on safe and unsafe spaces.

Remember, by asking, you open the door to possibilities and opportunities. At times, everything may seem impossible – until one day, it becomes a reality.

Menopause

Be mindful of how you treat your body long before perimenopause begins. Prioritise reliable information and disregard uninformed advice – educate yourself on how to access tools that support and improve your well-being. Retaining your mental and physical power, with or without medication, is essential.

5 Education

Igniting Dreams

Personal Note

My primary and secondary education were delivered between Madrid, Spain, and Darwin and Melbourne, Australia; each system – Spanish and English – demanded specific conduct based on cultural norms, but both had the same set of stereotypical sex-based expectations. I constantly resisted wearing a skirt, regardless of which side of the globe I was on.

Regardless, I was fortunate that my mother's connections within the Catholic Church and my father's talent for repairs – offering his services to the school in exchange for reduced tuition for his three daughters – provided a strong foundation that enabled my education. At the same time, I was somewhat unlucky, as the nuns and priests repeatedly reinforced sex differences, often to the detriment of our confidence and intellectual development.

For example, the restrictions on subjects based on our sex: *woodwork* was reserved exclusively for XYs – despite my attempts to join to no avail – while *home economics* (shopping and cooking) was only for XXs. I was constantly told to be a "lady" – an explanation superbly described in the piece to camera *Be a Lady They Said*, written by Camille Rainville (*GIRLS, GIRLS, GIRLS* magazine, n.d.), serving as a powerful reminder of Western phallocentric expectations and how XXs submit. After watching *Be a Lady They Said*, narrated by Cynthia Nixon, I understood exactly why I was so rebellious, angry, and confused for so long.

During my high school work experience, I quickly learned that impediments were ahead because of my XX chromosome makeup. During a placement at a government media department, whilst in the darkroom being shown how to process film and print images, the youngest of the XY photographers grabbed me and kissed me on the lips. I was stunned, speechless, and motionless. I reported it to no one; I did not tell my parents or teachers. I still do not know why, other than shame and Catholic guilt.

DOI: 10.4324/9781003516224-5

A few years later, I applied to work with the Australian military as an aerial photographer but was advised that only XYs could do that work. Eventually, I went where I was told I should be. Unable to stomach blood, nursing was not an option; hairdressing was. However, I quickly realised that the trade, dominated by XXs, would not pay enough to survive. I decided I needed an education.

When I told my mother about my plan, she reminded me that as an XX migrant, "you will not be allowed into a university." My father encouraged me to ignore her, suggesting that I visualise what I wanted, believe I could achieve it, and pursue it.

Before I finished my tertiary studies, I was offered a job with a magazine production company to which I had previously sold a story together with photos. The story featured several XX–run SMEs that were tanning, designing, and manufacturing fashion garments from fish and cane toad skins. I was paid AU$5000 (US$3100) for the cover photos, and AU$1 (US$0.63) per word.

Ironically, one of my first reporting assignments as a photojournalist employee was reporting on an aviation story. When I arrived at the meeting point, dressed in a skirt and heels, one XY from the crew handed me an oversized full-body suit – a comically ill-fitting ensemble. Once dressed, I was strapped into an aircraft, without doors, allowing me to hang out of the plane and photograph military air drills.

Seeing the images printed in the glossy magazine, to be distributed internationally, I realised that my father was indeed right – the fulfilment of my dream, however brief, was achieved as a result of my education. More than 30 years after completing my undergraduate degree, I was awarded my doctorate, which led to the writing of this little book that draws on a decade of research.

For many XXs across the world, opportunities like mine remain out of reach. While some fight simply for the chance to learn to read, others face relentless limitations throughout their educational journeys. Inequities in education persist, driven by socioeconomic disparities, political failures, and established cultural and/or religious gynophobia that continues to restrain XXs. Fortunately, many others are learning, succeeding, living their dream, advocating for change, leading, publishing, researching, teaching, and working across numerous diverse fields.

Introduction

The first university in the world was founded by an XX back in 800 CE in Morocco, but only for XY students.

Education is essential to strengthen XXs' participation in society and the economy and the foundation that creates opportunities. Yet, education remains one of the most challenging projects of social development, as access to knowledge has historically been restricted by entrenched patriarchal principles.

Access to education has significantly increased for XXs over recent decades, with global data indicating that enrolments in primary and secondary schools are almost equal between XXs and XYs, suggesting global progress towards reducing exclusion in obtaining an education. The multifaceted role of education shapes both individual lives and societies, interacting with cultural and religious norms, policies, and socioeconomic factors.

Debates surrounding single-sex versus coeducational schools are increasing; proponents of single-sex education argue that these environments can advance academic progress. Conversely, critics highlight the risk of reinforcing sex-based stereotypes and limiting social integration. Some studies indicate learning benefits for XXs in single-sex settings, while others suggest XYs are disadvantaged.

The implications of school uniforms are also reviewed, revealing that policies often reinforce phallocentric expectations, as skirts and dresses often limit the mobility of XXs and perpetuate their objectification.

The increasing prevalence of toxic masculinity in high schools is an urgent concern, demonstrating how school environments are becoming breeding grounds for misogynistic violence and harassment, perpetuated by cultural expectations that encourage dominance and aggression toward XX students (Drury, et al., 2013).

This chapter references the work of two students: Chanel Contos in Australia and Riley O'Keefe in the USA – both of whom brought attention to the widespread issue of sexual harassment and discrimination in schools, leading to positive legal changes.

Teachers, the majority of whom are XXs globally, are identified as central to advancing inclusive learning environments. However, they too face significant obstacles, including inadequate support, low salaries, and high levels of stress and burnout. Researchers are calling for comprehensive reforms, including enhanced professional development and systemic changes to improve teacher well-being and retention.

The underrepresentation of XX students in science, technology, engineering, and mathematics (STEM) courses is yet another global complication. Despite numerous initiatives to increase XX participation in STEM, androcentric cultural stereotypes, a lack of role models, and constraints persist. Additionally, disparities in universities endure, where XXs, despite obtaining PhDs at higher rates than XYs, continue confronting bigotry in systems that limit advancement and suppress opportunities.

The rise of artificial intelligence in education (AIED) and its potential to reduce administrative burdens on teachers also pose risks associated with biased algorithms and unequal access to technological resources, which can exacerbate inequalities; yet, AI can also provide educational tools for both students and teachers.

The toolkit section provides practical suggestions, based on years of academic research, illustrating that by incorporating self-defence training in schools, XX students could develop the skills and confidence necessary to combat sex-based violence. Self-defence training can also enhance personal safety techniques, reduce violence in schools, and restrict stereotypes that depict the XX body as inferior, weak, or feeble.

Additionally, self-defence sends a compelling declaration that XXs are capable and strong, deserving of the same respect and autonomy as XYs, while also instilling valuable life skills. The incorporation of self-defence programs is vital for changing the widespread normalisation of sex-based violence that too many students experience.

A holistic approach to educational reform – one that dismantles patriarchal structures and the adoption of equitable learning environments – is essential. Education must be recognised as both a means of individual advancement and as a collective endeavour to build balanced and inclusive nations.

The power of education highlights both its transformative impact and the unresolved concerns that require resolution to attain equity among the sexes.

The inclusion of several visionaries from Australia, the EU, India, the UK, and the USA serves as a reminder that, regardless of age or era, individual efforts do create transformative changes that generate *herstory*.

Looking Back, Moving Forward

The result of XY's writing history has often resulted in the exclusion of recognising and documenting the achievements made by XXs (Zorrilla, 2022; Vann, 2024), with few mentions of extraordinary *herstory* surfacing.

Africa

Fatima al-Fihri was born in Tunisia (800–880 CE), she is credited with opening the University of al-Qarawiyyin in Fez, Morocco, in 859 CE (Fejzić-Čengić, 2020). The institution was ground-breaking, introducing the degree-awarding system that continues to influence the structures of universities globally. Although al-Fihri established the world's first university using her inheritance, only XYs could attend – XXs had to wait until the 1940s.

Today, the university is recognised by the UN's Educational, Scientific and Cultural Organization (UNESCO) as the world's oldest continuously operating degree-granting educational institution (Mortimer, 2018). The University of al-Qarawiyyin, named after al-Fihri's birthplace, has been a source of guidance, knowledge, and culture for centuries. Since its inception, it has contributed to various fields of significant learning. al-Fihri's legacy is a powerful reminder of the crucial role XXs have historically played in the advancement of education and intellectual pursuits (Fejzić-Čengić, 2020).

Despite the numerous extraordinary and significant contributions, al-Fihri's achievements have been largely ignored for the past 1,165 years – yes, more than a millennium has passed since the first university was created by an XX.

Australia

Maybanke Anderson (1845–1927) was a prominent Australian activist for early childhood education and suffrage. Anderson was instrumental in advancing educational opportunities for XXs and advocated for changes to laws around divorce and property rights, which disproportionately disadvantaged XXs (Roberts & Oppenheimer, 1996).

Born in England, Anderson immigrated to Sydney in 1855 after facing personal adversity, including desertion by her XY partner. Prior to migrating, Anderson sustained her young family by working as a teacher. Between 1868 and 1879, Anderson endured seven births (Roberts & Oppenheimer, 1996).

She transformed her home into Maybanke College, a respected school for XXs, providing quality education at a time when opportunities were limited (Victorian Government, n.d.). In 1895, Anderson also co-founded the *Kindergarten Union of New South Wales*, establishing the first free kindergarten in Woolloomooloo, Sydney, to support working XXs and children living in impoverished areas, without any self-serving praise, acclaim, or recognition (Roberts & Oppenheimer, 1996). Anderson's efforts led to the expansion of kindergartens throughout Sydney's inner-city slums, providing children with a safe space for early development and care. Anderson continued her work into the 1920s (Pyrmont History, 2025), illustrating her unrelenting and tenacious commitment to improving education at the foundational community level.

Anderson's advocacy extended to tertiary education, where she wrote extensively to advance discussions on XXs' rights and education. Her handbook *Motherlore* offered guidance on early childhood education, emphasising the importance of nurturing learning from infancy (Britannica Kids, n.d.).

Hailed as "the most intellectual woman in Australia" at the peak of her influence (Pyrmont History, 2025)88, Anderson's contributions to education reform remain a testament to her belief that accessible education could revolutionise societies in beneficial ways, despite being excluded from many historical records and almost erased from significant narratives (Roberts & Oppenheimer, 1996). Maybanke died in Paris (Wikipedia, n.d.-a.).

The EU

There were numerous XXs who contested the patriarchy and advocated for educational rights across this continent; only a few are included in chronological order:

QUEEN ISABEL I OF CASTILE

Also known as Isabel la Católica, born in Ávila, Spain (1451–1504), one of the first queens to rule in her own right as the sole monarch of her realm, though not the first globally (Encyclopaedia Britannica, n.d.). As one of history's most influential rulers, her contributions included educational reforms, giving power to the Queen in the game of chess, and political conquests, including the establishment of the *College of Santa Cruz* in Valladolid, completed in 1491 (Spain.info, n.d.). This queen also provided wider accessibility to books by supporting the growth of printing presses in Spain (Braun, 2021) and was a patron of humanist scholars and artists, promoting literacy and the arts (Liss, 2008). Her sponsorship of Christopher Columbus's expedition led to the discovery of the "New World" (Royal Collection Trust, n.d.; World History Encyclopedia, n.d.). The investment secured substantial wealth for Spain and positioned it as a global imperial power (Sina, 2016).

Although not all historians agree, some claim the Queen of Castile changed the game of chess to reflect the reality of the time. In the original ancient game, there was no queen. Centuries later, when introduced, the queen piece was weak and had little power, able to move only one square at a time. An extraordinary transformation occurred when the queen became the most powerful piece on the board, reflecting the power of XX rulers – moving from symbolic subordination to one with the highest authority and the game's strategic centrepiece. In chess, as in society, the queen now holds the power to move in any direction – serving as the king's ally and as a versatile strategist with commanding influence (Andrews, 2004; Brown, 2015) – a transformation made possible by XXs who refused to be mere pawns.

ELENA CORNARO PISCOPIA

The first XX in the world to receive a doctoral degree was partly attributed to XX aristocrats who steered intellectual hubs influencing university policies, including Padua – where Cornaro Piscopia graduated in 1678 with a PhD in theology. She was born in Venice, Italy (1646–1684), where, like elsewhere at the time, universities prohibited entry to the "inferior sex", assigning XXs solely to the role of wife and mother. Cornaro Piscopia proved them wrong. Her academic excellence continues to inspire generations of XXs to pursue higher education (Bettella, 2018; Kalnická, 2021).

SOPHIE GERMAIN

Born in Paris, France (1776–1831), the self-taught mathematician, physicist, and philosopher accessed books from her father's library, as her sex prohibited her from academic institutions.

Germain corresponded under a male pseudonym, Monsieur Le Blanc, to gain access to the great minds of the time, but she was never permitted to work as a mathematician. An advocate for academic freedom for XXs in mathematics and science, Germain innovated various theories, including elasticity, plate vibrations, and numbers. Her paper on elasticity theory won the grand prize from the Paris Academy of Sciences. Germain died of breast cancer and was never awarded an honorary degree. Even so, 172 years after her death, in her memory, the French Academy of Sciences inaugurated the *Sophie Germain*

Prize for excellence in mathematics in 2003 (Musielak, 2020; Ramesh & Makeshwari, 2023; Wikipedia, n.d.-b.).

MARIE SKŁODOWSKA CURIE

Born in Poland (1867–1934) and migrating to France, Curie was primarily a teacher, and the daughter of a teacher, endorsing education and establishing research institutions. She advocated for XXs' involvement in science. Curie's groundbreaking work on radioactivity earned her the 1903 Nobel Prize in Physics. With philanthropic funds, Curie established the Curie Institutes in Paris and Warsaw, advancing scientific learning globally (Frontczak, 2023; Nobel Prize Outreach, n.d.).

India

Savitribai Phule (1831–1897) established the first school for XXs in Pune in 1848, marking a valuable historic moment for education, and earning her the title Flame of Education (Mondal & Baugh, 2024).

Accredited as India's first female headmistress, Phule dedicated her life to eradicating social injustices, understanding the transformative power of education to achieve significant social and economic change. Phule's relentless advocacy for universal access to educate led to significant strides, particularly for XXs from lower castes who have historically been marginalised. Nonetheless, regressive traditions endure, with some parents from lower castes continuing to prioritise XYs over XXs. Phule is also credited with introducing vocational training to promote self-reliance.

Despite the social resistance and harassment encountered, Phule persisted in her mission to promote education for children and advocate for a more equal society. The Krantijyoti Savitribai Phule Women's Studies Centre at Savitribai Phule Pune University, Maharashtra, continues to provide academic opportunities for XXs promoting feminist perspecitves (Mondal & Baugh, 2024; Sah, 2022).

The UK

Mary Wollstonecraft was born in London (1759–1797) and was one of the first English writers to advocate for XXs – an eminent individual who fiercely championed the cause of education (Ferguson, 1999).

Wollstonecraft's seminal book, *A Vindication of the Rights of Woman* (1792), argued that XXs should be able to access the same educational opportunities as XYs to obtain independence. Wollstonecraft's ideas were progressive at the time, linking the pursuit of XXs' freedom with broader socioeconomic criticisms.

In the 21st c., Wollstonecraft's work continues to resonate in both historical and contemporary human rights debates, solidifying her position as an authoritative figure (Emmett, 2018). Wollstonecraft's contributions remain foundational to discussions on equality, emphasising the essential role of education in empowering XXs to pursue parity with XYs, make progress, and achieve their goals.

The USA

Emma Willard was born in Connecticut (1787–1870), beginning her career as a teacher, aged 17, and continuing as a pioneering advocate for XXs' educational rights. Willard founded the *Troy Female Seminary* in 1821 in New York, the first institution dedicated to higher education for XXs in 19th c. America (Nelson, 1987). From the start the academic programmes matched the standards available to their XY counterparts.

Willard's philosophy continues to influence and inspire XXs through the *Emma Willard School*, a single-sex school for grades nine to 12 (Crocker, 2006), which upholds her legacy by providing a dedicated curriculum tailored to XX students.

Despite the thousands of kilometres and the 1,100-plus years separating Fatima, Maybanke, Isabel, Elena, Sophie, Marie, Savitribai, Mary, and Emma – as well as the countless others not mentioned in this little book – and despite the diverse cultural phallocentric contexts they traversed, these XXs have inspired millions by sharing their mission and executing their vision. Defying norms, traditions, policies, and the patriarchy while initiating, advocating, and reforming educational institutions in their respective nations, each one continues to inspire.

The Power of Knowledge

The phrase "knowledge is power" is attributed to Francis Bacon. In 1597, Bacon wrote *Meditationes Sacrae* (Drayton, 2022), addressing the role of human understanding and the moral duties of individuals. More than 370 years later, Michel Foucault, a historian, social theorist, and philosopher, explored the connection between knowledge and power in numerous works (Foucault, 1982, 1990, 1991). Foucault's insights laid the groundwork for contemporary discussions on the subject of power (Chapter 1).

The understanding of the importance of power gained from education facilitates many XX activists at the forefront of their advocacy work. Malala Yousafzai, born in 1997 in Pakistan, exemplifies this truth. After being denied access to education by the Taliban and surviving an assassination attempt, Yousafzai emerged as a powerful voice for the education of XXs worldwide (Yousafzai & Lamb, 2013). Yousafzai's bravery and activism captured global attention, and she became the youngest Nobel Prize laureate, sharing the honour with Kailash Satyarthi in 2014. Both were internationally recognised for their efforts to end the suppression of children and for promoting the right to education for XXs (Norwegian Nobel Institute, 2014).

Yet, long before the emergence of notable advocates mentioned, and the many others not included in this chapter, the Bible, central to both Judaism and Christianity (Chapter 2) – promoted the value of wisdom and knowledge. For example, in Proverbs 24:5 (New International Version, 1984), "A wise man is strong; yea, a man of knowledge increaseth strength." Both the oldest of texts and current research (Unterhalter, 2019) emphasise the undeniable power of knowledge.

Regardless of where we search for knowledge, the evidence affirms that educating individuals is a human right and a necessary foundation for any fair and thriving society (Holowchak, 2018). However, the question remains: where is the best place to provide education? The ongoing debates between home schooling, single-sex, and coeducational schools produce diverse viewpoints and conclusions.

Supporters of single-sex education argue that these schools cater to the unique developmental needs of students, enhancing focus by reducing distractions from the opposite sex. Conversely, critics assert that this approach is rooted in pseudo-science and perpetuates harmful sex-based stereotypes. The global debate is complex, with compelling arguments on both sides.

The Impact of Learning

Equal access to education is a basic human right and a fundamental pillar to achieve equality. However, "119.3 million girls" remain without access (UN Women, 2024:6). Furthermore, the expense of early childcare continues to impede early learning (Chapter 6).

CEDAW's Article 10 notes that nations are to ensure that XXs have "… equal rights with men in the field of education…" (CEDAW, 1979:4). The majority of XXs in nearly all developed nations do not face overt blocks to accessing education (OECD, 2020; Rincker et al., 2019; WEF, 2020a). International initiatives, including the UN's SDGs – Goal 4, "Quality Education," and Goal 5, "Gender Equality" (Eden & Wagstaff, 2020; OECD, 2020; UN, n.d.) – emphasise curricula that discourages stereotypes and promotes critical thinking (Aragonés-González et al., 2020).

On average, nations have closed the education gap between XXs and XYs by 95%, marking the greatest progress recorded to date (WEF, 2017, 2024a). The World Economic Forum (WEF) has been publishing international research on education progress from primary to tertiary levels since 2006, releasing annual *Global Gender Gap Index* reports. The WEF's findings draw attention to significant societal shifts, particularly since the onset of industrialisation, which enabled XXs to enter the workforce with improved literacy and educational attainment (Bush, 2011). This upward trend in education has been sustained well into the 21st c (WEF, 2020b, 2024b).

Over the past decades, the number of XXs graduating from tertiary institutions has increased worldwide, with much of the data suggesting that XX university students outnumber XY in "most industrialized societies" (Buchmann

& DiPrete, 2006:516). For example, XX medical students now outnumber XY students in the UK (The Press Association, 2014), but in numerous other STEM subjects, an imbalance remains.

The advantages of educating XXs include a healthier population, improved democratic rights and practices, and enhanced economic growth for communities and nations. However, the mere provision of education does not automatically produce the desired outcomes for XXs. Determining the most effective approach to education generates controversy among students, teachers, governments, and parents – irrespective of the delivery setting.

Global Realities

While progress is evident in the vast majority of democratic nations, less visible obstacles persist and remain a significant concern. In contrast, XX students in non-democratic nations, including Afghanistan, for example, face distinct and severe adversities deeply rooted in religious doctrines and phallocentric political ideologies. Under the Taliban's rule, these exclusions restrict access to education and opportunities for all XXs. The Taliban's "gender apartheid regime" enables XYs to impose ruthless and brutally oppressive dominance over XXs (Akbari & True, 2022:624).

International human rights laws (Chapter 2), teachers, academics, governments, and policymakers publicly advocate for equitable access to education. Most democratic nations agree that there are extensive advantages to educating XXs, and many have acknowledged the benefits of removing educational limitations (Pranevičienė, & Pūraitė, 2010). However, although research presents a reassuring argument, supported by the understanding that education is widely recognised as a human right and reinforced by existing legal frameworks, significant disparities remain between theory and practice (Khurshid, 2017).

The USA – a country promoted as the defender of equal rights and opportunity – is also labelled the "hypocrisy country" (Washington Post, 2013) due to its long history of injustices against all those who are not white, privileged XYs, including XXs. The double standards stem from entrenched ignorant misogynistic injustices. These discriminatory practices continue to occur in a democracy where a convicted XY felon can hold the highest office in the land, yet XXs without a criminal record still earn less than XYs (Watson, 2024).

This extraordinary phenomenon illustrates that what is often referred to as the most powerful democracy on Earth continues to prioritise the interests of XYs and the super-rich, while consenting to XXs being treated as second-class citizens – marginalised, constrained and denied equality rights and opportunities. For example, XXs who devote years to becoming experts in their chosen fields and completing doctoral research still face the harsh reality of earning less than an XY (Office for National Statistics, 2024).

So how is this possible, you ask? Despite a global consensus among researchers and governments on the importance of education and notable advancements around the world, a troubling regression is in progress.

Numerous discrepancies are exemplified by the rise of "exclusionary practices" (Anderson & Boyle, 2015:15), including a lack of access to necessary resources for individuals with XX chromosomes, curricula that fail to address their needs, and marginalisation that prevents parity and positive progress. Additionally, academic studies in the vast majority of developed nations have historically focused on Western research while neglecting other cultures and intellectual contributions.

Numerous activists over the centuries have proactively committed themselves to changing discriminatory practices by creating educational opportunities, often while confronting patriarchal constraints and systems of oppression. Discriminatory teaching practices, alongside cultural and religious norms, further alienate XXs. Therefore, it is essential that all stakeholders in education work to eliminate sex-discriminatory policies and practices that explicitly differentiate between the sexes (Rafferty, 2013).

Across the 146 countries included in the 2024 WEF index, the Educational Attainment gap has closed by 94.9%. Countries ranked in first place include France, Ireland, New Zealand, the Netherlands, the UK, and the USA, to name a few (WEF, 2024a). Rankings differ depending on how inequality is measured in various international reports – either by outcome or opportunity. The factors considered can significantly impact a country's ranking (Gromada et al., 2018). Nonetheless, the rankings provide some guidance to current realities.

Australia

Often perceived as a first-world nation symbolising excellence, Australia surprisingly faces significant educational challenges. Improving education in Australia, in theory, aligns with the country's pledge to provide every child with quality and equitable education by 2030. This commitment also reflects Australia's endorsement of Goal 4 of the SDGs (OECD, 2020; UN, 2017) – signed by all 193 UN member states – signalling a global commitment to achieving inclusive, equitable, and quality education for all by 2030. The reality, however, does not clearly reflect these commitments.

For example, the UN's Children's Fund (UNICEF) reveals that Australia's education system is one of the "most unequal in the world" (Chzhen et al., 2018:10). The study examined educational disparities across 41 nations. UNICEF's research specifically focused on reading proficiency among the 41 countries assessed (Chzhen et al., 2018). The CEDAW Committee (Chapter 2) recommended that Australia improve its education system (CEDAW, 2018). Australia was ranked 84th for educational attainment (WEF, 2024a).

One important factor adding to the confusing results is that a "single national system of education" has not been adopted in Australia, partly because "hostile" religious leaders openly oppose a nationwide approach (Barker, 2020:150).

The inclusion of religion in schools continues to be debated by scholars and in public forums, despite the claim that education in Australia is "free and secular" and has traditionally excluded general religious education (Peterson, 2016:217). However, there has been an ongoing national debate about tolerating religious schools that discriminate based on sex (Barker, 2020). An equitable solution has yet to be established.

The Australian SDA prohibits discrimination; nevertheless, there are "exemptions" for religious purposes (Peterson, 2016:146) that continue to enable prejudices. Living and learning in a wealthy nation does not inherently provide equal opportunity (Chapters 4, 6 & 7). The complexities of the various measurements and results also illustrate that XXs continue to face obstacles globally (Chzhen et al., 2018; OECD, 2020).

The EU

Sweden, for example, ranked 29th (WEF, 2024a), began transitioning to coeducational institutions in the 1920s, with the conversion largely completed by the late 1970s (Hjörne, 2016). In contrast, XXs in France retained single-sex schools until the end of the 20th c.

Finland, ranked 33rd, and Norway 74th (WEF, 2024a), also reveal evidence supporting single-sex education. Finland's coeducational programmes, which incorporate nationwide anti-bias training for educators, led to more than five in six (85%) schools reporting a more inclusive classroom environment. Similarly, coeducation reforms in Norway enhanced students' readiness to confront discriminatory practices, with around nine in ten (87%) students surveyed acknowledged the significance of equality in both academic and social settings (Aragonés-González et al., 2020).

In Poland, ranked 53rd (WEF, 2024a), researchers investigated whether single-sex schools provided XXs with a significant advantage compared to coeducational settings (Koniewski & Hawrot, 2022). The results were notable, illustrating that XXs in single-sex schools scored significantly higher in science – a difference that was statistically significant. In the humanities, XXs scored slightly higher, too, though these differences were statistically insignificant.

In Spain, ranked 41st (WEF, 2024a), studies also demonstrated that coeducational settings enhance social integration by providing opportunities for XXs and XYs to learn and collaborate, creating shared learning experiences that confront traditional sex-based roles. In Catalonia, northern Spain, a programme designed to promote sex-neutral behaviours reported that around nine in ten (93%) participating students showed significant improvement in respectful communication and collaborative problem-solving skills. Similarly, in Andalusia, southern Spain, a pilot study focused on coeducational team-based learning revealing that the vast majority of teachers (91%) observed a decline in sex-based conflicts and an increase in mixed-sex group participation during classroom activities. These findings suggest that coeducational reforms, when supported by structured interventions and comprehensive teacher training, can effectively break down sex-based hierarchies and create respectful and inclusive learning environments (Aragonés-González et al., 2020).

India

Ranked 112th (WEF, 2024a), despite significant differences in cultural and religious backgrounds, similar patterns are observed in India. For example, the emotional maturity of adolescents from coeducational and single-sex schools revealed that students from coeducational schools were more emotionally developed, socially adjusted, and independent. These differences were attributed to variations in school environments, traditions, and sex composition (Rawat & Singh, 2016).

Another study indicated that a lack of diverse peer interactions – considered crucial for disrupting sex-based stereotypes – limited opportunities for socialisation and reinforced existing sex and caste hierarchies in single-sex schools (Narwana & Rathee, 2019). Additionally, the intersection of poverty and caste-based patriarchal expectations, which often require young XXs to work, further restricts their freedoms and negatively impacts their school experiences (Yunus, 2021).

The UK

Educational attainment for XXs has improved significantly in the UK, ranked 34th in 2023 and climbing to 1st place in 2024 (WEF, 2024a).

Single-sex institutions, particularly those affiliated with the Catholic Church, maintained their single-sex philosophies even as coeducational schools became the predominant model by the late 19th century. Parents with conservative notions favoured single-sex schooling to reinforce traditional sex-based roles and uphold moral values. The shift towards coeducation was influenced by educational reform and socio-political factors that reflected broader cultural changes aimed at advancing equality in education. This approach was initially championed by the Victorian Board of Education in the late 1860s to enhance cost-effectiveness and widen educational access (Carole, 2021).

In 2023, the Independent Schools Council Census (2023) provided detailed insights into student enrolments and educational trends across England, Northern Ireland, Scotland, and Wales. Coeducational schools dominated the independent sector, representing four in five (81%) independent schools. A total of 159 schools catered exclusively to XXs and 106 to XYs in the UK (ISC, 2023), indicating a continued decline in single-sex educations as many institutions transition to coeducational models and/or announce plans to do so (Talk Education, 2024; ISC, 2023).

Past, current, and proposed policy changes suggest that discussions surrounding morality, economic considerations, and sex-based dynamics have influenced, and continue to influence, educational policies in the UK (Carole, 2021).

The USA

In the USA, the debate surrounding single-sex versus coeducational schooling also remains prominent (Charbonneau et al., 2022; Pahlke & Hyde, 2016; Riordan, 2015). Research indicates that students in single-sex schools typically achieve higher academic success and exhibit more favourable socio-emotional outcomes compared to students in coeducational schools, even when accounting for various economic and social determinants (Riordan, 2015). However, single-sex schools often operate under the assumption that impediments to success are unrelated to sex, race, class, ability, or religion.

Approximately 1,600 public schools in the USA offer single-sex classes or function as single-sex institutions. Critics argue that separating students by sex reinforces stereotypes and reduces opportunities for XXs and XYs to collaborate, which is vital for developing socio-emotional skills (Pahlke & Hyde, 2016).

One meta-analysis of 184 studies found that, after accounting for factors including socio-economic background, differences in academic performance between students in single-sex and coeducational schools were minimal. Additionally, socio-emotional outcomes, including self-esteem, body image, and peer relationships, showed little variation between the two school types. Research in the USA suggests that single-sex schooling does not consistently provide significant academic or social advantages over coeducation (Pahlke & Hyde, 2016).

Canada – ranked 55th (WEF, 2024a) – experiences similar obstacles to the USA, with research indicating that students in single-sex schools often feel restricted by traditional expectations and experience greater peer pressure to conform to stereotypical sex-based norms. This includes how a person's behaviour aligns with expectations of femininity and masculinity (Drury, et al., 2013). For example, assertiveness and rivalry were often associated with XYs, whereas caring and compassion were traits linked to XXs, suggesting that these sex-specific associations may lead to anxiety in single-sex school settings when students were surrounded by others perceived as similar to themselves (Charbonneau et al., 2022).

In contrast, XYs in coeducational schools in Canada reported experiencing less pressure and having more opportunities to explore a wider range of roles, while XXs in these environments experienced higher levels of classroom anxiety – a pattern not observed among XYs. Coeducational schools tended to place less emphasis on traditional feminine stereotypes than single-sex schools, with peer dynamics influencing both academic performance and social behaviour (Charbonneau et al., 2022).

Coeducational and single-sex schooling continue to be widely debated, while the homeschooling movement has also grown in popularity across several nations.

Homeschooling

The homeschooling movement emerged as a political and cultural reaction against compulsory schooling laws, gaining momentum in the late 1970s.

Where it originated is debated; nevertheless, its popularity is increasing in some nations.

In Australia, around 40,000 students are homeschooled – double the numbers recorded prior to 2019, partially attributable to the COVID-19 pandemic, marking an all-time high across the country. The growth of the homeschooling movement has been increasing by rising dissatisfaction with traditional schooling models (Blok et al., 2021; Cassidy, 2023a).

Exact numbers in the EU are inconsistent, with some data unavailable, partly caused by fragmented record-keeping systems. The regulation and participation rates vary significantly throughout; however, homeschooling is permitted in most countries. Between less than 0.1% and 1% of the student population is estimated to be homeschooled in the EU (Hána & Kostelecká, 2022).

Germany, for example, enforces strict regulations against homeschooling, permitting it only in exceptional cases. Similarly, Sweden allows homeschooling only under strict circumstances, including health or travel-related issues. France has legalised homeschooling but with some degree of oversight. In the Netherlands, school attendance is mandatory for all children, with homeschooling allowed solely through a religious exemption. The vast majority of countries require parents to inform authorities of their homeschooling activities (Blok et al., 2021; Hána & Kostelecká, 2022; Progressive Schooling, n.d.).

In India, homeschooling is also increasing in popularity, mainly in metropolitan areas, with an estimated annual growth rate ranging from approximately one in 50 (2%) to one in 12 (8%). There is also a rising interest in hybrid education models that combine home-based, digital, and traditional learning methods (Blok et al., 2021; Divekar et al., 2025).

In rural regions of India, students often struggle to resist deeply inculcated cultural norms due to limited exposure to progressive educational influences – a dynamic that can similarly occur in isolated homeschooling settings (Narwana & Rathee, 2019).

Additionally, there are those who still believe that educating XX individuals is a futile effort, operating under the assumption that XXs will eventually marry and rely on a man, rendering their education pointless. As a result, the education of XXs is often viewed as a waste of time, an unproductive use of parental effort, or an unjustifiable expense to community resources. In contrast, XYs are frequently granted access to educational facilities and resources, regardless of their abilities.

In India young XXs are pressured, assigned to, and/or confined to domestic and caregiving duties or child marriages (Chapters 2 & 3), many with no real alternatives, despite numerous laws and policies (Sah, 2022; Sahni & Shankar, 2012).

In the UK, legalised homeschooling is subject to some degree of oversight (Blok et al., 2021). The exact numbers for homeschooling are not available; again, due to issues around centralised records. However, estimates range from 50,000 to 150,000, with around one in seven (15%) students from working-class socioeconomic backgrounds (Kraftl, 2013), raising concerns about equity and educational access.

In the USA, homeschooling was legally recognised across all states by the 1980s and 1990s, supported by grassroots activism and legal victories. Distrust of public institutions led to homeschooling increasing as parents pursued more influence over their children's education (Blok et al., 2021). The US Census Bureau's *Household Pulse Survey* has identified new educational patterns across the country; the latest findings, from December 2024, reveal the prevalence of homeschooling between September 2022 and August 2023, with approximately one in 17 (6%) school-aged children reported as homeschooled during the same school period – compared to one in 36 (2.8%) in 2019, indicating an increase of more than 114%. In comparison, one in ten (10%) students attend private schools in the USA, while five in six (84%) are enrolled in public schools (Smith & Watson, 2024; U.S. Census Bureau, 2024).

Homeschooling, albeit providing more control for parents, is also raising concerns in the USA that it is "undermining national unity" (Blok et al., 2021:396), while others dread potential severe health ramifications (Thorell et al., 2022).

Single-Sex versus Coeducation

Educational equality is examined in terms of access to education, classroom engagement, subject choices, and achieving academic parity among the sexes. UNESCO (2017) has questioned whether XXs are safer and receive a better education in single-sex schools compared to coeducational schools. Nonetheless, there is no definitive resolution regarding the best way to educate XXs, as international research remains divided and fails to provide a clear consensus.

Some research suggests that single-sex schools offer small to moderate benefits, whilst other studies find no significant effects. One reason for the mixed results is the difficulty of randomly placing students into single-sex and coeducational schools; age differences further complicate meaningful comparisons (Pahlke & Hyde, 2016).

The varying results from across the globe over the past two decades suggest that the benefits of single-sex schools may depend on multiple contextual factors, including sociological and cultural elements, in addition to the effects of sex segregation. Studies conducted across different countries illustrate both the advantages and disadvantages of single-sex and coeducational schools.

Globally, the dominance of single-sex schools began to decline in the 20th c., with public coeducational schools becoming the standard in many Western countries. The modification away from single-sex schooling has been partly driven by the introduction of anti-discrimination laws and increased secularisation in nations that now predominantly favour coeducational schools.

The debate between single-sex and coeducational schooling has primarily focused on educational attainment and the impact on XXs and XYs in rectifying entrenched sex-based prejudice (Narwana & Rathee, 2019). This long-standing debate has raised numerous important questions for parents, teachers, governments, and the international community. Several developed nations continue segregating in primary and secondary schools, including Australia, Ireland, Israel, the UK, and numerous Muslim-majority countries.

Single-sex education frequently receives support from conservative and religious groups and is further reinforced by cultural traditions and societal norms. Reversely, coeducational schools are generally viewed as superior in cultivating advanced social and collaborative skills compared to single-sex educational settings. Coeducational schools are believed to improve critical thinking for XXs (Narwana & Rathee, 2019) and recognised as being more effective at promoting social and collaborative skills (Coren & Luthar, 2014).

The influence of different schooling approaches on confronting and dismantling entrenched sex-based stereotypes remains a central focus of international agendas (Narwana & Rathee, 2017). Moreover, the assumption that XXs obtain power through education alone ignores the fact that they continue to bear the historical burden of exclusion and entrenched sex-specific expectations (McCall, 2019).

Keeping students separated, nonetheless, is beneficial for XYs (Coren & Luthar, 2014), with some research suggesting their academic performance may decline in coeducational settings (Aragonés-González et al., 2020).

Others highlight that single-sex schools often create an environment where XXs feel more comfortable academically and emotionally, free from distractions that may arise in mixed settings. However, single-sex environments can also reinforce biases, as seen in classroom dynamics where greater emphasis is placed on sex differences (Pahlke & Hyde, 2016).

Advocates of single-sex education contend that sex divisions can improve educational outcomes by catering to distinct learning preferences. For example, XYs are believed to thrive in active, high-energy learning environments, whereas XXs are perceived to excel in calm, tranquil purposeful spaces (Pahlke & Hyde, 2016).

Sustained segregation in education often channels a majority of XY students towards STEM subjects. However, studies also indicate that segregated schooling does not benefit both sexes equally and may, in fact, reinforce sexism and perpetuate entrenched sex-based stereotypes (Sikora, 2014), negatively impacting XXs. In other words, the socio-emotional well-being of XXs appears to improve when the opposite sex is absent. However, peer pressure can also limit positive outcomes, even in a supportive learning environment, as peer dynamics among XXs reinforce competitive behaviours and expectations based on sex-based stereotypes.

Cultural stereotypes related to how either sex ought to present and conduct themselves, combined with peer pressure, suggest that XXs face more obstacles than XYs when pursuing an education. One of several restraints is the pervasiveness of sexual harassment, often described as a common aspect of interactions in coeducational schools and even perceived as a form of entertainment by some XY students (Edwards et al., 2024; Jones & Mahony, 1989; Murnen & Smolak, 2000; Robinson, 2005; UNESCO, 2017), leading to chauvinistic behaviours in schools, as reviewed in the "Masculine Toxic Traits in Schools" section in this chapter.

A study in Korea, for example, indicated that attending single-sex schools reduced the risk of depression among XX students, with no significant effect observed in XY students. Stress-related factors indicated that single-sex education eased the pressures associated with peer interactions, particularly for XXs, revealing that the social and emotional benefits of single-sex schooling may be greater than previously recognised by researchers and policymakers (Kim & Kim, 2024).

Proponents of single-sex education argue that separating XXs from XYs in classrooms or schools enhances academic performance by addressing sexism in coeducational environments instead of promoting sex-based differences. Conversely, critics claim that sex segregation reinforces negative stereotypes and has minimal impact on academic achievement. Although numerous empirical studies have been conducted on the effects of single-sex education, findings remain inconsistent. Nonetheless, single-sex schools have been associated with increased academic focus and social support (Pahlke & Hyde, 2016).

Students in single-sex schools also display higher educational outcomes compared to their coeducational peers, with XYs achieving a 5% to 10% advantage and XXs securing a 4% to 7% advantage (Charbonneau et al., 2022). Despite these gains, the persistence of sex-segregated practices continues to inhibit progress (Feniger, 2011).

Additionally, global research consistently illustrates that XXs outperform XYs in advanced degree programmes, both in terms of grades and completion rates (Institute for Women's Policy Research, 2015; Weaver-Hightower, 2010). These achievements are particularly noteworthy, given that adolescents (13 to 19 years) undergo significant hormonal changes that affect their bodies and minds, subsequently impacting their academic performance and overall physical and mental well-being (Latif, 2022).

Nevertheless, global data continues to reveal substantial disparities in STEM participation.

STEM Deficiencies

The 17 SDGs introduced by the UN in 2016 include initiatives to increase the number of XXs studying STEM subjects (OECD, 2020). Global data highlights persistent gaps in enrolment, graduation rates, and workforce involvement across diverse STEM disciplines, with XXs accounting for around one in three (35%) students pursuing STEM subjects in higher education and occupying less than one in three (29%) STEM jobs in the global workforce (Ro et al., 2022).

Pursuing a career in STEM remains difficult and arduous for many XXs, as they must perpetually resist institutional boundaries that suppress, undermine, and destabilise their potential and devalue their contributions. Addressing the numerous disparities requires sustained efforts to erode patriarchal concepts at all levels – students, graduates, employers, teachers, and policymakers. Developing and cultivating mindsets where equity is not merely promoted but expected, spanning from classrooms to boardrooms, is paramount, especially considering the speed at which technology is developing.

Some governments' strategies are addressing recommendations in response to criticisms from the CEDAW Committee and other stakeholders by increasing the representation of XXs in STEM fields. For example, the Advancing Women in STEM 2020 Action Plan (DISR, 2020; OECD, 2023) stated its aim to boost the number of XXs pursuing STEM careers and to increase the visibility of XXs in STEM roles.

Australia

One Australian conservative government's strategy to increase the number of XXs studying tertiary STEM courses reduced university fees for STEM courses in 2021. Stakeholders, however, held differing opinions on the initiative and its effectiveness.

The consequences of incentivising XXs to study STEM were expected to have a negative impact on students studying arts and humanities subjects. Research from one group of scholars, anticipating the proposed changes, indicated a dramatic decline in XX student enrolments in higher education overall when the cost of university humanities courses increased.

Fees rose to AU$15,152 (US$9,293) per year for business, law, and humanities courses – costing students four times more than STEM – AU$4,124 (US$2,529). The reforms, however, have been ineffective, with peak university bodies calling for their repeal (Cassidy, 2023b) as the numbers have barely increased. Less than a quarter of the total STEM student population are XXs, shirfting from 34% in 2015 to 37% in 2024 (DISR, 2022, 2024).

One factor contributing to the low number of XXs in STEM in Australia is differing preferences. For example, XX students excel in collaborative and interactive settings, where teamwork and engagement support their success. In contrast, XY students gravitate towards competitive, individualistic environments, where the desire to outperform peers serves as a central motivator (Fisher et al., 2020).

The EU

More than half of university students in the EU are XXs – between 49% and 56% depending on the country – yet their representation in technical disciplines remains stagnant, and they continue to be underrepresented in STEM fields, with XXs accounting for just above one in three (35%) of STEM students. General data indicates that around 70% of XXs and 66% of XYs in the EU, including the Europe and Central Asia (ECA) region, enrol in tertiary education (de las Cuevas et al., 2022; Munoz Boudet et al., 2021; World Bank, 2023).

Various assessments across EU school levels indicate that XX students excel in reading and specific areas of science, while XY students tend to perform better in advanced mathematics and physical sciences. Policy recommendations include early educational intervention to eliminate stereotypes, increase the visibility of XX role models, and stregthen support systems from primary schooling through to professional careers.

Numerous EU projects aimed at increasing XX participation in STEM – including coding camps to build interest in programming, robotics, and computer science among young XXs – have not translated into increased interest levels (de las Cuevas et al., 2022; Munoz Boudet et al., 2021).

Despite the various initiatives, the percentage of XXs in STEM remains disproportionately low compared to XYs. In Spain, for example, only one in four (25%) XX students pursue STEM subjects. Even after educational reforms, XX enrolment in engineering programmes decreased from 32% to 25% over a 13-year period. With three in five (60%) students perceiving engineering as an XY–dominated field, the lack of XX role models further exacerbates the exclusionary patterns. In high schools, 14% fewer XXs compared to XYs express interest in engineering, with this gap widening to 31% fewer XXs at university levels (de las Cuevas et al., 2022).

Overall, while progress has been made in increasing the representation of XXs in STEM, significant disparities persist due to entrenched stereotypes, self-efficacy issues, and structural obstructions. Further efforts are required across the EU to improve educational reform, increase role model visibility, and create supportive learning environments (de las Cuevas et al., 2022; Munoz Boudet et al., 2021).

India

Similar issues are being encountered in India to those in Australia and the EU. However, media reports indicate a rising trend in online STEM education enrolments among XXs, suggesting a growing preference for courses in AI, Machine Learning (ML), and IT (Information Technology) across India.

A 12% increase in enrolments was reported from 2023 to 2024. Retention rates, however, are a concern, with around three in five (62%) XX students completing online STEM courses compared to three in four (75%) XY students (India Today Education Desk, 2024).

The UK

As in other developed and developing economies, XXs in the UK continue to be underrepresented in STEM studies (Women in STEM, n.d.-a).

Around 17% of computer science undergraduates and less than 16% of engineering students are XXs, underscoring a persistent gap despite ongoing efforts to promote inclusivity (de las Cuevas et al., 2022).

The USA

At all school levels, the proportion of XXs and XYs taking math and science courses is approximately equal and remains largely consistent when students leave high school. However, this balance shifts at university, where XYs are more likely choose to pursue STEM-related degrees. Among first-year university students, XXs are significantly less likely than XYs to express an intention to major in STEM (Ro et al., 2022).

By the time students graduate, XXs are in the minority across most STEM disciplines, accounting for around one in three (36%) science graduates on average, with some areas within STEM fields showing even lower levels of XX representation (Women in STEM, n.d.-b).

Non-white students, encountering intersectional discrimination, are also significantly underrepresented in STEM fields in the USA (Ro et al., 2022).

Overall, global data reveals a gradual increase in the representation of XX students in specific STEM fields. However, in specific disciplines, including computer science and engineering, significant disparities remain between XXs and XYs.

Irrespective of the subject's students' study, expectations regarding their appearance in educational settings generate considerable debate, as attire can further restrict opportunities and impose additional constraints.

Debates about school uniforms are especially significant for XXs, as expectations surrounding dress and presentation often reinforce misogynistic norms and control behaviour.

School Uniforms

Restrictive uniforms that limit movement are a point of contention. Policies promoting traditionally feminine uniforms, often with specific hem-length requirements, deny XXs autonomy and restrict their ability to enjoy the same freedom of movement as their XY peers, with systems akin to those enforced in prisons (Friedrich & Shanks, 2023).

Under the guise of homogenising, while simultaneously differentiating and categorising students, uniform policies impose sexist standards for students, reinforcing traditional roles and limiting opportunities (Friedrich & Shanks, 2023). Strict regulations subject XXs to rules that control and sexualise their bodies (Reidy, 2021), reinforcing divisions among students – for example, while skirts and dresses are mandated for XXs, trousers are often restricted to XYs.

These practices further entrench power structures, inequalities, and distinctions, perpetuating androcentric disciplinary practices that dictate how XXs should present in public (Friedrich & Shanks, 2023). Moreover, uniforms that expose and constrain XXs contribute to their sexualisation (Aapola et al., 2005; Reidy, 2021), a practice often embedded in a school's philosophy.

School uniforms can also have adverse effects on health outcomes and negatively impact students. Poorly designed uniforms – including short dresses/skirts in winter, for example – or improper fit and synthetic fabrics can cause physical discomfort and distract students from learning (Reidy, 2021).

A study in Mongolia examined the impact of school uniforms on students' health and education (Sabic-El-Rayess et al., 2020), signaling that the cost of uniforms symbolically excludes students from less affluent backgrounds, resulting in higher dropout rates. Another study in NZ reported similar findings, illustrating that school uniforms impose a significant financial burden on families, particularly those from lower socioeconomic backgrounds (Reidy, 2021), with the high costs also contributing to dropout rates as families cannot afford the mandatory uniforms.

In Scotland, another study examined how uniforms dictate power relations, revealing that uniforms do more than create uniformity; instead, they regiment, divide, and classify students, demonstrating that old-school regulatory enforcement is prevalent and continues to cause harm (Friedrich & Shanks, 2023). Conservative policies often justify controlling practices as necessary for discipline, claiming that uniforms prepare students for the job market and help shape them into respectable, employable adults.

Additionally, uniform requirements for junior and senior students can create a visible power structure. Policies that fail to accommodate cultural or religious attire further marginalise students from diverse backgrounds, making them feel excluded or pressured to conform to dominant norms. The visible distinctions created by uniforms contribute to alienation and inferiority among less affluent students (Friedrich & Shanks, 2023). The competitive visual nature of uniforms often contributes to emotional and physical stress, further eroding some students' learning experiences.

The harmful effects that unequal policies initiate restrict the ability of students to learn – both in the present and in defining ambitions, future outcomes, and destinies (Sabic-El-Rayess et al., 2020). School policies are contributing to the objectification of XXs and creating unequal educational environments that, in some cases, increase VAW.

The persistent enforcement of patriarchal directives, differential treatment, and harmful stereotypes in schools underscore the urgent need for reform. A balanced and equitable lens is urgently needed to deliver justice, eliminate hazardous power imbalances, abolish discriminatory dress codes and eliminate language that reinforces sexism, while addressing the role of education in perpetuating VAW, misogyny, and control, which are increasingly exhibited through toxic masculine actions (Aragonés-González et al., 2020; Rajiva, 2023).

Toxic Traits

The spread of toxic masculinity in schools is not a new phenomenon, but rather a persistent manifestation of the patriarchy that has resurfaced in schools with alarming speed (Gukurume & Shoko, 2023; Orchard & Sangaraganesan, 2023), propelled by cultural narratives that determine attitudes and expectations of current and future generations.

A new wave of implicit and explicit sex-based violence in schools since the start of the 21st century has alarmed parents, governments, and teachers and motivated researchers to investigate the escalation of sexual violence (Pina et al., 2022). The data highlights the universal prevalence of sexual violence in schools, stressing the need for international engagement and immediate intervention (Pina et al., 2022).

The *Global Status Report on School Violence and Bullying* exposes the alarming frequency of sexual violence in schools, constituting a global violation of young people's rights (UNESCO, 2017). The prevalence of toxic behaviours reveals a deteriorating, and potential irreparable, reality. Sexual harassment is frequently normalised and inadequately addressed in educational settings, which is deeply unsettling, though unsurprising, given the widespread experiences of VAW and girls.

Violent actions often develop early in human behaviour (Pina et al., 2022). While individuals aged 10 to 25 have expressed intolerance for VAW by XYs, they have also justified sexual violence and coercion over the past 20 years (Edwards et al., 2024).

Considering diverse backgrounds, cultures, and socioeconomic environments that condition attitudes, it is evident that sex dictates perceptions and the identification of VAW. The alarming societal emergency, with its complex and vile expressions, is partly fuelled by stereotypical sex-based labels, patriarchal models, and toxic masculine expectations that exacerbate VAW (Chapters 2 & 4). This crisis includes sexual abuse, sex-based bullying, and sexual harassment among students.

The exact number of students experiencing sexual violence in schools is unconfirmed; few report their experiences due to fear of retribution, further exacerbating the violent pandemic and making it impossible to calculate the exact number of student assaults. What is confirmed is that XX students experience sexual violence at significantly higher rates than their XY counterparts, with UNESCO revealing that one in ten students has reported experiencing sexual violence, with higher prevalence rates in certain regions (UNESCO, 2017).

For example, in Sweden, around one in eight (12%) students report violations, followed by one in nine (11%) in both Norway and the USA; one in ten (10%) in France, around 9% in the UK, one in twelve (8%) in Spain, and one in seven (15%) students in India report experiencing sexual violence, the highest percentage among the countries reviewed (UNESCO, 2017). The true scale of unreported cases is typically at least three times higher than the recorded figures, revealing a deeply concerning and pervasive global crisis – comparable to the widespread violence that continues to devastate XX adults.

Although statistics represent only a portion of all incidents, one consensus exists: this violence is sex-based, with XYs being more prone to violent behaviour than XXs in classroom settings (Pina et al., 2022). Most experts agree that measures to dissolve toxic masculinity are needed now, more than ever.

Schools, intended to be safe spaces for education, can instead become sites of danger and harm for some students. The toxic masculine behaviours exhibited in schools disrupt educational practices and degrade the mental health of XXs, who may begin to internalise patterns of violence throughout their education. Without effective interventions, these destructive behaviours often persist into adulthood (Narusyte et al., 2017).

When gripped by fear and anxiety, XXs who experience violence and harassment in educational settings suffer declines in self-esteem and body image. These belligerent tactics reinforce toxic masculine power dynamics and often escalate into physical violence. In contrast, XY students' self-esteem typically remains unaffected, often interpreting harassment as flattering rather than distressing (Murnen & Smolak, 2000; Pina et al., 2022).

Violent behaviours are modelled by various factors, including social norms, peer influences, and the desire to establish dominance within social groups (Pina et al., 2022). Using violence for amusement, some XY students engage in aggressive actions to entertain themselves or enhance their self-esteem, much like the gratification derived from video games or films.

In environments where physical strength is valued, such as sports, and where peer pressure encourages schadenfreude (experiencing satisfaction from the suffering of others), viciousness becomes a means to gain attention, boost self-esteem, and affirm social status (Caro García & Monreal Gimeno, 2017; Murnen & Smolak, 2000; Pina et al., 2022).

By integrating sexual harassment into their identity, XY students gain and maintain social popularity at school. In some cultures, toxic masculine behaviours are also rationalised as flattery, signs of love or affection, with jealousy and possessiveness mistaken for romantic attraction (Caro García & Monreal Gimeno, 2017).

However, it is the XYs' perceptions and behaviours that demand change, not XXs'. For example, XY students often use sexual harassment as a tool to assert dominance and align with cultural expectations of masculinity (Robinson, 2005). Social norms and expectations can often appear as invisible rules that people practice and eventually adopt as default routines – habitual behaviours performed without conscious thought – that emerge from unconscious psychological patterns (Brekhus et al., 2024). These behaviours often develop from enduring toxic masculine philosophies based on phallocentric views that make VAW seem almost normal and thus accepted or ignored.

In India, for example, most adults believe that educating XXs to behave modestly in heterosexual relationships is the best way to ensure their safety (Diamant, 2022). Meanwhile, sex education in Australia and other nations has been criticised for its inadequacies, lacking real-life scenarios and relevant information. In the USA, for example, students reported a superficial understanding of sexual assault and noted that sex education perpetuated myths rather than correcting them (Muscari et al., 2023).

One student who refused to ignore school violence in Australia took action; what they discovered was both painful and frightening. Chanel Contos launched an anonymous online survey to understand the prevalence of sexual assault and harassment among high school students in 2021. The survey asked students if they had experienced sexual assault at school. More than 6,700 responses revealed sexual violence on school premises, at school events, and during social gatherings (Contos, 2021).

Many students exposed the misogyny and androcentric perspectives among XY students that were normalised, emphasising a lack of support for XX students. Fear of retaliation and scepticism often deterred XXs from reporting incidents. As a result, many XX students experienced shame, guilt, trauma, and academic setbacks.

Contos' survey revealed the pervasiveness of toxic masculinity and the urgent need for sexual consent education in schools across the nation. With the testimonials collected, Contos launched the *Teach Us Consent* campaign (Burns et al., 2024), which successfully advocated for the introduction of sexual consent education in all schools (McDonough, 2022).

By 2023, the Australian Government had legislated changes to the curriculum, aiming to address sex-based discrimination, stereotypes, and coercion. According to the Department of Education:

> The Consent and Respectful Relationships Education measure supports the wellbeing of Australian primary and secondary school students through expert-developed, high-quality, evidence-based, and age-appropriate consent and respectful relationships education.
>
> (Department of Education, 2022)

The actions of one XX adolescent demonstrate how a single individual can inspire others to speak out, raise awareness, mobilise a nation, and initiate legislative change that transforms lives.

Sexual violence in schools has short- and long-term personal, social, and economic consequences. Global studies indicate that sex-based violence in schools leads to increased absenteeism, higher dropout rates, declining grades, and emotional instability (Dunne et al., 2006; Pina et al., 2022). Ensuring secure, inclusive learning environments for all students, regardless of where, how, or what they study, is essential (UNESCO, 2023).

Who should be responsible for implementing the necessary changes is also a point of contention. Some argue that the responsibility lies with parents and teachers. While both play pivotal roles in influencing young minds, teachers are often at the frontline, tasked with complicated social and cultural stereotypes while attempting to develop positive student engagement (Kelly et al., 2023).

Teachers and parents alone, however, cannot change culture, conventions, practices, and behaviours, nor can they implement legislation or rectify systemic educational policy deficiencies. Hence, all stakeholders – policymakers, communities, teachers, principals, and religious leaders – must take immediate, decisive action to enforce urgent and irreversible changes in educational institutions around the globe to stop the violence.

Self-defence classes are one option researchers confirm is highly effective and can potentially reduce and/or prevent violence. For example, to understand the psychosocial effects of Taekwondo training on students, researchers conducted a meta-analysis of 28 studies carried out between 1985 and 2019, revealing that participants became more law-abiding, cooperative, and responsible after six months of Taekwondo training. The study also revealed that participants increased their sense of community and self-esteem and improved their psychosocial characteristics, resulting in better school-life adjustments (Kim et al., 2021). Potential for long-term, positive changes in attitudes and behaviours towards violence was also attained (Jordan & Mossman, 2019). More on this subject in the toolkit.

The Educators

Teachers, the overwhelming majority of whom are XXs globally (McGregor, 2020), are not adequately supported or equipped to overcome the regulations that sustain violence and discrimination in educational settings. Student perpetrated abuse – identified as teacher-directed violence (TDV) – is also profoundly problematic in various nations (Bounds & Jenkins, 2018; Reddy et al., 2013).

While teachers are essential in leading transformation, they require substantial support and training to enhance their work. Addressing their own norms and biases is also crucial for disbanding patriarchal structures and eradicating violence in schools, including instances where teachers themselves target XX students (Dunne et al., 2006).

Teacher training in sex-sensitive educational methods is inconsistently provided, limiting the effectiveness of coeducational reforms. While teachers play a key role in leading change and establishing classroom culture, teachers also require strategic support to reflect on and adjust their sex-based views and assumptions (Aragonés-González et al., 2020).

For example, in 2021, Riley O'Keefe (2021), a high school student in Florida, USA, criticised her school for promoting and perpetuating sexism towards XXs. O'Keefe expressed embarrassment and frustration after her yearbook photo, along with those of 80 other XX students, were modified to cover their chests. The yearbook coordinator responsible for the alterations was an XX teacher. O'Keefe observed that she was made to feel ashamed of her body, whereas images of XYs in swimwear were left unedited. O'Keefe launched a petition to question the discriminatory policies, which led to the St. Johns County School Board removing sex-specific language from the dress code. However, O'Keefe emphasised that a fundamental issue was the teachers' over-sexualisation of XX students and their perception of the XX body as inherently problematic (Tanenbaum, 2022).

Students and teachers alone cannot eliminate the misogynistic, sexist conditions under which many XXs work and learn (McGregor, 2020). Effective change requires a collaborative approach involving school management, parents, students, and teachers (Dunne et al., 2006). Consensus on necessary reforms is crucial for achieving fairness and creating an inclusive educational environment free from patriarchal power and dominance.

Globally, XX teachers report higher levels of stress and burnout compared to their XY counterparts (Agyapong et al., 2022; McGregor, 2020). Stress and burnout remain considerable impediments, with some reports indicating serious problems, as up to four out of five (77%) educators experience mental fatigue and/or depression. Several contributing factors include insufficient professional development, negative school cultures, emotional demands from parents and students, TDV, and long working hours dedicated to school-related activities (Agyapong et al., 2022).

The COVID-19 pandemic further intensified the distress of both teachers and students (Wilson et al., 2024). However, inefficiencies and systemic neglect predate the pandemic. An analysis of 28 studies conducted in the USA, beginning in 1975, reveals that educators have persistently and continuously managed competing objectives and values. In particular, teachers are expected to treat all students equitably while addressing the unique needs of individuals. They must stimulate students intellectually and guide, motivate, and teach them how to maximise abilities and potential, while simultaneously safeguarding that no student is left behind (Kennedy, 2016). Managing these responsibilities demands exceptional skill and dedication, as teachers strive to maintain high standards while supporting each student's growth and success.

The numerous interconnected complexities confronted by teachers are resulting in a global shortage. UNESCO estimates that by 2030, 44 million additional teachers will be required to meet the aims of SDG Goal 4, which prioritises fair, accessible education and lifelong learning for all. The global demand for teachers presents a critical issue in the efforts to achieve universal primary education by 2030 (UNESCO, 2025). Income disparities and repetitive administrative tasks deter many from joining and/or remaining in the education profession.

Numerous countries have already implemented measures to strengthen the teaching workforce, including providing educators with AI tools, introducing legislation to protect both teachers and students (Dunne et al., 2006), offering professional resources, promoting well-being initiatives (Stone et al., 2023), and encouraging self-regulation, including refining and fine-tuning professional responsibilities (Braeunig et al., 2018) to ensure their safety and well-being.

Perhaps, one day soon, teachers will receive the recognition and financial compensation they rightfully deserve.

AI in Education

AIED is expected to have significant impacts; both positive benefits and negative risks on students, teachers, and governments globally (Gillani et al., 2023; Harry & Sayudin, 2023; Schiff, 2022).

AI tools are transforming traditional teaching methods by providing real-time feedback and personalised learning experiences. By automating repetitive tasks, including marking and attendance tracking, for example, AIED is facilitating teachers to dedicate more time to students and curriculum development. Additionally, AI-powered tools offer real-time insights into student performance, replacing traditional periodic assessments with continuous and interactive response systems, thereby improving engagement and academic outcomes (Harry & Sayudin, 2023; WEF, 2024b).

For example, AI tools can include machine learning (ML) – algorithms that analyse large quantities of data to identify patterns and make predictions for predefined goals, assisting teachers in estimating future grades, detecting and tracking students at risk of withdrawing or those facing academic struggles. ML can also provide reinforcement learning systems to improve knowledge, albeit by trial and error, rewarding achievements and addressing failures and errors. Tutoring systems can also employ ML to adjust questions based on students' previous answers, reinforcing strategies that augment learning. Intelligent tutoring systems (ITS) (Selwyn, 2024), a popular application of AIED, can also be adapted to students' existing knowledge to increase new competencies in more personalised ways (Gillani et al., 2023).

Numerous countries have announced national strategies detailing AI policies, development goals, and regulations. AIED policy frameworks from 24 nations, including Australia, Austria, China, Denmark, Finland, France, Germany, India, Malta, Norway, Spain, Sweden, the UK, and the USA, primarily focus on education for AI – preparing the workforce and advancing AI expertise – rather than generating AI into learning.

For example, France and Finland aim to enhance public understanding of AI, encouraging public resilience, alleviating doubts, and reducing concerns (Schiff, 2022). Spain and Malta are taking a balanced approach, considering both technological advancements and potential risks. Privacy and transparency in AIED are emphasised, with policies often incorporating feedback from educators and researchers in several EU countries (Harry & Sayudin, 2023; Schiff, 2022). Meanwhile, India is focusing on using AIED to bridge educational gaps, including improving access for students in remote communities (Schiff, 2022).

Other nations are focusing on workforce preparation rather than addressing AIED's potential ethical issues or pedagogical improvements, emphasising the need for more comprehensive frameworks that align with broader societal and educational goals. In addition, several strategies are prioritising the development of AI talent pipelines and public AI literacy to enhance economic performance (Schiff, 2022).

Australia, the UK, and the USA are incorporating AI literacy into syllabuses and educational programmes to develop cognitive reasoning and logical analysis, including virtual tutors, enhancing personalised learning, and increasing grading efficiency. Developed nations, including the UK, for example, reported substantial AI adoption, with more than two in five teachers (42%) using generative AI tools at the end of 2023 (Harry & Sayudin, 2023; Schiff, 2022; WEF, 2024b).

Globally, schools are now also utilising robots to process repetitive tasks, assist with STEM education, support students' writing, and perform duties traditionally carried out by humans (Hsiao et al., 2024; Orhani, 2023). However, some policies risk de-professionalising teachers. Whether robots will eventually replace educators altogether is a question that remains unanswered.

One of the many concerns is that AI algorithms are feared to potentially perpetuate inequalities, particularly when trained on biased data. Data privacy is another pressing issue, as the collection of large volumes of student information raises the risk of potential breaches. Uncertainties also extend to teacher autonomy and the widening of education gaps due to unequal access to AI tools. Nonetheless, current policies are largely focusing on ethical considerations rather than directly addressing practical dilemmas (Selwyn, 2024).

AIED's potential to perpetuate biases in training data could disproportionately disadvantage vulnerable groups. Resource-poor nations also face the risk of adopting AI as a cost-cutting measure, which may undermine local education systems and exacerbate inequalities. Therefore, prioritising ethical safeguards and ensuring robust human oversight are paramount to ensuring students worldwide are able to thrive in technology-driven economies (Gillani et al., 2023; Harry & Sayudin, 2023; Schiff, 2022; WEF, 2024b).

Irrespective of technological advancements, schools for XYs continue to outnumber those for XXs in many parts of the world. This disparity is particularly evident in countries with entrenched cultural biases, phallocentric religious mandates (Chapter 2), or socioeconomic structures that prioritise the education of XYs over XXs.

Cultural norms often position XYs as dominant, sexually assertive, and physically stronger, while XXs are described as weak and overly emotional (Scarduzio et al., 2017). Patriarchal structures confine XXs to subordinate roles and limit their access to education (Edwards et al., 2024), justifying these injustices through entrenched societal stereotypes (MacKinnon, 2017). Regardless of educational attainment, XXs are frequently expected to prioritise caregiving, while XYs resist parity in both theory and practice (Jackson, 2010, 2012). The belief that XXs contribute nothing and that their education is futile is demonstrably false; on the contrary, research shows that educating XXs reduces corruption and strengthens national economies (Hudson et al., 2015).

More than half of the 1%

The key to entering the field of higher education is obtaining a doctoral degree, aka as a PhD, which remains the pinnacle of academic achievement (Black & Garvis, 2018; Watson, 2024).

"Education is key to economic growth" (Gray, 2017), as PhD researchers discover cures for illnesses, share knowledge globally, design cutting-edge products, invent disruptive technologies, discover scientific solutions, and more. Over the past decades, the participation of XXs in PhD programmes and research has increased significantly in several countries (Whiting, 2018).

On average, one in 77 (1.3%) adults worldwide is awarded a PhD. Australia and the UK hold the most PhDs per capita in the world (WPR, 2024). The nations with the highest percentage of PhD holders also vary in distribution between XXs and XYs.

Slovenia ranks first in the world, with 3.6% of its population holding a doctorate, where XXs outnumber XYs. Switzerland follows in second place, with 2.5% of individuals attaining PhDs, XYs exceeding XXs. Luxembourg ranks third, reporting 2% of the population holds a doctorate, with XXs and XYs being nearly equal in numbers (WPR, 2024).

The USA, in fourth position, has 1.8% of the total population holding a PhD, with XXs and XYs equally represented. Sweden has 1.6%, also exhibiting a balanced distribution between the sexes. Germany, ranked sixth, has 1.4% of its population conferred with doctorates, with XYs representing twice as many PhDs as XXs (WPR, 2024).

In the UK, 1.3% of the population has a PhD, with similar proportions between XXs and XYs. Australia, ranking eighth, also records 1.3% of its population holding doctorates, with an almost identical split between XXs and XYs (WPR, 2024). The data for India is unclear when comparing reports, but around 0.5% of student enrolments in Indian universities are studying for a doctoral degree (British Council, 2024).

However, inequities also persist at higher academic levels, with systemic biases impeding progress and recognition (OECD, 2024). For example, XXs are cited, funded, published, and promoted less frequently than their XY colleagues (Watson, 2024) and continue to earn lower salaries. Sexist and androcentric structures deprive XXs of opportunities (OECD, 2024; Watson, 2024; Whiting, 2018), with the OECD warning of the urgent need for equitable access, targeted funding, and institutional reforms to bridge the gaps globally (OECD, 2024).

The "toxic academic culture" (Black & Garvis, 2018:87) is draining many XXs and pressuring others to leave respected centres of learning. The resilience and dedication of those XXs who remain are focused on researching ways to improve lives, while collaborating with governments, foundations, and businesses to solve real-world problems, aiming to develop and implement practical solutions.

Power has historically been systematically denied to XXs – a pattern that, regrettably, persists at the tertiary education level, irrespective of the lens through which it is viewed. Justice and balance are urgently needed within education systems, as egalitarianism will serve as a positive foundation for economic, cultural and educational development (Mason, 2006).

Conclusion

Achievements in educational progress indicate triumphs but also expose the adversities encountered by XXs in the quest for opportunities and knowledge.

On a positive note, significant advancements in education have been achieved globally, as evidenced by increased access to primary and secondary education and higher enrolment rates for XXs across various regions. Initiatives, including school policies and the UN's SDGs of Goal 4 (Quality Education) and Goal 5 (Gender Equality), reinforce international commitments to educational equality. Additionally, progress has been made in promoting coeducational learning environments that encourage collaboration and disrupt misogynistic stereotypes.

The debate over which educational settings are more productive and beneficial for students – single-sex or coeducational schools – continues without a clear resolution. Single-sex schools provide some benefits, whereas students in coeducational settings may encounter pressures to conform to androcentric stereotypes while remaining vulnerable to sex-based violence. Both educational models, however, provide students with benefits and limitations.

Cultural and religious assumptions uphold perceptions that XXs are the feeble sex, devaluing their abilities and contributions, further reinforcing exclusion. Such prejudices are unjust, intolerable, illegal, and destructive. Laws promoting equitable practices must be implemented, monitored, and incessantly enforced for substantial changes to occur.

The critical role of individual and community engagement and advocacy in propelling enduring change is illustrated with examples, including the *Teach Us Consent* campaign, illustrating the power of grassroots movements in influencing national education policies and promoting cultural shifts that prioritise safety and respect in schools.

Harmful practices, including enforcing restrictive uniforms for XXs and the spread of phallocentric toxic masculine attitudes and behaviours leading to sexual violence and sexual harassment in schools, destabilise the learning experiences and safety of XX students.

Despite the numerous negative predicaments for XX students, global data indicates they are generally outperforming their XY peers.

Technological advancements, including AIED, have introduced innovative methods that personalise learning experiences and automate time-consuming tasks for educators, potentially enhancing the teaching process. However, the ethical use of AIED has yet to be prioritised to prevent the amplification of existing prejudices and to protect student data and privacy, thereby avoiding the worsening of educational disparities between resource-rich and resource-poor schools.

Despite the many successes, the chapter illustrates that equitable participation has not yet been achieved, particularly in STEM disciplines, where participation rates remain disproportionately low. The sex-based income pay gap further highlights the broader structural inequalities that remain unresolved.

Legislation is required to deliver reform, together with commitments to the ongoing training and support for educators, the majority of whom are XXs dealing with immense pressures that deter them from staying in the vocation. Providing educators with the required resources, competitive salaries, professional development opportunities, and protections against teacher-directed violence is essential for building resilience and assuring retention globally.

Targeted interventions by parents, principals, and governments are also necessary to strengthen teachers' skills, support them in amplifying the visibility of XX role models, and promote the adoption of sex-neutral teaching practices. Collaboration is crucial in instigating legislations that guarantee equitable funding and accountability, particularly in developing regions where XXs continue to be denied fundamental educational opportunities.

As history has shown through the initiatives and achievements of visionaries in Africa, Australia, the EU, India, the UK, and the USA, and the many others not cited in this little book, every individual has the power to contribute to transforming education to better prepare XXs and continue disbanding patriarchal exploitative and oppressive educational systems.

The achievements of educational advocates, both included and excluded in this chapter, are powerful reminders of XXs' power and their ability to transform lives through education. Their contributions, alongside current educational models, accentuate that progress requires an intersectional and justice-oriented approach, as well as ongoing vigilance and critical examination, to safeguard human rights.

Ultimately, achieving educational equality demands sustained individual and global commitment, alongside coordinated collaboration among governments, educators, researchers, and communities. By initiating inclusive syllabuses, promoting critical thinking, and removing systemic limitations, education can be a powerful tool to enable positive transformations, with benefits that extend beyond individual achievement to the collective progress of national economies.

By underlining the benefits of supportive educational environments that achieve parity and respect, the world can advance towards a future where knowledge is embraced as a universal right and a powerful force for justice. It is through education that educators can equip XXs with the tools required, not only to survive, but to influence and take control of their own destinies – real power begins with knowledge.

"Education is the key to unlocking the world, a passport to freedom".

Oprah Gail Winfrey, American television producer, author, actor, talk show host, and media owner (*Tribune India*. 2025)

Toolkit

Refuse to Conform

If an XX student is restricted by school uniforms, it is imperative to resolve this with urgency. Physical and psychological comfort affect students' school activities and must be prioritised. Mandating skirts/dresses may inadvertently limit a student's mobility, confidence, and sense of autonomy.

As a parent, your voice is critical in advocating for sensible policies. Request a meeting with school administrators and present the evidence of how inclusive dress codes can improve learning outcomes. Rejecting oppressive, sexist uniforms is not merely about dress codes; it is symbolic of broader systemic restrictions that impact educational engagement. When students feel physically restricted, their cognitive focus is also impacted.

Preventing Toxic Masculinity

To reduce the risk of XYs inflicting sex-based violence, parents should go beyond discipline and begin with emotional responsiveness – teaching XYs that empathy, vulnerability, and respect are characteristics of strength, not signs of weakness. These teachings should be taking place at home, where XYs are being guided to understand that consent and accountability are essential and non-negotiable values. This also involves actively dismantling the attitudes and behaviours associated with toxic masculinity, which equate manhood with dominance, aggression, and emotional suppression. That means prioritising emotional intelligence over bravado, empathy over entitlement, and connection over control, while also challenging everyday stereotypes and speaking candidly about power, sex, and consent. Education should include more than academic accomplishment; parents and educators must embed emotional intelligence, respectful sexual behaviours, and responsibility in relationships as core strengths. Parents who model equitable behaviour and collaborate with schools to challenge outdated patriarchal norms can support XYs in developing integrity, compassion, and respectful equitable relationships.

Self-Defence Training

Since the beginning of the 21st c., violence in school settings has increased. Considering the consensus that 'prevention is better than cure', teaching self-defence to XXs should commence as soon as a student enters the education system, if not earlier, as a proactive prevention strategy to increase confidence and prevent potential incidents.

There are five convincing reasons policymakers, parents, and teachers should consider students participate in self-defence training:

1. Personal Safety: Provides the skills necessary to recognise and resist potentially dangerous situations, decreasing the number of sexual assault incidents and other forms of violence against XXs (Jordan & Mossman, 2019; European Parliament, 2016; Hollander, 2014; Thompson, 2014).

2. Awareness: Helps students gain a deeper understanding of the primary causes that influence abuse and violence, enabling individuals to identify and learn that crimes committed against them are not their fault (Jordan & Mossman, 2019). Awareness raises an understanding of the root causes of abuse and violence, allowing students to absolve themselves of self-blame.
3. Confidence: Self-defence training increases confidence and self-discipline, offering a sense of control, freedom and autonomy. It challenges stereotypes that construct XXs as the weaker, feeble sex, developing a more confident connection with the body by dismantling myths of physical inferiority. An increase in confidence assists in preventing and/or stopping attacks, whilst learning to physically defend themselves, use their voice more effectively, recognise risks, and assert their boundaries. The positive ripple effect also encourages XX students to advocate for human rights, thereby contributing to a more just and equitable society (Jordan & Mossman, 2019; European Parliament, 2016; Hollander, 2014; Thompson, 2014).
4. Health: Self-defence training increases physical fitness and contributes to improved mental health outcomes by reducing fear and anxiety, building positive self-images, resilience, and a sense of control over one's body and environment. Additionally, it enhances the ability to seek help, make safe informed decisions, and support others (Jordan & Mossman, 2019; European Parliament, 2016; Hollander, 2014; Thompson, 2014).
5. Perpetrator Accountability: Self-defence training reinforces the principle that perpetrators are responsible for their actions – an important step in removing the common narrative that blames survivors for the violence they experience (Thompson, 2014).

6 Financial Influences

Personal Note

I attended five different primary schools, and at each one, I encountered bullies. I was teased with names like "wog", "four-eyed freak", "ugly duckling", and "big-eyed fly", to name a few. The typical animal instinctive response to threats includes fight, flight, and freeze – I chose fawn. Unable to change my appearance, ethnicity, sex, or identity, I came up with a protection plan. My resource? Sweets. My strategy? Survival – influencing through kindness and exerting power through understanding was my approach.

Whilst thinking about a survival plan, I noticed something peculiar about life in Australia: people vacuumed and washed their cars in their front gardens every weekend, unlike in Spain. Without considering my supply chain, I took my mother's vacuum cleaner, packed it into a large cardboard box, cut a hole in the box, tied a piece of rope to pull it along, and voilà – my first business was born.

I knocked on doors pitching my service. I was met with smiles and several enthusiastic "yeses". I charged AU$1 (US$.62) per car and made AU$5 (US$3) in one weekend. When my mother discovered her vacuum cleaner was missing, my first entrepreneurial endeavour ended, and so did my cashflow.

I then had to convince my mother to buy me a bag of sweets each week. She couldn't understand why I suddenly needed a steady supply – my preference was for savoury olives; I hated sugar. I insisted that having sweets at school was a necessity – and it truly was. The plan worked. When the bullies approached, I offered sweets; to my surprise, they never stole the entire bag.

Reflecting on my adventures, I realised that resources – be they sweets or a vacuum – are the lifeblood of any business. Without economic support to obtain the right tools, even the most ambitious ideas remain unrealised concepts.

DOI: 10.4324/9781003516224-6

Several decades later, seeking investors for the *Peacebeliever* John Lennon project – an endeavour to promote peace through music and raise funds for musical instruments in public schools – I found no interest from investors. Peace, music, and children were not a lucrative investment. So, I took out a loan and invested in myself – a decision that, in hindsight, was a really bad financial idea. As for the numerous other unpeaceful dramas – of which there were many – the sequence of events unfolded like a dark comedy. Reflecting, I acknowledge that I was naïve to think such a project would inspire XY capitalists looking for a quick ROI.

Economically, the business model was a complete disaster, despite being a creative triumph with 20 artists from around the world contributing to my mission. Most radio stations refused to play the song, resulting in limited listeners and no sales. Only one radio station in Madrid, Spain played the song once, to my knowledge.

Nevertheless, I accomplished an unprecedented feat, receiving permission from Yoko Ono and Paul McCartney to re-record *Give Peace a Chance*. For the first time in history, new lyrics (one new verse in Spanish) were allowed to be added to a John Lennon song, bringing his timeless message of peace into a contemporary context in two languages (ABC, 2010).

Equipped with valuable lessons and experience, I turned my focus to advising and supporting other XXs in their businesses at the AWCCI. I was constantly reminded of how often XXs start a business without a clear cash flow strategy and with minimal financial literacy. Nevertheless, it was inspiring to hear so many great ideas but also confusing to see so many corporate refugees having to work alone from home because the vast majority could not afford childcare after giving birth to a second child.

Research and advocacy became my primary focus. Despite nearly one million self-employed XXs trading in Australia, there was no existing data on their contributions, challenges, or successes at the time. It was as if they were invisible to the economic narrative.

I conceptualised and managed the first national piece of research focused on XX business owners in Australia. The research enabled me to amplify their voices, deliver workshops on topics they wanted to support their businesses, and advise government policy for small and medium enterprises (SMEs). My vision at the AWCCI was clear: to create equitable systems where XXs could thrive, not just for their own benefit, but as significant contributors to the economy.

Some entrepreneurs struggled to break even, and many did not pay themselves a wage or contribute to their superannuation, ultimately closing their businesses with a bittersweet mix of relief and regret. Nonetheless, several thrived and expanded their businesses, employing other XXs.

Introduction

Globally, XXs dominate online spending, contributing US$40 (AU$65) trillion, designating their consumer and economic power whilst embracing sustainability through reuse, repair, and recycling, influencing second-hand markets, and demanding eco-friendly products and fair labour practices. The *lipstick effect*, which describes the increase in cosmetic purchases during economic downturns based on survival instincts, is reviewed.

With the growing recognition of equal rights, XXs are now playing a crucial role in driving economic and social progress globally (Waqar et al., 2024). From Australia to the EU, to India, the UK, and the USA, the evidence is clear: a nation achieves its fullest economic potential when both sexes receive parity at home and at work.

Initiatives aimed at equipping XXs with the skills to manage money, save, and invest have made considerable progress. Financial education programs and targeted campaigns are helping to bridge the knowledge gap, enabling XXs to make informed economic decisions that enhance stability and provide freedom.

A powerful image can replace words, and humans leverage attire and cosmetics as instruments of self-expression, broadcasting identity, status, and intent. The historical and cultural significance of makeup reflects long-standing societal ideals of beauty. Practices aimed at obtaining pale skin continue today under the term "fairness mania", perpetuating harmful practices. Despite environmental and health risks, profit-driven industries continue to exploit beauty prospects, reinforcing phallocentric expectations and prejudices that lead to excessive consumption patterns.

The consumption of fast fashion is thriving with XXs' expending trillions, albeit their spending is misaligned with their environmental concerns. These consumer habits continue to perpetuate the excessive production of unsustainable items, exploiting workers and Mother Earth, and are being further fuelled by social networking sites (SNSs) and *femvertising*, which alleges an alignment of products with social causes and concerns.

The fashion industry ranks as the third-largest global polluter, generating more greenhouse gas emissions annually than both international aviation and shipping combined. This industry consumes enough water to sustain the needs of millions of people, produces vast amounts of waste, escalates carbon emissions, pollutes waterways, adds to landfills and exacerbates the global plastic crisis. These alarming consequences initiated the President of the French Republic, Emmanuel Macron, to introduce laws to abate the industry's harmful impact by prohibiting advertising for the most inexpensive and unsustainable fabrics. Activists are calling for other nations to adopt similar laws.

Household consumption is similarly predominantly conducted by XXs, accounting for the great majority (80%) of global spending. Various age groups are influencing sustainability trends, with XXs in several regions also actively reducing meat consumption to assist with the reduction of greenhouse gas emissions.

Although equal pay for equal work has demonstrated its effectiveness in improving economic growth and business performance, androcentric attitudes, corporate loopholes, and weak law enforcement continue to undermine equitable progress; for example, only around half (53%) of nations are allocating resources to address wage and income gaps.

Sex-based economic inequalities persist, with income and wage gaps negatively impacting XXs. Additionally, caregiving duties and inadequate financial literacy continue to exacerbate adversities. Poverty impacts XXs the most globally, with limited access to childcare, education, and employment furthering financial insecurity.

Childcare, both formal and informal, further complicates XXs' economic participation worldwide due to high costs and limited accessibility; this issue is reviewed in Australia, the EU, India, the UK, and the USA.

The toolkit at the end of the chapter provides practical ideas on how XXs can make conscious economic choices to advance financial independence and discontinue purchasing unsustainable products to participate in creating a more habitable world.

The Power of the Purse

With the increase in the number of XXs in the workforce reaching its highest levels and their increased levels of education (Chapter 5), XXs are now the most powerful consumers in the world (Raman, 2019).

Power is the capacity to influence outcomes, and XXs have significant influence through their dominant role in spending decisions, serving as the primary decision-makers across various sectors, including education, household goods, fashion, and cosmetics. In 2024, the spending of XXs was estimated at US$32 (AU$51) trillion globally; XXs are expected to control three in four (75%) discretionary purchases within five years, influencing the great majority (80%) of household purchases (NielsenIQ, 2024).

Consumers aged 35 to 54 have the greatest impact on consumption, particularly in education, housing, and various services. Meanwhile, those aged 55 and over allocate a larger portion of their spending towards healthcare (Jun et al., 2021).

Even in restrictive cultures, digital financial tools are increasing XXs' autonomy and bargaining power. For example, in India, rising mobile phone accessibility has equipped XXs to make more independent purchasing decisions and gain greater economic independence (Waghmare, 2025). However, many digital platforms facilitating these transactions are controlled by misogynistic oligarchies.

Across SNSs, XXs spend more time and engage with both transactional and non-transactional content compared to XYs. However, marketers exploit psychological values to influence XXs' choices through alluring packaging and branding, demonstrating that not all that glistens is gold.

With digital tools and knowledge, it is imperative for XXs to become more aware of how their financial power contributes to the patriarchy's economic dominance. For example, the luxury goods sector heavily relies on the spending of XXs; Bernard Arnault, owner of Louis Vuitton Moët Hennessy (LVMH), amassed an estimated net worth of US$194 (AU$309) billion in 2024 (Siampani, 2024; Murray, 2024). It is primarily XXs that purchase LVMH's fashion, leather goods, watches, jewellery, spirits, wines, perfumes, and cosmetics.

Imagine if those billions had been directed towards XX–owned businesses? A collective shift in purchasing power could profoundly redesign global economies and many lives.

Crowdfunding platforms are also enabling the support of XX entrepreneurs, with trends in Spain, for example, establishing XXs as more likely to fund projects led by other XXs, particularly in technology. This behaviour, attributed to "homophily" – the tendency to invest in individuals similar to oneself – is helping to close the financial funding gap for XXs' entrepreneurial networks (Groza, Groza, & Barral, 2020).

Despite these advancements, significant opportunities remain untapped for XX–led businesses. For example, more than one billion individuals globally are menopausal, yet products addressing their needs are scarce, despite the great majority (85%) actively managing their symptoms (NielsenIQ, 2024).

The good news is that new generations are supporting progress towards more socially responsible and ethical purchasing. Younger XX consumers are increasingly supporting fair trade products, advocating for safe working conditions and fair wages, and expanding sustainable markets. For example, XXs aged 18 to 21 favour brands that reflect inclusivity and diversity, enhancing the value of progressive products, including *femvertising* (Descouens & Gerbault, 2021; Waqar et al., 2024) reviewed in this chapter.

The proverb "A picture is worth a thousand words" appropriately captures the way humans use attire and cosmetics as tools for self-expression and to assert identity.

In the fashion and beauty industries, consumption is highest among XXs. Their spending power and habits reveal similarities across regions. As the largest consumer group, XXs possess significant purchasing power, setting trends and steering industries and markets. Fast fashion is a focal point for younger consumers, consequently contributing negatively to high levels of pollution (Cardona, 2024).

Revenue in the fashion market is projected to reach US$881 (AU$1400) billion in 2025 (Statista, 2025), whilst the cosmetics market revenue is projected to reach US$54.7 (AU$85.3) billion in 2025 (Statista, n.d.-a, n.d.-b).

One contributing revenue factor is the ***lipstick effect*** – the tendency to buy cosmetics during times of hardship – which reflects XX consumers' tendency to invest in small, affordable luxuries, including cosmetics, as a means of maintaining a sense of self-esteem and a sense of normalcy during difficult economic circumstances (Bahl et al., 2022; Hill et al., 2012).

The online consumption of XXs is growing rapidly, primarily driven by financial capability, convenience, and effective customer service. Globally, XXs account for almost half (42%) of online purchases, a substantial increase from one in five (20%) in 2015, emphasising XXs' expanding economic influence. This growth is evident across the EU, India, and the USA, where XXs are emerging as key players in the e-commerce sector (Raman, 2019).

In India, for example, the number of internet users is expected to reach 900 million in 2025, with XXs accounting for nearly 450 million (47%). This growth is partly attributed to the rise in content available in Indic languages, along with the increased number of users in rural India (IBEF, 2025; PTI, 2025).

Platforms are creating environments where using makeup is simultaneously framed as an empowerment tool, and yet users are subjected to scrutiny and criticism. For example, a single makeup tutorial was viewed more than 36 million times globally, reflecting the pervasive influence of SNSs in constructing beauty norms (White, 2017). These online interactions extend beyond outdated patriarchal values, revealing the complex pressures imposed on XXs, whose pursuit of beauty sometimes results in serious health implications (Rathi & D'Souza, 2018).

In the digital age, the craving for beauty has introduced significant challenges for XXs, as SNSs amplify Western attractiveness ideals and promote sexist cultural expectations of femininity.

The investment costs to attain beauty are not paying off.

In the USA, XXs account for around 85% of the US$115 (AU$186) billion beauty market (Ramati-Ziber et al., 2020). Fast fashion sales are also thriving as they are accessible and affordable, yet their environmental and societal costs fail to align. The consumer behaviour of Gen Z, for example, often contradicts the environmental values they promote and the sustainable future many claim to support and desire (Cardona, 2024).

Traditionally, the fashion and cosmetics industries have focused on younger consumers, however, many are reassessing their target markets and focusing on the "silver generation" – those aged 50 and above – who are becoming an increasingly influential demographic in population growth and fashion and cosmetics consumption (Balchandani et al., 2024).

Adorning to Be Adored

Concepts of beauty as harmony are embedded in the origin of the word "cosmetic", from the ancient Greek ***kosmētikos***, meaning "to adorn" or "arrange", reflecting ideals of beauty, physical perfection, and symmetry (Jain & Chaudhri, 2009).

Makeup, throughout human history, has been an essential aspect of numerous cultures, employed to enhance beauty, perform religious rituals, and denote social status and/or rank (Ramati-Ziber et al., 2020; Jain & Chaudhri, 2009).

The mass production of cosmetics in the 20th century increased accessibility around the world, making these products available to a global consumer base. In the 1980s, makeup became a worldwide phenomenon, influenced by pop culture that promoted dramatic tones, dense foundations, and bright blushes characteristic of the era (Townsend, 2019).

Power dressing emerged in the 1970s as XXs entered corporate roles, adopting elements of XY's attire to assert influence. Attire is selected to convey messages of authority, control, and influence in both social and professional settings. Perceptions of status and competence are partly based on attire and personal presentation; clothing functions as both a tool and symbol of power (Geczy & Karaminas, 2024). Fashion also has the intensity to regulate behaviour and reinforce societal hierarchies through specific clothing codes and trends.

Conditioned and encouraged to alter or modify appearance, including face, hair, and body, the deeply ingrained misogynistic expectations have designed societal norms that persuade XXs to differentiate themselves from XYs through distinctive identifiers; high-heel shoes, dresses, long hair, and lipstick, for example. The defined features reinforce sex-based stereotypes and at times provide tools for XXs to navigate oppressive settings (Ramati-Ziber et al., 2020).

For example, traditional elitist standards on professional dress codes in the legal profession – dictated by privileged white cisgender XYs that historically excluded all others – persist (DeLaney, 2023). "Undergarments" regulations are also applied to some XXs when visiting clients (Hill, 2023). Additionally, in some law firms, XXs are forbidden from wearing pants to align with the XY–dominated "stale pale male" perception of professionalism (Sommerlad, 2016:67), further reinforcing sexism in the legal profession (Foley, 2023) and raising concerns about anti-discrimination laws and the "right to privacy" (Cooper, 2019:4).

Archaic patriarchal expectations embedded in workplace attire regulations – together with pressures to wear makeup and conform to traditional notions of femininity – constrain self-expression, limit individuality, and reinforce the idea of an XXs body as a visual marker of identity, social status, and moral standing.

Blame It on History

The cultural significance of makeup extends across history, from Ancient Egypt and China to the European Renaissance, the Elizabethan era of the 16th century, 18th c. France, 19th c. Europe, and its mass production in the 20th century (Townsend, 2019).

Within the Roman Empire, imported beauty products became prevalent among the affluent. The acceptance of makeup then increased during the Renaissance period (from the 14th to the 17th c.) among European aristocracy, with cinnabar, a vivid red mineral, used to enhance colour, albeit with some religious groups claiming makeup was a tool of deception (Jain & Chaudhri, 2009; Townsend, 2019).

In ancient China, rice powder or white lead was applied to achieve a pale complexion, with beauty trends frequently set by emperors and concubines. In the UK, Queen Elizabeth I famously used ceruse – a toxic white lead foundation – along with vermilion rouge. By the 18th c. in France, foundation – originally used to conceal scars – and rouge became highly fashionable. By the early 19th c., makeup in Europe had become more natural, with rice powder replacing heavy foundations and the use of rouge decreasing, aligning with social norms of subtlety (Townsend, 2019).

The concept of fair skin being better than dark skin was regarded as a symbol of elevated social standing; the rich stayed indoors, whilst the poor worked outdoors in natural light. Culturally, throughout history, most societies favoured alabaster-like skin on XXs, partly based on concepts perpetuated by colonisation and slavery, instilling the belief that those with darker skin were primitive, inferior, unsophisticated, and uncultured. The Greeks also used substances, including olive oil and white lead, to achieve pale complexions (Jain & Chaudhri, 2009; Townsend, 2019). However, other cultures, including those in Africa, for example, associate light skin with "evil spirits," reflecting superstitions linking a pale complexion to dark forces (Rathi & D'Souza, 2018:viii).

Prejudicially, the colour of skin continues to allegedly determine the status of an individual in the 21st century. In India, for example, as in other Asian countries, the "fairness mania" is maintained, with fair skin aesthetics promoting the pervasive misuse of topical corticosteroid creams as cosmetic products, encouraged by collective pressure that influences and, at times, demands adherence to specific beauty standards. There is growing concern over the misapplication of corticosteroid creams, as some are hazardous and can lead to permanent damage (Rathi & D'Souza, 2018:viii).

Applying kohl around the eyes was also believed to ward off the evil eye and prevent eye infections. Widely used across the globe, kohl served both aesthetic and medicinal purposes because of its antimicrobial properties (Jain & Chaudhri, 2009; Townsend, 2019).

Currently, despite the evident dangers of product misuse and the detrimental effects on Mother Earth caused by excessive fast fashion consumption, profit-driven businesses continue to pursue growth – capitalising on the power of the XX purse and targeting their psychological vulnerabilities.

Femvertising and Fast Fashion

Femvertising uses pro–XX messaging to connect with consumers and sell products or services by aligning alleged brand values with social causes resonating with XXs – a marketing strategy that began around 2014. Tactics employed by brands, despite often lacking genuine commitment to sex-based equality, have proven effective (Gasulla Tortajada et al., 2024; Waqar et al., 2024).

Approximately one-third (30%) of XXs exposed to *femvertising* are more likely to purchase products linked to such campaigns (Waqar et al., 2024).

Instagram is widely used by XXs aged 21 to 41 in France, for example, who generally view *femvertising* positively, recognising its role in debunking stereotypes and promoting inclusivity. Nevertheless, concerns about the sincerity of brands raise questions regarding superficial commitments to equal rights causes made solely for profit. Despite scepticism, *femvertising* has influenced purchase intentions, reinforcing the marketing power of rhetoric within the cosmetic and fashion industries (Descouens & Gerbault, 2021).

Fast Fashion

Fast fashion refers to the rapid production of low-cost garments that imitate designer luxury brands. While it satisfies the aspirations of younger consumers in various regions, it simultaneously presents an unsustainable model of consumption (Joy et al., 2012).

The primary fast fashion buyers are young XXs, with the 18- to 24-year-old age group being the biggest consumers. For many, shopping is a social and enjoyable activity. However, almost half (41%) report feeling pressured to avoid wearing the same outfits. In contrast, XYs tend to shop less frequently and take more time adapting to changing fashion trends (Cardona, 2024).

The fast fashion section of the fashion industry generates around US$150 (AU$ 238) billion annually, constituting a major portion of the global fashion market (Cardona, 2024). It is projected to generate US$880.9 (AU$1405) billion in 2025 (Statista, 2025). Combined, the textiles and garment sectors employ more than "91 million workers globally", 50 million of whom were XX in 2019 (ILO, 2022:5).

Globally, the fashion industry contributes 10% of global annual carbon emissions. The industry also consumes an average of 141 trillion litres of water each year and is the leading culprit behind microplastic pollution in global waterways (Carbone, 2024).

Gen Z – born between 1997 and 2012 (Dimock, 2019) – has grown up in an era heavily influenced by the internet, smartphones, and SNSs. They are highly dependent on and skilled in the use of digital technology. They also represent the dominant consumer demographic for fast fashion (Bennett et al., 2022; Carbone, 2024; Pradhan et al., 2023).

Although the great majority (94%) of young consumers express support for sustainable fashion, their shopping habits reveal a disturbingly different reality – each one of the Gen Zs spends US$767 (AU$1239) annually on fast fashion. One in six (17%) XXs report weekly fast fashion shopping, and three in five (62%) shop every month (Cardona, 2024).

Companies including Shein and Zara are the biggest sellers of fast fashion. Unfortunately, their apparel is disposed of after being worn a maximum of 10 times (Agence France-Presse, 2024; Carbone, 2024).

What sets Gen Z apart from other consumers is their pursuit of truth, authenticity, and ethical alignment in their relationships with both influencers and brands, with some brands perceived as ethically unacceptable. However, influencers – individuals who gain large followings on SNSs – are often regarded as authentic, trusted sources who are relatable and influence purchasing decisions (Leung et al., 2022; Vrontis et al., 2021).

The global demand for clothing has surged over the past decade, causing significant negative effects, driven by the fast fashion industry and Gen Z – who, in 2025, will be aged 13 to 28 – pointing out a disturbing and conflicting reality within this generation (Munsch, 2021).

As a result of the unrestrained consumption, French President Emmanuel Macron passed legislation in 2024 focusing on environmental concerns, implementing a series of measures aimed at making fast fashion less appealing to consumers. The French government declared that this initiative was "legislating to limit the excesses of ultra-fast fashion" (Agence France-Presse, 2024). When the law is enforced, advertising for ultra-fast fashion brands and their products must disclose their environmental impact, with penalties imposed for non-compliance – "each item will come with a penalty of up to €10 (AU$16/US$10) by 2030." The fee is restricted to a "maximum of 50%" of the item's listed price (Agence France-Presse, 2024; Broom, 2024).

France's new tax is recognised as a progressive initiative that acknowledges the critical and urgent necessity to reduce the excessive consumption of non-natural fibres and their addition to landfill waste (Carbone, 2024; RMIT Communications, 2024). Ethical fashion activists are urging other nations to follow France's example to prevent further environmental damage caused by toxic chemicals, reduce the current fashion waste crisis, and halt the exploitation and slavery-like conditions in fashion supply chains (Broom, 2024; Australia Institute, 2024). The waste generated in France and the sales figures are expected to change substantially.

Irrespective of laws, online personalities and influencers, continue to impact consumer behaviour among XXs, particularly through SNSs, with influencers becoming integral in promoting and motivating purchasing decisions. This is especially evident among XXs aged 18 to 30, who are more responsive to non-traditional celebrities – including bloggers and "instafamous" figures – than traditional celebrities, indicating a shift in brand credibility and appeal (Djafarova & Rushworth, 2017; Pradhan et al., 2023).

There are also influencers advocating for more environmentally conscious fashion brands (Carbone, 2024), which contribute to reducing the environmental impact of the fashion industry's 21st c. consumption trends. Furthermore, influencers play a crucial role in harnessing peer pressure to motivate others to adopt specific behaviours. For example, in the USA, XXs account for seven in ten (70%) consumer purchases influenced by social media marketing, while in the EU, six in ten (60%) are similarly influenced (Djafarova & Rushworth, 2017).

Discovering brands and products has become significantly easier with the integration of AI–powered tools by companies that create content to increase customers and profits (Balchandani et al., 2024). Global patterns also indicate that personal traits influence XX consumers' spending habits, with economic status being a factor (Rehman et al., 2017), while instinctive tactics play a role in purchasing decisions.

Overall, influencers have increased the online purchasing behaviour of XXs, with half of consumers (50%) persuaded – reinforcing the substantial impact of SNS content on consumer behaviour and decision-making (Feng, et al., 2021; Martínez-López, et al., 2020).

The Lipstick Effect

During a crisis or recession, consumer spending generally decreases; however, even as overall spending declines, purchases of beauty items rise – a phenomenon termed the "lipstick effect", referring to the trend of purchasing cosmetics during economic downturns (Bahl et al., 2022:299).

To boost self-esteem, enhance social appeal, and adapt to financial stress, XXs aim to enhance their attractiveness to secure potential partners, where improving physical appearance serves as a coping mechanism during financial downturns (Hill et al., 2012). This subconscious strategy helps maintain desirability when resources are scarce (Hill et al., 2012). Instant gratification further influences the preference for economical luxury items, reinforcing the lipstick effect theory, as beauty product sales increase during unstable periods – an outcome driven by principles of evolutionary psychology (Bahl et al., 2022).

Although only recently identified, the *lipstick effect* phenomenon is not new. For example, despite the impacts of World War II, across the USA, cosmetic sales increased significantly in the 1940s (Townsend, 2019). The lipstick theory, however, was proposed by a cosmetics company, Estée Lauder, when statistics revealed an 11% increase in lipstick sales following the 9/11 attack (Bahl et al., 2022) – an extremist attack on September 11, 2001, targeting the Twin Towers of the World Trade Center in New York City and other locations in the USA.

During the global COVID-19 lockdowns, despite an 8.7% decline in overall purchases, the sale of beauty products again increased globally. For example, Sephora – a multinational beauty and personal care retailer – reported a 30% increase in online sales, while Amazon recorded a 70% rise in beauty and personal care products compared to pre-pandemic levels (Bahl et al., 2022).

Stress and self-esteem are key psychological forces impacting the *lipstick effect* and compulsive buying behaviour among XXs. Those aged 15 to 34 display a tendency towards more compulsive purchasing and discretionary spending behaviours (Jun et al., 2021).

Compulsive Buying Behaviour

Compulsive buying induced by stress triggers a surge in spending, with increases ranging between 25% and 30%, revealing how emotional factors act as powerful stimuli in the consumer behaviour of XXs, provoking customers towards immediate gratification in the form of online purchases (Zheng et al., 2020).

The global rise in spending among XXs underscores the link between psychological well-being and economic behaviour, with impulse buying acting as a mediator that increases spending by up to 25% (Pradhan et al., 2018).

In China, often referred to as the manufacturing hub of the world, XX consumers represent more than three out of five (60%) of online compulsive buyers, underscoring their substantial presence in digital markets (Zheng et al., 2020).

In urban India, compulsive purchases account for around one in three (35%) of consumer credit card debts among XXs. Compulsive buying behaviour increases by 40% when combined with materialistic desires and credit card availability (Balchandani et al., 2024). The e-commerce industry in India is projected to grow to US$200 (AU$323) billion by 2026 (Balchandani et al., 2024).

Shopping preferences also reveal that online purchases are both pleasure- and function-driven, indicating that XXs exhibit hedonic shopping habits at a rate more than three times (30%) higher than XYs (Wahyuddin et al., 2017). Essential elements, including trust, ease of use, and quality customer support, are factors contributing to XXs' online shopping patterns (Raman, 2019).

The consumer behaviour of XXs is also influenced by their level of financial literacy, bringing attention to the impact that financial knowledge can have on improving XXs' economic security. Addressing the financial literacy gap among XXs is an important step towards sex-based equality and would help unlock economic potential in a transformative way (Bucher-Koenen et al., 2017).

A new trend reveals shoppers are returning to physical stores to spend at pre-COVID levels, almost worldwide. The transition back to physical spending is negatively affecting the luxury market with forecasts indicating declining sales (Balchandani et al., 2024).

Reinventing Luxury

Reuse, repair, and recycling concepts are transforming how XX consumers redefine luxury item spending by incorporating circular economy principles – with the objective of optimising resource and reducing waste. The global luxury sector, valued at US$111.5 (AU$180) billion in 2023, is having to adapt to shifting preferences for sustainability and ethical consumption (Gasulla Tortajada et al., 2024; Statista, 2023).

In the EU, many XXs prioritise artisanry and tradition, with ethical consumption acting as a key factor in their purchasing decisions (Dhaliwal et al., 2020). While cultural differences are acknowledged, XXs generally purchase luxury products as symbols of success and social status (Dhaliwal et al., 2020) and are influencing the second-hand luxury market (Statista, 2023; Gasulla Tortajada et al., 2024).

In the USA, XXs are demanding greater transparency and ethical practices from luxury brands, their purchasing power applying pressure for fair labour practices and the production of environmentally friendly items (Gasulla Tortajada et al., 2024).

In Asia, while XX consumers continue to spend significantly on luxury goods, many are opting for circular fashion, a similar trend to the USA, including renting and upcycling fashion items (Gasulla Tortajada et al., 2024).

The UN and others in the fashion industry are encouraging upcycling – repurposing old garments into new apparel – and promoting the purchasing of durable, sustainably produced items designed to last (Carbone, 2024).

Household Consumption

Spending patterns on goods and services reflect the realities of household consumption, ranging from necessities including food and housing, as well as discretionary purchases including entertainment and travel. These patterns provide insights into consumer confidence and the financial stability of a nation (OECD, 2002).

Across 38 OECD countries, XXs are the key contributors to household consumption, accounting for the majority (70% to 80%) of total expenditures. In countries with higher XX labour force participation, including Sweden and Norway, for example, household consumption increases significantly due to the spending patterns of employed XXs compared to nations with lower employment rates (Gasulla Tortajada et al., 2024).

Largely motivated by ecological concerns, XXs are also leading the shift in global meat consumption trends, revealing a heightened awareness and commitment to sustainable spending choices through the reduction of animal protein.

Two in five (38%) XXs globally report cutting back on or avoiding meat for environmental reasons compared to approximately one in four (24%) XYs (Sanchez-Sabate & Sabaté, 2019). Efforts to limit meat intake have contributed to a global decline of between 5% and 15% in meat consumption (Sanchez-Sabate & Sabaté, 2019). In the USA, however, XXs are less inclined to reduce meat consumption. In EU countries including Belgium, Finland, Germany, and the Netherlands, around two-thirds (66%) of XXs recognise the environmental impact of meat.

Human Rights in Chains

The fashion industry supply chains have an obstinate lack of human rights, with workers frequently enduring abuse and exploitation. Appalling labour practices and widespread human rights violations by multinational corporations prioritise profits over worker well-being.

The purchasing habits of XXs inadvertently perpetuate exploitative practices entrenched in numerous industries, on a global scale. Despite the majority of garment workers and models being XXs, the industry remains predominantly controlled by XYs, who hold significant power and derive hefty profits. In contrast, XXs within the industry and supply chains frequently face human rights violations, patriarchal attitudes, and sex-based exploitation.

Additionally, the growing urgency to address environmental challenges, fuelled by the escalating frequency of extreme weather events in recent years, is expected to continue compelling companies to prioritise sustainability and enhance their resilience against climate impacts. Scorching temperatures and floods are some of the climate-related disasters that threaten global industries, making it increasingly untenable for businesses to ignore the crisis endangering workers' livelihoods and corporate stability, and the financial risks are mounting. For example, by 2030, an estimated US$65 (AU$105) billion in apparel exports are expected to be at risk (McKinsey & Company, 2024).

The abuse of workers is also highly concerning. Corporate headquarters, located in the EU and the USA, are where the abuse originates and permeates the entire production process, including unsafe working conditions, sex-based discrimination, excessive working hours, and child labour across major production regions, including Asia, Latin America, and Eastern Europe (Simmons, 2020).

In the USA, for example, employees in the fashion industry were paid less than the legal minimum wage. The US Department of Labor revealed that four in five (80%) contractors were violating laws on minimum wage and overtime pay, with one contractor paying workers as little as US$1.58 (AU$2.51) per hour instead of the minimum wage of US$15 (AU$24) per hour (Cardona, 2024). Paradoxically, the industries that target XX consumers are also exploiting them.

Often unknowingly or indifferently, consumers are contributing to the exploitation of XXs around the globe and neglecting the harsh realities faced by workers worldwide, where abuse, exploitation, and discrimination are prevalent (Crowley, 2023).

Employment laws in the fashion industry worldwide remain insufficient in safeguarding the rights of garment workers. Similarly, intellectual property laws, contract laws, international trade laws, and environmental regulations have failed to positively progress with the industry's expansion (Bhowmik & Anand, 2023).

The sexualisation of young XXs, another prevalent unlawful fashion industry practice, has been widely criticised by both the public and governments. Media representations further exacerbate the problem by frequently portraying XXs' bodies as objects, reinforcing phallocentric desires that erode equality. In the UK, for example, public backlash against the marketing of padded bras and G-string underwear to children led to their removal from retail stores (Edwards, 2020), reflecting societal concerns about the sexual exploitation and objectification of young XXs.

The rapid global expansion of the fashion industry has cultivated environments that fail to protect workers, with more than 24.9 million people exploited (Bhowmik & Anand, 2023). Garment workers in various countries, including Bangladesh, Cambodia, India, and China, for example, earn less than US$200 (AU$323) per month (Simmons, 2020). Australians are the world's leading purchasers of clothing (Broom, 2024).

The abuse and exploitation of models also persist in major fashion hubs, including Paris, Milan, New York, and London (Bhowmik & Anand, 2023). The great majority (95%) of XX models report experiencing harassment from XYs, including photographers and agents (Crowley, 2023).

The lack of job security, substandard salaries, and intense competition contribute to one in four models (25%) facing a higher risk of mental illness globally compared to other professions. Power imbalances further exacerbate conditions, with less than seven in ten (70%) models disclosing their experiences of harassment. More than two in five (40%) report struggling with eating disorders, depression, or substance abuse (Bhowmik & Anand, 2023; Crowley, 2023). In the worst-case scenarios, XX models are at risk of human trafficking, as traffickers exploit economic instability and poverty to lure ambitious individuals into unsafe jobs (Bhowmik & Anand, 2023).

Economic Realities

Over the past decades, incremental changes to policies have delivered mixed results; in some countries, within several industries, equal remuneration has been achieved. However, while inequalities have decreased at a global level over the past 30 years, the pay gap has widened in several developed countries (WEF, 2024). For example, research within OECD countries revealed that XXs' income inequality, prior to the COVID-19 pandemic, was at its highest level, indicating that five decades of efforts to address barriers to economic participation had not generated positive results (World Bank, 2020).

There have also been growing concerns in recent years about the negative impact of industrial automation. Although it offers opportunities, there are fears that it will disproportionately affect XXs, particularly those working in lower-paying sectors (WEF, 2021, 2024).

Financial knowledge deficits result in fewer financial resources, more career interruptions, and an inability to make sound financial decisions (Bucher-Koenen et al., 2017). Financial security is undermined by spending habits, as XXs often prioritise household expenditures and caregiving over personal savings or investments, further limiting their economic autonomy.

Sex-disaggregated poverty data is difficult to collect; nevertheless, all research illustrates that poverty impacts the financial standing of XXs, affecting their access to education, job prospects, and long-term health. Poverty disproportionately affects XXs, intensified by caregiving responsibilities and a lack of social support structures, making economic hardship exceedingly complex (Muñoz Boudet et al., 2018; World Bank, 2024).

International efforts to improve financial knowledge have been significant; however, XXs consistently trail behind XYs in understanding fundamental financial concepts, including interest rates and inflation, for example. Sociocultural trends in various countries including Germany, the Netherlands, and the USA indicate that XXs are less likely than XYs to answer financial questions correctly (Muñoz Boudet et al., 2018).

The lack of financial literacy and the pay gap remain a prevalent global issue, with XXs earning less than XYs for the same or similar work across various industries, ultimately diminishing their financial security and lifetime earnings.

Those aged between 25 and 34 with reproductive expectations encounter further severe economic disadvantages, experiencing substantially higher poverty rates compared to XYs of the same age. The poverty line is frequently measured on purchasing power parity. The inability to access essential services, including childcare, healthcare, and education, further limits economic engagement and restricts progress for future generations. Those living below the poverty threshold consistently assume caregiving responsibilities, with single XX parents being especially vulnerable. This disconnect restricts XXs' earning potential, limiting long-term economic stability and perpetuating financial insecurity (Gomes, 2015, World Bank, 2024).

The number of single XX parents varies globally, with the USA having the highest proportion among developed countries. Approximately one in 11 (9%) XXs in the USA are single parents, followed by the UK and Sweden with one in 14 (7%). In France, Canada, and Ireland, the rate of single XX parents is one in 17 (6%), while Norway and Finland report one in 20 (5%). In Belgium, Portugal, and Switzerland single XXs account for one in 25 (4%), whereas India, Germany, and Spain report one in 33 (3%). The lowest rates are found in Greece and Italy, where one in 50 (2%) of XXs are single parents (WPR, 2024).

Income Pay Gap

The terms "income gap", "gender pay gap", "wage gap" refer to the percentage difference between the median earnings of XYs and XXs. The term "income pay gap" or "gap" is employed in this book to ensure clarity.

Providing equal pay for equal work, regardless of sex, is not only fair but also strengthens financial performance in businesses and governance. It is also a legal requirement in the vast majority of nations. Yet, androcentric patriarchs continue to control the earning capacity of XXs.

Advocacy for equal pay and economic participation has been on global agendas for more than a century, since the ILO was established in 1919 (Bolle, 2013; ILO, n.d.). Nevertheless, the income pay gap – typically estimated based on earnings and represents the unadjusted gross income for full-time wages and employee salaries (OECD, 2024b) – continues to lack parity. These inconsistencies endure because governments fail to implement and monitor effective policies, citing constitutional reasons and ignoring international best practices (McConnell, 2016).

One reason for the persistent income pay gap is the inability of governments to control the actions of private employers. In practice, corporations often have the resources to bypass regulations or operate in jurisdictions with weak enforcement or laws that fail to protect XXs from discriminatory practices (Mun, 2016). Additionally, pro–XX policies often serve as symbolic gestures, masking broader economic issues that disadvantage XXs globally (Allsopp, 2012; Denniss et al., 2021). Persistent wage gaps restrict financial security, limit career advancement, and perpetuate cycles where lower earnings impede wealth accumulation (Bargain et al., 2019).

Despite the vast majority of countries (90%) globally implementing some form of sex-based pay equality legislation, only half (53%) have allocated resources to address income pay gap inequalities actively. Consequently, earnings differences prevail in all countries (WEF, 2024).

When XXs actively participate in the economy, economic growth accelerates, and the return on investment significantly improves. As a result, many countries have implemented pay equity laws, increasing from two in 1971 to 98 countries in the 21st century (WEF, 2024; WGEA, 2024a). However, equal pay policies often fail to deliver because of weak governmental objectives and a lack of enforceable penalties for employers who violate laws. This undermines the policies' effectiveness and perpetuates wage disparities.

Due to variations in publication dates and collection systems across countries by various organisations and governments, the following section, by region, is non-uniform. However, the data from *The Global Gender Gap 2024 Insight Report* is synchronised, providing a ranking based on the XX-to-XY ratio for "estimated earned income" (WEF, 2024).

Australia

As of December 2024, three out of five (63%) XXs aged 15 and over were employed in the Australian workforce (ABS, 2024a, 2024b).

Over the past two decades XXs have earned between 13% and 22% less than XYs. In some XY–dominated industries, the gap is above 28% (ABS, 2024a, 2024b; WGEA, 2024a), some of the worst in the developed world. Overall, XXs earn an average of 78 cents for every dollar received by XYs. Australia is ranked 75th in the "estimated earned income" subindex (WEF, 2024).

Some conservatives question the statistics, suggesting wage discrimination accounts for only 6% when factors including childcare are taken into account (Guest, 2018). However, full-time expertly skilled and knowledgeable XXs continue to be paid less than their XY counterparts for the same work (Watson, 2024). Additionally, segregation persists, with XXs making up only one in seven (15%) of STEM workers nationwide (DISR, 2022, 2024).

Legislations to promote Australia's economic growth, including equal pay for equal work, are intended to have a positive impact on wage equilibrium;

however, parity in wages between XXs and XYs is yet to be obtained in numerous industries (Macdonald & Charlesworth, 2013; Sheen, 2017; WEF, 2024).

The repeated failure of successive governments to enforce pro–XX policies reflects a patriarchal androcentric economic and social structure that maintains income inequalities. The nation that instigated world-leading women's budgets, reviewed in this chapter, continues to disregard its own successful initiative while also ignoring violence and harassment in its parliaments (Chapter 3) and other Australian workplaces.

The EU

Despite legislative progress on equal pay laws in more than half (57%) of EU countries, enforcement and policy implementation vary significantly, limiting effectiveness (European Commission, 2018, 2022).

The employment rate for XXs aged 20 to 64 across the EU averaged two in three (68%) in 2021, while the pay gap stood at 13% in 2020 (European Commission, 2022). Each country is progressing at distinct tempos.

The EU ranks highest among global regions, achieving 75% income parity. The leading nation in closing the gap is Iceland, with Finland, Norway, and Sweden also ranking in the top ten (WEF, 2024). Conversely, several countries, including Hungary, show less progress than other nations where XXs remain concentrated in lower-paid sectors (WEF, 2024).

Working hours, industry, and sex-based discrimination are notable factors. Contract type and firm size, along with educational and occupational segregation, are also key contributors to the income gap. Age is another factor, as older XX workers are increasingly leaving the workforce (European Commission, 2018, 2022). Job segregation widens the income disparity, as XXs are disproportionately represented in lower-paid sectors, including health and education. Additionally, many XXs hold part-time or temporary positions, placing them at a financial disadvantage (European Commission, 2018, 2022; WEF, 2024).

Economic migration is also contributing to the STEM brain drain in the EU, with professionals from Bulgaria and Poland, for example, migrating to higher-paying countries, including Germany and the UK. Nevertheless, STEM workers also experience remuneration disparities (Muñoz Boudet et al., 2018).

India

India remains among the countries with the lowest levels of income equality, and it is ranked 135th in the "estimated earned income" data (OECD, 2019; WEF, 2024).

In 2023–24, more than two in five (42%) XXs aged 15 and above were employed in India, indicating a continuous rise (23%) since 2017 (Ministry of Labour & Employment, 2024). In recent years, the income wage gap has narrowed by 7%. However, XYs still receive 82% of India's total labour income, while XXs earn only 18% of the nation's total (Kulkarni & Havaldar, 2024).

Progress in reducing the income pay gap has also been successful in several sectors, including healthcare, education, and the creative industries in parts of India. The alterations towards equal income have been partly achieved through government initiatives including women's budgets, which have been instrumental in directing income disparities changes. However, unconscious biases and occupational segregation have yet to fade out (Kulkarni & Havaldar, 2024).

Lower-income XXs experience smaller pay gaps compared to XYs in similar roles, but as income levels rise, the gap widens. The disparities are based on occupational segregation, restricted access to senior and higher-paying positions, and cultural norms that limit XXs' participation in certain fields, particularly in XY–dominated sectors where few XXs reach executive positions (Sengupta & Puri, 2022).

Cultural expectations also pressure XXs to leave the workforce or work part-time if they have family responsibilities. Limited access to maternity leave and career breaks further disrupts career progression, diminishing XXs' lifetime earnings and retirement security. Consequently, they are unable to pursue long-term careers in high-growth industries, limiting diversity and stifling innovation across various sectors including technology, finance, and applied sciences, where XXs are underrepresented and earning considerably less. Around one in five (19%) scientists and just over one in four (27%) STEM workers in India are XXs. Unconscious biases, insufficient childcare support, and limited diversity in leadership continue to prevent XXs from achieving income parity (Kulkarni & Havaldar, 2024).

The UK

At the end of December 2023, seven in ten (72%) XXs aged 16 to 64 were employed in the UK, representing a minimal increase from the previous year (House of Commons Library, 2024).

Although the income gap has narrowed over the past decade, XXs still earn 14% less than XYs. The UK is ranked 77th in the "estimated earned income" category (WEF, 2024). Although the hourly gap decreased from around 14% in 2017 to 13% in 2021, challenges persist. The largest proportion of low-wage earners is XXs (House of Commons Library, 2023; Office for National Statistics, 2023).

Disparities are influenced by geography, industry, occupation, and regional economic conditions, along with age. Significant differences remain, particularly among older age groups, across various sectors, and in regions including London and the South East (House of Commons Library, 2023; Office for National Statistics, 2023).

London reports a 12% gap for full-time XX workers, higher than Scotland's 3.7%. Age also plays a critical role, with XXs aged 40 to 49 facing an 11% gap compared to just 2% for those aged 30 to 39 (McIntosh, 2023; Office for National Statistics, 2023).

Occupational segregation remains a key issue, with XXs overrepresented in lower-paid caregiving and administrative roles. While part-time workers show near-parity in hourly wages, full-time roles in finance and related industries exhibit larger gaps.

The Equality Act 2017 mandated firms with more than 250 employees to report pay and bonus gaps, similar to Australia, but transparency alone has not resolved the inequalities. For example, XYs continue to receive bonuses that are, on average, 25% higher than those awarded to XXs, often due to less transparency in bonus structures (House of Commons Library, 2023; Office for National Statistics, 2023). Unlike in Ireland, where wage legislation reduced the income wage gap for low-wage earners, other areas noted minimal improvements due to poor compliance and enforcement (Bargain et al., 2019), as witnessed around the globe.

In STEM, XX representation has fluctuated over the decades, from an impressive almost half (44%) in 2019, decreasing to around one in four (27%) by 2022. Currently, only a quarter (26%) of the STEM workforce is XX, with parity unlikely before 2070 at current growth rates (Women in STEM, n.d.).

The USA

In 2024, XXs aged 20 and over reached a historic high of almost four in five (78%) in the USA labour force, the highest rate recorded since tracking began in 1948 (US Department of Labor, 2024).

High-income professionals in the top 5% have seen their wages grow at a rate surpassing gross domestic product (GDP) growth, while earnings for lower- and middle-income workers have stagnated (Akarsu, 2023; WEF, 2024).

The USA is ranked 63rd in the "estimated earned income" subindex (WEF, 2024), with XXs earning an average of 86 cents (16% less) for every dollar paid to XYs (Haan & Reilly, 2024). Wage disparities suggest that educational progress alone has not been enough to achieve equity, pointing to entrenched cultural and legal obstacles (PRC, 2023; US Census Bureau, 2022). For example, in 1970, XXs earned around 63 cents for every dollar paid to XYs. By 2010, it was around 80 cents. However, the momentum has slowed, with XXs in 2024 paid 84 cents for every dollar remunerated to an XY (Haan & Reilly, 2024; PRC, 2023; WEF, 2024).

Earnings, as in other nations, vary across industries and age groups: XXs aged 25–34 earned 8 cents less, those aged 35–54 earned 17 cents less, and those aged 55–64 earned 21 cents less for every $1 earned by an XY of the same age, illustrating that experience does not pay (Kochhar, 2023) and that age discrimination persists.

In 1980, occupational segregation accounted for 27% of the income gap; by 2010, it had risen to almost half (49%) (Meara et al., 2020). Generational patterns suggest similar trajectories for today's young XXs, with income gaps increasing between the ages of 35 to 64 when career progression, in theory, should peak. Family responsibilities, bigotry, and occupational segregation continue to disproportionately confine XXs to lower-paying sectors and limit career growth (Kochhar, 2023).

The economic disparities perpetuate a cycle of poverty among lower-income workers, restricting wage growth, increasing financial vulnerability, and leaving individuals exposed to a lower standard of living, reduced retirement savings, and poorer overall well-being (Akarsu, 2023; Meara et al., 2020).

The types of jobs XXs perform also affects occupational segregation (Kochhar, 2023), with sexist stereotypes, cultural norms, and family responsibilities within various ethnic groups contributing to the widening of the income gap across the USA. As seen in other regions, this reflects "the dynamics of structural intersectionality... [and the] intersections of racism and patriarchy" (Crenshaw, 1989:9–10).

Without targeted policy interventions, including tax reforms and minimum wage adjustments, income disparities will continue and potentially worsen under the regime of the 47th president. The economic changes proposed during and after the presidential election, alongside the introduction of tariffs and interventions by the richest people in the world, are expected to have devastating local and global repercussions.

Laws, governments, and businesses worldwide appear to have failed to enforce equal pay for equal work. Research into addressing these inequalities highlights that the first step to empowering XXs is closing the income gap with robust policies that are heavily enforced. Illustratively, numerous current tax systems support XYs, resulting in economic wealth being disproportionately skewed in their favour (Denniss et al., 2021).

Reforms are needed to ensure greater inclusion of XXs and address the social and economic realities faced, ultimately improving their short- and long-term financial security and economic participation (Vega, 2023). Additionally, the sisterhood needs to support XXs in the workplace by challenging discriminatory practices, promoting equitable opportunities, and cultivating a culture of solidarity and development in order to disband the patriarchy.

Queen Bee Syndrome

The Queen Bee label – a phenomenon where an XX in a position of power distances themselves from other XXs – is a stereotype that portrays XX leaders as unsupportive or obstructive, undermining their credibility and reinforcing and sustaining bigoted concepts.

Queen Bee behaviour is often determined by the scarcity of opportunities for XXs, stemming from a desire to retain power within androcentric systems, hence perpetuating prejudices by discouraging solidarity among XXs.

Global studies examining various industries, including banking, academia, and nursing, indicate Queen Bee behaviours emerge as a response to XY–dominated environments where XX leaders feel pressured to adopt hyper-competitive and individualistic attitudes to secure their positions, thereby maintaining the patriarchal *status quo* (Derks et al., 2016).

Key reasons for this behaviour include intense competition due to limited leadership opportunities, fear of being perceived as weak by XY counterparts, and a sense of superiority (Abalkhail, 2020). Additionally, XXs exhibiting Queen Bee attitudes often assume that their XX colleagues are less committed (Sutton, 2004).

The Queen Bee label propagates the notion that XX leaders are unsupportive, suggesting they may withhold mentorship, engage in exclusionary practices, or undermine other XXs to assert dominance and secure their roles. These behaviours are not inherent, they are designed and implemented based on misogynistic assumptions that dominate workplaces (Abalkhail, 2020; Derks et al., 2016).

Consequently, Queen Bee behaviour manifests in actions that exclude others from opportunities, creating and perpetuating negative and adversarial dynamics, leading to toxic workplaces, reducing job satisfaction, increasing absenteeism and employee turnover, and negatively impacting organisational performance and career progression (Abalkhail, 2020; Derks et al., 2016).

Narratives often characterise XX leaders as competitive and uncooperative queen bees, for example, in the black comedy film *The Devil Wears Prada* (Wikipedia, n.d.).

However, recent studies indicate XXs are enhancing cohesion and collaboration, deepening alliances and networks, supporting other XXs by encouraging and promoting their development; assisting career advancements for colleagues, subordinates, and teams; and developing pro-XX policies and programmes (Mufti et al., 2021).

Femocrats

Initially emerging in Australia during the late 1970s as pioneers of government-led feminist reforms, femocrats gained further influence in the 1980s with the global introduction and amplification of women's budgets. Australia's first "women's policy unit" was established to create "a feminist presence" and advance the social and economic status of XXs (Sharp & Broomhill, 2002:29). Their influence has left a lasting mark on governance worldwide (Bashevkin, 2014; Sawer, 2007, 2016).

Recognised as trailblazers and inspiring international best practices, femocrats have formed strategic alliances with NGOs, government agencies, academics, and political leaders, which have been pivotal in securing resources and holding governments accountable for equality commitments. Despite their significant contributions, these policymakers often remain overlooked, albeit being powerful forces driving the advancement of XXs' rights globally (Sawer, 2017; Vega, 2023).

In the 1970s and 1980s, femocrats were pivotal in driving feminist agendas by leveraging their positions. Their role was, and continues to be, vital. Operating within the machinery of government, femocrats focus on strengthening policy through strategic internal reforms, instigating progress and promoting inclusive governance, regardless of how many XXs are elected (Sawer, 2017).

Irrespective of the limited representation of XXs in parliaments, femocrats have revolutionised policymaking by reframing priorities, reconfiguring policies, and promoting international law, including CEDAW, while setting global standards for embedding equality-focused policies into governance (Chappell, 2002; Vega, 2023).

For example, between 1985 and 1996, the Australian government increased the budget allocation by 27% to XXs. By 2020, 0.04% of the federal budget was allocated – AU$48 (US$30) million annually over five years – to improve XX's financial security and workforce participation (Fitz-Gibbon et al., 2020).

For example, fiscal strategies, including women's budgets, equal pay initiatives, and reproductive rights protections, have been determined by their expertise and support, leading to substantial reforms and demonstrating their ability to enable effective and meaningful changes, even in the absence of XX power brokers.

The impactful women's budgets, which expanded globally, are recognised as one of the most enduring fiscal initiatives (Campbell, 2018; Edwards & Stewart, 2017). Their lasting impact stands as a testament to the femocrats' determination and ability to collaborate with inclusive leadership, catalysing transformational change within local and international systems (Vega, 2023).

Often operating in power-driven XY–dominated environments, where access to human and economic resources is scarce and highly regulated, they have been, and continue to be, key agents of change in progressing strategies that improve lives (Sapkota & Dahal, 2022; Vega, 2023). Even with significant resource constraints, they promote, endorse, and respond to the needs of XXs, exemplifying their commitment to advancing equality.

When government budgets limit financial and human resources to departments and agencies dedicated to advancing the rights of XXs, femocrats' progress continues, albeit at a slower pace and, at times, regressing. Governmental economic strategic oppression imposes financial constraints to disrupt, impede, and defer progress. These deliberate suppressions reflect a state's disruptive perspective towards XXs, measuring progress as a direct confrontation to deeply entrenched patriarchal systems (Vega, 2023).

Regardless of the ongoing marginalisation of XXs by governments (Vijeyarasa, 2021), femocrats continue to advance equality, defying and rejecting suppressive legal structures built against XXs (MacKinnon, 2005).

While their influence has evolved from reliance on the state to directing market forces – for example, naming non-compliant employers (Sawer, 2007; WGEA, 2024b) – femocrats remain key figures in advancing pro–XX policy whilst operating primarily under androcentric rule (Sapkota & Dahal, 2022), yet continue to influence local laws and IWRLs (Vega, 2023).

However, democratic nations have the potential to reverse previous femocrat achievements. For example, in 2025 the US administration, under Trump, established the Department of Government Efficiency (DOGE), led by Musk and his team, "DOGE kids", who were granted unvetted access to digital networks controlling billion-dollar budgets and classified information, thereby weakening the civil service and destabilising democratic institutions (Shuster & Bennett, 2025).

On the cover of *Time* magazine, January 2025, a bold red background frames Musk seated in a presidential setting, casually holding a cup of coffee – an image that exudes calculated dominance and erratic tyrannical supremacy. The XY who performed the fascist Nazi salute (Kriner, 2025), provoking crowds as he prepared to dismantle the US government and the femocrats within (Shuster & Bennett, 2025), seized unrestrained authority without accountability.

Musk's wealth, hunger for data, and consolidation of power have eroded governance and weakened state-run infrastructures. Long-standing policies were dismantled, indispensable programmes have been obliterated, and oversight bodies have been abolished, while independent agencies' ability to enforce accountability and hold the administration accountable have been eliminated (Shuster & Bennett, 2025).

Acting with despotic, autocratic, and enforced sovereignty, this oligarch suspended funding across numerous departments, terminating the US Agency for International Development (USAID) global services, as of January 2025 – which provided foreign aid and development assistance worldwide – consequently destabilising international support (Kindy & Slodysko, 2025; Reilly, 2025; USAID, 2025) and potentially instigating global public health disasters and humanitarian crises.

The dismissal of employees, including prosecutors and regulatory officials – who would typically be protected from capricious and unlawful terminations in a democracy (Kindy & Slodysko, 2025; Reilly, 2025) – is also expected to produce turmoil and instability.

These tactics by the 47th US president and his oligarch – designed to manipulate public perception and project an image of competence – includes propaganda and the strategic control of information, via traditional media and SNSs. These techniques are frequently employed by repressive dictators, referred to as "informational autocrats" (Guriev & Treisman, 2019:100).

The hostile restructuring of federal agencies by the world's richest oligarch illuminates the fragility of democracy when unrestricted executive power is permitted to expedite the collapse of key governmental institutions. Musk also had the power to halt regulatory probes into his companies, including ongoing investigations into inflated claims about Tesla's self-driving cars. Experts warn the unchecked impacts will have grave consequences, as independent scrutiny is essential for preventing disasters and protecting lives (Kindy & Slodysko, 2025; Reilly, 2025).

While progress has been made, primarily influenced by femocrats' resilience, resource constraints continue to impede pro–XX policies, revealing a lack of genuine government prioritisation for equitable outcomes (Vega, 2023). Nevertheless, the enduring dedication and perseverance of femocrats, even under restrictive circumstances, have overcome misogynistic systems and produced equitable outcomes, improving the lives of XXs around the world.

Women's Budgets

Irrespective of the turbulence in the USA, the introduction of women's budgets provides some hope for XXs in numerous regions, signalling advancements within the patriarchal *status quo.*

Referred to as "gender-responsive budgets", "gendered budgets", or "gender budgets" (Sawer et al., 2020; Sharp & Broomhill, 2013), these terms are collectively termed women's budgets in this book.

Women's budgets were introduced in Australia in the 1980s. Since Australia's pioneering initiatives, numerous countries have adopted sex-responsive budgeting to influence fiscal policies (Rubin & Bartle, 2023). UNIFEM embraced the model in the late 1990s (Elson, 2006).

The objectives of the women's budgets have been broad and ambitious, aiming to strengthen governments' capacity to analyse sex-specific needs when planning taxation and spending, hold governments accountable, and align legislation with global equality standards (Budlender et al., 2002).

Women's budgets are typically focused on three key goals: a) integrating sex considerations into policies, b) ensuring governments are held accountable for their commitments to reducing sex-based discrimination, and c) influencing budgets to address sex-based differences. Additionally, some frameworks encourage policymakers to focus on XXs' specific needs and promote a more equitable economy (Elson, 2006; Sawer, 2016).

The underlying principle is that taxpayer revenue should support equal opportunities for all citizens, regardless of sex (AWAVA, 2020; Fitz-Gibbon et al., 2021). Moreover, implementing women's budgets would ensure that XXs are not overlooked globally in national budgets (Peetz et al., 2020). Australia also led the way with its *Women's Budget Statement*, requiring federal agencies to evaluate the impact of their budgetary decisions on XXs (Rubin & Bartle, 2023).

Patriarchs claim that budgets are inherently neutral and unbiased (Sharp & Broomhill, 2002). However, how governments allocate and spend public funds significantly influences XXs' economic opportunities, access to essential services, and overall well-being. Resource allocation also impacts XXs' spending power and their ability to contribute to and participate in the economy.

Tax policies and public spending continue to disproportionately impact XXs negatively. Budgeting processes frequently overlook XXs' contributions, limiting their economic participation while benefiting XYs, who often receive more than double the financial gains (AIHW, Australia Institute, 2020).

Without a sex-sensitive approach, government expenditure and taxation often intensify negative outcomes for XXs, families, and communities, reinforcing an economic reality where XYs pay less than XXs, perpetuating the income gap and maintaining androcentric control over the economy (Campbell, 2018; Ramalho & Trumbic, 2020). Consequently, poverty continues to disproportionately affect XXs, obstructing their human rights. Recognising these economic inequalities, the UN prioritised "No Poverty" as SDG 1 (UN, 2017, 2018).

To eliminate poverty, achieve equal pay for equal work, and end economic discrimination, the CEDAW Committee (Chapter 2) recommends nations introduce or reinstate women's budgets. To enhance positive outcomes, CEDAW's guidelines have expanded to require all member nations to submit detailed reports on their budgeting initiatives. The lack of policy analysis on how budgets impact XXs continues to have detrimental effects, undermining their economic security (Campbell, 2018; Edwards & Stewart, 2017).

The lack of investment in XX–focused initiatives reflects a broader trend of systemic neglect rooted in patriarchal attitudes, revealing a government's capability to utilise fiscal policies and legal frameworks to marginalise XXs and consolidate control (Schultz, 2020; Lombardo & Alonso, 2020).

By failing to establish mechanisms to combat sex-based economic discrimination, governments preserve and reinforce institutionalised disparities (Vega, 2023). Moreover, inadequate fiscal support for government entities advocating pro–XX policies reveal the inherent misogyny in patriarchal governance.

The power of governments to enact biased laws continues to perpetuate exclusionary attitudes (Sapkota & Dahal, 2022), underlining the urgent need for reforms in both legal frameworks and societal attitudes to achieve Goals 1 and 5 of the SDGs.

The absence of sex-disaggregated data undermines the capacity to evaluate and implement holistic economic reforms, delaying meaningful progress. Expanding data compilation and examination, together with attitudinal adjustments, are crucial to overcoming financial discrimination and achieving substantive progress (Rubin & Bartle, 2023).

Government budgets often reveal that funding allocations for XXs are deprioritised. In Australia, for example, various NGOs have criticised budgets as inherently biased, arguing that XXs' needs are treated as an afterthought (Coleman, 2019; Oxley, 2020). This critique was reinforced by one of the nation's most powerful economic advisory entities, which admitted that the Australian Treasury Department failed to apply a "gendered lens" in its policy evaluations, despite its responsibility to predict and assess policy impacts from a holistic economic perspective (Schultz, 2020; The Treasury, 2022).

Governments often frame expenditures that benefit XYs as "investments" while categorising spending on XXs as "costs" rather than valuable contributions to economic growth (Elson, 1998; Rubin & Bartle, 2023; Sarraf, 2003; Sawer et al., 2020). These financial biases continue to negatively impact economies, communities, and XXs globally, further deteriorating egalitarian prospects.

Nevertheless, some governments are illustrating that policy changes and sensible budgets can improve quality of life for XXs. For example, budgeting for breast and ovarian cancer screening, increasing childcare subsidies, extending paid parental leave, removing luxury taxes from menstrual hygiene products (Chapter 3), legal consequences for VAW perpetrators, providing respiratory syncytial virus (RSV) vaccines – to protect XXs and foetuses from breathing problems, including pneumonia and bronchiolitis (Phadke et al., 2024) – are only a few examples. While some reforms indicate incremental progress, unclear funding mechanisms and limited systemic reform signify further improvements are necessary (Hodgson, 2022).

For example, while free period products had been introduced in public schools nationwide in Australia, remote Indigenous communities have limited availability, period poverty, high costs, and reduced access to services. Period poverty is a relatively new term to explain the adversities faced by XXs in managing their menstrual health based on various cultural expectations and taboos (Hall, 2021), attracting both political and media attention. However, menstrual health equity extends beyond product access – it requires education and community-driven initiatives to empower young XXs, reduce stigma, and increase period parity (Lansbury & King, 2024).

In the EU, Austria, for example, stands out with its *Organic Budget law*, which, since 2013, has required all federal ministries to integrate sex-based equality objectives into their budgets and reporting processes to create a benchmark for accountability. Austria has also reallocated funds from traditionally XY–dominated areas, including defence, to health and education (Rubin & Bartle, 2023).

On the Iberian Peninsula, Spain's *G+ Programme* indicates the transformative potential of pro–XX budgeting in national frameworks, reshaping fiscal policies and influencing the broader societal norms that underpin them. As a result, Spain has emerged as a leader in the EU, setting a precedent for other nations to adopt and adapt similar approaches, demonstrating the power of reflective reform when generating favourable policies for XXs (Rubin & Bartle, 2023).

Childcare

Childcare encompasses both paid and unpaid care for children under the age of five, delivered by individuals other than parents, either through formal arrangements – daycare centres, preschools, nannies – or informal setups – friends, relatives, neighbours. The various types of childcare continue to pose substantial obstacles for XXs globally, with policies and provisions varying significantly by region.

Childcare systems in Australia, India, the EU, the UK, and the USA are reviewed.

Australia

Around seven in ten (70%) households rely on some form of childcare in Australia, averaging 11 hours per week of informal care and 22 hours of formal care (Mumford et al., 2020).

Despite subsidies, paid childcare remains costly across all states, forcing many low-income families to depend on unpaid assistance (Arpino & Luppi, 2020). Among XXs aged 20–74, seven in ten (66%) participate in the workforce; however, less than a third (29%) of XX parents with young children are employed, compared to nine in ten (90%) XYs working full-time. These imbalances exemplify deeply rooted sex-based biases in Australia (Coombe et al., 2019).

Similar to the EU, formal childcare in Australia tends to benefit middle- and higher-income families, with employment security and work–family attitudes influencing childcare enrolments. Higher-educated parents with stable employment are 102% more likely to use formal childcare than lower-educated parents (Wood et al., 2023).

In line with trends in the UK, the use of nannies/au pairs in Australia is common among dual-earner households requiring flexible in-home care. Rising living expenses and extended work hours have increased demand, with XXs continuing to bear disproportionate parental responsibilities and facilitating in-home care to balance work and family life (Adamson & Brennan, 2017).

While some policies provide subsidised access to nannies, high costs and restrictive migration and working visa requirements limit availability, as observed in the UK and Canada (Adamson & Brennan, 2017). Nevertheless, in-home childcare is becoming an essential part of the system, particularly for high-income parents.

Conversely, families from low-income households experience substantial constraints to childcare access. Frequently prioritising childcare responsibilities over personal and professional goals, XXs are assuming the bulk of childcare and household tasks. This dynamic leads to elevated stress levels and reduced workforce engagement (Coombe et al., 2019).

Androcentric ideals of what constitutes a "good mother" often lead XXs to internalise guilt, pressuring them to adhere to residual patriarchal notions of "motherhood", with societal pressure often resulting in reduced working hours or complete withdrawal from the workforce (Coombe et al., 2019:305).

Around one-third of children under the age of three attend centre-based childcare in urban areas, while rural families rely heavily on unpaid childcare, provided by relatives or friends (Arpino & Luppi, 2020) facing even greater difficulties, with limited part-time work opportunities, fewer formal childcare services, and high costs. For example, the national average cost of long daycare is around AU$130 (US$81) per day – ranging from AU$200 (US$125) to AU$70 (US$44) per day (Monash Vale Early Learning Centre, 2024), totalling around AU$4,350 (US$2,731) annually per child, further straining the financial feasibility of XXs returning to work (Arpino & Luppi, 2020; Australian Institute of Family Studies, 2023; Coombe et al., 2019).

Another key issue in Australia's fragmented childcare system is low wages for childcare workers. The federated political structure and diverse ownership models create inconsistencies that restrict sustainable advancement. For example, the annual staff turnover rate is one in four (25%) to almost one in three (37%), with remote areas facing even higher exit rates, despite a 4% annual workforce growth and an 80% qualification rate among educators. The shortage of qualified staff is partly due to educators (Chapter 5) seeking better-paid employment (Cumming et al., 2015; OECD, 2024a).

Although childcare availability and affordability impact both XX and XY workforce participation, XXs' labour supply is more sensitive to changes in wages and childcare costs. As a result, work opportunities for XX parents are often constrained, while XYs' employment hours remain largely unaffected (Mumford et al., 2020).

The disparity extends to informal childcare, particularly grandparental care, where sex-based norms restrict caregiving roles. Grand XYs typically play a less direct role and face fewer constraints, whereas grand XXs have greater responsibilities. In urban areas, grandparents provide regular care to support working parents and mitigate the high costs, while rural grandparents offer more occasional care, reflecting lower parental employment rates (Craig & Jenkins, 2016).

Grandparents with higher education and socio-economic status are more likely to provide regular care. However, grand XXs assume caregiving roles regardless of financial standing, while grand XYs' involvement remains flexible and unaffected by employment status. Understanding grand XXs' struggles is crucial for policies supporting caregivers and work–life balance (Craig & Jenkins, 2016).

The EU

Childcare deterrents in the EU include logistical impediments in accessing services. Despite various policies, practical obstacles persist across the EU, including mismatched schedules, inefficient geographical distribution, and affordability issues. Affordability, accessibility, and cultural expectations remain the primary barriers affecting XXs' workforce participation and financial status.

Childcare dilemmas in the EU also include inadequate access. Despite the existence of various policies, practical barriers remain, including misaligned schedules, inefficient geographical distribution, and prohibitive costs. Cultural expectations and affordability remain the principal obstacles for XXs' workforce participation and financial stability. Policy efforts to eliminate traditional sex-based roles have continued across most EU countries, leading to some advancements in promoting equality. However, childcare policies vary, conditioned by economic, cultural, and political contexts (Szelewa & Polakowski, 2023).

Grandparents' involvement in childcare across the EU also differs in intensity and frequency, determined by each nation's labour force participation rates, childcare provisions, family planning decisions, and cultural norms (Di Gessa et al., 2016; Rutigliano, 2020).

In Southern Europe, including Italy, Spain, and Greece, for example, one in three (30%) grandparents provide regular daily childcare, driven by limited formal childcare services and cultural expectations for family-based caregiving. Reliance on grandparents often stems from limited government-sponsored childcare options, making them essential to informal childcare arrangements (Di Gessa et al., 2016).

In Spain, familial bonds play a significant role in childcare, with nearly one in two (45%) grandparents in urban areas actively involved, compared to one in three (35%) in rural areas. Most caregivers are grand XXs, with around two in three (65%) holding a tertiary education. Although many Spanish grandparents find caregiving rewarding, the intensity of their responsibilities negatively impacts their health and quality of life, with one in three (30%) reporting a moderate quality of life, while one in seven (15%) experiences a low quality of life (García-Sanjuán et al., 2024).

Belgium and France, along with Spain, have also implemented pro-birth policies. In contrast, Austria, Germany, Greece, Italy, and Switzerland show a strong correlation between grandparental childcare availability and family planning decisions. The likelihood of having a first child increases with the expectation of grandparental support. Conversely, in countries with comprehensive formal childcare systems, including Denmark, Sweden, and the Netherlands, grandparental involvement plays a minimal role in family planning (Rutigliano, 2020).

The differences between Northern, Western, and Southern European nations are largely attributed to well-developed childcare systems, which support high XX labour force participation. In Sweden, for example, between one in 20 and one in ten (5% to 10%) grandparents provide daily childcare. This low rate reflects policies that promote shared parental caregiving responsibilities, thereby reducing reliance on grandparents (Di Gessa et al., 2016).

In Germany, despite progress towards sex parity in parental leave, early childcare remains traditional, with part-time work being more common for XXs than XYs. Although substantial parental leave is offered, access to childcare services is inconsistent, particularly for younger children (Escriva et al., 2024).

Operating hours often clash with work schedules, and lengthy waiting lists further complicate arrangements for working parents (McLeana et al., 2017). Furthermore, services are frequently limited and lack the flexibility required to accommodate modern working demands (Szelewa & Polakowski, 2023).

Robust maternal leave policies in Germany, for example, reduce the need for intensive grandparental care during the early years. As a result, around two in five (40%) grandparents provide some form of childcare, but only around one in ten (10%) provide daily care, averaging 15 hours per week, indicating that in countries with pro–XX childcare policies, grandparental care is typically supplementary rather than intensive (Di Gessa et al., 2016).

Italy, like Ireland and Poland, exhibits prejudices, prioritising maternal leave over paternal leave. In contrast, Sweden and Denmark offer progressive policies, including extensive parental leave that encourages both parents to share caregiving responsibilities. Universal childcare coverage with flexible arrangements aligns with work demands while supporting child development and parental employment (Szelewa & Polakowski, 2023; McLeana et al., 2017).

For migrants and expats across the EU, childcare limitations are exacerbated by cultural motherhood expectations and inadequate institutional support. Despite many XXs holding tertiary qualifications, their access to childcare and ability to balance parental responsibilities remain defined by legislative restrictions and family support systems. Inflexible work schedules and the persistence of XXs' caregiving expectations continue to preclude XYs' involvement (Escriva et al., 2024).

Overall, inflexible schedules, geographical issues, androcentric policies, and government budgets limit access to childcare for parents in many EU countries, making it difficult to balance work and family responsibilities. Around one in four (24%) parents in urban areas are more likely to use formal childcare compared to those in rural regions, highlighting considerable disparities across the EU (Wood et al., 2023).

India

The childcare system lacks a cohesive structure in India, defined by socioeconomic stratification rather than equitable policy frameworks. This disparity affects both the quality and accessibility of childcare, with economic, social, and institutional factors heavily influencing the financial security of XXs (Motwani, 2024; Palriwala & Neetha, 2011).

Informal childcare is entrenched with sex-based expectations and familial responsibilities, reflecting hierarchical methods where caregiving duties fall disproportionately on XXs. Social class and economic disparities further disadvantage XXs with culture reinforcing caregiving as their primary responsibility, perpetuating patriarchal expectations and undervaluing care work. Limited access to childcare services compounds fiscal inequalities, particularly for low-income families (Palriwala & Neetha, 2011).

Global exposure, however, is changing mindsets, resulting in XYs increasingly engaging in childcare responsibilities. For example, in urban India, around two in five (40%) XYs are involved in childcare activities, with one in ten (10%) XYs indicating that they share childcare equally with their partners, particularly among young educated XYs.

Although perspectives are changing, restrictive workplace policies, inadequate paternity leave, and societal expectations impede the involvement of XYs (Motwani, 2024).

The UK

Treasury data from 2021 indicates a £2.4 (AU$4.7/US$2.9) billion underspend on tax-free childcare, reflecting low uptake and difficulties in accessing financial support across England, Scotland, Wales, and Northern Ireland, impacting XXs' employment decisions as many families struggle to navigate schemes (McIntosh, 2023).

Delivering childcare remains a dilemma in the UK, despite progressive parental leave policies (Szelewa & Polakowski, 2023). While childcare availability has improved over recent decades, the system is comparatively more privatised than in the EU, resulting in inconsistencies in both service quality and accessibility (Lyonette et al., 2011; McLeana et al., 2017).

Childcare costs are key in defining parental decisions about work and family, significantly influencing career choices. On average, childcare costs consume nearly £30 of £100 (30%) – AU$59 of AU$197 / US$37 of US$122 – of household income, imposing substantial financial burdens, particularly on lower-income families. For example, one in three (30%) XXs are employed, and nearly half of parents (46%) make use of free childcare entitlements, while more than half (53%) pay for childcare services (Lyonette et al., 2011; McIntosh, 2023).

The lack of affordable and accessible childcare disproportionately impacts XXs, who are more likely to reduce their working hours or exit the workforce to manage childcare responsibilities, as in other nations. This trend, referred to as the "motherhood penalty", leads to setbacks in earnings and career progression (McIntosh, 2023), thereby widening the pay gap as XXs age. The issue is especially acute in London and the South East, where childcare expenses are the highest, resulting in the lowest maternal employment rates (McIntosh, 2023; Viitanen, 2005).

Employment is less economically viable for low-income households; hence, many parents turn to informal care, with approximately one in seven (15%) grandparents regularly providing childcare (Di Gessa et al., 2016) in the UK.

Grandparental participation is influenced by socio-economic status and cultural norms, which vary across the UK's diverse multicultural communities. In South Asian households, for example, multi-generational living arrangements enable grandparents to provide regular childcare.

In contrast, African and Caribbean families, though they include grandparents in childcare roles, often seek support outside the immediate family due to distinct cultural factors and the legacies of migration (Bordone et al., 2020).

In the UK, XYs' perspectives on XXs returning to work after childbirth continue to be affected by practical considerations, including childcare availability, costs, and access to healthcare (Lyonette et al., 2011). Additionally, the absence of policies that address the specific needs of non-British families further complicates access to childcare services (Bordone et al., 2020).

Nanny services, similar to Australia, are becoming increasingly popular among families who can afford them, partly influenced by policies designed to make in-home care more accessible and affordable in the UK for higher-income households (Adamson & Brennan, 2017).

USA

Working XX parents are more prevalent in the USA than in the UK, reflecting a shift in XY attitudes towards motherhood and a stronger societal expectation for XXs to participate in full-time employment. In support of this trend, three out of five (60%) preschoolers spend around 25 hours each week in care (Lyonette et al., 2011; Herbst, 2023), reflecting the reliance on external care to enable parental workforce participation.

One of the numerous impediments with the childcare system in the USA is that healthcare is frequently employer provided, and parents rely on the private sector for childcare, creating additional obstacles and influencing XXs' employment decisions. Additionally, XX parents aged 25 to 44 are less likely to be in the labour force and, when employed, tend to work fewer hours each week compared to those of the same age who do not have children (Kochhar, 2023; Lyonette et al., 2011). Data from 2019 indicates that two out of three (64%) mothers with babies under one year were in the workforce, compared to seven in ten (71%) of those with children aged five (Herbst, 2023).

Across the 50 states, costly childcare services generate disruptions in employment for XXs, with regulations varying widely. Weekly childcare expenses increased by 71% over a 25-year period, with annual costs exceeding public university tuition fees within 28 states, stagnating fertility rates, workforce participation, and economic security (Fraga, 2018; Herbst, 2023; Laughlin, 2013).

Rising child poverty rates are exacerbated by the high cost of childcare, changes in subsidies, and persistent inequalities in labour markets. Suppliers and sectors vary in quality, restricting XX parents' employment and disrupting economic growth (Landivar et al., 2021; Herbst, 2023). Inadequate childcare policies in the USA further exacerbate financial insecurity for families, deepening poverty rates (Hartley et al., 2022; Herbst, 2023).

More than three in four (75%) parents reported difficulties in finding affordable, high-quality childcare, which negatively impacts employment opportunities and the child's education, raising concerns about the ramifications on child development in the USA (Pilarz et al., 2022).

Reducing childcare costs would allow more XXs to engage in consistent work and lower child poverty rates by 5% to 10%, with single XXs benefiting the most. Additionally, capping childcare expenses could increase XX labour participation by more than 12%, with the resulting wages helping to reduce child poverty (Hartley et al., 2022).

The grand XXs play a crucial role in enabling employment across urban and rural areas in the USA, with geographical proximity being a key factor. For example, one in four (25%) XXs who live close to their XX parent benefit from work-related childcare, compared to only one in 25 (4%) whose XX parent resides farther away. Likewise, one in five (20%) XXs receive childcare assistance from nearby XX-in-laws (Compton & Pollak, 2014).

The childcare sector experiences an annual employee exit rate exceeding one of every four (25%) in the USA, around four times higher than that of primary schools (Bassok et al., 2013; Herbst, 2023).

Conclusion

The economic capacity of XXs is a testament to their unparalleled ability to transform economies, disrupt societal norms, and redefine the dimensions of global markets.

The spending power of XXs through the rise of fast fashion, online consumerism, and their reduction of meat consumption portrays the varied and emerging market trends that XX consumers are changing; many are also demanding accountability and transforming industries to align with values of equity and sustainability.

Cultural, psychological, and marketing factors induce XX's consumer habits. The *lipstick effect*, for example, reveals the psychological elements of shopping activities linked to obtaining beauty and security. These behaviours also highlight the resilience and adaptability of XXs when negotiating complex fiscal realities.

The "power of the purse" represents more than just economic capacity; it signifies the ability to propel transformation in industries long dominated by sexist, illegal, and inhumane practices. However, this change is not without difficulties. As awareness of environmental costs and exploitative labour practices grows, so does the urgency for more sustainable and ethical production and consumption practices, with legal provisions already implemented in France restricting fast fashion.

Egalitarians have made progress in challenging systemic bigotry, from narrowing the pay gap to implementating women's budgets – setting global precedents by integrating sex-based perspectives into government resource allocations and tax regulations. These initiatives have amplified XX voices, enabling femocrats to make progress on international platforms and to deliver pro–XX legislation.

Childcare, long recognised as an essential element for XX's workforce participation, has seen notable improvements in accessibility and affordability in some regions. However, significant disparities remain. Many are forced to carry a disproportionate load in balancing professional and personal responsibilities, while others struggle with cost of childcare and motherhood expectations – leading many to start their own businesses.

The role of XXs as formal and informal carers often results in economic penalties that can reverberate through generations, accentuating the need for comprehensive policies that support family-friendly workplaces, improve equitable government resources allocation, and deliver appropriate remuneration and recompense for grand–XXs.

Narrowing in some areas, the lack of parity is a stark reminder of the widespread illegal actions of millions of employers continuously making excuses for underpaying XXs. Despite the proliferation of equal pay laws, the lack of enforcement mechanisms and bigotry perpetuate wage disparities. The underrepresentation of XXs in high-paying sectors and leadership roles further exacerbates these inequities. Nonetheless, numerous XXs are leading and initiating positive changes, and where progress is visible, so too are the benefits obtained by communities and nations.

The Queen Bees are being displaced as collaborative leaders drive transformation across numerous industries. Removing sticky floors and breaking glass ceilings, whilst proving ethical leadership and consumer activism, are powerful forces for change, from the femocrats shaping change on a global scale to the numerous breakthroughs achieved internationally with XXs initiatives.

While patriarchs and their mates perpetuate misogyny, this chapter affirms that XX's economic agency is a transformative force that, when united and redirected, will further power global changes.

"When we invest in women – the most critical and under-resourced asset in the world – we unlock a better future not only for women themselves, but also for the next generation."

Melinda French Gates, American philanthropist and former multimedia product developer and manager at Microsoft (Gates, 2016)

Toolkit

Not all XXs are affected by childcare and not all can be femocrats either; however, each one of us has the power to contribute to improving our economic well-being. Following are a few practical tools to help you take meaningful steps for yourself, your loved ones, colleagues, and Mother Earth.

Be Aware of Your Economic Power

This toolkit is not a one-time effort but a guide for consistent, regular actions. By implementing the suggested practices listed here, XXs can collaboratively restructure and eliminate ineffective philosophies and inefficient systems, leading the way to a fairer fiscal, more equitable, and healthier planet – one deliberate economic choice at a time.

Speak About Money and Negotiate

Societal and cultural norms often assert that money is a taboo topic. Androcentric concepts disproportionately disadvantaged XXs, with fewer promotions and less pay for equal work. Hence, it is important to demand transparency and equity to establish authentic merit. Breaking the silence on money will be both liberating and transformative.

When you ask for a pay rise, or a promotion, it goes beyond personal ambition; it is a direct challenge to the systemic undervaluation of your work. Communicating clearly demonstrates self-respect, recognises contributions, and sets a precedent for other XXs to follow. Normalising conversations about wages promotes transparency, encourages self-assurance, and cultivates workplace equity, where XXs feel empowered to advocate for themselves and others, without fear of retribution.

Economic independence is more than an individual achievement; it drives XXs into positions of leadership, where policies and actions can prioritise and include their needs. Moreover, economic independence facilitates the breakdown of patriarchal power that controls the actions and lives of all XXs.

If you do not ask, the answer is always "no", so ask!

Promoting fair and equal wages is not just an act of self-empowerment; it is a vital step towards a more balanced and progressive equitable world. If you are aware that your employer is ignoring equal wage laws, suggest the necessary changes. If they ignore you, consider reporting the matter. Discuss money openly – bonuses also form a substantial part of total compensation and should be included in all negotiations.

Adopt mindful consumer habits: Developing thoughtful purchasing habits is key to reducing demand for unsustainable items that pollute waterways and add to landfills. While cheap items may seem cost-effective, the cumulative expense of items used only a few times quickly adds up. Before buying new things, evaluate their long-term value for both your personal use and the environment. Opting for recycled alternatives can also deliver surprising finds while benefiting the planet and your budget.

Verify the recipients of your purchases: Before buying, donating, or investing, research to ensure your hard-earned cash will not disadvantage other XXs or further empower oligarchs. In today's digital world, spending a few moments to gather information before you buy can create a domino effect, positively impacting people, communities, and the environment, in the short and long term.

Support female entrepreneurs: Consider purchasing from XX–led businesses, whether for items, utilities, or services. This approach not only facilitates a more equitable redistribution of wealth but also supports ethical practices. Reflect on how your choices will affect your future and the planet. Are the companies you are supporting treating their employees and the planet responsibly? Will your purchase contribute to landfill waste? Reflect on the origins of the product and who stands to benefit from your decision, before you buy!

Hire and Promote XXs

If you are in a leadership role, lead with inclusivity. Think about how your decisions reflect fairness and empathy. Build teams where XXs feel valued and supported so they can climb the ladder and attain economic security.

Strive to prioritise XXs in hiring decisions; aim to provide fair opportunities for XXs wherever possible. At times, we may inadvertently hold one another back. Consider asking yourself, "Am I acting like a Queen Bee?"

Advocate for XXs into leadership roles and provide mentorship to help them succeed. Use your voice to amplify their achievements and create visibility for their contributions. The Queen Bee syndrome is not beneficial for anyone, so consider your future and the struggles of others before adopting exclusionary behaviours.

7 Polity and Law

Personal Note

While representing Australia at a G20 meeting, I approached an XY CEO who had just spoken about the alleged impossibility of finding XXs for leadership roles. Standing beside the Minister for Small Business, I offered to introduce him to qualified XXs and handed him my business card. Instead of accepting it, he patted me on the head and said, "Give your card to my Sherpa," and walked away. The minister and I were left speechless.

The year before the 2022 federal election was announced in Australia, I was approached by one of the two major parties, as well as a minor party, to run as a candidate. After some negotiations, I realised that my values did not align with the androcentricities of the major party and decided to stand as a Senate candidate with the minor party.

Having spent time in parliament advocating for self-employed XXs with the AWCCI, the experiences taught me that change within government is exhausting and often insurmountable, further reinforcing my understanding that, to secure balanced outcomes, one needs power and the ability to work within the machinery of government.

My decision to run was partly driven by fear. A well-funded right-wing minor party was making loud and alarming statements, and I feared that if they gained control of the Senate, they would profoundly transform the nation.

Throughout the election campaign, I was regularly unsettled by the abuse I received. The insults and sex-based stereotypes were both alarming and disheartening. I was also disturbed by the sheer volume of malinformation, misinformation, and disinformation that severely distorted voters' understanding and decisions. Equally surprising were the many XXs who openly admitted to voting as directed by their XY partner or father.

DOI: 10.4324/9781003516224-7

In contrast, I was astonished, moved, and grateful for the generosity of strangers who dedicated countless hours to the election campaign as volunteers.

Throughout the campaign, the media were interested only in providing coverage on a single occasion, specifically when they could use the word "sex", while ignoring my policy platform, which addressed critical issues including XXs health and climate change.

Unfortunately, my concerns materialised – though not catastrophically – as the party I feared won the seat I was targeting. However, it was the only seat they secured nationwide, leaving them without any control or influence, and incapable of affecting legislation.

The experience reaffirmed the bitter reality that political power remains elusive, and that this sought-after domain is still skewed in favour of XYs. It also taught me that every single vote makes a difference.

My experiences are minuscule relative to the obstructions and impediments encountered by so many XXs in politics globally, as illustrated in this chapter.

Introduction

Democracy is premised on government by the people, yet historically and currently, many democracies are exclusive and patriarchal in practice. Nonetheless, laws, legislation, and policies regulate every aspect of life for citizens.

Over time, XXs have contributed significantly to democratic advancements, though often overlooked, ignored, and/or undervalued.

Across the globe, XX politicians withstand precarious situations: sexism, violence, harassment, and at times death. Political leaders, including Gillard (Australia), Merkel (Germany), Marin (Finland), Gandhi (India), Cox and Abbott (UK), and Giffords (USA), for example, are a few of the many who sacrificed their well-being to improve their respective countries, albeit enduring unremitting adversities. These heroines demonstrate that, despite ongoing constraints, XXs continue to lead change and inspire progress for both current and future generations around the world.

Increasing XX representation is vital to achieving fairer, more inclusive legislation and to building equitable societies, despite enduring patriarchal opposition to diversity, equity, and inclusion efforts.

Eliminating paternalistic dominance begins with informed voting, accountability, and support for pro–XX policies, all of which are integral to democratic systems. Collective contributions from XXs are generating reforms and, XXs together possess the electoral strength to redesign current and future political realities. By understanding how governing systems are functioning, effective tools are being employed to disband the patriarchy. But first, it is essential to understand how democracy operates.

Politicians are the architects of laws. The polity holds the authority to create policies, enact legislation, and establish the rule of law to which citizens must abide; the judiciary interprets and applies them accordingly. Because the great majority of politicians are XYs, misogyny within politics has been verified for decades and continues to be central in public debates globally, long after suffrage began in the late 1800s. The fight for suffrage, however, demonstrates the perseverance of XXs' demands for equality, spurring the first feminist wave that has swelled into the current tsunami.

Most democracies have three main branches of power: legislative, judicial, and executive. These systems, in theory, ensure balance and accountability but can also be subject to malpractice and exploitation, affecting trust in governance. Progress towards equality has begun, albeit after centuries of waiting, while societies continue to witness the misuse of androcentric power, which often leads to corruption.

There is a significant gap between the ideals of DEI, political rhetoric; and the lived realities of XXs. Those in power mandate and impose restrictions that limit XXs' progress and retain traditional oppressive hierarchies.

Nevertheless, voting is the key mechanism of democracy, enabling citizens to select leaders and influence laws. Yet disparities in voting patterns persist, influenced by sex, age, education, and racial demographics.

Compulsory voting boosts participation, as seen in several countries, including Australia and Belgium, for example. In contrast nations including the USA, where voting is optional, experience significantly lower voter turnout.

While debates on mandatory voting as an undemocratic practice linger, it also demonstrates the capacity to increase electoral participation. Engagement and informed voting from XXs – half of the population – can steer legislative changes that impact current and future generations.

The underrepresentation of XXs in legislative bodies, and their absence from leadership roles worldwide, remains a pressing global issue that requires evolution – current trends indicate it will take over a century to obtain proportional representation. For example, in 2024, just over one in four parliamentary seats were held by XXs.

Nonetheless, XXs who have gained a seat at the table are defining pro–XX policies, albeit facing structural obstacles, systemic bigotry, unequal power dynamics, workplace discrimination, and violence. Their influence is paving the way for greater representation and advancing democratic standards. However, their governance has also divided opinion: "*Do XX politicians increase and support pro–XX policies?*"

Advocacy and international law also have notable roles in advancing DEI, at times compelling governments to honour contractual commitments – voters also influence how nations are represented on the international stage.

By engaging with political systems and amplifying voices, individuals can lobby and/or vote for laws that uphold human rights, pushing for a diverse and ethical world. When voters lack essential knowledge of democratic systems, they remain unaware and vulnerable to the influence of autocratic regimes.

Heroines

Australia

Julia Gillard, Australia's first XX PM (2010–2013), endured exceptional levels of misogyny, vilification, and violence throughout her tenure. The media's relentless denigration, abuse, and explicit sexualisation of Gillard (Dowse, 2014; Summers, 2012) was brutal, unrelenting and gynophobic. Subjected to derogatory nicknames, including "Juliar" – a term coined by an Australian radio broadcaster, accused of 34 sexual assault charges in 2024 (Beazley, 2024). The same broadcaster suggested that Gillard should be placed in a chaff bag and thrown out to sea. Others referred to Gillard as "Bob Brown's Bitch" – Brown was the leader of the Australian Greens party at the time.

The "Ditch the Witch" campaign against Gillard was ruthless. Protesters displayed insulting signs during rallies, while the conservative opposition leader stood nearby, ensuring the media captured the vicious scene – blatantly attempting to undermine Gillard through misogynistic tactics (Walsh, 2013). The slur "Juliar" was frequently used in parliament by the opposition to undermine Gillard's credibility.

The media also employed XY chauvinistic tactics by referring to her as "Julia" instead of "PM Gillard", deviating from the traditional respect afforded to previous XY PMs (Summers, 2012). Instead of focusing on her legislative achievements, the media and others fixated on her appearance. For example, Germaine Greer, the author of *The Female Eunuch* (1971), commented on live television, "You've got a big arse, Julia …" and compared her dress style to that of an "organ grinder's monkey" (ABC News, 2013; Goodall, 2013). Cartoonists depicted Gillard in vulgar and sexualised ways – one drawing featured Gillard with a strap-on penis, while another showed her alone in a wedding dress (Stevenson, 2019).

The persistent disparaging depictions of Gillard had a profound mental and emotional impact and tarnished her public image. Reluctant to play the "gender card", Gillard avoided explicitly focusing on "women's issues" (Wright & Holland, 2014:459). However, her stance altered demonstrably when delivering her famous "misogyny speech" in 2012, responding to a Bill presented by the leader of the opposition (Sawer, 2017). The speech generated international headlines and inadvertently transformed Gillard into a global feminist icon overnight (Wright & Holland, 2014).

The famous speech brought new challenges for Gillard, who later reflected: "It [sexism] definitely will not take us to being a nation where at every level and in every way, women and men participate in our society and are judged by the same, not different, standards" (Gillard, 2014:112).

Prior to entering politics, Gillard worked as an industrial lawyer. Elected to parliament in 1998, she thereafter held several portfolios, including education and social inclusion, before becoming the 27th PM of Australia. Her achievements were numerous, including fairer industrial relations systems, the first national paid parental leave scheme, new school funding models, and the implementation of Australia's first national school curriculum. Gillard also established the foundation for the National Disability Insurance Scheme (NDIS), amongst many other progressive pieces of legislation (National Archives of Australia, n.d.) that positively affected the majority of the population.

The EU

Angela Merkel

Germany's first XX Chancellor overcame formidable resistance when promoting equal opportunity policies, including sexism within her own party. The Conservative Christian Democrats often misjudged Merkel as an unsuitable leader for being a childfree divorcee. Merkel held the portfolio of Women's Affairs before becoming Chancellor (Boysen, 2005) and was recognised as a prominent figure in EU politics from 2005 to 2021.

Despite opposition, Merkel implemented numerous policies that benefited XXs in Germany, demonstrating resilience and a commitment to equality. Similar to Gillard, Merkel did not openly champion XXs' issues (Davidson-Schmich, 2011) and often hesitated to label herself a feminist (Mushaben, 2018), partly because she required the support of polity XYs (Boysen, 2005) to advance her agenda.

Merkel often ignored the androcentric and patriarchal attitudes frequently exhibited by XY leaders. For example, Russian President Vladimir Putin took his large dog to a meeting with Merkel, knowing she was afraid of dogs after being attacked in 1995 (Hume, 2016). Similarly, the former president of the USA, George W. Bush, inappropriately rubbed Merkel's shoulders at a G8 summit without her consent (ABC News, 2006).

The media frequently sought to weaken Merkel's authority by using language that diluted her leadership credibility and attempted to erode her integrity with chauvinistic rhetoric (Van Halsema, 2019). Diminutive terms, including "Helmut's Mädchen" (Helmut's girl), condescendingly linked her identity to her mentor, former Chancellor Helmut Kohl, suggesting reliance on an XY. Similarly, "Mutti" (Mommy) reinforced phallocentric stereotypes, framing her as nurturing and domestic rather than a decisive leader. "Pfarrerstochter" (pastor's daughter) further implied traditional family values and subservience (Van Halsema, 2019).

Merkel often used humour to reflect; in 2018, for example, during the celebration of 100 years of suffrage in Germany, Merkel remarked: "These days, no one ridicules a young girl when she says she would like to be a minister or even federal chancellor when she grows up. I have even heard that some people ask if a man can become federal chancellor – no, I'm not making that up!" (Merkel, 2018).

Irrespective of the dismissive treatment from XYs in power and the media, Merkel became one of the most powerful and influential politicians in the world. She was globally admired for her strategic leadership, measured restraint, and remarkable ability to manage systemic bigotry and contempt.

Sanna Marin

In November 2022, Sanna Marin, Finnish PM and Jacinda Ardern, NZ PM, held a joint press conference in Auckland. Various issues were discussed, including the situations in Afghanistan and Ukraine, as well as the significant economic relationship between the two countries, with NZ importing NZ$199 (AU$179.5 / US$114) million worth of goods from Finland.

A young XY reporter, ignoring the significant trade deals, asked, "... are you two meeting just because you're similar in age and got a lot of common stuff there?" (Ripper, 2022).

Ardern's face showed shock, but she responded by questioning whether XY leaders would ever face the same question. Marin echoed Ardern's sentiments, emphasising the presence of a business delegation and the focus on cooperation between the two nations. The incident made global headlines, again revealing the persistence of misogyny even towards those holding the most powerful positions in politics (Crewe, 2022; Mata, 2022; Patterson, 2022).

Prior to becoming PM, Ardern held several portfolios, including Arts, Culture & Heritage and Child Poverty Reduction. Ardern announced her resignation in January 2023. In the same year, Marin, the youngest PM of Finland when elected, left politics following her party's defeat in 2023 (Bland, 2023). Marin had previously held the portfolios of Transport and Communications.

India

Indira Gandhi, the first XX PM of India (1966 to 1977 and again 1980 to 1984), faced sexism, patriarchal arrogance, and death threats throughout her political career. Her tenure was marked by intense scrutiny, accusations of adultery, and criticism for being audacious, decisive, and strong (Chaudhury, 2022). Gandhi was assassinated by her two bodyguards in New Delhi (History.com, 2021; Kumari, 2021).

Despite significant contributions and extraordinary adversities, Gandhi asserted her influence in a nation deeply ingrained with patriarchal values (Gangoli, 2016; Nigam, 2022).

Gandhi's experiences were horrific and ultimately fatal. Yet she was not the only one to confront gynophobes. Mamata Banerjee, for example, became one of the youngest parliamentarians in West Bengal in 1984, aged 29, defeating a veteran XY politician and securing a seat in the *Lok Sabha*. Banerjee founded the All India Trinamool Congress (AITC) and, in 2011, gained a historic victory, ending 34 years of communist rule and becoming the first XX Chief Minister of West Bengal.

Banerjee withstood hostility and vilification, including physical assaults causing serious injuries. There were also coordinated attempts on her life by political rivals. Nonetheless, Banerjee persevered. As of 2025, the AITC remains an active and influential political force (Chaudhury, 2022; History.com, 2021; Ruud & Heierstad, 2016); the outcome of the election in 2026 will decide her future.

The UK

Jo Cox and Diane Abbott

The rise of violent, confrontational intimidation towards politicians in the UK is reminiscent of US–style aggression, imposing profound risks, resulting in assassination attempts, deaths, and withdrawals from election campaigns (Syal, 2024). Violence against women in politics (VAWIP), reviewed later in this chapter, is progressively emerging as an additional impediment, further interfering with efforts for XXs and other underrepresented groups to run for office (Ballington & Borovsky, 2023).

Between 2010 and 2015, the great majority (81%) of UK parliamentarians experienced some form of degradation while in office (James et al., 2016); all had been subjected to trolling and various forms of harassment (Akhtar & Morrison, 2019). The sentiment for some is that there is little justification for sacrificing both personal safety and private life to serve constituents, given there is no assurance that adequate support or safety will be provided by any political party (Khan, 2024).

Jo Cox, a British Labour MP, was stabbed 15 times and shot three times during the 2016 European Union referendum campaign, an event that sent shockwaves through the UK and the EU (BBC News, 2016).

An inquiry into the extent of VAWIP was conducted by the Committee on Standards in Public Life (CSPL), initiated under former PM Theresa May (2016–2019), following appeals for intervention. The publication of the 2017 CSPL report outlined recommendations aimed at the government, SMCs, polity, law enforcement and the media (Ballington & Borovsky, 2023; Collignon et al., 2017; CSPL, 2017).

In the years that followed, despite the release of the Online Harms White Paper (UK DCMS Committee, 2019) and growing governmental pressure, alongside increased media scrutiny, meaningful improvements failed to materialise. As the 2019 UK national election approached, many candidates chose not to run, citing persistent threats as their primary reason (Ballington & Borovsky, 2023).

The climate of aggression extended beyond threats and was reinforced by influential figures, including political financiers. In 2019, the largest donor to the UK's Conservative Party, an XY, was reported as stating that seeing Diane Abbott on television – the first black XX elected to parliament and the UK's longest-serving black MP (1987 to 2020) (Wikipedia, n.d.) – made him "want to hate all black women" and that she "should be shot". The PM at the time condemned the remarks as "racist" and "wrong"; however, the £10

(AU$ 19.5 / US$12) million donation remained with the party (Khan, 2024; Al Jazeera, 2024).

Amnesty International revealed that Abbott received nearly half of all abusive tweets analysed, highlighting the extreme levels of anti-black racism and sexism she faced. The trolling exemplifies the relentless and ferocious antagonism black XXs encounter in predominantly white spaces, including law and politics (Ballington & Borovsky, 2023; Khan, 2024) – demonstrating how intersectionality intensifies the discrimination directed on the basis of both race and sex (Crenshaw, 1989).

The USA

Gabrielle Giffords

The third XX in Arizona's history to be elected to the US Congress (2007–2012), Giffords faced a heinous ordeal when she was shot in the head at point-blank range by a young XY in 2011 (Cowan & Brissenden, 2011). Against the odds, the Democrat survived, but was severely wounded, forcing her to retire from politics.

Giffords recovery process included relearning to speak, walk, and write. Despite the life-altering event, Giffords demonstrated remarkable determination by founding an organisation that has become a leading voice in the gun control debate throughout the USA. Giffords.org advocates for common-sense reforms aimed at saving lives, promoting a responsible approach to gun ownership (Giffords et al., 2011) and supporting the reduction of annual tolls of the 44,000 lives lost to gun violence in the USA (Giffords, n.d.).

The few cases reviewed in this section expose the reality of VAWIP around the globe. However, barbaric and atrocious crimes continue, with XYs employing violent tactics to obstruct XXs from attaining political power across numerous democratic nations.

Democracy & Justice

The Oxford Dictionary offers various definitions of democracy. The applicable meaning for this chapter is "government by the people ..." (Oxford University Press, n.d.), as opposed to the perceived authority of XYs over XXs.

History often credits the Greeks as vanguards of democratic political societies, for being the "first political people in the history of mankind" (Ehrenberg, 1950:515). Their approach was based on establishing and governing by the people, with foundational principles emphasising the civic duty of individuals – engaging in actions that benefit communities and societies – and participating in decision-making, including the freedom for all to vote (Alexandre-Collier & Drolet, 2022; Gillin, 1919).

Democracy was originally formulated and defined by XYs for their exclusive benefit, and XXs had to fight to be included. Other forms of democracy are structured around communal similarities rather than formal patriarchal political ideologies. For example, among the Minangkabau in Indonesia – a matrilineal society in which lineage is traced through the XX's family – heirlooms are collectively owned by XXs, ensuring they hold equal rights to XYs in decision-making. However, in religious dogmas (Chapter 2), XXs are not considered central to the decision-making process (Chairiyah, 2020; Sari et al., 2024).

Nonetheless, historical evidence indicates that XXs performed influential roles in advancing democratic principles. For example, since the 1500s, XXs have been instrumental in international politics (Sluga & James, 2016). Although XXs were not officially recognised or employed as diplomats, they were selected as diplomats' wives. Their intellect and networking abilities enabled them to serve as intermediaries and leveraged international power. Meetings between paid and unpaid diplomats often took place in salons; Madame de Staël's salon, in Paris, for example, was renowned for hosting philosophers and politicians who devised plans against Napoleon Bonaparte. Figures including Germaine de Staël and Dorothea Lieven facilitated critical political dialogues, navigating numerous obstacles and leaving impactful legacies. Despite their results, the contributions of XXs have often been ignored in historic narratives (Sluga & James, 2016).

As androcentric filters are removed, XXs are being acknowledged for their pivotal roles in democratic processes, and their previously unacknowledged contributions behind XYs are becoming clearer as more XXs engage in writing and reviewing historic and political records.

The blood, sweat, and tears of those who refused to be silenced – and the many that continue to resist the patriarchy – built the foundation for the right to vote, a right that was once unthinkable.

Their victory in securing suffrage initiated trajectories that remind democracies that understanding the past is key to dissolving patriarchal values in the present, and indispensable for creating a sustainable future for all – irrespective of sex, age, political ideology, or nation.

Suffrage

Active suffrage movements appeared between the 1890s and 1920s (Bader-Zaar, 2011; Ramirez et al., 1997). A global demand for autonomy witnessed XXs campaigning for the right to vote using eclectic strategies from peaceful protests to extreme measures.

In June 1913, for example, Emily Wilding Davison, a member of the Women's Social and Political Union in the UK, died after stepping onto a horse track while attempting to seize the reins of the King's horse. Whether her actions were a deliberate suicide or an attempt to broadcast the suffrage cause remains unconfirmed (Kay & Mendes, 2020; Purvis, 2013).

Exchanging strategies and celebrating victories across borders, XXs established and advanced the global movement, informed by international examples and solidarity. In Asia, suffrage efforts, while influenced by Western ideas, faced unique challenges. Battling patriarchs was not the only impediment; many strained to determine which government to lobby (Edwards & Roces, 2004).

Australia's suffrage success in 1902 had global impacts, becoming a worldwide model (Ramirez et al., 1997), and marking the first instance of other nations employing an Australian policy (Wright, 2018).

Between 1890 and 1990, a total of 133 countries granted XXs the right to vote, solidifying suffrage as a core element of democratic rights. The USA granted XXs the right to vote in 1920, the UK in 1928, and India in 1947 (Edwards & Roces, 2004).

Finland became the first to grant all XXs the right to stand for election in 1906 (Larsen et al., 2022). Australia was the first to allow non-Indigenous XXs to vote and stand for parliament, but it took 41 years before XXs were federally elected: in 1943, Enid Lyons became the first federal MP, and Dorothy Tangney the first federal senator (National Museum of Australia, n.d.).

While progress has sometimes been gradual and frustrating – with improvements met by resistance, and triumphs at times followed by setbacks – suffrage laid the foundation for political advancements. Each breakthrough, despite the pace, has contributed to gradual but undeniable alterations in XXs representing their constituents in the great majority of nations.

Nonetheless, progress remains frustratingly slow, with regressions revealing a lack of genuine political will to advance DEI.

Legislative, Judicial, and State Power

It will take another 134 years – roughly five generations – at the current rate of progress to achieve full sex-based equality (WEF, 2024). Although XX's political representation has advanced, it remains inconsistent and uneven across regions. This slow pace stresses the pressing need for decisive action, particularly in political spheres, and makes it crucial to recognise the power of an individual vote and the consequences of not voting.

Most democratic nations have three main systems of formal power: legislative, judicial, and executive (Newman, 2017; Nourse, 2018; Ouyang, 2019). Countries lacking these systems typically practise non-democratic governance, often descending into dictatorship or absolute monarchy.

Vatican City, for example, operates as an elective monarchy where the Pope (Chapter 1) holds ultimate power (Kelly, 2003). Similarly, the United Arab Emirates is a monarchy in which the King exercises control over the legislative, executive, and judicial branches, while in Brunei, the Sultan exerts total executive authority, and legislative powers are similarly concentrated (Saunders, 2002).

In the USA, the 47th president signing executive orders is profoundly disturbing; for example, withdrawing from the WHO could endanger the global population – the WHO's global coordination is essential to prevent diseases from rapidly spreading across borders, as demonstrated by the COVID-19 pandemic (MacIntyre, 2025).

Legislative power enables the creation of laws leading to either positive or negative outcomes, depending on the prevailing political agenda (Jenkins & Monroe, 2015). Meanwhile, judicial power grants courts the authority to interpret laws by clarifying their meaning and resolving discrepancies or disputes (Gerangelos, 2018; Newman, 2017).

The judiciary, as a result of its controlling abilities, also carries the risk of misapplication – when judges use their dominance and values to deviate from the integrity of the law, undermining justice and fairness. These abuses of power erode trust in the judicial system and compromise democratic foundational principles.

State power is held by the executive branch, which authorises government officials and agencies to administer public policy and enforce laws on behalf of the state. The potential for reforms often depends on the executive's capacity and willingness to implement and/or ratify changes, consequently either limiting the scope of reforms (Forrester et al., 2018) or in some cases, contributing to the deconstructing of democracies.

Casting a Ballot

The scrutiny process begins well before an electorate votes, with political parties selecting prospective contenders and retaining the power to veto individuals before candidates can be formally approved to stand in elections. Since most political parties worldwide are controlled by XYs, the vetoing process is often embedded with patriarchal biases, determining who is allowed to run and often excluding XXs and other marginalised groups from being represented (Dahlerup, 2007).

Even when XXs are selected and elected, they often encounter structural disadvantages that XYs do not, including overt sexism and sexual harassment (AHRC, 2021; IPU, 2016). These constraints limit not only participation but the sustainability of XXs' political careers.

Nonetheless, voting is one of the few unique privileges and a direct mechanism allowing citizens to influence political decisions that alter, define, and transform lives. However, many XXs in various parts of the world are still not voting freely, even in compulsory voting nations. Studies illustrate that some XXs vote based on advice or pressure from an XY (Mancosu & Hopmann, 2019), indicating continuing patriarchal power imbalances.

Compulsory voting dates back to medieval Switzerland's *Landsgemeinde* (XY citizen assemblies), where citizens faced penalties for non-compliance (Malkopoulou, 2014). In the 17th century, several American colonies, including Plymouth in 1636 and Virginia in 1649, imposed fines on XYs who failed to vote (Keyssar, 2000); no such laws exist in the 21st century in the USA.

Despite the foundational role of voting in democracies, its practice varies significantly across nations. In several countries, including Belgium, Australia and parts of South America, compulsory voting helps maintain higher voter turnout. In contrast, optional voting in the USA for example, contributes to declining participation, raising concerns about the legitimacy of electoral representation (Hill & Rutledge-Prior, 2016).

Irrespective of whether voting is compulsory or optional, once all ballots are cast and elected representatives are declared, officials begin legislating, amending existing laws, and, in some cases, overturning laws that protect XXs.

Compulsory and Optional Voting

Research suggests that compulsory voting laws around the world are among the most effective means of ensuring the majority of eligible citizens participate. Casting a ballot is regarded as a civic duty (Birch, 2009). However, there are differing perspectives on compulsory voting. Proponents argue that it enhances electoral legitimacy by ensuring higher voter turnout, leading to more representative outcomes (Singh, 2021).

Various democratic nations implemented compulsory voting alongside suffrage to reverse voter apathy, reduce electoral fraud, ensure election results reflect the majority's will, and increase political participation. For example, Belgium adopted compulsory voting in 1893, Australia at the federal level in 1924, and Greece in 1926 (Birch, 2009, 2016).

Among the 195 countries internationally recognised, around 13% have some form of compulsory voting, including Australia and several EU countries; however, enforcement varies by region (Bonotti & Strangio, 2021; McCarthy, 2015; WPR, n.d.).

Critics with a conservative view argue that compulsory voting infringes on personal freedoms and increases invalid or protest votes. However, evidence suggests that compulsory voting enhances democratic engagement. In countries where voting is mandatory, invalid votes range from one in 20 (5%) to one in eight (12%), with around 90% of the eligible population participating in elections (Kouba & Lysek, 2019; Singh, 2021).

Research also indicates that when citizens are disconnected from social organisations, their likelihood of abstaining rises significantly (Medel, 2024). In numerous democracies, polling attendance has been decreasing (Hooghe & Kern, 2017), with people from lower-income groups participating less often; consequently, their votes and voices are excluded (Horni, 2023).

Nations with optional voting experience much lower participation rates. For example, in 2002, only two in five (40.5%) eligible Americans voted (Ballotpedia, 2024), increasing to around three in five (60%) in 2016 (Ballotpedia, 2024; McDonald, 2020). In 2020, despite variations in reported figures, voter turnout reached unprecedented levels. Estimates indicate that approximately three in five citizens (62.8%), or around 158.4 million people, cast their ballots (DeSilver, 2022), while other reports placed the turnout above two in three (66.6%). In 2024, around two-thirds (64%) cast their ballots in the USA (Ballotpedia, 2024; Lindsay, 2024; Riccardi, 2024).

Former Vice President Kamala Harris received more votes from XXs than from XYs in 2024. However, like their XY counterparts, XX voters are not a monolithic group. For example, Black, Latina, white college-educated, and young XXs showed the highest levels of support for Harris, whereas non–college-educated and white evangelical XXs continued supporting Trump (CAWP, 2024; CNN, 2024).

A key focus of Harris' campaign was reproductive health (Shortis, 2024). Harris received more than half (56%) of the overall Asian vote, around three in four (77%) of the Black vote, around two in five (38%) of the white vote, seven out of ten (70%) Jewish votes, and two in three (64%) voters with no religious affiliation (CAWP, 2024; Sherman, 2024a).

Her opponent received four out of five (78%) of the Protestant vote and two in three (66%) of the Catholic vote (CNN, 2024). Overall, more than half (53%) of white XXs cast their votes for Trump, compared to three of five (60%) white XYs (CAWP, 2024). Trump is now reported to hold the unparalleled record for securing the largest tally of popular votes by any presidential candidate in the history of the USA (Lindsay, 2024).

The election result was disappointing for millions worldwide. The long-held hope of seeing the first XX lead the free world vanished, reinforcing a stark reality: XXs remain chronically underrepresented in leadership roles around the world.

In 2024, the presence of XXs in political leadership remained alarmingly low. Out of 31 elections held globally, only five XXs were elected as Heads of State – with wins in Iceland, Mexico, Namibia, the Republic of Moldova, and North Macedonia. With the exception of Iceland, the elections in the other four countries were landmark moments, resulting in the appointment of their first female heads of state. Overall, XXs' representation in parliaments around the world remained largely stagnant, with XXs holding around one in four seats (27%) (UN Women, 2024). However, in several countries – France, Belgium and Australia, for example – XXs make up half or more of parliamentary representatives.

But why is it necessary for XXs to vote or be in politics? Because politicians – overwhelmingly XYs – design and enforce laws often modelled on phallocentric perspectives. Trump demonstrated this perspective at his January 2025 inauguration, declaring that his administration would recognise only two genders: XYs and XXs (Olson & Miller, 2025), and proclaimed himself to be a divinely chosen saviour, nominated and "saved by God" (SBS News, 2025).

Law, Policy, and Legislation

The world is governed by laws and regulatory frameworks that affect every part of daily life. For example: in health, laws determine the prices of medication, who is eligible for specific care, when, and where services are available; in education, laws influence childcare fees, school curricula, teacher availability, and programme delivery; in the economy, laws regulate taxation, the pricing of goods and services, budgets, and more, In the area of human rights (Fredman, 2006), laws dictate basic protections, police authority, access to justice, freedom of expression, and freedom of and from religion. Laws also determine which ideologies prevail, and how they are enacted and enforced.

Politicians enact laws, but distinctions between laws, policies, and legislation are often obscured and vary across regions and political systems. These variations can result in outcomes that are directly influenced by the priorities of polity agendas (Jenkins & Monroe, 2015) as well as the power and interests of external actors (Vega, 2023).

Law is defined as a rule, usually made by a government, that is used to regulate the way in which a society behaves (CUP. n.d.-a). However, laws have become so voluminous and complex that few individuals know their full contents (Crawford, 2024).

Defining "law" is debated among jurisprudence scholars, leading to disagreements and making a universal definition difficult. Nevertheless, for the purpose of this little book, three general definitions are noted: a) "Law is made by political actors, not by lawyers, throughout political procedures, for political ends" (Henkin, 1990:183); b) laws are rules established and/or ratified and imposed through social and/or governmental institutions to regulate human behaviour; and c) laws are tools employed in a court of law that assist in mediating relationships (Hart, 1961; Njiri, 2020; Simpson, 2011).

Because XYs predominantly continue to design and dominate government frameworks, including the judiciary, laws and legislation can marginalise and undermine XXs. Governments hold the power to disregard or exploit XXs while neglecting laws and conditions that sustain entrenched patriarchal hierarchies (MacKinnon, 2013, 2017, 2020). However, polity also has the capacity to enact meaningful reforms and fulfil commitments made to citizens and the international community to deliver equality by the 2030 deadline (Thompson & Hedman, 2020; UN, 2017).

Legislation refers to a law or set of laws proposed by a government and formally enacted by a parliament (CUP. n.d.-b). The objectives of legislation are to create legal documents that achieve the intended regulatory outcomes as determined by policymakers (Bar-Siman-Tov, 2021; Kosti et al., 2019).

There exists an overwhelming volume of legislation, which tends to increase and can be rapidly amended, making it difficult for citizens to interpret and understand. As a result, finding out how legislation affects our legal position is hugely demanding – hence, some argue that "the rule of law has failed" (Crawford, 2024:2).

The multiple roles that legislation performs directly influence the systems established for its monitoring and evaluation. Although the definition of legislation is relatively simple, it serves a range of diverse purposes, including budgets and multiple regulations (Kosti et al., 2019).

Policy is defined as a set of ideas or a plan of what to do in particular situations that has been agreed to officially by a group of people, a business, an organisation, a government, or a political party (CUP. n.d.-c). Policies are not laws per se, but they often influence the creation of legislation and the application of laws. For example, legislation consists of "internal government instructions" issued by the legislature to guide government policies and direct their implementation for administrative agencies and departments (Rubin, 1989:374) – including the judiciary and, more frequently, the executive arms of government (Crawford, 2024).

Polity refers to a system of civil government, a constitution, or a political entity (Oxford University Press, n.d.), establishing the framework for laws, legislation, and policies which despite their distinct roles, are often mistakenly conflated and not always understandable, even though all citizens are required to comply (Crawford, 2024; Kosti et al., 2019). Nevertheless, "the rule of law can prevail even if legislation is not reasonably knowable to the people" (Crawford, 2024:2).

Ratifying, codifying, enacting, and enforcing policies and laws are, for the most part, effective means of rectifying injustices. Unfortunately, the terms "sex" and "gender" are also often erroneously applied in political and legal contexts (Fleming, 2007; Werbinski, 2008); these misinterpretations can lead to damaging repercussions in both legislation and policies.

Research reveals that politicians often inject androcentric constructs into lawmaking and policy construction, which benefits XYs and often ignores the needs and rights of XXs. Additionally, individuals act with specific intentions, which can obstruct progress and policy innovation (Bachrach & Baratz, 1962; Denniss et al., 2021).

Nations including Italy, Israel, India, Hungary, Poland, and the USA, for example, have extreme discriminatory right-wing policies undermining democratic and human rights (Fredman, 2006). Many of these transactional leaders with gynophilic tendencies introduce laws that differ little from those imposed on XXs in Afghanistan by the Taliban – the fundamentalist Muslim militia – where the persecution of XXs constitutes monstrous human rights violations (de Silva de Alwis, 2024). Tyrannical policies suppress XXs, deny them autonomy, prevent their progress, and deprive them of fundamental freedoms, including access to secure healthcare (Macklin, 2022), and political participation.

Nevertheless, in the USA, for example, an XY can serve as Commander-in-Chief despite being found guilty of violating numerous national and international laws (Sisak et al., 2024), demonstrating an inability to communicate or understand democratic governance, and can pardon individuals convicted of violent crimes (Pengelly & Leingang, 2025). Meanwhile, XXs face relentless oppression simply for seeking essential healthcare (ABC Radio National, 2025; Our Bodies Ourselves Today, n.d.). Alarmingly, this oppressive reality is set to further intensify, with countless human rights breaches and legal battles looming under Trump (ABC Radio National, 2025). Additionally, other conservative politicians are taking note, with the intention to replicate Trump's bigoted policies (Barlow, 2025).

The persistent repression and dehumanisation of XXs has grave consequences; hence, a democratic nation has an obligation to encourage laws that support everyone (MacKinnon, 2005). In principle, policies can incrementally lead to the changes needed to ensure a nation adheres to human rights laws (Cope et al., 2019) and IWRLs (Chapter 2). International law, also known as "international contracts" (Henkin, 1990:188), is complex yet essential for regulating interactions between countries. UN member states often uphold shared principles and values. Most importantly, IWRLs influence, and in some cases informs domestic legislation (Guzman, 2012; Crawford et al., 2017).

For example, in Australia, the establishment of the first federal SDA (Commonwealth of Australia, 1984) was inspired by international law, specifically CEDAW (Vega, 2023). Thanks to the advocacy work of the late Susan Ryan, then Minister Assisting the PM for the Status of Women, PM Bob Hawke's cabinet ratified CEDAW in 1983 (DFAT, 2020). A year later, in 1984, the SDA was legislated (Charlesworth & Charlesworth, 2004; Commonwealth of Australia, 1984), despite opposition from religious leaders. Although the SDA prohibits discrimination, there are exemptions on religious grounds (Peterson, 2016).

Nevertheless, progress influenced by IWRLs is evident. The UN's classification of rape as a war crime, for example, recognising it as more than just a wartime inevitability, along with the strengthening of VAW and harassment laws in various nations following the #MeToo movement (Chapters 2 & 3), represent key examples of progress based on international law.

However, non-compliant nations face few, if any, repercussions for ignoring international law, which are only effective if ratified, legislated, and monitored with "enforcement" (Devereux & McCosker, 2017:24).

International Political Participation

Despite many nations adopting democratic processes, joining the UN, and signing international human rights agreements, progress toward sex-based equality has been slow, albeit with polity often spreading propaganda claiming that all citizens will be treated equally remaining as unfulfilled promises. The gap between theoretical equality and real-world outcomes highlights the ongoing patriarchal endemic constraints that prevent achieving genuine equality between the sexes (Ford, 2018).

There is a significant gap between democratic ideals and the lived realities of XXs in democracies. XYs construct and maintain phallocentric patriarchal systems that enforce restrictions and uphold broader discriminatory values. Consequently, democratic nations gravitate towards XY ideals based on perceived external threats, which negates XX strengths and perspectives (Agius et al., 2021).

With the continued assumption that XYs are the most potent and powerful of the sexes, XYs assert their authority and perceived superiority to exert control over XXs, imposing pervasive limitations that prevent entry, block progress, and enforce androcentric laws embedded with ideologies that restrict progress and deter advancements (Dolan et al., 2021; MacKinnon, 2020; Rollins, 2011). Yet, laws empowering XXs have altered partly thanks to XX activists, advocates, and femocrats' ability to persuade (Bustelo, 2016; Vega, 2023) and transform exclusionary patriarchal systems.

The concept of power (Chapter 1) has been examined since humans first started trying to understand it. Power can reside in the hands of groups or individuals (McConnell, 2016) – individuals with a voice that is heard, including oligarchs, billionaires, or media moguls – and/or individuals who have access to other resources that grant them influence, including political power. The dilemma with people who hold power is that they can obstruct political systems from within and/or be persuaded by powerful individuals external to politics. Given that the overwhelming majority of power resides with XYs globally, instigating reforms based on IWRLs is complex and, at times, unattainable (Arat, 2015; Bailliet, 2016).

A substantial and significant body of research examines why egalitarianism has yet to prevail and questions a) the dynamics of political power; b) barriers faced by XXs in politics; c) the importance of numerical representation; and d) whether XXs effectively support one another – often referred to as the sisterhood.

Representation

The number of XXs in parliaments has more than doubled in 30 years globally; hence, laws during this period have at times considered XXs. Therefore, it is paramount for XXs to vote, be represented, and have their concerns prioritised.

In 1995, around one in ten (11%) XXs held seats in parliament; by 2015, it was just under one in six (16%) (Congressional Research Service, 2024), rising to around one in four (25%) in 2020 (IPU, 2021). By 2023, it increased to 27% (IPU, 2023).

With nearly half of the global population voting in 2024, the year started with optimistic expectations for a rise in XXs' representation (IPU, n.d.). However, the global percentage remained unchanged at 27% (IPU, n.d.). In one-third of chambers, the proportion of XX MPs stayed the same, while in another third, it dropped by more than one percentage point in 2024 (IPU, n.d.). This stagnation, however, excludes Australia's recent historic advancements.

A record number of XXs were elected to federal parliament by Australians in 2025 (Manfield, 2025). For the first time, XXs outnumber XYs and comprise 56% of the Labor Party, demonstrating the tangible outcomes of quota implementation. Anthony Albanese's new cabinet – the highest echelon of decision-making power – comprises 12 XXs and 11 XYs, marking a historic majority (Stephenson & Williams, 2025).

In the conservative Liberal and National parties, XXs remain underrepresented, making up 28.5%, with the parties continuing to consider quotas. Following the Coalition's 2025 defeat, Sussan Ley became the first XX to lead the Liberal Party in its 80-year history (Staszewska, 2025). Overall, XXs now represent a record 49.1% of federal parliament across all parties including the crossbench (Stephenson & Williams, 2025).

In the EU, by 2024, XXs held 35% of seats, reflecting a 7.4-point rise from around 28% in 2014. However, the numbers vary across countries (Eurostat, 2025). For example, following the 2023 Spanish elections, XXs held about two in five (44%) seats in the lower house and almost 43% in the upper house (Senate). In comparison, XXs made up 55% of parliamentarians in Belgium, and 50% in both Estonia and France (Eurostat, 2025).

In India, the Women's Reservation Bill was passed in September 2023, mandating that XXs occupy at least one in three (33%) seats in state legislative assemblies and the *Lok Sabha* (lower house of Parliament, also known as the House of the People) (UN Women, 2023). However, by January 2024, the proportion decreased from roughly 15% to 13.5% (IPU, 2023).

In the 2024 UK election, XXs secured 41% of seats in the House of Commons, the highest level of representation in its history, with 263 XXs elected to Parliament overall (Commons Library, 2024).

The January 2025 US Congress included 170 XXs, with 45 in the Senate and 125 in the House of Representatives. Sarah McBride is now the first openly transgender person elected to Congress in the nation's history (CAWP, 2024).

Future global progress is anticipated to fall below that of recent years, with raising concerns over dormancy, decline, and/or regression in the advancements achieved (IPU, n.d.). Additionally, ideological gaps between XXs and XYs are widening globally, with young XXs becoming increasingly progressive while XYs shift further toward conservatism.

For example, in the USA, XXs aged 18 to 30 exhibit stronger liberal (politically left leaning) alignments compared to XYs of the same age. Less than a decade ago, the cultural and political landscape was markedly different. A similar trend is evident in Germany, the UK, and various Asian nations, where these ideological divisions are expanding at an accelerating rate (Sherman, 2024b; Charrel, 2025). Some attribute this shift to the #MeToo movement (Chapter 3), which exposed and legitimised the prevalence of systemic injustices worldwide.

Discriminatory behaviours and systems that obstruct XXs' advancement in politics are well-documented in international and national democratic political structures; hence, it is important for XXs to be in politics because those who can influence policies and institutions are those who hold power and have the ability to enable or impose barriers to equality (Silve, 2015).

Visibility Strategies

Over the years, there have been some positive outcomes for XXs, including increased representation through quotas and the introduction of legislation focusing on XXs participation.

One strategy for increasing the number of XXs in politics has been quotas. In political frameworks, there are two types: candidate quotas and reserved seat quotas. Research suggests that quotas influence and contribute to the rising number of XXs in parliaments globally (IPU, 2019), as illustrated in Australia. Around 130 countries have implemented quotas as part of electoral reforms (Zetterberg et al., 2022).

Candidate quotas require political parties to include a specified percentage of XXs in the candidate selection process. Those advocating for equity favour candidate quotas (Zetterberg et al., 2022). In theory, the quota system guarantees that XXs can run for office alongside XYs.

Reserved seat quotas differ in that they guarantee a predetermined number of legislative seats to be occupied by XXs (Acheampong et al., 2024); popular standards are around three in ten (30%). However, this approach fails to contest existing patriarchal structures, as seen in India. By operating alongside the standard electoral process, representation is secured without altering political competition dynamics. Countries with lower levels of electoral contestation are more likely to adopt reserved seats as a mechanism to increase XXs' political participation (Zetterberg et al., 2022).

When nations adopt quotas, positive outcomes also emerge on the international stage, as XXs unite to ensure gains are achieved (Paxton & Hughes, 2014). However, XXs are usually appointed to less authoritative or junior ministerial portfolios that lack influence and power; often assigned to stereotypical ministries, including Education and Women's Affairs for example. Hence, increasing the number of XXs "would translate into substantive policy influence" (Bashevkin, 2014:442).

One of the many reasons why XXs are needed in parliaments, especially in portfolios that have influence (Bashevkin, 2014), is to deliver pro–XX policies that respect half of the global population. But do XXs advocate for pro–XX policies from within?

The Sisterhood

How XX parliamentarians use their political power has divided scholars internationally. One cohort maintains that XXs advocate for pro–XX policies, arguing that those in positions of power effectively advance equal rights. The other cohort contends that XXs do not advocate for pro–XX policies (Currell, 2024; Shaw et al., 2013; Mackay et al., 2011).

The sisterhood argument indicates that XXs in power support other XXs more than XYs (Shaw et al., 2013). For example, in Canada, XXs raised awareness of global feminist issues twice as often as XYs, increasing the country's spending on XXs' programmes (Bashevkin, 2014).

The former Swedish Foreign Minister, Margot Wallström, launched the first feminist foreign policy (FFP) in 2014, arguing that many XX leaders were outperforming XYs. Wallström cited examples, including the tendency of XYs to view VAW as inevitable or as a "relatively minor crime" (Wallström, 2021:73).

Since the introduction of the FFP in Sweden, at least 16 other nations have adopted similar policies, including France, Germany, the Netherlands, Norway, and Spain (Foster & Markham, 2024; Thompson & Clement, 2024). FFPs aim to reduce sex-based discrimination and inequality through strategic foreign and development policies by supporting the delivery and fulfilment of international commitments to eliminate biased policies (GenderNet, 2016; Kusuma & Babu, 2017).

A study of 191 countries, from 1990 to 2020, revealed that XXs in parliament influenced education policies, particularly by promoting policies that focus on sex-based disparities and improving access to tertiary, secondary, and primary education. The impact of XXs on educational equality was more evident in countries with reserved seat quotas compared to candidate quotas (Acheampong et al., 2024). The findings suggest that XXs significantly contributed to the increase in XXs receiving an education.

Securing more XXs in legislatures results in more policy initiatives that benefit XXs, indicating that greater representation of XXs in parliaments leads to broader inclusivity (Caiazza, 2002; Toshkov & Cretti, 2024). Additionally, XXs fulfil a vital and significant role in peace and security negotiations (Thomson, 2017). Although states endorse the women, peace and security (WPS) agenda, ongoing funding gaps continue to undermine its effective implementation (Davies & True, 2022).

While conclusive evidence remains mixed on whether XXs advocate for pro–XX policies, what is clear is that voter perceptions of XX politicians across the EU indicate strong support for increasing XX representation in politics (Toshkov & Cretti, 2024), a trend confirmed by Australian voters at the 2025 federal election.

Many voters also endorse the use of quotas as a means to achieve parity in political representation. Additionally, one study revealed that XXs are more likely to trust XX politicians over their XY counterparts (Toshkov & Cretti, 2024).

Becoming increasingly vocal and prominent in both social and political arenas, XXs' contributions have gained recognition for advancing the well-being of citizens, nations, and the environment. Their emphasis on these important issues has provided significant societal benefits, enhancing their reputation as highly effective leaders. Nevertheless, XXs continue to confront prejudices that XYs do not face in the public domain, particularly in misogynistic political environments.

VAWIP

In politics, many face threats irrespective of sex or gender; however, XXs experience violence and harassment at escalated levels, leading the UN to recognise that VAWIP significantly deters the sustainability of peace and development within nations (UN, 2024). The proliferation of VAWIP in the 21st century has also led to the coining of the acronym to define and address this distinct form of violence.

There are powerful obstacles for XXs in politics, as reflected in survey findings where a majority of XX respondents revealed experiencing persistent and damaging discrimination, yet only a minority of XYs acknowledged this reality (Fingerhut, 2016).

One-quarter of XX politicians have experienced physical or sexual violence, and more than eight in ten (82%) disclosed having been affected by psychological violence, including death threats, beatings, rape, and/or abduction (IPU, 2016). Fear plays a central role in the continuous oppression of XXs, including brutal sexual assaults, harassment, and intimidation (Krook, 2017; Kumari et al., 2024).

VAWIP is often strategically employed to discourage, restrain, or deter XXs from participating in or maintaining positions of power. Those contesting seats in traditionally XY–dominated constituencies often trigger gynophobic responses, as XYs perceive XXs as threats to their established dominance (Kumari et al., 2024).

A decade ago, around one in five (20%) parliaments worldwide had sexual harassment policies in place for MPs and staff, reflecting a troubling lack of recognition of the necessity of workplace basic workplace protections. This is especially concerning considering that XX MPs regularly endure oppression, derogatory remarks, and threats at work, creating a hostile environment that undermines their ability to actively and equally partake without fear (Khalid, 2023).

Since the first global study of VAWIP was published in 2016, nations have begun implementing strategies to regulate workplaces and improve safety (Khalid, 2023). Some nations have introduced reforms, with Latin America becoming the first region to criminalise VAWIP (Restrepo Sanín, 2018).

Although VAWIP is widespread, it often goes unreported. Fear of retaliation, a culture of silence embedded within political institutions, and the normalisation of violence remain entrenched in the political lives of many XXs. Additionally, VAWIP is frequently underreported by the media and ignored by law enforcement and political parties (Kumari et al., 2024).

The juncture of two pandemics – COVID-19 and VAW – drastically increased the risk of VAWIP, while simultaneously exposing and intensifying long-standing systemic failures. These include the exclusion of XXs from the formulation of pandemic response strategies, reflecting their persistent under-representation and further exacerbating the neglect of sex-sensitive approaches in decision-making processes (Šimonović, 2020).

UN member states are contractually obligated to uphold international human rights and are expected to "prevent, investigate, and penalise all acts of VAW" (Bjarnegård & Zetterberg, 2023, p.191). In theory, parliaments should uphold the highest standards, serve as exemplary workplaces, (Ballington & Borovsky, 2023; UN Women & ILO, 2019) and promote the right to live and work free from violence and harassment – a fundamental human right.

Beyond its physical and psychological toll, VAWIP undermines democratic participation and governance. It can derail careers, endanger lives, and dissuade potential candidates from standing for election. The threat and reality of VAWIP create a hostile environment that limits XXs' political engagement and erodes democratic integrity. Less visible forms of violence include economic violence, which constrains access to funding and campaign resources, further restricting XXs' participation (Kumari et al., 2024).

Additionally, portraying XXs as sexual objects and making derogatory remarks about their abilities are key tactics of symbolic VAWIP, intended to discredit and marginalise (Krook, 2017). Both symbolic and physical forms of VAWIP frequently manifest within parliamentary settings (Giorgi, 2024; Palmieri et al., 2021).

Various preventative methods, programmes, tools, and policies around the globe have been initiated. For example, in November 2021, the AHRC tabled the *Set the Standard: Report on the Independent Review into Commonwealth Parliamentary Workplaces*, critically examining the culture within the Australian federal parliament (Chapter 3), providing recommendations to ensure Commonwealth parliamentary workplaces are "safe and respectful", setting a benchmark for best practices in preventing and addressing "bullying, sexual harassment, and sexual assault" (AHRC, 2021:11). However, alcohol consumption remains permitted in the workplace, despite the proposal for an *Independent Parliamentary Standards Commission* – designed to enforce the behavioural code of conduct through complaint procedures and enforcement mechanisms (AHRC, 2021; Giorgi, 2024).

In the EU, the Council of Europe's Gender Equality Strategy (2024–2029) includes measures to prevent and combat VAWIP (Council of Europe, 2018). In India, numerous programmes are in place to support XXs in entering politics and to reduce VAW in public life (Jha & Choubey, 2024). In the USA, the National Democratic Institute's #NotTheCost campaign was launched in 2016 to directly address VAWIP (Krook & Restrepo Sanín, 2020).

In the face of relentless violence, threats, and systemic barriers, many XXs across all regions have survived and thrived, continuing to legislate and inspire. Their resilience and achievements benefit their constituents and are paving the way for future generations and more inclusive democracies.

Conclusion

The contributions of XXs in politics, propelled by the suffrage movement, represented a pivotal turning point for democratic nations, marking a historic triumph. However, obtaining the right to vote was only the first step. Since then, numerous structural, cultural, and institutional barriers have had to be dismantled to enable XXs to enter parliaments – some of whom have gone on to attain the highest offices of authority.

The increasing presence of XXs at decision-making tables has enriched political processes and introduced varied perspectives to leadership. The resulting improvements in numerous areas of legislation have been significant and transformative.

The successes of the many global MPs and legislators mentioned, and the many excluded, serve as evidence of the advancements and milestones accomplished toward a more balanced representation that continues to inspire and initiate productive reforms, albeit with the unbalanced distribution of power being evident in most regions and with overt and subtle bigotry enduring. Yet, the achievements of XXs in power are permanently retained in the history of Australia, the EU, India, the UK, and the USA.

Regrettably, national and international laws intended to prevent VAWIP have not yet stopped the heinous crimes that kill, deter and oppress XXs globally, highlighting the risks they face at work – much of which is underreported or inadequately addressed by the media and the polity.

VAWIP affects not only the individuals targeted but also has a chilling effect on families, other candidates, and voters. The perpetuating cycle of intentional underrepresentation – rooted in phallocentric philosophies and often sustained by gynophobic tendencies and illusions that XXs are less suited for leadership roles or deserve only feminine portfolios – is also shifting.

The use of quotas has been a positive strategy to increase the representation of XXs. While quotas have proven effective in ensuring a minimum level of XX participation, quotas are not a lasting or universal remedy. The effectiveness of quotas depends on the broader political and social environment, particularly the willingness of those with power.

Achieving a balanced representation requires a multifaceted approach that mitigates the symptoms as well as the root causes of misogyny. Increasing the number of XXs in politics is one way to increase pro–XX policies; however, XXs also require access to influential ministerial portfolios to be effective and to balance power dynamics.

International laws, including treaties and conventions promoting human and political rights, are crucial in setting standards and achieving parity. However, their ratification, implementation, and enforcement need to improve. The nations that sign international contracts but fail to adhere to them should be prosecuted.

Only time will reveal how the younger XX population continues to surpass XYs in advancing progressive politics. The malicious actions of Trump in the USA may also sway many towards less androcentric leaders, as his administration is having catastrophic ramifications nationally and internationally.

Awareness through educational campaigns needs to influence voting behaviour to transform societal attitudes by rectifying misinformation, malinformation, and disinformation. However, to annihilate cultural bigotry it is essential to engage both citizens and the polity in delivering governance that is representative, free from corruption, conducive to peace, and committed to equilibrium and stability.

> "When one woman is a leader, it changes her. When more women are leaders, it changes politics and policies".
>
> **Michelle Bachelet**, former President of Chile, UN High Commissioner for Human Rights, and Executive Director of UN Women (UN Women, 2012)

Toolkit

The onus and responsibility to eradicate patriarchal political systems start with voters who take intentional actions based on informed decisions. To effect meaningful transformation and cultivate a more sustainable, resilient, and inclusive society, consider the following actions:

- Understand the policies of the candidates you vote for and ask, "Are they pro-XXs?" Do not base your vote solely on the opinions of others or on the candidate's physique.
- Support and vote for XXs who advocate for policies that benefit and strengthen your community.
- Hold governments, political parties and politicians accountable for their promises: write letters, attend public meetings, and use SNSs to ensure your voice and concerns are heard.
- Launch campaigns that raise awareness of the importance of XX representation, actively challenge harmful stereotypes, and encourage public support for XX candidates.
- Mentorship and networking programmes can be established to connect aspiring XX politicians with experienced leaders to provide guidance, build confidence, and expand professional networks.
- Offer targeted training programmes focused on leadership, public speaking, campaign strategy, and policy analysis to prepare XXs for success.
- Push for the implementation of quotas, ensuring a minimum percentage of XX candidates and elected officials. This has been a successful strategy in numerous countries to increase XX representation in politics.
- Develop financial support systems for XX candidates to help overcome the financial obstacles that often prevent them from running in local, state, and/or national elections.
- Advocate for the elimination of legal constraints that deter XX political participation, and campaign for the implementation of family-friendly policies to increase inclusivity.
- Promote public education that enables XXs to better understand the law and actively engage with legislation that impacts their lives.

By employing these tools, individuals and communities can initiate changes to progress and disband patriarchal systems to establish a political environment that reflects fairness and inclusivity for all.

8 Conclusion

Throughout history, a single chromosome has been used to claim that those with XY are stronger, more capable, and better suited to power, and that XXs are the weaker sex.

Spreading like wildfire since Aristotle first declared his assumptions in the third century BCE, and later accelerated by Darwin in the 19th century, the patriarchy has sustained its manufactured power for millennia.

Patriarchal power is not just a relic of the past – it is a living architecture that organises societies and all within. It operates on a spectrum, from overt domination to subtle manipulations disguised as tradition, morality, or concern – all in service of XYs preserving control, while XXs are suppressed, exploited, and excluded.

Seizing the authority to dominate, marginalise XXs, and propagate misogynistic ideologies, XYs sustain dominance through an intricate web of structural, cultural, political, and psychological forces. Power imbalances are deeply entrenched in the institutions that structure everyday life – health, the economy, education, law, the media, politics, religion, and workplaces.

These foundations impose XY-centric norms and suppress dissent. Those who challenge the system are rapidly dismissed or methodically discredited. It makes no difference which nation is examined, which dataset is assessed, which cohort is studied, or which doctrine, ideology, or principle is interrogated – the pattern remains constant: those with XY chromosomes dominate those with XXs across systems, societies, and time.

It is no surprise, then, that XXs have persistently demanded the right to live under conditions equal to those afforded to XYs – to be recognised as human, to speak and be heard, and to challenge the unjust, inequitable, and ultimately indefensible authority of the patriarchy.

From the first wave to the tsunami, each feminist movement has built upon the momentum of its predecessor – confronting entrenched discrimination while expanding the instruments through which XXs demand equal rights, recognition, and access to power.

Each movement offers a clear lens on global realities. From Australia to the EU, India, the UK, and the USA, resistance has taken many forms – from quiet demands to mass protests, collective outcries, and digital hashtag campaigns.

DOI: 10.4324/9781003516224-8

All expose the same enduring truth: sex-based discrimination remains deeply embedded, denying XXs bodily autonomy, equal access to opportunity, and the fundamental right to live free from violence.

The capacity of XXs to energise, support, and inspire others into action – while serving as role models – is evident across nations and throughout the centuries.

Collective actions have created lasting legacies of resistance and progress, cutting across geographical, political, and cultural boundaries – not as abstract ideals, but as guiding principles that inform how societies should govern, lead, and function.

Beginning with political campaigns for suffrage and property rights, the first wave laid the groundwork that was further developed during the second and third waves, which expanded the movement through education and advocacy on labour rights, reproductive autonomy, intersectionality, and the ongoing struggle to eradicate VAW.

The second wave expanded feminist advocacy to include workplace discrimination, reproductive autonomy, and VAW. Legal reforms – including Australia's SDA and the USA's Equal Pay Act – signalled the movement's capacity to influence legislation. It also deepened cultural critique, introducing terms like *herstory* to challenge androcentric historical accounts and establishing academic fields that legitimised XXs' voices and lived realities. However, this wave faced criticism for its exclusivity, with many noting the alienation of non-white XXs and those from disadvantaged socioeconomic groups.

The third wave, emerging in the 1990s, amplified intersectionality by addressing the overlapping systems of oppression affecting individuals across race, sex, and class. It was distinguished by the growth of grassroots campaigns, digital platforms, and cultural expression aimed at redefining femininity.

The fourth feminist wave – aptly described as a "tsunami" – was propelled by the erosion of justice and accelerated by digital technology, enabling the rapid global circulation of information and the amplification of XXs' narratives.

This tsunami culminated in several monumental movements in modern history, as national and transnational campaigns mobilised public consciousness, unmuted generational silence, and intensified awareness of the oppression faced by XXs through the rise of hashtag activism.

Among the most enduring and widely publicised was the #MeToo movement, which exposed the systemic scale of workplace harassment, assault, and sexual exploitation. Survivors' narratives demanded accountability and ended the careers of numerous dangerous patriarchs, leading to workplace sexual harassment being treated as a serious legal and reputational concern in multiple regions.

In Australia, the #LetHerSpeak campaign directly challenged legal frameworks that silenced survivors of sexual abuse, advocating for – and successfully achieving – legislative reform. In India, #DelhiBraveheart and #IWillGoOut sparked national and international outrage by exposing extreme VAW, demanding justice, and confronting victim-blaming androcentric narratives. #LahuKaLagaan (tax on blood) centred on economic justice, successfully leading to the removal of the tampon tax.

In the EU, the #StopBildSexism campaign targeted misogyny in journalism and advertising, while in the UK, #NoMorePage3 confronted the normalisation of objectification in tabloid media, ultimately ending the publication of nude images that catered to a phallocentric appetite.

The #FreeTheNipple campaign gained traction across several regions, challenging censorship, objectification, and the sexualisation of XXs' breasts, while defending the right to breastfeed in public. These legal and cultural restrictions reveal a deeply rooted and pathological form of discrimination – one that tolerates the sexualisation of XXs' bodies while simultaneously penalising their natural and essential functions.

The digital campaigns mentioned – and the many not included in this little book – share a unifying purpose: the rejection of patriarchal expectations, the affirmation of XXs' agency, and the insistence on meaningful transformation in how societies are organised and governed.

From each feminist wave to the multitude of hashtag campaigns, the collective action of XXs is transcending borders. Their efforts are disrupting oppressive practices and redistributing power, revealing the capacity and determination of XXs to reform global narratives and institutional structures. While the aim – to disband the patriarchy – remains consistent, the message is expressed in different tones and languages across every region of the world.

Although some claim feminism is obsolete – an erroneous argument repeated since the first wave – global realities suggest otherwise. Each feminist movement has built on its predecessor, confronting persistent discrimination whilst striving towards equality, securing equal human rights and justice for XXs – rights historically extended to XYs, long before the first recognised feminist wave formally emerged.

Feminist narratives are expressed through diverse artistic and cultural forms – from visual storytelling in film and documentary to live performance, including theatre, dance, choreography, photography, and installation art. XXs are conveying *herstory* through narratives and music, using the power of words and lyrics to express lived experiences of injustice, amplifying resistance, and challenging the constructs and practices imposed by patriarchal systems.

For example, Wollstonecraft's *A Vindication of the Rights of Woman* (1792) laid the foundations of feminist thought. Simone de Beauvoir's *The Second Sex – Facts and Myths* and *Lived Experience* (1946–1949) and Germaine Greer's *The Female Eunuch* (1970) provoked critical debate on the suppression of XX sexuality in Western societies. Alice Walker's *The Color Purple* (1982) explicitly addressed VAW, while Judith Butler's *Gender Trouble: Feminism and the Subversion of Identity* (1990) challenged identity politics and reframed sex and gender. Naomi Wolf's *The Beauty Myth: How Images of Beauty Are Used Against Women* (1990) exposed the media's role in pressuring XXs to conform to feminine ideals, and Eve Ensler's *The Vagina Monologues* (1996) confronted systemic sexism, from genital mutilation to menstruation.

In the 21st century, Malala Yousafzai's *I Am Malala* (2013) and Chimamanda Ngozi Adichie's *We Should All Be Feminists* (2014) continue to call out injustices while amplifying the lived experiences of previously silenced, traditionally underrepresented voices. Collectively, these texts offer powerful narratives of feminist resistance – each a testament to truth-telling on XXs' own terms, influencing public discourse, educating, and challenging patriarchal rules and narratives.

For example, as the sexual revolution gained momentum in pop culture – particularly through music – Helen Reddy's "I Am Woman" (1971) emerged as an anthem, released at the height of the countercultural movement.

Today, new generations continue to protest patriarchal rule – from "White Boy" (1992) by *Bikini Kill*, which confronts everyday sexism, condemns toxic masculinity and power imbalances, and critiques how society often dismisses or tolerates XY privilege and aggression, urging listeners to recognise and challenge patriarchal injustice. "Battlefield" (2022) by SkyDxddy expresses life as a combat zone, conveying distrust in authority and systems of power, asserting the need for self-protection and bodily autonomy, and presenting a courageous posture against injustice. "Labour" (2024) by Paris Paloma is a powerful feminist anthem that critiques the unequal emotional and physical labour disproportionately imposed on XXs in society and intimate relationships.

These voices, and the many others not mentioned, must continue to expand and intensify to overpower the calculated, widespread, and deeply embedded regimes of XY-centred manipulation that persist without pause – grotesque in both construction and outcome. Their destruction is unrelenting, and the consequences catastrophic. It must end!

The patriarchy cannot be allowed to continue accumulating power. If you are still not convinced, consider the discrimination and harm enacted with their stronghold on HEEP, law, media, and religion – these realities should be more than enough to wake you up. And if not, review the evidence – starting with the systemic denial of access to health services and the assault on bodily autonomy, and ending with the way the law is weaponised to silence, subjugate, and strip away the basic rights of XXs.

Given that health is the first of the four core determinants (HEEP), without access to mental and physical healthcare, progress in education, employment, or political participation is almost impossible.

Nonetheless, health systems in the 21st century continue to disregard the XX body, perpetuating cycles of medical negligence that result in misdiagnosis, dismissal, or inadequate treatment. Additionally, with the intent to maintain dominance over the more resilient sex, VAW has become a global health pandemic – one that threatens the physical, mental, and reproductive well-being of XXs worldwide.

Meanwhile, behind closed doors, XYs are killing their children, mothers, and partners to assert their assumed supremacy, mask misogynistic gynophobia, and conceal their own ineptitudes. On average, one XX dies every ten minutes from DV or IPV – at the hands of their father, brother, or lover somewhere in the world.

Those subjected to DV and IPV are routinely sidelined or disbelieved. Institutional failure to meet survivors' needs frequently results in long-term suffering, including traumatic brain injury and chronic pain. These outcomes are made worse by enduring myths that link violence to biology, despite clear evidence that environmental and social conditions play a greater role than sex, genetics, or hormones.

Health practitioners often minimise or dismiss XXs' symptoms – from PTSD linked to violence to gynaecological conditions – offering little more than a pain relief tablet and a condescending dismissal. Meanwhile, nurses – the vast majority of whom are XXs – are overworked, underpaid, and ill-equipped to support their sisters to the extent required.

Efforts to address VAW have gained momentum. Global movements have increased visibility, prompting some governments to strengthen reporting – notably, police stations staffed by XX officers are linked to higher reporting and lower femicide rates. Still, many governments continue to ignore the evidence.

Even more concerning is that the data fails to capture the full scale of VAW, as many cases go unreported, undocumented, or misclassified. Additionally, survivors are retraumatised by legal and institutional systems that routinely fail to protect them, while perpetrators often go unpunished.

Although just a drop in the ocean within the global context, a significant milestone was marked in 2008, when the UN formally recognised rape as a war crime – rejecting long-standing assumptions that sexual violence in conflict is somehow inevitable. Yet sexual violence against XXs in conflict remains rampant, with perpetrators rarely held accountable for such atrocities.

As if that were not enough, reproductive freedoms are under relentless attack. Hardline conservatism, religious fundamentalism, autocratic leaders, and judicial overreach are combining to curtail XXs' autonomy – even in nations once regarded as defenders of democracy.

In many nations, XXs are reduced to reproductive vessels, with institutions determining the fate of their uterus – a dystopian reality echoed in Atwood's *The Handmaid's Tale*.

These androcentric ideologies are visible in the overturning of *Roe v. Wade* in the USA and mirrored in other countries that restrict abortion, contraception, and access to healthcare – many underpinned by religious dogma, wilful denial, and negligent cruelty.

However, thanks to the relentless advocacy of XXs, healthcare systems are beginning to change. Research and policy reform are redesigning medical frameworks to meet the distinct needs of XX populations.

Access to contraception and abortion continues to expand in some regions, reaffirming reproductive autonomy as a fundamental human right. Yet in other nations – including the USA – critical protections are being dismantled, threatening XXs' rights globally. Amid these constraints, telehealth and XX-led digital platforms are offering alternative pathways to healthcare and information.

Sex-disaggregated data is now being collected in various regions, moving beyond XY-centric models towards treatments grounded in biological reality. Several countries have mandated the inclusion of XXs in clinical trials, enhancing the accuracy of care long dismissed due to the perceived complexity of XX hormones, and increasingly placing the XX body at the centre of clinical inquiry.

Evidence-based care is finally emerging, including for conditions long ignored by medical frameworks that were never designed to understand, prioritise, or serve the health needs of XXs. For example, while menopause continues to be medicalised, it is increasingly recognised as a natural life stage that requires informed, individualised support rather than clinical correction. National strategies are under review, and dialogue is increasing across workplaces and communities. While barriers persist, there is genuine potential to redress centuries of neglect.

Placing XXs' well-being at the centre of healthcare policy and practice requires policymakers, clinicians, pharmaceutical companies, and patients to recognise their legal and ethical responsibilities – a collective obligation that must be embedded in training, professional practice, and education, and demanded by all XXs, regardless of sex, gender, economic status, or circumstance. To do so, however, XXs require accurate information to support informed decision-making – a need that further exposes systemic medical injustices.

The evidence is clear: knowledge is vital for advancing XXs' engagement and access to opportunity. Yet education remains one of the most obstructed pathways to progress, as access to learning has long been restricted by entrenched patriarchal structures.

In recent decades, however, XXs' access to education has improved, with global figures showing near parity in primary, secondary, and tertiary enrolments between XXs and XYs – indicating progress towards broader inclusion.

Interestingly, and further illustrating the power of XXs, global data indicates that XXs are surpassing XYs in academic achievement across all educational levels in most countries. However, cultural expectations in some areas still prevent XXs from obtaining an education, with a focus instead on preparing them for caregiving and domestic work.

Additionally, discussions continue around which educational setting is more effective – single-sex or coeducational. While supporters highlight enhanced academic outcomes for XXs in single-sex environments, others raise concerns about reinforcing traditional stereotypes and limiting peer interaction, with some research suggesting that single-sex settings may disadvantage XYs.

Coeducational learning – embedded in national education policies across several regions – is also advancing efforts to dismantle sexist attitudes. Yet the question remains: if we have not achieved equality between the sexes, how will societies achieve gender-based equity?

The implications of "feminine" school uniforms further reveal how policies reinforce phallocentric expectations, as skirts and dresses frequently limit the mobility of XXs and perpetuate their objectification.

As though the existing brutality inflicted on XXs were not already enough, some XY students are resorting to aggression as entertainment – gaining a distorted sense of power and approval through displays of misogynistic dominance and targeted acts of harassment, intimidation, and violence, mirroring the simulated rewards reinforced in video games.

In environments where physical prowess is glorified – including sports and other school activities – and where social pressures normalise amusement in others' suffering, cruelty becomes a currency for recognition and self-inflation, mistaking brutality for strength. These attitudes reflect not only individual conduct but also societies that continue to incentivise violence as a form of social capital.

Educational institutions that tolerate XY violence and control must undergo urgent reform to eliminate toxic masculine ideals. Policies for schools should advance progress and cultivate environments where fairness, respect, and equity are not just aspirations but fundamental principles.

This vision is not abstract – young XXs across the globe are personifying these principles through bold actions and leadership.

The initiatives of XX adolescents exemplify how a single individual can raise awareness, animate a nation, and propel legislative reform to advance equity and justice. Grassroots campaigns like *Teach Us Consent* show that individual action can meaningfully improve lives – offering a powerful reminder that anyone can be inspired to confront structural inequality, speak out, and demand the eradication of sex-based discrimination.

The fundamental rights to learn, work, and exist free from violence or harassment are no longer up for debate. As violence spans all age groups, introducing self-defence education early is argued to be imperative, urgent, and warranted – signalling the capability of XXs, their resilience, and their equal entitlement to the respect and autonomy granted to XYs. Beyond building confidence and practical skills, self-defence helps confront the entrenched normalisation of sex-based violence that many continue to face.

Another concern is the ongoing global underrepresentation of XXs in STEM in schools, universities, and workplaces. Despite various campaigns and programmes, cultural bias, limited representation, and structural barriers remain. Even in universities, XXs – though earning PhDs at higher rates than XYs in various countries – face discrimination that prevent progress and restricts access to economic advancement.

The growing role of technological advancements – AIED, for example – presents opportunities to reduce the workload of educators yet simultaneously raises concerns about algorithmic bias and unequal digital access, both of which risk amplifying existing disparities in education. AI also carries the potential to enhance learning for both educators and students – provided it is implemented with equity, transparency, and human oversight at its core.

However, this potential must be approached with caution, as misuse or poorly regulated use risks deepening inequalities.

If nations are serious about transforming education systems to improve economies and their citizens' capacities, they must acknowledge and implement changes that demonstrate an understanding of how the power of education lies in its ability to change lives. Nations must adopt comprehensive strategies with equitable policies and tools for development – for both students and educators – supported by unapologetically bold, equitable interventions.

At an international level, progress continues, with policies and global frameworks – including the UN SDGs (Goal 4: Quality Education and Goal 5: Gender Equality) – reaffirming global commitments to equal education access, irrespective of sex, gender, age, class, or geography.

Progressive legal changes are essential to achieving structural reforms, alongside sustained investment in professional development and support for educators – most of whom are XXs facing unsustainable workloads that lead many to exit the profession.

Ensuring educators have adequate tools, clear pathways for career progression, protection from violence, and equal pay for equal work is essential to improving the education sector and retaining talent globally.

The evidence is clear: economies and nations advance when all sexes are given equal opportunity – yet income inequality remains central to national and international agendas, as no country has achieved equal pay for equal work – despite clear evidence that when XXs participate in the economy, everyone benefits.

Since 1919, when the ILO was established, equal pay for equal work has been repeatedly delayed and resisted by patriarchal institutions – more than a century later, the same discussion continues in most nations.

Equal remuneration for equal work has been shown to boost economic performance and business productivity. Yet even in countries where equal pay laws exist, weak enforcement, entrenched prejudice, sex-based bias, and the exploitation of legal loopholes continue to sustain wage disparities and derail accountability mechanisms.

Meanwhile, XXs worldwide continue appealing to those in power to act ethically and impartially. The ongoing exclusion of XXs from top-earning industries and leadership positions further cements these structural inequalities into the foundations of economic and political life.

Nations that have legislated for equal pay demonstrate measurable progress – due in part to sustained advocacy and pressure from femocrats advancing equity through national and international platforms, including the successful implementation of "women's budgets" in numerous economies. Nonetheless, the allocation of national budgets continues to reinforce patriarchal attitudes, as funding allocated to XXs is categorised as "expenses", while financial commitments benefiting XYs are deemed "investments".

Childcare, for example, remains largely unaffordable and inaccessible – reinforcing structural inequalities by placing a disproportionate burden on XXs and forcing many to scale back their careers or exit the workforce entirely to assume caregiving responsibilities.

The "motherhood penalty" not only lowers earnings and prevents advancement but also deepens long-term financial disparities, widening the gap as XXs age. For low-income households and single mothers, the situation is even more severe, as childcare costs often exceed the financial benefits of work, making workforce participation increasingly unviable. The result? A system that punishes caregivers and entrenches economic inequality.

Nonetheless, it is important to recognise that amid persistent inequalities, XXs – once classified as property – are now, in many contexts, property owners, exercising control over assets and financial decisions.

Programmes and efforts to build XXs' capabilities in budgeting and asset growth have contributed meaningfully to economic literacy, helping to bridge the financial gap between the sexes. These initiatives have enabled XXs to make more confident financial choices that support their economic security and autonomy.

Additionally, XXs have become the most powerful consumer group in the world, partly propelled by record-breaking workforce participation. For many, economic power offers leverage – and when harnessed collectively and strategically, it has demonstrated the capacity to disrupt industries, modernise outdated hierarchies, and redesign global markets.

Whilst wealth operates as both a resource and a tool of influence, consumption also functions as a marker of identity and status. However, some financial decisions raise concerns, with biological factors contributing in complex but significant ways to patterns of consumer behaviour – revealing vulnerabilities that are often exploited by targeted marketing and profit-driven industries.

Psychological factors – including the need for self-esteem and survival – combined with manipulative marketing strategies, including *femvertising*, are fuelling compulsive consumerism. The *lipstick effect* – a pattern of increased consumption during times of crisis, which occur with unsettling regularity – and fast fashion all reveal their destructive consequences, while simultaneously reinforcing systemic exploitation under the guise of empowerment.

In 2024, XXs were responsible for $31.8 trillion of global spending – partly driven by manipulated consumption that reinforces entrenched misogynistic expectations of "femininity" – all while expanding landfills, perpetuating labour abuses, disregarding human rights, and accelerating environmental destruction.

Many consumers remain unaware of these manipulative tactics; hence, XXs are inadvertently sustaining industries that exploit workers – most of whom are XX – deceive consumers, and pollute waterways, land, and air, all while making the rich even wealthier. Meanwhile, a significant number of consumers are focusing on pre-owned products.

In response to the overconsumption of fast fashion, legislation has begun to target excess – with France banning advertising for the most polluting and disposable materials. Activists are now calling for the global adoption of similar measures to hold these industries accountable, educate consumers, and reduce pollution.

The real question is not whether XXs can transform the world, but how long those in power can postpone the inevitable revolution that will extinguish the economic power of the patriarchy?

That transformation is actively unfolding and gaining momentum – evidenced by the growing presence of XXs at the highest levels of power – demonstrating that with equal participation, societies can implement equitable legislation, reinforce institutional integrity, and advance collective well-being for both the people and the planet.

Supporting XXs – the world's most critical yet underutilised resource – is essential to creating more egalitarian societies, including elevating greater numbers of XXs into politics.

Choosing ignorance or claiming indifference to politics equates to self-sabotage. Politicians design and dictate the laws that govern every aspect of life. Understanding how power operates – and how small, deliberate actions can ignite profound transformation – is not just important, but essential for survival in the face of escalating injustices.

These principles are not novel – they form the foundation of democracy. Yet in many democratic nations, patriarchal systems continue to privilege only a portion of the population, using laws to enforce daily life activities, while erecting persistent barriers for XXs.

Despite the many hurdles, XXs have consistently been at the forefront of democratic progress – championing pro-XX reforms, expanding rights, and creating more inclusive spaces.

Still, paternal authority continues: by mid-2025, only 27 (14%) of the 193 UN member nations were led by XXs, with just 31 holding the highest political positions – in stark contrast to 162 XYs.

The XXs entering politics often face hostile conditions – including sexism, harassment, violence, and in extreme cases, death. Political leaders including Gillard (Australia), Merkel (Germany), Marin (Finland), Gandhi (India), Cox and Abbott (UK), and Giffords (USA) are among those XXs who have risked their well-being to serve their nations, despite relentless challenges. Their courage highlights how, even under constant pressure, XXs continue to lead progress and inspire positive change.

Greater XX representation in politics is essential. Ending paternalistic conventions starts with informed voting, accountability, and supporting policies that uphold XXs – all central to democratic governance. Collective action is already generating change, and XXs hold the electoral power to reshape political futures. Achieving this begins with understanding the mechanics of democracy.

The polity holds the power to define the legal frameworks that govern society, while the judiciary interprets and enforces them. As most political positions are still occupied by XYs, misogyny within governance has been well-documented and remains a matter of global concern.

However, XXs make up half the global population, and voting remains the cornerstone of democratic systems – enabling citizens to choose representatives and shape legislation, whether participation is compulsory or voluntary. When XXs engage and vote with awareness, they influence outcomes that affect both present and future generations. For this reason, it is crucial that XXs support and elect other XXs into office.

The assumption that "boys will be boys" is no longer defensible – yet many continue to accept it, even as the ideological divide between XXs and XYs widens at an unprecedented pace. Young XXs are aligning with progressive values, while XYs increasingly entrench themselves in conservative ideologies. The time for debate has passed; these divisions are real – but how they will redefine power, justice, and societies remain uncertain.

The good news is that more XXs are in favour of electing politicians like themselves and support increasing XX representation in parliaments. There is also growing support for quotas as a necessary mechanism to achieve parity in political leadership, with XXs expressing greater confidence in XX politicians. These preferences signal a shifting political landscape, where representation is increasingly regarded as a requirement for legitimacy rather than a symbolic aspiration. As attitudes evolve, institutions face mounting pressure to implement structural reforms that reflect the electorate's demands.

While a few argue that XXs in leadership fail to advocate for other XXs, legislative outcomes in many regions suggest otherwise. Even when confronting structural barriers, entrenched discrimination, and unequal power dynamics, XXs in politics continue to introduce pro-XX laws, improve governance, reduce corruption, and promote equality and human rights.

Quotas have been a useful tool for increasing XX representation. Though effective in securing minimum levels of participation, they are not a permanent or universal solution. Their success depends heavily on the surrounding political and social context, particularly the commitment of those in power.

Obtaining equal representation requires a comprehensive strategy that addresses both the symptoms and root causes of bigotry. Simply increasing XX numbers in politics is not enough; access to senior portfolios is equally necessary to alter power dynamics.

History shows that when a single XX takes office, their perspectives change – but when many XXs lead together, they initiate pro-XX laws and advance progress towards egalitarian societies.

International laws – including treaties and conventions promoting human and political rights – play a critical role in setting benchmarks for equality. Yet, their approval, application, and enforcement remain inconsistent. Nations that sign international contracts but ignore their obligations must be prosecuted.

Campaigns to educate must guide voting behaviour and shift public attitudes by correcting misinformation, malinformation and disinformation. To dismantle deep-seated prejudice, both the electorate and political leaders must actively contribute to governance that is inclusive, transparent, peaceful, and committed to social balance.

Political participation – whether through voting, advocacy, or leadership – is not optional; it is paramount. Without XX active engagement, the *status quo* that serves only XYs will tighten its grip and continue to intensify.

Disguised as governance, oppressive laws operate as instruments of patriarchal rule. When that authority is contested, patriarchs respond with calculated force, enforcing sexist doctrines to reassert masculine hegemony.

Additionally, progressive laws are being deliberately dismantled. The sacking of DEI and various other officials across government departments and agencies in the USA, and the aggressive severance from global health frameworks, including the WHO, for example, are not isolated events.

These actions illustrate a broader ideological assault designed to undo decades of hard-won social advancement and are producing profoundly damaging, far-reaching consequences across the globe. Hence, IWRLs – including CEDAW and the UN's SDGs – remain foundational to any serious strategy for global justice. But recognising rights on paper is not enough; translating them into lived realities demands stronger legal mechanisms, firmer accountability for violations, and broader ratification.

As history illustrates, laws do change for the better when more XXs hold political power. Matriarchal societies once thrived as inclusive, egalitarian communities grounded in care-based principles. These systems emphasised ecological harmony, interpersonal connection, and collective welfare – offering a clear contrast to prevailing patriarchal frameworks. Although patriarchal tyranny led to the widespread erasure of matricultures, aspects of matricultural life endure, offering valuable models of sustainable, cooperative governance rooted in consensus.

To advance genuine egalitarianism, the revitalisation and reconstruction of matriarchal systems – or their equivalents – are both necessary and urgent, as clearly illustrated by rich and powerful patriarchies – including oligarchs, corporations, political and religious leaders – who often ignore the law and escape culpability through influence, economic power, and tax exemptions.

Centuries ago, XX changed the game of Chess by legitimising the queen's power – authorising her to move in all directions – transforming her into the most commanding piece on the board, reflecting the power of reigning XX monarchs at the time. It is now time to apply that same logic beyond the board to redesign every patriarchal pillar. Why? Because, as confirmed by the UN, XXs are expected to wait another 286 years to obtain legal parity – an unacceptably ridiculous, unlawful, and deplorable timeline.

Central to maintaining the androcentric *status quo* and delaying the equal participation of XXs is language – one of the most powerful tools employed by lawmakers, the media, and others to subjugate, restrain, and control.

Words possess the power to distort perception, reinforce supremacy, and perpetuate archaic beliefs, all while enforcing and propagating patriarchal expectations. The language used by lawmakers and the media does more than inform – it dictates debate, distorts behaviour, deepens harmful stereotypes, and manipulates political outcomes with far-reaching consequences.

Despite ongoing bias and institutional resistance, progress is possible. Rewriting narratives and moving societies closer to justice and equality has been confirmed by the numerous movements and campaigns around the world and further illustrating that feminism remains as urgent now as it was at its inception.

For example, traditional media continues to frequently portray XXs in leadership, sport, politics, and other domains as less capable, despite them often possessing stronger qualifications and more skills than their XY counterparts.

Deeply alarming is the rise of SMCs and their unregulated SNSs, controlled by oligarchs who are weaponising and reconfiguring global communication systems – transforming social platforms into mechanisms of distortion, dependency, and ideological submission, and creating powerful channels for unfiltered messaging and influence across social, cultural, and political domains.

While these XY-owned platforms have amplified perspectives from previously marginalised voices, they have simultaneously become breeding grounds for harmful information.

Oligarchs are encouraging violence and legitimising ideologies rooted in ageism, antisemitism, colonialism, heterosexism, misogyny, nationalism, racism, religious extremism, sexism, transphobia, and xenophobia, to name a few. Each of these forms of oppression reinforces systemic inequality and discrimination, deepening societal exclusion, entrenched negative stereotypes, and prejudices.

Investigative XX journalists are uncovering and exposing systemic exploitation, often operating under legal restrictions, yet continuing to reveal the dirty secrets of the powerful – including oligarchs, political and religious figures who exploit, violate, control, and dehumanise. These acts of truth-telling are not merely cultural expressions; they are feminist movements in motion – resisting authoritarian rule and fighting to preserve democratic rights.

The unchecked power of oligarchs poses a grave threat to democracy, citizen engagement, and social cohesion. Oligarchic dominance and their relentlessly manipulated narratives suggest that meaningful change is increasingly out of reach. Hence, immediate and uncompromising global regulation is no longer optional – it is a democratic imperative.

The power to strip oligarchs of influence lies with the people – we, the users. Rather than remaining on platforms owned by XY oligarchs, shift to those led and owned by XXs. Every individual holds the capacity to lead meaningful changes; what is needed now is the courage to act and detox from the highly toxic.

More inclusive digital environments are emerging as XX-led SNSs amplify diverse perspectives. By entering and expanding global markets, XXs are not only generating economic opportunities but also accelerating progress towards equality – demonstrating the transformative potential of inclusive and ethical innovations in virtual environments.

As previously noted – and requiring further emphasis – language operates as a powerful mechanism for influencing perception and leading societal constructs. As cultures evolve, linguistic adaptation must also continue to reflect social advancement, affirming a wider range of identities. By adopting inclusive terms – for example, "humankind" instead of "mankind" – and rejecting biased expressions, communication becomes a tool for dismantling barriers and advancing equity. Although opposition persists, the flexibility of language supports the creation of more balanced, inclusive narratives – as demonstrated by terms like *herstory*.

Linguistic shifts are crucial to disrupt entrenched XY-default narratives propagated by dominant institutions, notably the media and religious dogma. Both are frequently evading accountability through influence, patriarchal entitlement, and tax exemptions. These institutions exercise immense global power – continuing to reinforce outdated ideologies that invalidate, vilify, and dehumanise. Their so-called leaders must be relentlessly exposed, rigorously challenged, and held accountable – both economically and philosophically.

For example, countless redundant and illegal practices persist under the guise of tradition – from the stigmatisation of menstruation to child marriage – serving only to block progress and dismantle rights that XXs have fought to secure over generations. These dogmas continue to erode autonomy by restricting personal freedoms and decision-making power.

Although legal prohibitions against sex-based discrimination exist in most nations, religious figureheads routinely resist reforms, claiming they threaten long-standing customs. Their interpretations frequently justify exclusion and excuse abuse.

Despite international pressure, entrenched cultural and religious doctrines – supported by legal loopholes – continue to impede advancements across both developing and developed nations.

The fusion of theological dogma with patriarchal concepts has enabled systemic violence, degraded XXs' societal position, and entrenched XY-centric scripts. While secularisation is increasingly questioning religion's legitimacy in public life, many still hold disproportionate influence, resisting equity and DEI reforms.

Nevertheless, XXs are making gradual progress – gaining leadership roles, defying sexual conduct codes, negotiating cultural expectations, navigating restrictive dress rules, and, in some cases, leaving religion behind in pursuit of autonomy and freedom from religion.

Unfortunately, however, even when XXs are freed from religious constraints, they encounter entrenched authorities wherever they go, as power remains concentrated in the hands of privileged XYs that govern all the pillars of the patriarchy.

Additionally, a new wave of XX leaders is replacing the Queen Bee model and redefining power and influence. XXs are cleaning up sticky floors and cracking glass ceilings through ethical leadership. While patriarchs and their mates continue to perpetuate misogyny, the educational and economic agency of XXs is a transformative force that – when united and strategically redirected – has proven capable of driving positive global reforms with resilience, cooperation, and innovation.

Matriarchal societies, embedded in equality, cooperation, and ecological harmony, also offer compelling alternatives. Though largely displaced, elements of matricultural life endure, presenting sustainable models of collective well-being. Exploring gynocratic governance highlights the capacity of XX-led systems to challenge and change existing phallocentric power.

Change demands active, daily participation. Disbanding the patriarchy is neither simple, nor linear, nor a spectator sport – but it is urgent, and it must begin now. Everyone – regardless of sex, gender, race, age, or geography – has a necessary role in ensuring XXs are present at every decision-making table.

XXs have endured, disrupted, and advanced with resilience – leading movements, governing, researching, caring, giving life, writing, and more. As pervasive irrational behaviour and abuses of authority continue, increasing numbers are rising to challenge all that can no longer be tolerated. Knowledge enables influence, and every act of XX-driven momentum, however small, erodes the systems that sustain XY dominance.

From factory floors to parliamentary offices, VAW persists. The rise of gynophobia – driven by an unwillingness to accept that XXs are educated, capable, and leading global progress – remains a serious threat to patriarchal interests. Still, XXs continue to resist outdated narratives, championing peace, equity, and sustainability in the face of enduring hostility.

History has shown that the collective strength of the sisterhood delivers results. From securing suffrage to challenging the tampon tax, feminists, advocates, and activists have consistently instigated reforms through persistence and intersectional advocacy. The same determination that once delivered hard-won victories must now ignite the next phase of progress – because mere resistance is no longer enough. It is outrageous that after generations of struggle, we are still resisting the same enemy.

Our obligations are clear: XXs must act decisively to prevent the rollback of hard-won freedoms and human rights. Meaningful change is not achieved by waiting – it is obtained when XXs uplift, support, and inspire one another.

The issue is no longer capacity, but clarity. XXs have the financial means; what is now essential is a conscious refusal to spend or invest in those who support the patriarchy. Influence lies not only in what is spent – but in the deliberate decision to withhold spending from brands, businesses, and industries that profit from misogyny, exploitation, and/or exclusion.

And for those who believe equality has already been obtained – be warned: the moment an XX steps into a leadership role, enters a boardroom, or the beauty of youth fades, the patriarchal backlash intensifies, aiming to silence, suppress, and marginalise with force.

Advancing equality is not merely urgent – it is critical, and the patriarchy must be disbanded. Every delay damages, injures, destroys, deepens injustice, and costs lives. Change must now move with speed, precision, clarity, and intent – because what is at stake is nothing less than everything!

References

Chapter 1

ABC News. (2024, February 1). Meta, TikTok, and X CEOs grilled at US Senate child safety hearing. Australian Broadcasting Corporation News. https://www.abc.net.au/news/2024-02-01/meta-tiktok-x-ceos-grilled-at-us-senate-child-safety-hearing/103412442

Abjorensen, N., & Docherty, J. C. (Eds.). (2014). *Historical Dictionary of Australia* (4th ed.). Rowman & Littlefield Publishers.

Agius, C., Rosamond, A. B., & Kinnvall, C. (2021). Populism, ontological insecurity and gendered nationalism: masculinity, climate denial and Covid-19. *Politics, Religion & Ideology*, *21*(4), 432–450.

Akbari, A., & Gabdulhakov, R. (2019). Platform Surveillance and Resistance in Iran and Russia: The Case of Telegram. *Surveillance & Society*, *17*(1/2), 223–231.

Alvarez, J. E. (2006). *International organizations as law-makers*. Oxford University Press.

Anderlini-D'Onofrio, S., & Alexander, J. (2009). Introduction to the Special Issue: Bisexuality and Queer Theory: Intersections, Diversions, and Connections. *Journal of Bisexuality*, *9*(3–4), 197–212.

AzQuotes. (n.d.). Justine Musk quotes. https://www.azquotes.com/author/38582-Justine_Musk

B & T Weekly. (2022, September 12). *WeAre8 announces string of change makers for Australia's newest social media app*. https://www.bandt.com.au/weare8-announces-string-of-change-makers-for-australias-newest-social-media-app/

Bailliet, C. M. (2016). A Nordic approach to promoting women's rights within international law: internal v. external perspectives. *Nordic Journal of International Law*, *85*(4), 368–394.

Barnett, M., & Duvall, R. (2005). Power in International Politics. *International Organization*, *59*(1), 39–75.

BBC News. (2020, November 17). *Twitter and Facebook CEOs grilled by Senate over election misinformation*. BBC News. https://www.bbc.com/news/education-54974819

Beecher, E. (2024). *The Men Who Killed the News*. Scribe Publications.

Bloomberg. (n.d.). *Bloomberg Billionaires Index* (May 2025). https://www.bloomberg.com/billionaires/

Booth, R. (2025, January 8). Meta to get rid of fact-checkers and recommend more political content. The Guardian. https://www.theguardian.com/technology/2025/jan/07/meta-facebook-instagram-threads-mark-zuckerberg-remove-fact-checkers-recommend-political-content

Burroughs, W. S. (1962). *The Ticket that Exploded*. Olympia Press.

Butler, J. (2004). *Undoing gender* (1st ed.). Routledge.

Cassidy, E. (2016). Social networking sites and participatory reluctance: a case study of gaydar, user resistance and interface rejection. *New Media & Society*, *18*(11), 2613–2628.

Choucair, T. (2024, September 2). *Brazil just banned X. Could other countries follow suit?* The Conversation. https://theconversation.com/brazil-just-banned-x-could-other-countries-follow-suit-237960

Čickaric, L. (2016). Reconsidering gender and women in politics. *South-East European Journal of Political Science*, *IV*(I), 95–103.

Colker, R. (1990). Feminist consciousness and the state: a basis for cautious optimism. *Columbia Law Review*, *90*(4), 1146–1170.

Cooperrider, D. L., & Srivastva, S. (1987). Appreciative inquiry in organizational life. *Research in Organizational Change and Development*, *1*(1), 129–169.

Corcos, A., & Hodara, L. (2023). How social media are collecting more of users' data: A behavioral model of platform retention strategies. *SN Business & Economics*, *3*(7), Article 117, 1–18.

Dawkins, R. (2016). *The Selfish Gene* (40th anniversary edition). Oxford University Press.

Dembroff, R., & Wodak, D. (2021). *How much gender is too much gender?* In R. Sterken & J. Khoo (Eds.), *The Routledge handbook of social and political philosophy of language* (pp. 362–376). Routledge.

Dent, G. (2019, August 20). *The Mad Witches Orchestrating the Alan Jones boycott.* Women's Agenda. https://womensagenda.com.au/latest/the-mad-witches-orchestrating-the-alan-jones-boycott/

Derico, B., & Wells, I. (2024, October 9). *Brazil lifts ban on Musk's X after it pays $5m fine.* British Broadcasting Corporation, BBC News. https://www.bbc.com/news/articles/c5y06vzk3yjo

Derrida, J. (1998). Faith and knowledge: The two sources of 'religion' at the limits of reason alone. In J. Derrida & G. Vattimo (Eds.), *Religion* (pp. 1–78). Stanford University Press.

Douglass, C. H., Wright, C. J. C., Davis, A. C., & Lim, M. S. C. (2018). Correlates of in-person and technology-facilitated sexual harassment from an online survey among young Australians. *Sex Health*, *15*(4), 361–365.

Dunn, S. (2023). *Spill app emerges as a Twitter alternative.* Time. https://time.com/6292622/spill-app-twitter-alternative/

Easteal, P., Holland, K., Breen, M. D., Vaughan, C., & Sutherland, G. (2019). Australian media messages: critical discourse analysis of two intimate homicides involving domestic violence. *Violence Against Women*, *25*(4), 441–462.

Eckert, P., & McConnell-Ginet, S. (2003). *Language and Gender.* Cambridge University Press.

Eden, L., & Wagstaff, M. F. (2020). Evidence-based policymaking and the wicked problem of SDG 5 gender equality. *Journal of International Business Policy*, *4*(1), 28–57.

Emens, E. F. (2007). Changing Name Changing: Framing Rules and the Future of Marital Names. *The University of Chicago Law Review*, *74*(3), 761–863.

Enache, C. (2024, April). *Digital taxation around the world.* Tax Foundation. https://taxfoundation.org/wp-content/uploads/2024/04/FF833.pdf

Evans, J. (2024, December 13). *Social media tax follows hundreds of news jobs cut since Meta's refusal to pay.* ABC News. https://www.abc.net.au/news/2024-12-13/social-media-tax-delay-hundreds-of-news-jobs-cut-meta-refusal/104719760

Faludi, S. (1992). *Backlash: The undeclared war against American women.* Crown Publishers.

Fan, M., Qalati, S. A., Khan, M. A. S., Shah, S. M. M., Ramzan, M., & Khan, R. S. (2021). Effects of entrepreneurial orientation on social media adoption and SME performance: The moderating role of innovation capabilities. *PLOS ONE*, *16*(4), e0247320.

Fausto-Sterling, A. (2000). *Sexing the body: gender politics and the construction of sexuality* (1st ed.). Basic Books.
Fawole, O. I., Okedare, O. O., & Reed, E. (2021). Home was not a safe haven: women's experiences of intimate partner violence during the COVID-19 lockdown in Nigeria. *BMC Women's Health, 21*(1), 32–37.
Fenichel Pitkin, H. (1967/2019). *The Concept of Representation* (Reprint 2019). University of California Press.
Fileborn, B., & Loney-Howes, R. (Eds.) (2019). *#Metoo and the politics of social change.* Palgrave Macmillan.
Forbes. (n.d.). *Real-time billionaires.* https://www.forbes.com/billionaires/
Foster, R. (2023). *Oligarchic material power and the implications for democratic systems* (Master's thesis). University of British Columbia.
Foucault, M. (1982). The subject and power. *The University of Chicago Press Journals, 8*(4), 777–795.
Foucault, M. (1999). *Religion and culture.* Routledge.
France 24. (2024, August 29). *Telegram chief Durov freed on bail after being formally charged over crime on messaging app.* https://www.france24.com/en/europe/20240829-telegram-chief-durov-freed-on-bail-after-being-formally-charged-over-crime-on-messaging-app
Frimer, J. A., Brandt, M. J., Melton, Z., & Motyl, M. (2019). Extremists on the left and right use angry, negative language. *Personality and Social Psychology Bulletin, 45*(8), 1216–1231.
Fung, B., & Duffy, C. (2024, January 31). *CEOs of Meta, X, Discord, TikTok, and Snap testify before the Senate Judiciary Committee.* CNN. https://edition.cnn.com/tech/live-news/meta-x-discord-tiktok-snap-chiefs-testimony-senate/index.html
Garay, A. (2010). Taxing Religious Organizations: A European Perspective. *The Review of Faith & International Affairs, 8*(2), 49–52.
Gay, V., Hicks, D. L., & Santacreu-Vasut, E. (2020). Migration as a window into the coevolution between language and behavior. *Journal of Economic Behavior & Organization, 180*, 529–557.
Goettner-Abendroth, H. (2022). *Matriarchal societies of the past and the rise of patriarchy: West Asia and Europe.* Peter Lang.
Göhler, G. (2009). *'Power to' and 'Power over'.* In M. Haugaard & S. R. Clegg (Eds.), *The SAGE Handbook of Power* (pp. 27–39). SAGE Publications.
Gomes, B. (2020). Masculinity and the patriarchal treatment of women in Shakespeare. *Conspectus Borealis, 5*(1), 15.
Gradwohl, R., Heller, Y., & Hillman, A. (2022). Social media and democracy. *arXiv.*
Grand View Research. (n.d.). *Digital advertising market report.* https://www.grandviewresearch.com/industry-analysis/digital-advertising-market-report
Grim, B. J., & Grim, M. E. (2016). The Socio-economic Contribution of Religion to American Society: An Empirical Analysis. *Interdisciplinary Journal of Research on Religion, 12.*
Harris, A. (2010). Mind The Gap: Attitudes and Emergent Feminist Politics since the Third Wave. *Australian Feminist Studies, 25*(66), 475–484.
Hart, C., & Gilbertson, A. (2018). When does violence against women matter? Gender, race and class in Australian media representations of sexual violence and homicide. *Outskirts, 39*, 1–31.
Harvey, D. (2005). *A brief history of neoliberalism* (1st ed.). Oxford University Press.
Hawkesworth, M. E. (2012). *Political worlds of women: activism, advocacy, and governance in the 21st century.* Westview Press.
Helberger, N., Pierson, J., & Poell, T. (2018). Governing online platforms: From contested to cooperative responsibility. *The Information Society, 34*(1), 1–14.
Hoffnung, M. (2006). What's in a name? Marital name choice revisited. *Sex Roles, 55*(11–12), 817–825.

Holton, S. S. (1987). *Feminism and democracy: Women's suffrage and reform politics in Britain*, 1900–1918. Cambridge University Press.

Hoskins, B. B. (1980). Gynocracy?: Who should advise women's lives? *Bioethics Quarterly*, *2*(4), 245–246.

Hudson, V., Leidl, P., & Hunt, S. (2015). *The Hillary doctrine: Sex and American foreign policy*. Columbia University Press.

HuffPost. (2012, March 26). *Sex workers punishing banks by not sleeping with employees.* https://www.huffpost.com/entry/spanish-sex-workers_n_1380404

Husain, T. (2024). Shattered innocence: uncovering the epidemic of sexual violence against women workers in Dhaka, Bangladesh. *Journal of Aggression, Conflict and Peace Research*, *16*(4), 414–426.

Inter-Parliamentary Union. (2022). *Global parliamentary report 2022.* IPU. https://www.ipu.org/resources/publications/reports/2022-03/global-parliamentary-report-2022

Jaworska, S., & Larrivée, P. (2011). Women, power and the media: Assessing the bias. *Journal of Pragmatics*, *43*(10), 2477–2479.

Jia, S., Lansdall-Welfare, T., Sudhahar, S., Carter, C., & Cristianini, N. (2016). Women are seen more than heard on online newspapers. *PLOS ONE*, *11*(2), 1–11.

Jordan, S. R., & Gray, P. W. (2019). American Bureaucracy in an Age of Oligarchy. *International Journal of Politics, Culture, and Society*, *32*(3), 279–300.

Kantola, J. (2006). *Feminists Theorize the State* (1st ed.). UK: Palgrave Macmillan.

Khalil, U., & Mookerjee, S. (2019). Patrilocal Residence and Women's Social Status: Evidence from South Asia. *Economic Development and Cultural Change*, *67*(2), 401–438.

Khan, M. R. (2021). A critical analysis of Elon Musk's leadership in Tesla Motors. *Journal of Global Entrepreneurship Research*, *11*(1), 213–222.

Koskie, T. (2024, August 26). *French police have arrested the founder of Telegram. What happens next could change the course of big tech.* The Conversation. https://theconversation.com/french-police-have-arrested-the-founder-of-telegram-what-happens-next-could-change-the-course-of-big-tech-237462#:~:text=Durov%20is%20currently%20only%20being,platforms%2C%20but%20also%20their%20owners

Lakoff, R. T. (2000). *The Language War*. University of California Press.

Lam, H. (2016). Social media dilemmas in the employment context. *Employee Relations*, *38*(3), 420–437.

Lewis, J. (2012, March 28). *High class Spanish prostitutes tell wealthy bankers 'No loans, no lay'.* International Business Times UK. https://www.ibtimes.co.uk/striking-spanish-prostitutes-beauties-boycott-bankers-320813

Liguori, M., & Steccolini, I. (2018). The power of language in legitimating public-sector reforms: When politicians "talk" accounting. *The British Accounting Review*, *50*(2), 161–173.

Lister, R. (2013). "Power, not Pity": Poverty and Human Rights. *Ethics and Social Welfare*, *7*(2), 109–123.

Lomas, N. (2022, May 13). *WeAre8 launches crowdfunder for its social media app where users are paid to watch ads.* https://techcrunch.com/2022/05/13/weare8-launches-crowdfunder-for-its-social-media-app-where-users-are-paid-to-watch-ads/#:~:text=On%20the%20WeAre8%20app%20consumers,business%20model%20for%20social%20mediaTechCrunch

MacKinnon, C. A. (2005). *Women's lives, men's laws* (2007 paperback ed). Harvard University Press.

MacKinnon, C. A. (2013). Creating international law: gender and leading edge. *Harvard Journal of Law & Gender*, *36*(1), 105–122.

MacKinnon, C. A. (2017). Introduction to symposium on Toward a feminist theory of the state. Law and Inequality: *A Journal of Theory and Practice*, *35*(2), 255–264.

MacKinnon, C. A. (2020). Equality. *Daedalus, 149*(1), 213–221.
Macquarie Dictionary. (2024). *Word of the Year.* https://www.macquariedictionary.com.au/word-of-the-year/word-of-the-year-2024/
Maher, H. (2025, January 27). *Elon Musk now has an office in the White House. What's his political game plan?* The Conversation. https://theconversation.com/elon-musk-now-has-an-office-in-the-white-house-whats-his-political-game-plan-248011
Mancosu, M., & Hopmann, D. N. (2019). Political disagreement and vote volatility: The role of familism across different European countries. *European Political Science Review, 11*(3), 301–317.
Margolis, H. (2017, March 13). *17 times politicians have resorted to wildly sexist speech over the last year. Human Rights Watch.* https://www.hrw.org/news/2017/03/13/17-times-politicians-have-resorted-wildly-sexist-speech-over-last-year
Márquez, U. R., Tovar Cabañas, R., & Herrera Meza, G. (2022). Covert Hegemonic Masculinities and other Androcracies. *Masculinidades y Cambio Social, 11*(2), 162–184.
Martin, S. (2024, October 10). *Kyle and Jackie O Show advertisers back out amid violent misogyny accusations.* The Guardian. https://www.theguardian.com/media/2024/oct/09/kyle-and-jackie-o-show-advertisers-back-out-violent-misogyny-accusations-campaign-mfw-ntwnfb
Martyn, J. A., Scott, J., van der Westhuyzen, J. H., Spanhake, D., Zanella, S., Martin, A., & Newby, R. (2019). Combining participatory action research and appreciative inquiry to design, deliver and evaluate an interdisciplinary continuing education program for a regional health workforce. *Australian Health Review, 43*(3), 345–351.
Meaker, M. (2024, August 28). *Telegram founder Pavel Durov charged over alleged criminal activity on the app.* WIRED. https://www.wired.com/story/telegram-pavel-durov-indictment/
MFW [Mad Fucking Witches]. (n.d.). Home. https://www.mfw.org.au/
Moore, D., Fraser, S., Törrönen, J., & Tinghög, M. E. (2015). Sameness and difference: metaphor and politics in the constitution of addiction, social exclusion and gender in Australian and Swedish drug policy. *International Journal of Drug Policy, 26*(4), 420–428.
Naas, M. (2016). Television and modernity: Jacques Derrida and the religion of the media. *Media, Culture & Society, 38*(1), 96–106.
Nasr Abdelhalim, E. H., Ibrahim, A. M., Hassan, H. E., Wahba, N. M., & Moawd, S. A. A. (2024). Silent struggles: Unveiling the unspoken epidemic of domestic violence against infertile women in Egypt. *International Journal of Africa Nursing Sciences, 20*, 100663.
Neuwirth, J. (2005). Inequality before the law: holding states accountable for sex discrimination laws under the Convention on the Elimination of All Forms of Discrimination against XXs and through the Beijing platform for action. *Harvard Human Rights Journal, 18*, 19–64.
Newman, G. M. (2019). The Taxation of Religious Organizations in America. *Harvard Journal of Law and Public Policy, 42*(2), 681–710.
NielsenIQ. (2024). *Women's Spending Power Grows as Values Shift.* NielsenIQ. https://nielseniq.com/global/en/insights/analysis/2024/shaping-success-a-deep-dive-into-womens-impact-on-the-cpg-landscape/#:~:text=Women's%20Spending%20Power%20Grows%20as%20Values%20Shift&text=As%20of%202024%2C%20women%20control,in%20the%20next%205%20years
Norris, P., & Inglehart, R. (2001). Cultural obstacles to equal representation. *Journal of Democracy, 12*(3), 126–140.
Onmanorama. (2022). *How women entrepreneurs are taking over social media.* https://www.onmanorama.com/lifestyle/women/2022/12/30/women-entrepreneurs-taking-over-social-media.html

Payne, S. B. (1996). The Iroquois League, the Articles of Confederation, and the Constitution. *The William and Mary Quarterly*, *53*(3), 605–620.
Phillips, A. (2024, November 14). *Why is Elon Musk becoming Donald Trump's efficiency tsar?* BBC News. https://www.bbc.com/news/articles/cpqd4vw0ejeo
Pleines, H. (2009). The political role of the oligarchs. In *Ukraine on its way to Europe. Interim results of the orange revolution*, 103–120.
Raday, F. (2018). CEDAW and the jurisprudence of UN human rights mechanisms. *Canadian Woman Studies*, *33*(1–2), 60–69.
Rankin, J. (2024, August 28). *European Union law and the arrest of Telegram's Pavel Durov: An analysis.* The Guardian. https://www.theguardian.com/world/article/2024/aug/28/european-union-arrest-telegram-pavel-durov-law-analysis
Reid, M. (2013). Unjust signifying practices: submission and subordination among Christian fundamentalists. *Journal of Feminist Studies in Religion*, *29*(2), 154–161.
Remy, J., Morgan, D., & Hearn, J. (Eds.). (1990). *Patriarchy and fratriarchy as forms of androcracy.* In *Men, Masculinities & Social Theory* (1st ed., Vol. 46, pp. 43–54). Routledge.
Rentschler, C. A. (2014). Rape culture and the feminist politics of social media. *Girlhood Studies*, 7(1), 65–82.
Renzetti, C. M. (2010). *Feminist theories.* Oxford Bibliographies Online. DOI: 10.1093/OBO/9780195396607-0013
Ricketson, M., & Dodd, A. (2024, September 8). *Murdoch to Musk: How global media power has shifted from the moguls to the big tech bros.* The Conversation. https://theconversation.com/murdoch-to-musk-how-global-media-power-has-shifted-from-the-moguls-to-the-big-tech-bros-237985
Romm, T. & Timberg, C., (2018, December 11). *Google CEO Sundar Pichai testifies before Congress: Highlights from the hearing.* The Washington Post. https://www.washingtonpost.com/technology/2018/12/11/google-ceo-sundar-pichai-testifies-congress-hearing/
Ross, A. M., Morgan, A. J., Jorm, A. F., & Reavley, N. J. (2019). A systematic review of the impact of media reports of severe mental illness on stigma and discrimination, and interventions that aim to mitigate any adverse impact. *Social Psychiatry and Psychiatric Epidemiology*, *54*(1), 11–31.
Rozgonyi, K. (2023). Accountability and platforms' governance: The case of online prominence of public service media content. *Internet Policy Review*, *12*(4), 1–36.
Ryan, K. (2013). The media's war on women: gendered coverage of female candidates. *Xavier Journal of Politics*, *4*(1), 1–13.
Santos, M., Saldaña, M., & Tsyganova, K. (2024). Subversive affordances as a form of digital transnational activism: The case of Telegram's native proxy. *New Media & Society*, *26*(1), 131–153.
Sapkota, M., & Dahal, K. (2022). Gender and politics: a feminist critique of the state. *Journal of Political Science*, *22*(1), 75–91.
Sawer, M. (2007). *Australia: the fall of the femocrat.* In J. Outshoorn & J. Kantola (Eds.), *Changing state feminism* (pp. 20–40). Palgrave Macmillan, UK & USA.
Sawer, M., & Radford, G. (2008). *Making women count: a history of the Women's Electoral Lobby* (1st ed.). UNSW Press.
SHEROES. (n.d.). *SHEROES: A women's social network.* https://sheroes.com/
Sia, S., Cornish, R., & Tranter, K. (2021). Fired for Facebook…terminated for Tinder: dismissal for social media misconduct in New Zealand. *International Journal of Law and Information Technology*, *29*(3), 204–224.
Sills, S., Pickens, C., Beach, K., Jones, L., Calder-Dawe, O., Benton-Greig, P., & Gavey, N. (2016). Rape culture and social media: young critics and a feminist counterpublic. *Feminist Media Studies*, *16*(6), 935–951.
Silve, A. (2015). Democratic spillovers – rent-seeking elites, mobile capital, and the coevolution of political institutions. *The Journal of Economic Literature*, *53*(3), 48–103.

Smith, L., & Niker, F. (2021). What Social Media Facilitates, Social Media should Regulate: Duties in the New Public Sphere. *The Political Quarterly*, *92*(4), 613–620.
Snyder, R. C. (2008). What Is Third-Wave Feminism? A New Directions Essay. *Signs: Journal of Women in Culture and Society*, *34*(1), 175–196.
Spill. (n.d.). *Spill: The Social Platform*. https://www.spill.com/
Statista. (n.d.). *Global digital population as of July 2023*. Statista. https://www.statista.com/statistics/617136/digital-population-worldwide/
Steels, L. (2011). Modeling the cultural evolution of language. *Physics of Life Reviews*, *8*(4), 339–356.
Steensland, B. (2008). Why do policy frames change? Actor–idea coevolution in debates over welfare reform. *Social Forces*, *86*(3), 1–28.
Stephanopoulos, N. O. (2015). Political powerlessness. *New York University Law Review (1950)*, *90*(5), 1527–1608.
Strassmann, B. I., & Kurapati, N. T. (2016). What Explains Patrilineal Cooperation? *Current Anthropology*, *57*(S13), S118–S130.
Tasker, Y., & Negra, D. (2005). In Focus: Postfeminism and Contemporary Media Studies. *Cinema Journal 44*(2), 107–110.
The New York Times. (2018, April 10). *Mark Zuckerberg testifies before Congress on Facebook's privacy practices*. The New York Times. https://www.nytimes.com/2018/04/10/us/politics/mark-zuckerberg-testimony.html
Thornthwaite, L., Balnave, N., & Barnes, A. (2018). Unions and social media: Prospects for gender inclusion. *Gender, Work & Organization*, *25*(4), 401–417.
Tickner, J. A. (1988). Hans Morgenthau's Principles of Political Realism: A Feminist Reformulation. *Millennium*, *17*(3), 429–440.
Tidmarsh, P., & Hamilton, G. (2020). Misconceptions of sexual crimes against adult victims: Barriers to justice. *Trends and Issues in Crime and Criminal Justice*, *611*, 1–18.
Tracxn. (n.d.). *SHEROES – Funding and investors*. https://tracxn.com/d/companies/sheroes/__ZPGIWZ8Mz9BRJCFaxYuyny9Ahw_Tiw_VT1BbxeHTUkU
Turley, E., & Fisher, J. (2018). Tweeting back while shouting back: Social media and feminist activism. *Feminism and Psychology*, *28*(1), 128–132.
Twenge, J. M., Campbell, W. K., & Gentile, B. (2012). Male and female pronoun use in U.S. books reflects women's status, 1900–2008. *Sex Roles*, *67*(9–10), 488–493.
United Nations. (2019). Official languages. https://www.un.org/en/our-work/official-languages
United Nations. (2020, March 2). *Use of religious beliefs to justify rights violations must be outlawed, says UN expert*. UN News. https://news.un.org/en/story/2020/03/1058411
United Nations, Department of Economic and Social Affairs, Population Division. (2023). World population prospects 2023: Summary of results. UN.
United Nations. (n.d.). *Member States*. UN. https://www.un.org/en/about-us/member-states
Valeriani, A. S. (2023). Navigating surveillance capitalism: A critical analysis through philosophical perspectives in computer ethics. *arXiv:2305.03787* DOI: 10.48550/arxiv.2305.03787
Vega, Y. K. (2023). *Sex, Policy and Power: The Australian Experience* (Doctoral thesis, unpublished). Swinburne University of Technology, Melbourne, Australia.
WeAre8. (2022). *WeAre8 launches self-serve ad-buying engine; eponymous app rewards users financially for watching ads*. https://www.weare8.com/post/weare8-launches-self-serve-ad-buying-engine-eponymous-app-rewards-users-financially-for-watching-ads#:~:text=WeAre8%20prompts%20and%20pays%20its,20p%20for%20each%20ad%20watched
Wendling, M., & Epstein, K. (2025, January 20). *Trump makes 'two sexes' official and scraps DEI policies*. BBC News. https://www.bbc.com/news/articles/czx84en1yp4o

Wikipedia (n.d.). *Justine Musk*. https://en.wikipedia.org/wiki/Justine_Musk
Wilding, D., Fray, P., Giotis, C., Molitorisz, S., Koskie, T., Hynes, D., Jakubowicz, A. (2020). *News in Australia – impartiality and commercial influence: review of literature and research*. University of Technology, Sydney, Australia.
Winters, J. A. (2017). Wealth defense and the complicity of liberal democracy. *Nomos, 58*, 158–225.
Wolfstone, I. W. F. (2018). *ReMembering Matricultures: Historiography of Subjugated Knowledges*. University of Alberta.
Wood Daly, M. (2021). Taxing Faith: Halo Effect and the Implications of Taxing Canadian Places of Worship. *Studies in Religion/Sciences Religieuses, 50*(3), 397–418.
Woodbridge, L. (2024). The Power of Language. *Journal for Social Action in Counseling and Psychology, 15*(2), 36–49.
Wu, P. (2015). Impossible to Regulate? Social Media, Terrorists, and the Role for the U.N. *Chicago Journal of International Law, 16*(1), 281–281.
Young, L., & Fitzgerald, B. (2006). *The power of language: how discourse influences society*. Equinox Publishing ltd.

Chapter 2

Ademiluka, S. O. (2020). 'Be fruitful and multiply': Examining Genesis 1:28 as a basis for the adoption of polygamy as a solution to childlessness amongst Nigerian Christians. *Verbum et Ecclesia, 41*(1), a2116.
Adler, R. (1998). *Engendering Judaism: An inclusive theology and ethics*. Beacon Press.
Aeberhard-Hodges, J., & McFerran, L. (2018). An International Labour Organization instrument on violence against women and men at work: the Australian influence. *Journal of Industrial Relations, 60*(2), 246–265
Ahmed, L. (1992). *Women and gender in Islam: Historical roots of a modern debate*. Yale University Press.
Alger, C. F. (2013). *The emerging roles of NGOs in the UN System: From Article 71 to a People's Millenium Assembly*. In Chadwick F. Alger (Vol. 7, pp. 129–151). Springer International Publishing AG.
Allen, S. L. (2014). The Anomaly of Tony Alamo Christian Ministries: A New Testament-based Call for Christian Polygamy. *Nova Religio: The Journal of Alternative and Emergent Religions, 17*(4), 61–82.
Arat, Z. F. K. (2015). Feminisms, women's rights, and the UN: would achieving gender equality empower women? *American Political Science Review, 109*(4), 674–689.
Arosoaie, A., & Osman, M. N. M. (2018). Islam beyond religion and politics: Islamisation in Southeast Asia. *Journal of Religious and Political Practice, 4*(3), 209–213.
Arthur, M., Earle, A., Raub, A., Vincent, I., Atabay, E., Latz, I., Kranz, G., Nandi, A., & Heymann, J. (2018). Child marriage laws around the world: Minimum marriage age, legal exceptions, and gender disparities. *Journal of Women, Politics & Policy, 39*(1), 51–74.
Asia-Pacific Economic Cooperation. (2011). *High level policy dialogue on women and the economy — the APEC declaration*. APEC. https://www.apec.org/meeting-papers/sectoral-ministerial-meetings/women/2011_women
Australian Human Rights Commission (AHRC). (2022). https://humanrights.gov.au/
Australian NGO Coalition. (2018). *Australia's compliance with the Convention on the Elimination of All Forms of Discrimination against Women: Shadow report*. UNSW. https://www.unsw.edu.au/content/dam/pdfs/law/klc/law-reform-submissions/

2018/2018-Australian-NGO-Coalition-Shadow-Report-on-Australia%E2%80%99s-Compliance-with-the-Convention-on-the-Elimination-of-All-Forms-of-Discrimination-Against-Women.pdf

Bailliet, C. M. (2016). A Nordic approach to promoting women's rights within international law: internal v. external perspectives. *Nordic Journal of International Law*, *85*(4), 368–394.

Baldez, L. (2011). The UN Convention to Eliminate All Forms of Discrimination against Women (CEDAW): a new way to measure women's interests. *Politics & Gender* 7, 419–423.

Baldez, L. (2013, June 26). U.S. drops the ball on women's rights. Cable News Network. https://home.dartmouth.edu/news/2013/03/us-drops-ball-womens-rights-cnn

Băluţă, O. (2015). Women, mobilization and political representation. *Journal of Gender and Feminist Studies* (5), 3–7.

Ban, K.M. (2014). *Beijing Declaration and Platform for Action.* Beijing+5 political declaration and outcome [Report]. UN Women. https://www.unwomen.org/en/digital-library/publications/2015/01/beijing-declaration

Banerjee, S. (2010). Women, Muscular Nationalism and Hinduism in India: Roop Kanwar and the Fire Protests. *Totalitarian Movements and Political Religions*, *11*(3–4), 271–287.

Barclay, F. P., Karippara, M. S., Sasidharan, A., Barclay, F. P., & Laskar, K. A. (2024). Fourth-Wave Feminism: World View and the Indian Context. In F. P. Barclay & K. A. Laskar (Eds.), *Gender and Popular Visual Culture in India* (1st ed., Vol. 1, pp. 74–84). Routledge.

Barnett, M., & Duvall, R. (2005). Power in international politics. *International Organizations Law Review*, *59*(1), 39–75.

Basu, S. (2016). Gender as national interests for the UN Security Council. *The Royal Institute of International Affairs*, *92*(2), 255–273.

Beck, L. (2021). Our father who art in town hall: do local councils have power to pray? *Alternative Law Journal*, *46*(2), 128–133.

Beck, L. (2023, April 6). *Many local councils still officially pray to God. Here's why this may be unlawful and should be abandoned.* The Conversation. https://theconversation.com/many-local-councils-still-officially-pray-to-god-heres-why-this-may-be-unlawful-and-should-be-abandoned-203192

Bengtsson, N. (2023). Default options and tax avoidance: Evidence from the church tax. *Journal of Public Economics Plus*, *4*, 100018.

Blaney, I. (2022). Pious Causes: The Boundaries between Charity Law and Ecclesiastical Law. *Ecclesiastical Law Journal*, *24*(3), 309–331.

Boxer, M. J. (1982). 'First wave' feminism in nineteenth-century France: Class, family and religion. *Women's Studies International Forum*, *5*(6), 551–559.

Boyne, K. (2011). UN Women: jumping the hurdles to overcoming gender inequality, or falling short of expectations? *Cardozo Journal of Law & Gender*, *17*(3), 683–716.

Broinowski, A., & Wilkinson, J. (2005). *The third try – can the UN work?* Scribe Publications.

Bronner, L. L. (1993). From veil to wig: Jewish women's hair covering. *Judaism*, *42*(4), 465.

Bull, A. L., Bhachu, D., & Blier-Carruthers, A. (2022). *Slow Train coming?: Equality, diversity and inclusion in UK higher education.* The University of York.

Bush, S. S. (2011). International politics and the spread of quotas for women in legislatures. *International Organization Journal*, *65*(1), 103–137.

Caglar, G., Prügl, E., & Zwingel, S. (2013). *Feminist strategies in international governance.* Routledge.

Casas, A., Menchen-Trevino, E., & Wojcieszak, M. (2023). Exposure to Extremely Partisan News from the Other Political Side Shows Scarce Boomerang Effects. *Political Behavior*, *45*(4), 1491–1530.

CEDAW. (1979). *Convention on the Elimination of All Forms of Discrimination against Women*. UN. https://treaties.un.org/Pages/ViewDetails.aspx?src=TREATY&mtdsg_no=IV-8&chapter=4&clang=_en

Chatterjee, C. (2002). *Celebrating women: Gender, festival culture, & Bolshevik ideology, 1910–1939*. University of Pittsburgh Press.

Chaudhuri, M. (2022). *International Women's Day: New Avatars and Forgotten Beginnings*. *Journal of Women & Society*, *2*, 1–30.

Chavura, S. A., Gascoigne, J., & Tregenza, I. (2019). *Reason, religion and the Australian polity: a secular state?* Routledge.

Choi, J., & Park, J. (2023). Exploring inbreeding dynamics by considering reproductive bound and polygyny. *Chaos (Woodbury, N.Y.)*, *33*(8).

Clinton, H. R. (2011). *Secretary Clinton's remarks to the APEC Women and the Economy Summit* [Speech]. https://2009-2017.state.gov/secretary/20092013clinton/rm/2011/09/172605.htm

Colgan, F., & Colgan, F. (2011). Equality, diversity and corporate responsibility: Sexual orientation and diversity management in the UK private sector. *Equality, Diversity and Inclusion an International Journal*, *30*(8), 719–734.

Colley, L., & van Acker, E. (2021). Women's selection into parliament: the interplay between formal rules and informal practices. *Journal of legislative studies*, *27*(2), 185–206.

Commission on the Status of Women. (2019). *Short history of the Commission on the Status of Women*. CSW. UN Women. https://www.unwomen.org/en/digital-library/publications/2019/02/a-short-history-of-the-commission-on-the-status-of-women

Commonwealth of Australia. (1984). *Sex Discrimination Act 1984*. SDA. https://www.legislation.gov.au/Details/C2014C00002

Cooke, L. (2023). *Bitch: What does it mean to be female?* Penguin Books.

Cope, K. L., Creamer, C. D., & Versteeg, M. (2019). Empirical studies of human rights law. *Annual Review of Law and Social Science*, *15*(1), 155–182.

Cornwall, A., & Rivas, A.-M. (2015). From 'gender equality' and 'women's empowerment' to global justice: reclaiming a transformative agenda for gender and development. *Third World Quarterly*, *36*(2), 396–415.

Crawford, E., Rothwell, D. R., Charlesworth, H., Bailey, P., Baird, R., Bartsch, R., . . . Triggs, G. (2017). *International law in Australia*. Thomson Reuters (Professional) Australia.

Crowther-Heyck, K. (2002). 'Be fruitful and multiply': Genesis and generation in Reformation Germany. *Renaissance Quarterly*, *55*(3), 904–935.

Dawkins, R. (2016). *The selfish gene* (40th anniversary edition.). Oxford University Press.

de Alwis, R. S., & Verveer, M. (2021). 'Time Is A-Wasting': Making the Case for CEDAW Ratification by the United States. *The Columbia Journal of Transnational Law*, *60*(1), 1.

Department of Foreign Affairs and Trade. (2020). *The Australian Treaty Series: Convention on the Elimination of All Forms of Discrimination against Women*. DFAT. Australian Government. https://www.info.dfat.gov.au/info/treaties/treaties.nsf/alldocids/333d22b9ed69b058ca256b300024f1ba

Department of Prime Minister and Cabinet. (2022). *International forums*. Australian Government. DPMC. https://www.pmc.gov.au/office-women/international-forums

Dowse, S. (2014). The prime minister's women. *Australian Feminist Studies*, *29*(82), 391–402.

Edgar, A., & Thwaites, R. (2018). Implementing treaties in domestic law: translation, enforcement and administrative law. *Melbourne Journal of International Law*, *19*(1). 24–51.
Efevbera, Y., & Bhabha, J. (2020). Defining and deconstructing girl child marriage and applications to global public health. *BMC Public Health*, *20*(1), 1547–1611.
El-Ali, L. (Ed.). (2021). *Sexual Misconduct: What the Qur'an Tells Us about Pre-Marital vs Extra-Marital Sex. In No Truth Without Beauty* (pp. 249–261). Springer.
El-Ali, L., & El Fadl, K. A. (2022). *No Truth Without Beauty: God, the Qur'an, and Women's Rights*. Springer Nature.
Englehart, N. A., & Miller, M. K. (2014). The CEDAW Effect: International Law's Impact on Women's Rights. *Journal of Human Rights*, *13*(1), 22–47.
Esposito, J. L. (2011). *What everyone needs to know about Islam* (2nd ed.). Oxford University Press.
Fader, A. (2009). *Mitzvah girls: Bringing up the next generation of Hasidic Jews in Brooklyn*. Princeton University Press.
Fan, S., & Koski, A. (2022). The health consequences of child marriage: a systematic review of the evidence. *BMC Public Health*, *22*(1), 309–309.
Farrior, S. (2009). Human rights advocacy on gender issues: challenges and opportunities. *Journal of Human Rights Practice*, *1*(1), 83–100.
Fleming, P. (2007). Sexuality, power and resistance in the workplace. *Organization Studies*, *28*(2), 239–256.
Foucault, M. (1982). The subject and power. *The University of Chicago Press Journals*, *8*(4), 777–795.
Frawley-O'Dea, M. G. (2007). *Perversion of power: Sexual abuse in the Catholic Church*. Vanderbilt University Press
Gengler, S. W., & Lee, J. W. (2002). Ministers' Understanding of Battered Women: Differences Among Catholic Male Priests, Protestant Female Ministers and Protestant Male Ministers. *Journal of Religion & Abuse*, *3*(3–4), 41–59.
Gibson, N. (2007). Faith in the courts: Religious dress and human rights. *Cambridge Law Journal*, *66*(3), 657–697.
Gordan, R., Kurtzer, Y., & Sufrin, C. E. (2020). Blu Greenberg, *On Women and Judaism: A View from Tradition*. In Yehuda Kurtzer and Claire E. Sufrin (Eds.), *The New Jewish Canon* (pp. 326–329). Academic Studies Press.
Grabham, E., & Hunter, R. (2008). Encountering human rights: gender/sexuality, activism and the promise of law. *Feminist Legal Studies*, *16*(1), 1–7.
Green, D. (1999). Engendering Judaism: An Inclusive Theology and Ethics. Rachel Adler. *The Journal of Religion*, *79*(4), 685–686.
Gregg, S. (2016). Does religion support the free society? *Policy: A Journal of Public Policy and Ideas*, *32*(4), 42–48.
Grigat, D., & Carrier, G. (2007). Gender Transgression as Heresy: The Trial of Joan of Arc. *Past Imperfect*, *13*, 188–207.
Grint, K. (2010). The cuckoo clock syndrome: addicted to command, allergic to leadership. *European Management Journal*, *28*(4), 306–313.
Gross-Wyrtzen, L. (2023). "There is no race here": on blackness, slavery, and disavowal in North Africa and North African studies. *The Journal of North African Studies*, *28*(3), 635–665.
Gudorf, C. E. (2011). Feminist approaches to religion and torture. *The Journal of Religious Ethics*, *39*(4), 613–621.
Haliczer, S. (1996). *Sexuality in the confessional: A sacrament profaned*. Oxford University Press.
Hand, J., Davis, B., & Feast, P. (2012). Unification, simplification, amplification? An analysis of aspects of the British Equality Act 2010. *Commonwealth Law Bulletin*, *38*(3), 509–528.

Hanhimaki, J. M. (2008). *The United Nations: a very short introduction*. Oxford University Press.
Harlan, L. (1992). *Religion and Rajput women: The ethic of protection in contemporary narratives*. University of California Press.
Hauptman, J., & Greenspahn, F. E. (2009). *Women and Jewish Law*. In *Women and Judaism* (Vol. 5, pp. 64–90). NYU Press.
Hawkesworth, M. E. (2012). *Political worlds of women: activism, advocacy, and governance in the 21st century*. Westview Press.
Hawley, J. S. (Ed.). (2023). *Sati, the blessing and the curse: The burning of wives in India*. Oxford University Press.
Haworth, N., & Hughes, S. (2010). Surfing History's Waves: On the resilience of the International Labour Organisation as an international institution. *New Zealand Journal of Employment Relations*, *35*(3), 16–26.
Heideman, K., Nietsche, C., Romano, J. C., Parker, E., White, E., & Fetterly, M. (2014). *Beijing+20: looking back and the road ahead—reflections on milestones in women's leadership in the 21st century*. The Woodrow Wilson International Center for Scholars.
Henkin, L. (1990). Law and politics in international relations: state and human values. *Journal of International Affairs*, *44*(1), 183–208.
Henkin, L. (1995). Human rights and state sovereignty. *Georgia Journal of International and Comparative Law*, *25*(2), 31–46.
Henne, P. S. (2018). Does the UN Human Rights Council help or hurt religious repression? *Journal of Church and State*, *60*(4), 705–724.
Hessini, L. (2007). Abortion and Islam: Policies and Practice in the Middle East and North Africa. *Reproductive Health Matters*, *15*(29), 75–84.
Hobbins, D. (2005). *The trial of Joan of Arc*. Harvard University Press.
Hodges, J. (2014). The role of the International Labour Organization in balancing work and family in the 21st century. *Journal of Industrial Relations*, *56*(4), 566–576.
Holub, M. A. (2012). Immersion and Transformation: A Community Explores the Mikveh. *Liturgy*, *27*(4), 14–19.
Homolka, W., & Schöttler, H.-G. (2013). *Rabbi, pastor, priest: their roles and profiles through the ages* (1st ed.). De Gruyter.
Htun, M., & Weldon, S. L. (2010). When do governments promote women's rights? A framework for the comparative analysis of sex equality policy. *Perspectives on Politics*, *8*(1), 207–217.
Hudson, V., Leidl, P., & Hunt, S. (2015). *The Hillary doctrine: Sex and American foreign policy*. Columbia University Press.
Hunsberger, B., & Jackson, L. M. (2005). Religion, meaning, and prejudice. *Journal of Social Issues*, *61*(4), 807–826.
Hunt, S. (2013). Negotiating equality in the Equality Act 2010 (United Kingdom): Church-state relations in a post-Christian society. *Journal of Church and State*, *55*(4), 690–711.
Institute for Women's Policy Research. (2015). The status of women in the states: 2015 poverty and opportunity. IWPR. https://iwpr.org/iwpr-publications/report/the-status-of-women-in-the-states-2015/
International Labour Organization (ILO). (n.d.). *About the ILO*. https://www.ilo.org/about-ilo
International Monetary Fund (IMF). (2018). *Pursuing women's economic empowerment*. https://www.imf.org/en/Publications/Policy-Papers/Issues/2018/05/31/pp053118pursuing-womens-economic-empowerment
International Women's Rights Action Watch Asia-Pacific. (2022). *IWRAW Asia Pacific*. https://www.iwraw-ap.org/

Inter-Parliamentary Union. (2024). *World e-Parliament report 2024.* IPU. https://linktr.ee/WEPR2024

James, K. (2022). Removal of the tampon tax: A costless or Pyrrhic victory? *Australian Feminist Law Journal, 48*(2), 193–220.

Jansen, C., Cammock, P., & Conner, L. (2010). Leaders building professional learning communities: appreciative inquiry in action. *Journal of Educational Leadership, Policy and Practice, 25*(1), 41–54.

Jaworska, S., & Larrivée, P. (2011). Women, power and the media: Assessing the bias. *Journal of Pragmatics, 43*(10), 2477–2479.

Johnson, T. M., & Grim, B. J. (2013). *The world's religions in figures: an introduction to international religious demography.* John Wiley & Sons.

Kaplan, T. (1985). On the Socialist Origins of International Women's Day. *Feminist Studies, 11*(1), 163–171.

Keck, M. E., & Sikkink, K. (1998). *Activists beyond borders: advocacy networks in international politics.* Cornell University Press.

King, C. S. (2000, November 9). Remarks at the 13th annual 'Creating Change' *Conference of the National Gay and Lesbian Task Force.* Atlanta, GA. https://www.azquotes.com/author/8030-Coretta_Scott_King

Kirchgaessner, S. (2016, November 2). *Pope Francis says women will never be Roman Catholic priests.* The Guardian. https://www.theguardian.com/world/2016/nov/01/pope-francis-women-never-roman-catholic-priests-church

Kolbaba, T. (2003). Pernoud & Clin, Joan Of Arc – Her Story. *Teaching History (Emporia, Kan.), 28*(2), 97-.

Korbatieh, S. (2018). Adultery Laws in Islam and stoning in the modern world. *Australian Journal of Islamic Studies, 3*(2), 1–20.

Koski, A., & Heymann, J. (2018). Child Marriage in the United States: How Common Is the Practice, And Which Children Are at Greatest Risk? *Perspectives on Sexual and Reproductive Health, 50*(2), 59–65.

Krook, M. L., & Restrepo Sanín, J. (2020). The cost of doing politics? Analyzing violence and harassment against female politicians. Perspectives on Politics, *18*(3), 740–755.

Kusuma, Y. S., & Babu, B. V. (2017). Elimination of violence against women and girls as a global action agenda. *Journal of Injury and Violence Research, 9*(2), 117–122.

La Fornara, L. M. (2018). Islam's (in)compatibility with the West?: Dress code restrictions in the age of feminism. *Indiana Journal of Global Legal Studies, 25*(1), Article 18.

Lekha, N. B., & Kumar M. P. (Eds.). (2025). *Routledge Handbook of Gender, Culture, and Development in India* (1st ed.). Routledge.

Low, B. S. (1988). Measures of Polygyny in Humans. *Current Anthropology, 29*(1), 189–194. https://doi.org/10.1086/203627

MacCulloch, D. (2024). *Lower than the angels: A history of sex and Christianity.* Allen Lane.

Mackay, F. (2008). 'Thick' conceptions of substantive representation: women, gender and political institutions. *Representation, 44*(2), 125–139.

MacKinnon, C. A. (2005). *Women's lives, men's laws* (2007 paperback ed). Harvard University Press.

Macy, G. (2008). *The Hidden History of Women's Ordination: Female Clergy in the Medieval West.* Oxford University Press Inc

Mansouri, F., Kivisto, P., Imbert, P., Grossman, M., Roose, J. M., Armillei, R., . . . Phillips, M. (2015). *Cultural, religious and political contestations: the multicultural challenge.* Springer International Publishing.

McConnell, A. (2016). A public policy approach to understanding the nature and causes of foreign policy failure. *Journal of European Public Policy, 23*(5), 667–684.

McCrudden, C. (2015). Why do national court judges refer to human rights treaties? A comparative international law analysis of CEDAW. *American Journal of International Law*, *109*(3), 534–550.

Mernissi, F. (1991). *The veil and the male elite: A feminist interpretation of women's rights in Islam*. Perseus Books.

Merry, S. E. (2003). Constructing a global law–violence against women and the human rights system. *Law & Social Inquiry*, *28*(4), 941–977.

Merry, S. E. (2009). *Human rights and gender violence*. University of Chicago Press.

Miéville, C. (2005). *Between equal rights: a Marxist theory of international law*. Brill.

Misra, G. (2020, August 7). *Roop Kanwar: The last known case of Sati in India and its relevance today*. Feminism in India. https://feminisminindia.com/2020/08/07/roop-kanwar-last-known-case-sati-india-relevance-today/#google_vignette

Moxon, D. (2007). Book review. Between equal rights: a Marxist theory of international law by China Miéville. *The Society of Legal Scholars*, *27*(2), 343–346.

Muller, F. M., & Bühler, G. (Eds.). (2001). *The laws of Manu*. Routledge, Taylor & Francis Group.

Narayan, A., & Gurung, S. H. (2016). *Living our religions: Hindu and Muslim South Asian American women narrate their experiences* (A. Narayan & B. Purkayastha, Eds.). Kumarian Press.

Nawaz, M., & Deegan, T. (2018, July 24). *UN delivers strong rebuke to Australian government on women's rights*. The Conversation. https://theconversation.com/un-delivers-strong-rebuke-to-australian-government-on-womens-rights-100089

Nelson, J. B. (1983). *Between two gardens: Reflections on sexuality and religious experience*. The Pilgrim Press.

Neuwirth, J. (2005). Inequality before the law: holding states accountable for sex discrimination laws under the Convention on the Elimination of All Forms of Discrimination against Women and through the Beijing platform for action. *Harvard Human Rights Journal*, *18*, 19–64.

Newman, G. M. (2019). The taxation of religious organizations in America. *Harvard Journal of Law and Public Policy*, *42*(2), 681–710.

Noor, A. (2010). Stoning for Adultery in Christianity and Islam and its Implementation in Contemporary Muslim Societies. *Intellectual Discourse*, *18*(1), 97–113.

Nussbaum, M. C. (2016). Women's progress and women's human rights. *Human Rights Quarterly*, *38*(3), 589–633.

O'Brien, K., Fitzsimmons, T. W., Crane, M., & Head, B. (2017). Workplace gender inequality as a wicked problem: implications for research and practice. *Academy of Management Annual Meeting Proceedings*, *2017*(1), 14717.

O'Toole, L. J. (2000). Research on policy implementation: assessment and prospects. *Journal of Public Administration Research and Theory*, *10*(2), 263–288.

O'Toole, L. J., & Montjoy, R. S. (1984). Interorganizational policy implementation: a theoretical perspective. *Public Administration Review*, *44*(6), 491–503.

Padoux, A. (1984). The Hindu World and Sex: Symbolism, Attitudes, and Practices. *Cahiers internationaux de sociologie*, *31*(76), 29–49.

Parliament of Australia. (2022). Acknowledgement of Country and Prayers. https://www.aph.gov.au/About_Parliament/House_of_Representatives/Powers_practice_and_procedure/Practice7/HTML/Chapter8/Acknowledgement_of_country_and_Prayers

Pew Research Center. (2016a). The Gender Gap in Religion Around the World. PRC. https://www.pewresearch.org/religion/2016/03/22/the-gender-gap-in-religion-around-the-world/

PEW Research Center. (2016b). Women more likely than men to affiliate with a religion. PRC. https://www.pewresearch.org/religion/2016/03/22/women-more-likely-than-men-to-affiliate-with-a-religion/

Pintchman, T. (2007). *Women's lives, women's rituals in the Hindu tradition*. Oxford University Press.

Poulos, E. (2019). Constructing the problem of religious freedom: an analysis of Australian Government inquiries into religious freedom. *Religions*, *10*(10), 1–17.

Priest, N., & Biddle, N. (2017, August 21). *The verdict on domestic violence data and the Church: believe the women*. Australian Broadcasting Corporation (ABC). https://www.abc.net.au/news/2017-08-21/the-verdict-on-domestic-violence-data-and-the-church-believe/8804790

Raday, F. (2018). CEDAW and the jurisprudence of UN human rights mechanisms. *Canadian Woman Studies*, *33*(1–2), 60–69.

Rafferty, Y. (2013). International dimensions of discrimination and violence against girls: a human rights perspective. *Journal of International Women's Studies*, *14*(1), 1–24.

Ram, A. (2021). Ritual, Romance, and Royalty: Bollywood Remakes of Hindu Femininity.

Ratcliff, S., & Haltom, T. M. (2023). Not on the Same(-Sex) Page: How Religion Shapes Opposition to Same-Sex Marriage Among Sexual Minorities and Heterosexuals. *Sexuality Research & Social Policy*, *20*(4), 1360–1377.

Reid, M. (2013). Unjust signifying practices: submission and subordination among Christian fundamentalists. *Journal of Feminist Studies in Religion*, *29*(2), 154–161.

Reilly, N. (2019). *International human rights of women* (N. Reilly, Ed.; 1st ed.). Singapore: Springer.

Reza, F. (2022). The role of NGOs in promoting education: Successes and challenges. *International Journal of Education, Learning and Development*, *10*(1), 24–43.

Rincker, M., Henderson, M., Vidigal, R., & Delgado, D. (2019). Evaluating the representation and responsiveness of the United Nations Commission on the Status of Women (CSW) to diverse women populations worldwide. *Frontiers in Sociology*, *4*, 1–15.

Robinson, J., & Yoshida, K. (2024). *Silenced women: Why the law fails women and how to fight back*. Octopus Publishing Group

Rompis, N. H., Kasim, N. M., & Bakung, D. A. (2020). Polygamy in the perspective of Christianity. *Estudiante Law Journal*, *2*(1), 180–193.

Rosenblum, D. (2011). Unisex CEDAW, or what's wrong with women's rights. *Columbia Journal of Gender and Law*, *20*(2), 98–194.

Rothwell, D., & Crawford, E. (2017). *International law: is Australia a good international citizen?* Australia: Australian Institute of International Affairs. https://www.internationalaffairs.org.au/australianoutlook/international-law-australia-good-citizen/

Rustici, C. M. (2006). *The afterlife of Pope Joan deploying the Popess legend in early modern England*. Michigan, USA: University of Michigan Press.

Ryder, G. (2015). The International Labour Organization: the next 100 years. *Journal of Industrial Relations*, *57*(5), 748–757.

Sanders, O. (2024, March 5). *Pressure grows on Victorian councils to ditch opening prayer amid claims of human rights violation*. ABC News. https://www.abc.net.au/news/2024-03-05/vic-councils-face-pressure-opening-prayer-human-rights-violation/103516516

Sapkota, M., & Dahal, K. (2022). Gender and politics: a feminist critique of the state. *Journal of Political Science*, *22*(1), 75–91.

Sarkar, B. (2014). Murderous Ritual versus Devotional Custom: The Rhetoric and Ritual of Sati and Women's Subjectivity in Amitav Ghosh's Sea of Poppies. *Humanities (Basel)*, *3*(3), 283–298.

Sauer, B., & Wöhl, S. (2011). Feminist perspectives on the internationalization of the state. *Antipode*, *43*(1), 108–128.

Shaw, E., McCormick, D., Hartmann, H., & Gault, B. (2013). *Enhancing the status of women: how engaging women in leadership creates a more inclusive democracy and improves women's lives.* (IWPR #L002, Updated June 2013). Institute for Women's Policy Research. https://iwpr.org/enhancing-the-status-of-women-how-engaging-women-in-leadership-creates-a-more-inclusive-democracy-and-improves-womens-lives/

Shlain, L. (2003). *Sex, time and power: how women's sexuality shaped human evolution.* Penguin Books.

Siddiqi, M., & Greene, M. E. (2022). Mapping the Field of Child Marriage: Evidence, Gaps, and Future Directions From a Large-Scale Systematic Scoping Review, 2000–2019. *Journal of Adolescent Health*, *70*(3), S9–S16.

Sipe, A. W. R. (1995). *Sex, priests, and power: Anatomy of a crisis.* Brunner/Mazel Publisher, Inc.

Søland, B. (2019). International Women's Day. *Origins: Current Events in Historical Perspective.*

Sotarauta, M., & Srinivas, S. (2015). *The co-evolution of policy and economic development: a discussion on innovative regions.* Massachusetts Institute of Technology.

Spinedi, M. (2002). State responsibility v. individual responsibility for international crimes: *tertium non datur? European Journal of International Law*, *13*(4), 895–899.

Statista. (2022). *Share of global population affiliated with major religious groups 2022.* https://www.statista.com/statistics/374704/share-of-global-population-by-religion/

Statistics & Data. (2023). Most popular religions in the world from 1950 to 2023. https://statisticsanddata.org/data/most-popular-religions-in-the-world-1950-2023/

Stephanopoulos, N. O. (2015). Political powerlessness. *New York University Law Review (1950)*, *90*(5), 1527–1608.

Suri, G. (2017). Performance, Appropriation and Adaptation: A Case of Vrat Kathas. Bharatiya Pragna*: An Interdisciplinary Journal of Indian Studies*, *2*(2).

Swedish Parliament. (2000). *Act on equality between women and men: The Equal Opportunities Act (SFS 1991:433) (Including amendments up to and including SFS 2000:773).* Women's Caucus for Gender Justice. https://www.wcwonline.org/pdf/lawcompilation/Sweden-genderequality.pdf

The UK Equality Act. (2010). *Equality Act 2010.* Legislation.gov.uk; https://www.legislation.gov.uk/ukpga/2010/15/contents

Thomas, H., & Turnbull, P. (2021). From a 'moral commentator' to a 'determined actor'? How the International Labour Organization (ILO) orchestrates the field of international industrial relations. *British Journal of Industrial Relations*, *59*(3), 874–898.

Thomson, J. (2017). Thinking globally, acting locally? The women's sector, international human rights mechanisms and politics in Northern Ireland. *Politics*, *37*(1), 82–96.

Thornton, M. (2010). *Sex discrimination in uncertain times.* ANU Press.

Torrance, D. (2021). *The relationship between church and state in the United Kingdom.* House of Commons Library. *Commons Library Research Briefing*, 14 September 2023. Pages 1–46. https://commonslibrary.parliament.uk/research-briefings/cbp-8886/

UN Chronicle. (2008). *Rape as a war crime.* https://www.un.org/en/chronicle/article/rape-war-crime

UN Women. (1981). *A short history of the CEDAW Convention.* https://www.un.org/womenwatch/daw/cedaw/history.htm

UN Women. (2015). *Collective failure of leadership on progress for women.* https://asiapacific.unwomen.org/en/news-and-events/stories/2015/03/collective-failure-of-leadership-on-progress-for-women

UN Women. (2019). *Commission on the Status of Women*. https://www.unwomen.org/en/csw

UN Women. (2020). *Global norms and standards: Ending violence against women*. https://www.unwomen.org/en/what-we-do/ending-violence-against-women/global-norms-and-standards

UN Women. (2022). *NGO participation at CEDAW sessions*. https://www.un.org/womenwatch/daw/ngo/cedawngo.html

UN Women. (2024, December 20). *International Women's Day 2025 For ALL women and girls: Rights. Equality. Empowerment*. UN Women. https://www.unwomen.org/en/news-stories/announcement/2024/12/international-womens-day-2025-for-all-women-and-girls-rights-equality-empowerment

UN Women. (n.d.). *Members of the Executive Board*. UN Women. https://www.unwomen.org/en/executive-board/bureau#:~:text=UN%2DWomen%20Board%20consists%20of,members%20from%20top%20contributing%20countries

UNICEF. (2014). *Ending child marriage: Progress and prospects*. UNICEF Division of Policy and Research. https://data.unicef.org/resources/ending-child-marriage-progress-and-prospects/

UNICEF. (2023). *Child marriage*. United Nations Children's Fund. https://www.unicef.org/protection/child-marriage

United Kingdom Parliament. (2010). *The Building Regulations 2010*. Legislation.gov.uk; https://www.legislation.gov.uk/uksi/2010/2214/contents

United Nations. (1975). *Declaration of Mexico on the equality of women and their contribution to development and peace*. http://www.un-documents.net/mex-dec.htm

United Nations. (1995). *Report of the Fourth World Conference on Women, Beijing*. https://www.un.org/womenwatch/daw/beijing/pdf/Beijing%20full%20report%20E.pdf

United Nations. (2017). *17 Goals to transform our world*. http://www.un.org/sustainabledevelopment

United Nations. (2018). *The Sustainable Development Goals report*. https://www.un.org/sustainabledevelopment/progress-report/

United Nations. (2020). *Stop Rape Now, UN Action Against Sexual Violence in Conflict*. UN. https://www.un.org/sexualviolenceinconflict/wp-content/uploads/2020/05/report/14-agencies-committed-to-ending-sexual-violence-in-conflict/UN-Action-14-Agencies-Committed-to-Ending-SVC.pdf

United Nations. (2021). *Glossary of terms relating to treaty actions and international agreements*. https://treaties.un.org/pages/overview.aspx?path=overview/glossary/page1_en.xml

United Nations. (2025). *Member states*. https://www.un.org/en/about-us/member-states

United Nations. (n.d.-a). *Human rights*. United Nations. https://www.un.org/en/about-us/universal-declaration-of-human-rights

United Nations. (n.d.-b). *We must achieve it now: Current and future generations*. Department of Economic and Social Affairs. https://www.un.org/en/desa/we-must-achieve-it-now-current-and-future-generations

United Nations. (n.d.-c). Background: International Women's Day. UN. https://www.un.org/en/observances/womens-day/background

United Nations Committee for Development Policy. (2014). *Global governance and global rules for development in the post-2015 era*. UN. https://www.un.org/development/desa/dpad/publication/cdp-policy-note-2014/

United Nations General Assembly. (1948). *Universal Declaration of Human Rights*. United Nations. https://www.un.org/en/about-us/universal-declaration-of-human-rights

United Nations Security Council. (2024). *Current members*. https://www.un.org/securitycouncil/content/current-members

United Nations Security Council. (n.d.). *Current members.* UNSC. https://main.un.org/securitycouncil/en/content/current-members

Urbaniak, J., & Willman, D. (2023). Women's priestly ordination in the Catholic Tradition with the focus on the subversive praxis of the Roman Catholic Women Priests. *International Journal for the Study of the Christian Church*, *22*(4), 277–295.

Vega, Y. K. (2023). *Sex, policy and power: The Australian experience* (Doctoral thesis, unpublished). Swinburne University of Technology, Melbourne, Australia.

Vijeyarasa, R. (2019). Making the law work for women: standard-setting through a new Gender Legislative Index. *Alternative Law Journal*, *44*(4), 275–280.

Vijeyarasa, R. (2020). CEDAW's General Recommendation No. 35: a quarter of a century of evolutionary approaches to violence against women. *Journal of Human Rights*, *19*(2), 153–167.

Vijeyarasa, R. (2021a). Gender equality in Australia: looking for the silver bullets in the short and long term. *Australian Journal of Human Rights*, *27*(1), 170–177.

Vijeyarasa, R. (2021b). *International women's rights law and gender equality: making the law work for women*. Taylor & Francis Group.

Vijeyarasa, R. (2021c). Quantifying CEDAW: concrete tools for enhancing accountability for women's rights. *Harvard Human Rights Journal*, *34*, 37–80.

Vijeyarasa, R. (2021d). What is gender-responsive legislation? Using international law to establish benchmarks for labour, reproductive health and tax laws that work for women. *Griffith Law Review*, *29*(3), 334–350.

Vijeyarasa, R. (2024). Institutionalising women's experiences in law: Possibilities and pitfalls of parliamentary gender audit committees. *Alternative Law Journal*, *49*(2), 114–119.

von Bogdandy, A., & Steinbrück Platise, M. (2012). ARIO and Human Rights Protection: Leaving the Individual in the Cold. *International Organizations Law Review*, *9*(1), 67–76.

Walker, B. G. (1994). Science: the feminists' scapegoat? *Research on social work practice*, *4*(4), 510–514.

Walker, B. G. (2011). Religion as the root of sexism. *Freethought Today*, *28*(5), 1–5.

Watt, M. (2013). Fundamental rights and recognition in private international law. *European Journal of Human Rights*, *13*, 411–435.

Weiss, T. G. (2016). *What's wrong with the United Nations and how to fix it* (3rd ed.). Cambridge University Press.

Wilkinson, O., McDonald, K., Trotta, S., Eggert, J. P., & de Wolf, F. (2024). A Social Norms Analysis of Religious Drivers of Child Marriage. *Global Health Science and Practice*, *12*(2), e2300339.

Winkler, G. (1998). *Sacred Secrets: The Sanctity of Sex in Jewish Law and Lore.* Jason Aronson, Incorporated.

Wiseman, G. (2015). Diplomatic practices at the United Nations. *Cooperation and Conflict*, *50*(3), 316–333.

Wøjdemann, K. R., Benedetto, C., & Grénman, S. (2017). International Women's Day – all changes matter. *Acta Obstetricia et Gynecologica Scandinavica*, *96*(3), 261–262.

Wood, E. J. (2018). Rape as a Practice of War: Toward a Typology of Political Violence. *Politics & Society*, *46*(4), 513–537.

Woodiwiss, A. (2006). International law. *Theory, Culture & Society*, *23*(2–3), 524–525.

World Bank Group. (2020). *Women, business and the law 2020.* https://openknowledge.worldbank.org/server/api/core/bitstreams/6c2b5974-9a3b-5249-995b-2b22e5fd7909/content

World Economic Forum. (2023). *Global Gender Gap Report 2023.* https://www.weforum.org/reports/global-gender-gap-report-2023/

World Economic Forum. (2024). *Global Gender Gap Report 2024.* WEF, https://www3.weforum.org/docs/WEF_GGGR_2024.pdf
World Economic Forum (WEF). (2020a). *The global risk report 2020.* https://www.weforum.org/reports/the-global-risks-report-2020/
World Economic Forum (WEF). (2020b). *The global gender gap report 2020.* https://www3.weforum.org/docs/WEF_GGGR_2020.pdf
World Health Organization. (2019). *World health statistics 2019: monitoring health for the Sustainable Development Goals.* https://www.who.int/publications/i/item/9789241565707
World Population Review. (2024). *Religion by country.* https://worldpopulationreview.com/country-rankings/religion-by-country

Chapter 3

ABC News. (2021, February 15). *Staffer Brittany Higgins allegedly raped in office of senior government minister Linda Reynolds inside Parliament House.* Australian Broadcasting Corporation. https://www.abc.net.au/news/2021-02-15/brittany-higgins-rape-claim-parliament-house-defence-minister/13154736
Abrams, D. E. (2012). The twelve-year-old girl's lawsuit that changed America: the continuing impact of now v. little league baseball, inc. at 40. *Virginia Journal of Social Policy & the Law, 20*(2), 241–270.
Abrams, M., & Bartlett, M. L. (2019). #SportToo: Implications of and Best Practice for the #MeToo Movement in Sport. *Journal of Clinical Sport Psychology, 13*(2), 243–258.
Al Jazeera. (2025, January 28). *Caroline Kennedy sends letter to US senators calling RFK Jr a 'predator'.* Al Jazeera. https://www.aljazeera.com/news/2025/1/28/caroline-kennedy-sends-letter-to-us-senator-describing-rfk-jr-as-predator
Alter, C. (2017, January 20). The pussyhat: How a pink knit cap became a symbol of resistance. *Time.* https://time.com/magazine/us/4649884/february-6th-2017-vol-189-no-4-u-s/
Ang, I. (2001). I'm a Feminist But: 'Other' women and postnational identities. In I. Ang (Ed.), *On Not Speaking Chinese* (1st ed., pp. 177–192). Routledge.
Arnold-Forster, A. (2021). Medicine and the body in second-wave feminist histories of the nineteenth century. *History, 106*(372), 668–686.
Aune, K., & Holyoak, R. (2018). Navigating the third wave: Contemporary UK feminist activists and 'third-wave feminism'. *Feminist Theory, 19*(2), 183–203.
Australian Associated Press. (2022, December 13). *Brittany Higgins reaches confidential settlement with the Commonwealth.* ABC/AAP. https://www.abc.net.au/news/2022-12-13/brittany-higgins-settles-compensation-case-with-commonwealth/101769012
Baghel, E. (2022). Analysis of death sentence in Nirbhaya rape case. *International Journal of Law Management & Humanities*, 5, 2265.
Baptista, A. (2023, May 24). *What is the tampon tax and which countries have axed it?* Reuters News. https://www.reuters.com/article/markets/commodities/what-is-the-tampon-tax-and-which-countries-have-axed-it-idUSL1N33O24Z/
Barclay, F. P., Karippara, M. S., Sasidharan, A., Barclay, F. P., & Laskar, K. A. (2024). *Fourth-Wave Feminism: World View and the Indian Context.* In *Gender and Popular Visual Culture in India* (1st ed., Vol. 1, pp. 74–84). Routledge.
BBC News. (2017, January 3). *India outrage after minister blames 'Western dress' for groping.* BBC News. https://www.bbc.com/news/world-asia-india-38494433
BBC News. (2020, July 15). *Five shocking passages in Mary Trump's tell-all book.* BBC News. https://www.bbc.com/news/world-us-canada-53328654
Biennale of Sydney. (2024). *Biennale of Sydney.* https://www.biennaleofsydney.art/

Boston Women's Health Book Collective. (1968). *Our Bodies, Ourselves*. Simon & Schuster.

Bowie, N. (2024, Autumn). *Greta Thunberg. School Librarian, 72*(3), 57.

Boxer, M. J. (1982). 'First wave' feminism in nineteenth-century France: Class, family and religion. *Women's Studies International Forum, 5*(6), 551–559.

Boyer, K. (2011). "The way to break the taboo is to do the taboo thing": Breastfeeding in public and citizen-activism in the UK. *Health & Place, 17*(2), 430–437.

Bradford, S., & Cullen, F. (2014). Youth policy in austerity Europe. *International Journal of Adolescence and Youth, 19*(1), 1–4

Brooks, R. E. (2002). Feminism and international law: An opportunity for transformation. *Yale Journal of Law and Feminism, 14*(345), 345–361.

Buchanan, R. A. (2016, May 27). *Friday essay: How Shakespeare helped shape Germaine Greer's feminist masterpiece*. The Conversation. https://theconversation.com/friday-essay-how-shakespeare-helped-shape-germaine-greers-feminist-masterpiece-59880

Bulbeck, C. (1997). *Living feminism: the impact of the women's movement on three generations of Australian women*. Cambridge University Press.

Cambridge University Press. (n.d.). Wave (away, on, etc.). In Cambridge English Dictionary. https://dictionary.cambridge.org/dictionary/english/

Carbado, D. W., Crenshaw, K. W., Mays, V. M., & Tomlinson, B. (2013). Intersectionality: Mapping the Movements of a Theory. *Du Bois Review: Social Science Research on Race, 10*(2), 303–312.

Casebriefs. (n.d.). *Fisher v. University of Texas*. 136 S. Ct. 2198, 195 L. Ed. 2d 511 (2016). https://www.casebriefs.com/?s=Fisher+v.+University+of+Texas+

Cassidy, E. (2016). Social networking sites and participatory reluctance: A case study of gaydar, user resistance and interface rejection. *New Media & Society, 18*(11), 2613–2628.

Catalini, L., & Fedder, J. (2020). Characteristics of the endometrium in menstruating species: lessons learned from the animal kingdom. *Biology of Reproduction, 102*(6), 1160–1169.

Caughie, P. L. (2010). Theorizing the 'First Wave' globally. *Feminist Review, 95*(1), 5–9.

Chawla, N., Gabriel, A. S., O'Leary Kelly, A., & Rosen, C. C. (2021). From #MeToo to #TimesUp: Identifying Next Steps in Sexual Harassment Research in the Organizational Sciences. *Journal of Management, 47*(3), 551–566.

Chidgey, R. (2020). Postfeminism™: celebrity feminism, branding and the performance of activist capital. *Feminist Media Studies, 21*(7), 1055–1071.

Chiu, B. (2020, March 8). 2020s mark a new wave of feminist mobilization. *Forbes*. https://www.forbes.com/sites/bonniechiu/2020/03/08/2020s-mark-a-new-wave-of-feminist-mobilization/?sh=5bb068d4485e

Clark, T., Dodson, S., Guivarra, N., & Widders Hunt, Y. (2021). "We're not treated equally as Indigenous people or as women": The perspectives and experiences of Indigenous women in Australian public relations. *Public Relations Inquiry, 10*(2), 163–183.

Colley, L. (2019). (Un)Restricting feminism: High school students' definitions of gender and feminism in the context of the historic struggle for women's rights. *Theory & Research in Social Education, 47*(3), 426–455.

Cosic, M. (2016, April). *Reading Australia: 'The Female Eunuch' by Germaine Greer. Australian Book Review*, (380).

Countries of the World. (n.d.). *Current list of all 27 European Union countries*. https://www.gov.uk/eu-eea

Cox, L. (2018, November 7). *Australian students plan school strikes to protest against climate inaction*. The Guardian. https://www.theguardian.com/australia-news/2018/nov/07/australian-students-plan-school-strikes-to-protest-against-climate-inaction

Crawford, B. J., & Spivack, C. (2019). Human Rights and the Taxation of Menstrual Hygiene Products in an Unequal World. In P. Alston and N. Reisch (Eds.), *Tax, Inequality, and Human Rights*. Oxford University Press.

Crenshaw, K. (1989). Demarginalizing the intersection of race and sex: A Black feminist critique of antidiscrimination doctrine, feminist theory, and antiracist politics. *University of Chicago Legal Forum, 1989*(1), 139–167.

Crenshaw, K., Maschke, K. J., & Maschke, K. (1997). Demarginalizing the Intersection of Race and Sex: A Black Feminist Critique of Antidiscrimination Doctrine, Feminist Theory and Antiracist Politics. In *Feminist Legal Theories* (1st ed., pp. 23–51). Routledge.

Cronau, P., & Milligan, R. L. (2020, November 9). *Inside the Canberra Bubble* (*Four Corners*, Australian Broadcasting Corporation). https://www.abc.net.au/news/2020-11-09/inside-the-canberra-bubble/12864676

Crossley, A. D. (2015). Facebook feminism: Social media, blogs, and new technologies of contemporary US feminism. Mobilization: *An International Quarterly*, 20(2), 253–268.

Crozier-De Rosa, S., & Mackie, V. (2018). *Remembering Women's Activism*. (1st ed.). Routledge.

Cushman, C. (Ed.). (2012). *The supreme court justices: Illustrated biographies, 1789–2012*. CQ Press.

Daniels, N. (1978). Merit and Meritocracy. *Philosophy & Public Affairs, 7*(3), 206–223.

Davidson, H. (2018, December 31). *Australia's new laws taking effect on 1 January: From axed tampon tax to credit card changes*. The Guardian. https://www.theguardian.com/law/2018/dec/31/australias-new-laws-taking-effect-on-1-january-from-axed-tampon-tax-to-credit-card-changes

de Beauvoir, S.. (1953). *The Second Sex* (H. M. Parshley, Trans.). Jonathan Cape. (Original publication: de Beauvoir, S. (1949). *Le Deuxième Sexe*. Gallimard.

Dean, J. (2009). Who's afraid of third-wave feminism? On the uses of the 'third wave' in British feminist politics. *International Feminist Journal of Politics, 11*(3), 334–352.

Department of Justice. (2001). Fact sheet on changes to the *Tasmanian Evidence Act 2001*—section 194K. Tasmanian Government. https://www.justice.tas.gov.au/__data/assets/pdf_file/0004/466033/Discussion-Paper-section-194K-Evidence-Act-2001-version_2.pdf

Dey, A. (2020). Sites of Exception: Gender Violence, Digital Activism, and Nirbhaya's Zone of Anomie in India. *Violence Against Women, 26*(11), 1423–1444.

Diwanji, V. S., Saleem, A., & Lee, J. (2021). 'A night of shame': A quantitative content analysis of newspaper narratives of the mass molestation event in Bangalore, India. *Journal of International Women's Studies, 22*(9), 343–360.

Dore, B. (2016, July 27). *A small group of campaigners is attacking sexism in Europe's largest-selling newspaper*. https://scroll.in/article/812018/a-small-group-of-campaigners-is-attacking-sexism-in-europes-largest-selling-newspaper

Dowse, S. (2014). The prime minister's women. *Australian Feminist Studies, 29*(82), 391–402.

Drewett, C., Oxlad, M., & Augoustinos, M. (2021). Breaking the silence on sexual harassment and assault: An analysis of #MeToo tweets. *Computers in Human Behavior, 123*, 106896.

Dyrenfurth, N. (2007). John Howard's hegemony of values: the politics of 'mateship' in the Howard decade. *Australian Journal of Political Science, 42*(2), 211–230.

Edwards, L., & Roces, M. (2004). Introduction: Orienting the global women's suffrage movement. In L. Edwards & M. Roces (Eds.), *Women's suffrage in Asia: Gender, nationalism, and democracy* (pp. 1–21). Routledge.

Elisburg, D. (1978). Equal Pay in the United States: The Development and Implementation of the Equal Pay Act of 1963. *Labor Law Journal (Chicago), 29*(4), 195–208.

Evans, E. (2015). *The politics of third wave feminisms: Neoliberalism, intersectionality, and the state in Britain and the US*. Palgrave Macmillan.

Evans, E., & Chamberlain, P. (2014). Critical Waves: Exploring Feminist Identity, Discourse and Praxis in Western Feminism. *Social Movement Studies*, *14*(4), 396–409.

Eveline, J. (1994). Normalization, leading ladies, and free men: Affirmative actions in Sweden and Australia. *Women's Studies International Forum*, *17*(2/3), 157–167.

Faludi, S. (1992). *Backlash: The undeclared war against American women*. Vintage Books.

Fasting, K. (2015). Assessing the sociology of sport: On sexual harassment research and policy. *International Review for the Sociology of Sport*, *50*(4–5), 437–441.

Faupel, A., & Werum, R. (2011). The individualization of first-wave feminism, 1910–1930. *Mobilization: An International Quarterly*, *16*(2), 181–200.

Fileborn, B., & Loney-Howes, R. (Eds.) (2019). *#Metoo and the politics of social change*. Palgrave Macmillan.

Finlayson, L. (2018, December 13). *Germaine: The life of Germaine Greer by Elizabeth Kleinhenz review – A career of controversy*. The Guardian. https://www.theguardian.com/books/2018/dec/13/germaine-the-life-of-germaine-greer-by-elizabeth-kleinhenz

Fisher v. University of Texas, 570 U.S. 297 (2013). https://supreme.justia.com/cases/federal/us/570/297/

Flinders, M., & Lowery, G. (2023). Period politics and policy change: The taxation of menstrual products in the United Kingdom, 1996–2021. *Contemporary British History*, *37*(2), 238–265.

Fox, S. (2020). Advocating for affordability: The story of menstrual hygiene product tax advocacy in four countries. *Gates Open Research*, *4*, 134.

Free the Nipple. (July 1, 2015). *Campaigns of the World*. https://campaignsoftheworld.com/ooh-campaigns/free-the-nipple/

Friedan, B. (1963). *The Feminine Mystique*. W.W. Norton & Company.

Gallagher, L., Brady, V., Kuliukas, L., Dykes, C., Rubertsson, C., & Hauck, Y. L. (2023). Australian, Irish, and Swedish women's comfort levels when breastfeeding in public. *BMC Public Health*, *23*, 2535.

Garrido Ortolá, A. (2022). Reivindicaciones feministas de la cuarta ola: la transnacionalización de la protesta. *Asparkía: Investigación Feminista*, *40*, 191–216.

Gibbs Knotts, H., Wofford, C. B., & Griesedieck, C. G. (2018). The politics of marital name change. *The Social Science Journal (Fort Collins)*, *55*(4), 510–516.

Gillis, S., Howie, G., & Munford, R. (Eds.). (2007). *Third Wave Feminism: A Critical Exploration* (2nd ed. 2007). Palgrave Macmillan UK.

Ginzberg, L. D. (2002). Re-viewing the first wave. *Feminist Studies*, *28*(2), 418–434.

Godayol, P. (2022). The translation of socialist feminisms in post-Francoism: Juliet Mitchell and Sheila Rowbotham. *International Journal of Iberian Studies*, *35*(1), 59–78.

Gökarıksel, B. and Smith, S. (2017). Intersectional feminism beyond U.S. flag hijab and pussy hats in Trump's America. *Gender, Place & Culture*, *24*(5), 628–644.

Goldin, C., & Shim, M. (2004). Making a name: Women's surnames at marriage and beyond. *The Journal of Economic Perspectives*, *18*(2), 143–160.

Gorman, A. (2021, March 15). "*Enough is enough!" Where, when and why March4Justice protests are taking place across Australia. The Guardian*. https://www.theguardian.com/australia-news/2021/mar/15/march-4-justice-where-when-womens-march-protests-australia-march4justice-sydney-melbourne-canberra-brisbane

Grant, A. (2016). "I …don't want to see you flashing your bits around": Exhibitionism, othering and good motherhood in perceptions of public breastfeeding. *Geoforum*, *71*, 52–61.

Grant, A., McEwan, K., Tedstone, S., Greene, G., Copeland, L., Hunter, B., Sanders, J., Phillips, R., Brown, A., Robling, M., & Paranjothy, S. (2018). *Maternal and Child Nutrition*, *14*(1), 52–61.

Greenslade, R. (2012, March 9). *Bild banishes its topless model pictures after 28 years. The Guardian*. https://www.theguardian.com/media/greenslade/2012/mar/09/international-womens-day-germany

Greer, G. (1971). *The Female Eunuch*. McGraw-Hill.

Grimshaw, P. (2000). Settler anxieties, indigenous peoples, and women's suffrage in the colonies of Australia, New Zealand, and Hawai'i, 1888 to 1902. *Pacific Historical Review*, *69*(4), 553–572.

Guerrilla Girls. (n.d.). *Guerrilla Girls*. https://www.guerrillagirls.com/

Gupta, S., & Trehan, K. (2021). Digital advocacy by non-governmental organizations for menstrual activism: A framing analysis of #LahukaLagaan (Blood Tax) campaign by SheSays India. *Journal of Content, Community & Communication*, *13*(7), 291–304.

Haavio-Mannila, E. (1979). How Women Become Political Actors: Female Candidates in Finnish Elections. *Scandinavian Political Studies*, *2*(4), 351–372.

Harbke, C. R., & Lindemann, D. F. (2023). Objectification and reactions toward public female toplessness in the United States: Looking beyond legal approval. *Sexuality & Culture*, *27*, 104–130.

Harris, A. (2004). *Future girl: Young women in the twenty-first century*. Routledge.

Harris, A. (2010). Mind the gap: Attitudes and emergent feminist politics since the third wave. *Australian Feminist Studies*, *25*(66), 475–484.

Hart, C., & May, R. M. (2018). Really fake or faking reality? The Riot Grrrls project. In V. Geroimenko (Ed.), *Augmented reality art* (pp. 371–382). Springer.

Hartman, A. (1992). It Was Not Our Finest Hour. *Social Work (New York)*, *37*(1), 3–4.

Haugseth, J. F., & Smeplass, E. (2023). The Greta Thunberg Effect: A Study of Norwegian Youth's Reflexivity on Climate Change. *Sociology (Oxford)*, *57*(4), 921–939.

Heilmann, A. (2005). First-Wave Feminist Engagements with History: Introduction. *Victorian Review*, Introduction. *Victorian Review*, *31*(1), 1–4.

Henderson, M. A., Taylor, A. (2020). *Postfeminism in Context: women, Australian popular culture, and the unsettling of postfeminism*. Routledge, Taylor & Francis Group.

Herr, R. S. (2014). Reclaiming Third World Feminism: or Why Transnational Feminism Needs Third World Feminism. *Meridians (Middletown, Conn.)*, *12*(1), 1–30.

Historical Dictionary of Australia. (2014). *Mateship*. Rowman & Littlefield Publishers. https://rowman.com/ISBN/9781442245020/Historical-Dictionary-of-Australia-Fourth-Edition

Horne, D. (1964). *The lucky country*. Penguin Books. (Original work published by Angus & Robertson).

Humphries, A. (2020, Tue 3 Mar). *Sexual assault survivors in Tasmania win right to speak out publicly*. Australian Broadcasting Corporation. https://www.abc.net.au/news/2020-03-03/sexual-assault-survivors-free-to-speak-after-law-changes/12021122

Ichitani, T. (2007). *A trajectory for future feminist praxis in Australian indigenous women's writing: Melissa Lucashenko's Steam pigs as a third wave feminist text* (Doctoral dissertation, Doshisha University).

Jain, S. (2020). The rising fourth wave: Feminist activism on digital platforms in India. *ORF Issue Brief*, *384*, 1–16.

James, K. (2022). Removal of the tampon tax: A costless or Pyrrhic victory? *Australian Feminist Law Journal*, *48*(2), 193–220.

John, M. E. (2005). Women's studies in India and the question of Asia: Some reflections. *Asian Journal of Women's Studies, 11*(2), 41–66.
Johnson, C. (2024). The politics of gender equality: Australian lessons in an uncertain world. Palgrave Macmillan.
Kakroda, N., & Sole, N. A. (2023). Through the lens of feminism: Concept, origin, and the four waves. *International Journal of Political Science, 9*(2), 87–94.
Karpf, D. 2010. 'Online Political Mobilization from the Advocacy Group's Perspective: Looking beyond Clicktivism', *Policy & Internet* 2, 7–41.
Kaur, R. (2017). Mediating Rape: The Nirbhaya Effect in the Creative and Digital Arts. *Signs: Journal of Women in Culture and Society, 42*(4), 945–976.
Kelly, E. A. (2005). Review Essay: A New Generation of Feminism? Reflections on the Third Wave. *New Political Science, 27*(2), 233–243.
Kinser, A. E. (2004). Negotiating spaces for/through third-wave feminism. *NWSA Journal, 16*(3), 124–153.
Kitts, S.A. (1994). Mary Wollstonecraft's *A Vindication of the Rights of Woman*: A judicious response from eighteenth-century Spain. *The Modern Language Review, 89*(2), 351–359.
Koerber, A. 2001. 'Postmodernism, Resistance, and Cyberspace: Making Rhetorical Spaces for Feminist Mothers on the Web', *Women's Studies in Communication 24* (2), 218–240.
Korn, J. U., & Kneese, T. (2015). Feminist approaches to social media research: history, activism, and values. *Feminist Media Studies, 15*(4), 15.
Lake, M. (2016). "Revolution for the hell of it": the transatlantic genesis and serial provocations of The Female Eunuch. *Australian Feminist Studies, 31*(87), 7–21.
Lam, H. (2016). Social media dilemmas in the employment context. *Employee Relations, 38*(3), 420–437.
Lamas, I., Barca, S., Ferreira, B. S., & Yanez, I. (2021). Ecofeminist Horizons. *Ambiente & Sociedade, 24.*
Larrondo Ureta, A. (2020). (In)visibility of feminism in the media: The depiction of the second-wave women's movement in Spain. *Feminist Media Studies, 20*(1), 70–85.
Legge, E. (2017). On being a second: Grace Wambolt, legal professionalism and "inter-wave" feminism in Nova Scotia. *Dalhousie Law Journal, 40*(1), 221–238.
Lekha, N. B., & Kumar M. P. (Eds.). (2025). *Routledge Handbook of Gender, Culture, and Development in India* (1st edition.). Routledge.
Lelea, M. A., & Voiculescu, S. (2017). The production of emancipatory feminist spaces in a post-socialist context: organization of Ladyfest in Romania. *Gender, Place and Culture: A Journal of Feminist Geography, 24*(6), 794–811.
Lister, R. (2005). Being Feminist. *Government and Opposition (London), 40*(3), 442–463.
Lotz, A. D. (2003). Communicating third-wave feminism and new social movements: challenges for the next century of feminist endeavor. *Women and Language, 26*(1), 2–2.
Mack-Canty, C. (2004). Third-Wave Feminism and the Need to Reweave the Nature/Culture Duality. *NWSA Journal, 16*(3), 154.
Mahoney, K. (2016). Historicising the 'third wave': Narratives of contemporary feminism. *Women's History Review, 25*(6), 1006–1013.
Malinowska, A. (2020). Waves of feminism. In K. Ross et al. (Eds.), *The International Encyclopedia of Gender, Media, and Communication* (pp. 1–7). John Wiley & Sons.
March4Justice. (2021). *Hear me. See me. Act!* https://www.march4justice.org.au
Matich, M., Ashman, R., & Parsons, E. (2018). #freethenipple – digital activism and embodiment in the contemporary feminist movement. *Consumption Markets & Culture, 22*(4), 337–362.

McBride, D. E., & Mazur, A. G. (2010). *The politics of state feminism: innovation in comparative research*. Temple University Press.

McCray, D. (2025, January 23). *Bruce Lehrmann to seek judge-only trial over Toowoomba rape charges*. ABC News. https://www.abc.net.au/news/2025-01-23/bruce-lehrmann-judge-only-trial/104849498

McCulloch, J. (2023, August 2). *New report into Lehrmann prosecution mires case in yet more controversy*. The Conversation. https://theconversation.com/new-report-into-lehrmann-prosecution-mires-case-in-yet-more-controversy-211033

Meade, A., & Cassidy, C. (2024, April 2). *Bruce Lehrmann defamation trial: Channel Seven reimbursed Lehrmann for drugs and sex workers, court documents allege*. The Guardian. https://www.theguardian.com/law/2024/apr/02/bruce-lehrmann-defamation-trial-channel-seven-reimbursed-lehrmann-for-drugs-and-sex-workers-court-documents-allege-nfbntw

Miller, C. C., & Willis, D. (2015). *Maiden names, on the rise again*. The New York Times, June 27. https://www.nytimes.com/2015/06/28/upshot/about-the-maiden-name-analysis.html

Milligan, L. (2021, March 15). *Bursting the Canberra Bubble*. Australian Broadcasting Corporation. https://www.abc.net.au/news/2021-03-08/bursting-the-canberra-bubble/13227810

Misra, K. (1997). Indian Feminism and the Post-Colonial State. *Women & Politics*, *17*(4), 25–43.

Moreton-Robinson, A. (2020). *Talkin' up to the white woman: indigenous women and white feminism* (20th anniversary edition.). University of Queensland Press.

Morgan, R. (Ed.). (1970). *Sisterhood is powerful: An anthology of writings from the women's liberation movement*. Random House.

Mulvey, L. (1975). Visual Pleasure and Narrative Cinema. *Screen*, *16*(3), 6–18.

Munford, R., Munford, R., Howie, G., & Gillis, S. (2007). Wake Up and Smell the Lipgloss: Gender, Generation and the (A)politics of Girl Power. In *Third Wave Feminism* (pp. 266–279). Palgrave Macmillan UK.

Munro, E. (2013). Feminism: A fourth wave? *Political Insight*, *4*(2), 22–25.

Murphy, K. (2021, May 13). *Scott Morrison says investigation by department head has resumed into Brittany Higgins matter*. The Guardian. https://www.theguardian.com/australia-news/2021/may/13/scott-morrison-says-investigation-by-department-head-has-resumed-into-brittany-higgins-matter

Murray, M. (2021). Race-ing Roe: Reproductive justice, racial justice, and the battle for *Roe v. Wade*. *Harvard Law Review*, *134*(2025), 2027–2043.

National Archives of Australia (NAA). (April 8, 1973). *Appointment to Prime Minister's Staff*. Series number: A1209. Control symbol: 1976/2370

National Australia Day Council. (2021, 28 Jan). *2021 Australian of the Year awards announced*. https://australianoftheyear.org.au/

Ng, E. S., & McGowan, R. A. (2023). Breaking the glass ceiling: Views of women from the second-wave feminist movement. *Canadian Journal of Administrative Sciences*, *40*(2), 173–187.

Nicholson, L. (2010). Feminism in "Waves": Useful Metaphor or Not? *New Politics*, *12*(4), 34–39.

Nieder, C., Muck, C., & Kärtner, J. (2019). Sexual Violence Against Women in India: Daily Life and Coping Strategies of Young Women in Delhi. *Violence against Women*, *25*(14), 1717–1738.

Noordewier, M. K., van Horen, F., Ruys, K. I., & Stapel, D. A. (2010). What's in a name? 361.708 Euros: The effects of marital name change. *Basic and Applied Social Psychology*, *32*, 17–25.

Nordberg, E. M. K., Skirbekk, H., & Magelssen, M. (2014). Conscientious objection to referrals for abortion: Pragmatic solution or threat to women's rights? *BMC Medical Ethics*, *15*(1), 15–15.

Office of the Mayor, New York City. (2016, July 13). *Mayor de Blasio signs legislation increasing access to feminine hygiene products for students, shelters, and inmates.* NYC. gov; http://www.nyc.gov/office-of-the-mayor/news/611-16/mayor-de-blasio-signs-legislation-increasing-access-feminine-hygiene-products-students

Ooi, J. (2018). Bleeding women dry: Tampon taxes and menstrual inequity. *Northwestern University Law Review, 113*(1), 109–153.

Pande, R. (2018). The history of feminism and doing gender in India. *Revista Estudos Feministas, 26*(3), e58567.

Pant, N., & Sharma, A. (2024). Equity initiatives for sustainable development: A comparative study of affirmative action in the USA and India. *Social Sciences & Humanities Open, 10*, 101102.

Parliamentary Debates. (2021, March 15). *House of Representatives official Hansard. Forty-sixth parliament. First session-fifth period.* Parliament of Australia. Commonwealth of Australia. https://www.aph.gov.au/Parliamentary_Business/Hansard

Payne, A. (2019). *Living in Australia: a snapshot of Australian society and how it is changing over time. HILDA survey.* Melbourne Institute: Applied Economic & Social Research. The University of Melbourne.

Pedwell, C. (2006). Third-Wave Feminism: A Critical Exploration [Review of *Third-Wave Feminism: A Critical Exploration*]. *Feminist Review, 82*(82), 138–140. Palgrave Macmillan.

Petray, T., O'Brien, J., Gregory, B., Maloney, H., & Radcliffe, N. (2022). *School strikers enacting politics for climate justice: Daring to think differently about education Australian Journal of Environmental Education. 38*(1), 26–39.

Phillips, R., & Cree, V. E. (2014). What does the 'fourth wave' mean for teaching feminism in twenty-first-century social work? *Social Work Education, 33*(7), 930–943.

Pollack, E. (2019), Sweden and the# MeToo movement, Interactions: *Studies in Communication and Culture, 10*(3), 185–200.

Puri, N. (2015). Feminist waves: An Indian perspective. *International Journal of Law and Society, 2*(3), 117–119.

Rajgopal, S. S. (2022). Fiery sparks of change: A comparison between first wave feminists of India and the U.S. *Journal of International Women's Studies 24*(2), 3.

Rampton, M. (2015, October 25). *Four waves of feminism.* Pacific University-Oregon Mag azine. https://www.pacificu.edu/magazine/four-waves-feminism

Rana, S. (2020). Visualizing the Semiotics of Protest: The 'Nirbhaya' Rape Case. *Indian Journal of Gender Studies, 27*(1), 141–153.

Reingold, R. B., & Gostin, L. O. (2023). New legal frontiers for safeguarding reproductive freedoms. *JAMA, 329*(11), 877–878.

Rhode, D. L. (2021). Myths of Meritocracy Comment on M. Sandel's the Tyranny of Merit. *American Journal of Law and Equality, 1*, 27–32.

Riot Grrrl. (n.d.). *About.* https://riotgrrrlonline.wordpress.com/about/

Rolling Stone. (2001). Biography: Bikini Kill. In *The Rolling Stone Encyclopedia of Rock & Roll.* Simon & Schuster.

Rome, A. S., O'Donohoe, S., & Dunnett, S. (2019). Rethinking feminist waves. In L. Dobscha (Ed.), *Handbook of Research on Gender and Marketing* (pp. 251–270). Edward Elgar Publishing.

Roser, M., Ritchie, H., & Ortiz-Ospina, E. (2023). *World Population Growth.* Our World in Data. https://ourworldindata.org/population-growth

Roy, A. (2024). The personal is political: An activist's memoir. HarperCollins India.

Runyan, A. S., & Peterson, V. S. (2014). *Global gender issues in the new millennium* (4th ed.). Routledge.

Ruthchild, R. G. (2012). From West to East: International Women's Day, the first decade. *Aspasia, 6*(1), 1–24.

Sabherwal, A., Ballew, M. T., Linden, S., Gustafson, A., Goldberg, M. H., Maibach, E. W., Kotcher, J. E., Swim, J. K., Rosenthal, S. A., & Leiserowitz, A. (2021). The Greta Thunberg Effect: Familiarity with Greta Thunberg predicts intentions to engage in climate activism in the United States. *Journal of Applied Social Psychology*, *51*(4), 321–333.

Saeed, D. (2024, June 21). *'Should have owned it': Seven chief admits paying Lehrmann's rent eroded trust*. Crikey. https://www.crikey.com.au/2024/06/21/bruce-lehrmann-seven-jeff-howard-news-corp-michael-miller/

Sah, S. (2022). Patriarchy and the Identity of Women in Indian Society. *Journal of Emerging Technologies and Innovative Research*, *9*(8), 563–603.

Sahu, S. (2023). *Unfolding Feminism in India: Women*, Power and Politics. Routledge.

Saunders, K. (2024, April 24). Sexual assault victims give evidence in court, but alleged perpetrators don't have to: Bruce Lehrmann's case shows what must change. The Conversation. https://theconversation.com/sexual-assault-victims-give-evidence-in-court-but-alleged-perpetrators-dont-have-to-bruce-lehrmanns-case-shows-what-must-change-228278

Shreemati Nathibai Damodar Thackersey Women's University (SNDT). (n.d.). *Home*. https://sndt.ac.in/

Simic, Z. (2016). Mateship: a very Australian history book review. *Australian Historical Studies*, *47*(2), 348–349.

Simons, M. (2013, October 28). *Germaine Greer sells archive to University of Melbourne*. The Guardian. https://www.theguardian.com/books/2013/oct/28/germaine-greer-sells-archive-to-university-of-melbourne

Singer, N. R. (2020). Toward Intersectional Ecofeminist Communication Studies. *Communication Theory*, *30*(3), 268–289.

Snyder, R. C. (2008). What is third-wave feminism? A new directions essay. *Signs: Journal of Women in Culture and Society*, *34*(1), 175–196.

Statista. (2024). *Number of internet users worldwide 2024*. https://www.statista.com/statistics/273018/number-of-internet-users-worldwide/

Subramanian, S. (2015). From the streets to the web: Looking at feminist activism on social media. *Economic and Political Weekly*, *50*(17), 71–78.

Sümer, S., & Eslen-Ziya, H. (2017). New waves for old rights? Women's mobilization and bodily rights in Turkey and Norway. *European Journal of Women's Studies*, *24*(1), 23–38.

Tasker, Y., & Negra, D. (2008). *Interrogating Postfeminism: Gender and the Politics of Popular Culture*. Duke University Press.

Taylor, A. (2020). "The Most Revolting Ideas I've Read in a Woman's Magazine": The Female Eunuch, Affective (dis)investments, and McCall's Reader-writers'. *Australian Feminist Studies*, *35*(103), 20–36.

Thaker, Y. Y. (2023). Feminism and Women's Movement in India. *Vidhyayana-An International Multidisciplinary Peer-Reviewed E-Journal*-ISSN *8*(4), 2454–8596.

The f word. (n.d.). The f word: Contemporary UK Feminism. https://thefword.org.uk/

The Grace Tame Foundation. (n.d.). *The Foundation*. https://www.thegracetame foundation.org.au/

Titus, D. (2018). Social media as a gateway for young feminists: lessons from the #IWillGoOut campaign in India. *Gender and Development*, *26*(2), 231–248.

Trump, M. L. (2020). *Too much and never enough: How my family created the world's most dangerous man*. Simon & Schuster.

UK Government. (2010). *Equality Act 2010, c. 15*. Legislation.gov.uk. The National Archives. https://www.legislation.gov.uk/ukpga/2010/15/contents

Varela, N. (2019). *Feminismo 4.0: La cuarta ola* (Tapa blanda ed.). Edición en español. Penguin Random House Grupo Editorial.

Varela, N. (2020). El tsunami feminista. *Revista Nueva Sociedad, 286*, 93–106.

Vega, Y. K. (2023). *Sex, Policy and Power: The Australian experience* (Doctoral thesis, unpublished). Swinburne University of Technology, Melbourne, Australia.

VNS Matrix. (n.d.). *A tender hex.* https://vnsmatrix.net/

Volkova, I. (2014). "I Have Looked Steadily around Me": The Power of Examples in Mary Wollstonecraft's A Vindication of the Rights of Woman. *Women's Studies, 43*(7), 892–910.

Walby, S. 2011. *The Future of Feminism.* Polity Press.

Walker, R. 1992, 'Becoming the third wave', *Ms. Magazine, 11*(2), 39–41.

Ward, M. (2017, February 7). *Group behind Women's March announce strike day for all women.* Sydney Morning Herald. https://www.smh.com.au/lifestyle/group-behind-womens-march-announce-strike-day-for-all-women-20170207-gu6wzk.html

Watkins-Hayes, C., & Adams-Santos, D. (2023). Women's health in post-*Roe v. Wade* America: Injuries of inequality and the promise of safety nets. *American Journal of Sociology, 129*(3), 983–991.

Weiss, P.A. (2018). Series of Resolutions: First International Congress of Women's Rights; Paris, France; Summer 1878. In *Feminist Manifestos* (pp. 105). NYU Press.

Whelehan, I. (2000). Overloaded: Popular culture and the future of feminism. The Women's Press.

White, P. J., Ferguson, J. P., O'Connor Smith, N., & O'Shea Carre, H. (2022). School strikers enacting politics for climate justice: Daring to think differently about education. *Australian Journal of Environmental Education, 38*(1), 26–39.

Wikipedia. (n.d.-a). *Australian Women Chamber of Commerce & Industry.* Wikipedia. https://en.wikipedia.org/wiki/Australian_Women_Chamber_of_Commerce_%26_Industry

Wikipedia. (n.d.-b) *Women's March. Wikipedia*, https://en.wikipedia.org/wiki/2017_Women%27s_March

Wikipedia. (n.d.-c). *Aruna Roy.* Wikipedia. https://en.wikipedia.org/wiki/Aruna_Roy

Willness, C. R., Steel, P., & Lee, K. 2007. A meta-analysis of the antecedents and consequences of workplace sexual harassment. *Personnel Psychology*, 60, 127–162.

Wockner, C. (2024, December 12). *Former Liberal Party staffer Bruce Lehrmann alleged rape indictments presented to court.* ABC Southern Qld. https://www.abc.net.au/news/2024-12-12/bruce-lehrmann-rape-charges-indictment-qld-toowoomba-court/104716668

Wollstonecraft, M. (1792). *A vindication of the rights of woman.* J. Johnson.

Wollstonecraft, M., & Blick, A. (2024). Extract from A Vindication of the Rights of Woman. In Documents on the Nineteenth Century United Kingdom Constitution: Vol. II (1st ed., pp. 3–4). Routledge.

Women's March. (n.d.). *Women's March.* https://www.womensmarch.com/

Worldometers. (n.d.). *India population (live).* https://www.worldometers.info/world-population/india-population/

Wright, C. (2018). *You Daughters of Freedom: Australians Who Won the Vote and Inspired the World.* Text Publishing.

Wright, M. (2009). 'An Impudent Intrusion?' Assessing the life of Elizabeth Wolstenholme Elmy, first-wave feminist and social reformer (1833–1918). *Women's History Review, 18*(2), 243–264.

Wrye, H. K. (2009). The Fourth Wave of Feminism: Psychoanalytic Perspectives. *Studies in Gender and Sexuality, 10*(4), 185–189.

Young, I. M. (1992). Breasted experience: The look and the feeling. In D. Leder (Ed.), *The body in medical thought and practice.* (1st ed., pp. 215–230) Springer.

Chapter 4

Abeyratne, R., & Jain, D. (2012). Domestic violence legislation in India: The pitfalls of a human rights approach to gender equality. *American University Journal of Gender, Social Policy & the Law*, *21*(2), 333–378.

Abrunhosa, C., Rodrigues, A. C., Cruz, A. R., Gonçalves, R. A., & Cunha, O. (2021). Crimes against women: From violence to homicide. *Journal of Interpersonal Violence*, *36*(23–24), NP12973–NP12996.

Aeberhard-Hodges, J., & McFerran, L. (2018). An International Labour Organization instrument on violence against women and men at work: the Australian influence. *Journal of Industrial Relations*, *60*(2), 246–265

Ainsworth, C. (2015). Sex redefined. *Nature (London)*, *518*(7539), 288–291.

Akhtar, C. (2013). Sexual harassment at workplace and in educational institutions: A case study of District Srinagar, Kashmir. *International NGO Journal*, *8*(3), 54–60.

Aldridge, J. (2020). Not an either/or situation: The minimization of violence against women in United Kingdom “domestic abuse” policy. *Violence Against Women*, *27*(11), 1823–1839.

Alves, M. J. V., Manita, C., Caldas, I. M., Fernández-Martinez, E., Gomes da Silva, A., & Magalhães, T. (2019). Evolution and analysis of cultural and cognitive factors related with domestic violence against women. *Journal of Interpersonal Violence*, *34*(3), 621–641.

Arain, M., Haque, M., Johal, L., Mathur, P., Nel, W., Rais, A., Sandhu, R., & Sharma, S. (2013). Maturation of the adolescent brain. *Neuropsychiatric Disease and Treatment*, *9*, 449–461.

Arguedas-Ramírez, G., & Wenner, D. M. (2023). Reproductive justice beyond borders: Global feminist solidarity in the post-Roe era. *Journal of Law, Medicine & Ethics*, *51*(3), 606–611.

Atwood, M. E. (1987). *The Handmaid’s Tale*. Virago.

Australian Bureau of Statistics (ABS). (2022a). Sexual assaults increase for tenth year in a row. https://www.abs.gov.au/media-centre/media-releases/sexual-assaults-increase-tenth-year-row

Australian Bureau of Statistics (ABS). (2022b). *Recorded crime – Victims*. Sexual assault. https://www.abs.gov.au/statistics/people/crime-and-justice/recorded-crime-victims/latest-release

Australian Institute of Health and Welfare. (2019). Family, domestic and sexual violence in Australia: continuing the national story 2019 – In brief (Cat. no. FDV 4). https://www.aihw.gov.au/reports/family-domestic-and-sexual-violence/family-domestic-sexual-violence-australia-2019/contents/summary

Baber, R. (2023). World Menopause Day. *Climacteric*, *26*(5), 409–410.

Baird, B. (2017). Decriminalization and Women’s Access to Abortion in Australia. *Health and Human Rights Journal*, *19*(1), 197–208.

Baird, S. L., Tarshis, S., & Messenger, C. (2022). The use of neuroscience in interventions for intimate partner violence (IPV): A scoping review. *Clinical Social Work Journal*, *50*, 194–206.

Basile, K. C., Hertz, M. F., & Sitterle, D. (2006). *Measuring intimate partner violence victimization and perpetration: A compendium of assessment tools*. Centers for Disease Control and Prevention, National Center for Injury Prevention and Control. https://stacks.cdc.gov/view/cdc/11402

Baumeister, H. (2024). Preventing and combating violence against women and domestic violence: A commentary on the Istanbul Convention [Review of the book *Preventing and combating violence against women and domestic violence: A commentary on the Istanbul Convention*, by S. De Vido & M. Frulli (Eds.)]. *Liverpool Law Review*. Edward Elgar.

Bearak, J. M., Alkema, L., Kantorová, V., & Casterline, J. (2023). Alignment between Desires and Outcomes among Women Wanting to Avoid Pregnancy: A Global Comparative Study of "Conditional" Unintended Pregnancy Rates. *Studies in Family Planning*, *54*(1), 265–280.

Beck, V., Brewis, J., & Davies, A. (2018). The medicalization of menopause: Critique and consequences. *Journal of Organizational Ethnography*, *7*(3), 247–262.

Beck, V., Brewis, J., & Davies, A. (2021). Women's experiences of menopause at work and performance management. *Organization*, *28*(3), 510–520.

Beecher-Monas, E., & Garcia-Rill, E. (2006). Genetic Predictions of Future Dangerousness: Is There a Blueprint for Violence? *Law and Contemporary Problems*, *69*(1/2), 301–341.

Beharry, M. S. (2015). Menstruation. *Pediatric Annals*, *44*(9), 371–371.

Berenbaum, S. A., & Beltz, A. M. (2016). How early hormones shape gender development. *Current Opinion in Behavioral Sciences*, *7*, 53–60.

Berent-Spillson, A., Marsh, C., Persad, C., Randolph, J., Zubieta, J.-K., & Smith, Y. (2017). Metabolic and hormone influences on emotion processing during menopause. *Psychoneuroendocrinology*, *76*, 218–225.

Bhandari, S., & Hughes, J. C. (2017). Lived experiences of women facing domestic violence in India. *Journal of Social Work in the Global Community*, *2*(1), 1–14.

Brizendine, L. (2022). *The upgrade: How the female brain gets stronger and better in midlife and beyond*. Harmony.

Brizendine, L. (n.d..). *Louann Brizendine official website*. https://www.louannbrizendine.com/

Brunton-Smith, I., Flatley, J., & Tarling, R. (2020). Prevalence of sexual violence: A comparison of estimates from UK national surveys. *European Journal of Criminology*, *19*(5), 891–910.

Burke, E., Watson, K., Eva, G., Gold, J., Garcia-Moreno, C., & Amin, A. (2024). Is addressing violence against women prioritised in health policies? Findings from a WHO policies database. *PLoS Global Public Health*, *4*(2), e0002504.

Burrell, S. R. (2018). The contradictory possibilities of engaging men and boys in the prevention of men's violence against women in the UK. *Journal of Gender-Based Violence*, *2*(3), 447–464.

Calderone, K. L. (1990). The influence of gender on the frequency of pain and sedative medication administered to postoperative patients. *Sex Roles*, *23*(11/12), 713–725.

Callander, E., & Fox, H. (2018). Changes in out-of-pocket charges associated with obstetric care provided under Medicare in Australia. *Australian and New Zealand Journal of Obstetrics and Gynaecology*, *58*(3), 362–365.

Campbell, J. C. (2002). Health consequences of intimate partner violence. *The Lancet*, *359*(9314), 1331–1336.

Capinha, M., Rijo, D., Pereira, M., & Matos, M. (2022). The Prevalence, Directionality, and Dyadic Perpetration Types of Intimate Partner Violence in a Community Sample in Portugal: a Gender-Inclusive Inquiry. *European Journal on Criminal Policy and Research*, *30*, 1–18.

CEDAW. (1979). *Convention on the Elimination of All Forms of Discrimination against Women*.

Changfoot, N. (2009). The second sex's continued relevance for equality and difference feminisms. *European Journal of Women's Studies*, *16*(1), 11–31.

Chao, F., Guilmoto, C. Z., & Ombao, H. (2020). Probabilistic projection of the sex ratio at birth and missing female births by State and Union Territory in India. *PloS One*, *15*(8), e0236673.

Chawla, N., Gabriel, A. S., O'Leary-Kelly, A. M., & Rosen, C. C. (2021). From #MeToo to #TimesUp: Identifying next steps in sexual harassment research in the organizational sciences. *Journal of Management*, *47*(3), 805–833.

Chen, J., Walters, M. L., Gilbert, L. K., & Patel, N. (2020). Sexual Violence, Stalking, and Intimate Partner Violence by Sexual Orientation, United States. *Psychology of Violence*, *10*(1), 110–119.

Chin, Y.-M., & Cunningham, S. (2019). Revisiting the effect of warrantless domestic violence arrest laws on intimate partner homicides. *Journal of Public Economics*, 179, 104072.

Cioffi, A., Cecannecchia, C., Cioffi, F., Bolino, G., & Rinaldi, R. (2022). Abortion in Europe: Recent legislative changes and risk of inequality. *International Journal of Risk & Safety in Medicine*, *33*(4), 281–286.

Coates, A., & Allotey, P. (2023). Global health, sexual and reproductive health and rights, and gender: Square pegs, round holes. *BMJ Global Health*, *8*, e011710.

Cohen, D. S., Donley, G., & Rebouché, R. (2023). The New Abortion Battleground. *Columbia Law Review*, *123*(1), 1–100.

Commonwealth of Australia. (2020). *Religious discrimination (Consequential Amendments) Bill 2019.* https://www.ag.gov.au/sites/default/files/2020-03/explanatory-notes-second-exposure-draft-religious-discrimination-consequential-amendments-bill-2019.pdf

Cooke, L. (2023). Bitch: What does it mean to be female? Penguin Books.

Cortés, Y. I., & Marginean, V. (2022). Key factors in menopause health disparities and inequities: Beyond race and ethnicity. *Current Opinion in Endocrine and Metabolic Research*, *26*, 100389.

Costello, K., & Greenwald, B. D. (2022). Update on Domestic Violence and Traumatic Brain Injury: A Narrative Review. *Brain Sciences*, *12*(1), 122.

Council of Europe (CoE). 2011. Council of Europe Convention on Preventing and Combating Violence Against Women and Domestic Violence, May 11. CoE. https://www.coe.int/en/web/istanbul-convention

Critchley, H. O. D., Babayev, E., Bulun, S. E., Clark, S., Garcia-Grau, I., Gregersen, P. K., Kilcoyne, A., Kim, J.-Y. J., Lavender, M., Marsh, E. E., Matteson, K. A., Maybin, J. A., Metz, C. N., Moreno, I., Silk, K., Sommer, M., Simon, C., Tariyal, R., Taylor, H. S., … Griffith, L. G. (2020). Menstruation: Science and society. *American Journal of Obstetrics and Gynecology*, *223*(5), 624–664.

Cullen, P., Vaughan, G., Li, Z., Price, J., Yu, D., & Sullivan, E. (2019). Counting dead women in Australia: an in-depth case review of femicide. *Journal of Family Violence*, *34*(1), 1–8.

Dawson, E., Kovac, T., & Lewis, A. (2020). *Measure for measure: gender equality in Australia*. Per Capita. https://percapita.org.au/our_work/measure-for-measure-gender-equality-in-australia/

De Meyer, F. (2020a). Abortion law reform in Europe: The 2018 Belgian and Irish acts on termination of pregnancy. *Medical Law International*, *20*(1), 3–30.

De Meyer, F. (2020b). International trends towards the liberalization of abortion law. *BMJ Global Health*, *378*(o2025), 1–9.

De Zordo, S., Zanini, G., Mishtal, J., Garnsey, C., Ziegler, A. K., & Gerdts, C. (2020). Gestational age limits for abortion and cross-border reproductive care in Europe: A mixed-methods study. *BJOG: An International Journal of Obstetrics & Gynaecology*, *128*(5), 838–845.

Decker, M. R., Peitzmeier, S., Olumide, A., Acharya, R., Ojengbede, O., Covarrubias, L., … & Blum, R. W. (2014). Prevalence and health impact of intimate partner violence and non-partner sexual violence among female adolescents aged 15–19 years in vulnerable urban environments: A multi-country study. *Journal of Adolescent Health*, *55*(6), S58–S67.

Department of Health and Aged Care. (2018). *National Women's Health Strategy 2020–2030*. Australian Government.

Department of Health and Social Care. (2022). *Women's health strategy for England.* UK Government.

Der-Ohannesian, N. (2021). Female Negotiations of Affect in Domestic and Public Space in the Television Series, 'The Handmaid's Tale'. *Ilha Do Desterro*, *74*(1), 577–588.

Dheensa, S., Morgan, K., Love, B., & Cramer, H. (2024). Researching men's violence against women as feminist women researchers: The tensions we face. *Violence Against Women*, *30*(2), 347–371.

Dhillon, M., & Bakaya, S. (2014). Street Harassment: A Qualitative Study of the Experiences of Young Women in Delhi. *SAGE Open*, *4*(3).

Dhiman, B. (2023). *Education's role in empowering women and promoting gender inequality: A critical review. SSRN Electronic Journal.* Advance online publication. https://doi.org/10.2139/ssrn.4556375

Dibben, A., Stabile, I., Gomperts, R., & Kohout, J. (2023). Accessing abortion in a highly restrictive legal regime: characteristics of women and pregnant people in Malta self-managing their abortion through online telemedicine. *BMJ Sexual & Reproductive Health*, *49*(3), 176–182.

Dockray-Miller, M. (2008). Old English literature and feminist theory: a state of the field. *Literature Compass*, *5*(6), 1049–1059.

Dunlevy, G. (2020, June 25). Sex and gender differences in medical research impact patients and the economy. https://www.unsw.edu.au/newsroom/news/2020/06/sex-and-gender-differences-in-medical-research-impact-patients-a

Dyer, O. (2021). Demonstrations erupt in Poland after new abortion law is blamed in woman's death. *BMJ (Online)*, *375*, n2698.

Encyclopaedia Britannica. (n.d.). *Amartya Sen.* https://www.britannica.com/money/Amartya-Sen

Etymonline. (n.d.). *Menopause.* https://www.etymonline.com/word/menopause

Evans, M. L., Lindauer, M., & Farrell, M. E. (2020). A Pandemic within a Pandemic — Intimate Partner Violence during Covid-19. *The New England Journal of Medicine*, *383*(24), 2302–2304.

Ferguson, L., Anderson, M. E., Liang, M., & Filmer-Wilson, E. (2024). Why a good law is not always good enough: A global review of restrictions to supportive laws for sexual and reproductive health and rights. *BMJ Global Health*, *9*, e014100.

Fitz-Gibbon, K., True, J., & Pfitzner, N. (2021). More help required: The crisis in family violence during the coronavirus pandemic. *The Conversation.* https://theconversation.com/more-help-required-the-crisis-in-family-violence-during-the-coronavirus-pandemic-144126

Fleming, P. (2007). Sexuality, power and resistance in the workplace. *Organization Studies*, *28*(2), 239–256.

Footman, K., Bright, S., Kavanagh, J., Parnham, E., Bury, L., & Hoggart, L. (2024). Exploring provider preference and provision of abortion methods and stigma: Secondary analysis of a United Kingdom provider survey. *Perspectives on Sexual and Reproductive Health*, *56*(1), 50–59.

Franklin, C. A., Garza, A. D., Goodson, A., & Bouffard, L. A. (2020). Police perceptions of crime victim behaviors: A trend analysis exploring mandatory training and knowledge of sexual and domestic violence survivors' trauma responses. *Crime and Delinquency*, *66*(8), 1055–1086.

Fredman, S. (2022). *Discrimination law* (3rd ed.). Oxford University Press.

Gangoli, G. (2007). *Indian feminisms: law, patriarchies and violence in India* (1st ed.). Ashgate.

Gebhard, C. (2017). Women and acute coronary syndromes: still up to no good. *European Heart Journal*, *38*(14), 1066–1068.

Gholamrezayi, A., Aryaeian, N., Rimaz, S., Abolghasemi, J., Fallah, S., Moradi, N., & Taghizadeh, M. (2019). The effect of Cornus mas fruit extract consumption on lipid profile, glycemic indices, and leptin in postmenopausal women — A randomized clinical trial. *Phytotherapy Research*, *33*(11), 2979–2988.

Gosangi, B., Park, H., Thomas, R., Gujrathi, R., Bay, C. P., Raja, A. S., Seltzer, S. E., Balcom, M. C., McDonald, M. L., Orgill, D. P., Harris, M. B., Boland, G. W., Rexrode, K., & Khurana, B. (2021). Exacerbation of physical intimate partner violence during COVID-19 pandemic. *Radiology*, *298*(1), E38–E45.

Gracia, E., Martín-Fernández, M., Lila, M., Merlo, J., & Ivert, A. K. (2019). Prevalence of intimate partner violence against women in Sweden and Spain: A psychometric study of the 'Nordic paradox'. *PLoS ONE*, *14*(5), e0217015.

Graham, L. M., Ranapurwala, S. I., Zimmer, C., Macy, R. J., Rizo, C. F., Lanier, P., & Martin, S. L. (2021). Disparities in potential years of life lost due to intimate partner violence: Data from 16 states for 2006–2015. *PLoS ONE*, *16*(2), e0246477.

Grey, D. J. R. (2021). "It is impossible to judge the extent to which the crime is prevalent": infanticide and the law in India, 1870–1926. *Women's History Review*, *30*(6), 1028–1046.

Hamoda, H., & Sharma, A. (2024). Premature ovarian insufficiency, early menopause, and induced menopause. *Baillière's Best Practice & Research. Clinical Endocrinology & Metabolism*, *38*(1), 101823.

Harada, T., Momoeda, M., Taketani, Y., Hoshiai, H., & Terakawa, N. (2008). Low-dose oral contraceptive pill for dysmenorrhea associated with endometriosis: A placebo-controlled, double-blind, randomized trial. *Fertility and Sterility*, *90*(5), 1583–1588.

Hardy, C., Griffiths, A., Thorne, E., & Hunter, M. (2019). Tackling the taboo: Talking menopause-related problems at work. *International Journal of Workplace Health Management*, *12*(1), 28–38.

Healy, B. (1991). The Yentl Syndrome. *The New England Journal of Medicine*, *325*(4), 274–276.

Heron, R. L., Eisma, M. C., & Browne, K. (2022). Barriers and facilitators of disclosing domestic violence to the UK health service. *Journal of Family Violence*, *37*(2), 533–543.

Hickey, M., Hunter, M. S., Santoro, N., & Ussher, J. (2022). Normalising menopause. *BMJ*, *377*, e069369.

Hrdy, S. B. (1999). *The woman that never evolved* (Rev. ed.). Harvard University Press.

Humbert, A. L., Strid, S., Hearn, J., & Balkmar, D. (2021). Undoing the 'Nordic Paradox': Factors affecting rates of disclosed violence against women across the EU. *PLoS ONE*, *16*(5), e0249693.

Jackson, R. M. (2010). *Destined for equality: the inevitable rise of women's status*. Harvard University Press.

Jagori. (2011). *Safe cities free of violence against women and girls initiative: A draft strategic framework for women's safety in Delhi 2010*. New Delhi, India: http://jagori.org/wp-content/uploads/2006/01/Strategic_Framework.pdf

Jain, D. (2023). Supreme Court of India judgement on abortion as a fundamental right: breaking new ground. *Sexual and Reproductive Health Matters*, *31*(1), 2225264.

Jain, K., & Mathur, N. (2024). Analyzing the impact of education on women's empowerment: A systematic literature review and meta-analysis. *Research Review International Journal of Multidisciplinary*, *9*(6).

Jha, P., Kumar, R., Vasa, P., & Dhingra, N. (2006). Low male-to-female sex ratio of children born in India: national survey of 1.1 million households. *The Lancet (British Edition)*, *367* (9506), 211.

Johnson, A., Roberts, L., & Elkins, G. (2019). Complementary and Alternative Medicine for Menopause. *Journal of Evidence-Based Integrative Medicine*, *24*, 2515690X19829380.

Johnson, S. B., Blum, R. W., & Giedd, J. N. (2009). Adolescent maturity and the brain: The promise and pitfalls of neuroscience research in adolescent health policy. *Journal of Adolescent Health*, *45*(3), 216–221.

Kalokhe, A., del Rio, C., Dunkle, K., Stephenson, R., Metheny, N., Paranjape, A., & Sahay, S. (2017). Domestic violence against women in India: A systematic review of a decade of quantitative studies. *Global Public Health, 12*(4), 498–513.

Kalra, G., & Bhugra, D. (2013). Sexual violence against women: Understanding cross-cultural intersections. *Indian Journal of Psychiatry, 55*(3), 244–249.

Kaniuka, A. R., Nanney, E. M., Robertson, R., Hoff, R., Smith, M., Bowling, J., Basinger, E. D., Dahl, A. A., & Cramer, R. J. (2024). A grounded theory of sexual and gender minority suicide risk: The sexual and gender minority suicide risk and protection model. *Psychology of Sexual Orientation and Gender Diversity.*

Kaufman, R. E., & Mayall, K. (2023). One Year Later: Dobbs v. Jackson Women's Health Organization in Global Context. In *Human Rights 48*(4), 18–19. American Bar Association.

Keogh, L. A., Gillam, L., Bismark, M., McNamee, K., Webster, A., Bayly, C., & Newton, D. (2019). Conscientious objection to abortion, the law and its implementation in Victoria, Australia: perspectives of abortion service providers. *BMC Medical Ethics, 20*(1), 1–10.

Khadem, N. (2022, July 29). Sexual assault reports in Australia hit all-time high. *What's driving the increase? Australian Broadcasting Corporation (ABC).* https://www.abc.net.au/news/2022-07-29/sexual-assaults-australia-record-high/101281802

Kimuna, S. R., Djamba, Y. K., & Ciciurkaite, G. (2012). Domestic violence in Kenya: Implications for social policy. In Y. K. Djamba & S. R. Kimuna (Eds.), *Gender-Based Violence: Perspectives from Africa, the Middle East, and India* (pp. 29–47). Springer.

Kirby, M. (2016). Whitlam as internationalist: A centenary reflection. *Melbourne University Law Review, 39*(3), 850–894.

Kotb, M. A. M., Ragab, H. M., Elwan, Y. A., & Hussein, Y. H. H. (2022). Oral contraceptive pills use and adverse effects. *The Egyptian Journal of Hospital Medicine, 86*(1), 286–290.

Krahé, B., Tomaszewska, P., Kuyper, L., & Vanwesenbeeck, I. (2014). Prevalence of sexual aggression among young people in Europe: A review of the evidence from 27 EU countries. *Aggression and Violent Behavior, 19*(5), 545–558.

Krook, M. L., & Restrepo Sanín, J. (2020). The Cost of Doing Politics? Analyzing Violence and Harassment against Female Politicians. *Perspectives on Politics, 18*(3), 740–755.

Krusz, E., Hall, N., Barrington, D. J., Creamer, S., Anders, W., King, M., . . . Hennegan, J. (2019). Menstrual health and hygiene among Indigenous Australian girls and women: barriers and opportunities. *BMC Women's Health, 19*(1), 2–7.

Kudon, H. Z., Herbst, J. H., Richardson, L. C., Smith, S. G., Demissie, Z., & Siordia, C. (2024). Prevalence estimates and factors associated with violence among older adults: National Intimate Partner and Sexual Violence (NISVS) Survey, 2016/2017. *Journal of Elder Abuse & Neglect, 36*(1), 67–83.

Kumar, C. (2022). The Fallout of Forbidding Female Foeticide in India: A Human Rights Analysis. *Indonesian Journal of International & Comparative Law, 9*(3), 387.

Kumar, N., Darshan, B. B., Unnikrishnan, B., Kanchan, T., Thapar, R., Mithra, P., Kulkarni, V., & Holla, R. (2014). Awareness and Attitudes Regarding Prenatal Sex Determination, Pre-Conception and Pre-Natal Diagnostic Techniques Act (PCPNDTA) among Pregnant Women in Southern India. *Journal of Clinical and Diagnostic Research, 8*(10), JC09–JC11.

Kusuma, Y. S., & Babu, B. V. (2017). Elimination of violence against women and girls as a global action agenda. *Journal of Injury and Violence Research, 9*(2), 117–122.

Kwee, S. H., Tan, H. H., Marsman, A., & Wauters, C. (2007). The effect of Chinese herbal medicines (CHM) on menopausal symptoms compared to hormone replacement therapy (HRT) and placebo. *Maturitas, 58*(1), 83–90.

La Ferle, C., Muralidharan, S., & Kim, E. (2019). Using guilt and shame appeals from an Eastern perspective to promote bystander intervention: A study of mitigating domestic violence in India. *Journal of Advertising*, *48*(5), 555–568.

Lake, M. (2013). Women's and gender history in Australia: A transformative practice. *Journal of Women's History*, *25*(4), 190–211.

Law, H.D., Marasinghe, D., Biddle, N., Butler, D., Lancsar, E., Desborough, J., & Korda, R. (2022). Progressivity of out-of-pocket costs for Medicare-subsidised services and medicines in Australia. *International Journal of Population Data Science*, *7*(3).

Lee, B. X. (2019). The Biology of Violence. In *Violence* (pp. 23–44). John Wiley & Sons, Inc.

Little, W. (2023). *Introduction to Sociology* –3rd Canadian edition. Nova Scotia Community College.

López Ferreruela, I., Obón Azuara, B., Malo Fumanal, S., Rabanaque Hernández, M. J., & Aguilar-Palacio, I. (2024). Gender inequalities in secondary prevention of cardiovascular disease: a scoping review. *International Journal for Equity in Health*, *23*(1), 146.

Luebke, J., Kako, P., Lopez, A., Schmitt, M., Dressel, A., Klein, K., & Mkandawire-Vahlmu, L. (2023). Barriers faced by American Indian women in urban Wisconsin in seeking help following an experience of intimate partner violence. *Violence Against Women*, *29*(11), 2080–2103.

Lyons, K. (2024, May 5). *Horror and fury in Australia as epidemic of violence against women sweeps across the country: Anger and grief have erupted, with women demanding action from the government on what has become a national emergency.* The Guardian *(London)*. https://www.theguardian.com/australia-news/article/2024/may/05/horror-and-fury-in-australia-as-epidemic-of-violence-against-women-sweeps-across-the-country

Lyons, K. (2025, January 27). *Older women allegedly killed by family members a 'silent crisis', experts say.* The Guardian. https://www.theguardian.com/global/2025/jan/27/older-women-killed-by-family-members-a-silent-crisis-no-one-is-talking-about-experts-say-ntwnfb

Macêdo, P., Cavalcante, A., Fernandes, S., Salustiano, M., Lima, M., Jerez-Roig, J., & Câmara, S. (2023). Association between menopausal status and physical function: A systematic review protocol. *PLoS ONE*, *18*(1), e0280786.

Madsen, T. E., Bourjeily, G., Hasnain, M., Jenkins, M., Morrison, M. F., Sandberg, K., McGregor, A. J. (2017). Article commentary: sex- and gender-based medicine: the need for precise terminology. *Gender and the Genome*, *1*(3), 122–128.

Mahapatro, M., Gupta, R. N., Gupta, V., & Kundu, A. S. (2011). Domestic violence during pregnancy in India. *Journal of Interpersonal Violence*, *26*(15), 2973–2990.

Mantler, T., Jackson, K. T., Walsh, E. J., Tobah, S., Shillington, K., Jackson, B., & Soares, E. (2022). Sharing personal experiences of accessibility and knowledge of violence: A qualitative study. *Journal of Interpersonal Violence*, *37*(3–4), 1206–1222.

Marks, L. (2010). *Sexual chemistry: A history of the contraceptive pill* (Paperback edition). Yale University Press.

MenoLabs. (n.d.). *A historical perspective on menopause*. https://menolabs.com/blogs/menolife/a-historical-perspective-on-menopause

Meurer, A. (2021). The end of the "Bad seed" Era? Epigenetics' contribution to violence prevention initiatives in public health. *The New Bioethics*, *27*(2), 159–175.

Meyer, S. R., Lasater, M. E., & García-Moreno, C. (2020). Violence against older women: A systematic review of qualitative literature. *PLoS ONE*, *15*(9), e0239560.

Meyer, V. F. (2001). The Medicalization of Menopause: Critique and Consequences. *International Journal of Health Services*, *31*(4), 769–792.

Michals, D. (Ed.). (2017). Gloria Steinem (1934–). *National Women's History Museum.* https://www.womenshistory.org/education-resources/biographies/gloria-steinem

Miller, A. R., & Segal, C. (2019). Do female officers improve law enforcement quality? Effects on crime reporting and domestic violence. *Review of Economic Studies*, *86*(5), 2220–2247.

Montinari, M. R., Minelli, S., & De Caterina, R. (2019). The first 3500 years of aspirin history from its roots – A concise summary. *Vascular Pharmacology*, *113*, 1–8.

Moore, D., Fraser, S., Törrönen, J., & Tinghög, M. E. (2015). Sameness and difference: metaphor and politics in the constitution of addiction, social exclusion and gender in Australian and Swedish drug policy. *International Journal of Drug Policy*, *26*(4), 420–428.

Morgan, J. (2012). Abortion law reform: The importance of democratic change. *University of New South Wales Law Journal*, *35*(1), 142–174.

Moulding, N., Franzway, S., Wendt, S., Zufferey, C., & Chung, D. (2021). Rethinking women's mental health after intimate partner violence. *Violence Against Women*, *27*(8), 1064–1090.

Muehlenhard, C. L., & Peterson, Z. D. (2011). Distinguishing Between Sex and Gender: History, Current Conceptualizations, and Implications. *Sex Roles*, *64*(11–12), 791–803.

Myhill, A. (2019). Renegotiating domestic violence: Police attitudes and decisions concerning arrest. *Policing and Society*, *29*(1), 52–68.

Narayan, S. (2018). Religion and Female–Male Ratios in India. *Indian Journal of Human Development*, *12*(3), 441–452.

National Today. (n.d.). World Menopause Day. https://nationaltoday.com/world-menopause-day/?utm_source=chatgpt.com

New South Wales Government. (2019). *Abortion Law Reform Act 2019 No. 11.* https://legislation.nsw.gov.au/view/pdf/asmade/act-2019-11

Nieder, C., Muck, C., & Kärtner, J. (2019). Sexual Violence Against Women in India: Daily Life and Coping Strategies of Young Women in Delhi. *Violence Against Women*, *25*(14), 1717–1738.

Nigam, S. (2020). *Women and domestic violence law in India: a quest for justice* (1st ed.). Routledge.

Nolen, E., Siegel, J. A., Mendoza, R. R., Cubbin, C., Vohra-Gupta, S., Dosanjh, L. H., & Lewis-Smith, H. (2024). The Impact of Dobbs v. Jackson Women's Health Organization on Young Women's Experiences of Objectification and Sexual Well-Being. *Psychology of Women Quarterly*, *48*(3), 319–334.

Office for National Statistics. (2022). Domestic abuse prevalence and trends, England and Wales: year ending March 2022. Office for National Statistics. https://www.ons.gov.uk/peoplepopulationandcommunity/crimeandjustice/bulletins/domesticabuseinenglandandwalesoverview/latest

Orgad, S., & Rottenberg, C. (2024). The rising visibility of 'the change': UK news coverage of menopause. *European Journal of Cultural Studies*, *27*(4), 519–539.

Our Watch. (2018). *Change the story.* https://www.ourwatch.org.au/change-the-story/

Oxford English Dictionary. (n.d..). *Menopause.* https://www.oed.com/dictionary/menopause_n

Oxley, G., & Lipscombe, S. (2025, January 7). *Tackling violence against women and girls.* House of Commons Library. https://commonslibrary.parliament.uk/research-briefings/cdp-2024-0183/

Palmieri, S. (2013). Sympathetic advocates: male parliamentarians sharing responsibility for gender equality. *Gender & Development*, *21*(1), 67–80.

Pell, B., Melendez-Torres, G. J., Buckley, K., Evans, R., & Robinson, A. (2024). A realist evaluation of a "whole health" response to domestic violence and abuse in the UK. *Violence Against Women*, *30*(4), 567–589.

Perry, M. J., & Albee, G. W. (1998). The deterministic origins of sexism. *Race, Gender & Class*, *5*(3), 122–134.
Price, E., Sharman, L. S., Douglas, H. A., Sheeran, N., & Dingle, G. A. (2022). Experiences of Reproductive Coercion in Queensland Women. *Journal of Interpersonal Violence*, *37*(5–6), NP2823–NP2843.
Price, J. (2017). *Counting dead women: the hard truth about Australia's domestic violence victims. UTS Social Impact*. The University of Technology Sydney.
Proudman, C., & Lloyd, F. (2023). The impact of COVID-19 on women and children in the UK who were victims of domestic abuse: A practitioner perspective. *Journal of Aggression, Conflict and Peace Research*, *15*(3), 234–241.
Raeder, F., Heidemann, F., Schedlowski, M., Margraf, J., & Zlomuzica, A. (2019). No pills, more skills: The adverse effect of hormonal contraceptive use on exposure therapy benefit. *Journal of Psychiatric Research*, *119*, 95–101.
Rankin, M. J. (2018). Abortion law in New South Wales: the problem with necessity. *Monash University Law Review*, *44*(1), 32–70.
Reed, B. G., & Carr, B. R. (2018). The Normal Menstrual Cycle and the Control of Ovulation. *Endotext*.
Resnik, J. (2013). Opening the door: Ruth Bader Ginsburg, law's boundaries, and the gender of opportunities. *Columbia Journal of Gender and Law*, *25*(1), 81.
Riach, K., & Jack, G. (2021). Women's health in/and work: Menopause as an intersectional experience. *International Journal of Environmental Research and Public Health*, *18*(20), 10793.
Riaz, S., & Pervaiz, Z. (2018). The impact of women's education and employment on their empowerment: An empirical evidence from household level survey. *Quality & Quantity*, *52*(6), 2855–2870.
Roe v. Wade, 410 U.S. 113 (1973). Justia US Supreme Court. https://supreme.justia.com/cases/federal/us/410/113/
Rollins, J. (2011). Political science, political sex. *Political Science & Politics*, *44*(01), 27–30.
Romanis, E. C. (2023). Abortion access and the benefits and limitations of abortion-permissive legal frameworks: Lessons from the United Kingdom. *Cambridge Quarterly of Healthcare Ethics*, *32*(3), 378–390.
Rushton, G. (2019, July 12). *Australian doctors already have signs up saying they won't provide contraception or pregnancy terminations. BuzzFeed Inc.*
Sabri, B., & Campbell, J. C. (2015). Intimate partner violence against women in slums in India. *Indian Journal of Medical Research* (New Delhi, India: 1994), *141*(6), 757–760.
Sah, S. (2022). Patriarchy and the identity of women in Indian society. *Journal of Emerging Technologies and Innovative Research*, *9*(8), 563–603.
Samango-Sprouse, C., Counts, D., & Gropman, A. (2021). Insight versus hindsight: What we have learned after 17 years of research with sex chromosome abnormalities. *American Journal of Medical Genetics. Part A*, *185*(3), 1004–1005.
Sánchez-Prada, A., Delgado-Álvarez, C., Bosch-Fiol, E., Ferreiro-Basurto, V., & Ferrer-Pérez, V. A. (2022). Bystanders of intimate partner violence against women and their willingness to intervene: An analysis of secondary data in Spain (2005–2020). *PLoS ONE*, *17*(9), e0274822.
Sanz-Barbero, B., Barón, N., & Vives-Cases, C. (2019). Prevalence, associated factors and health impact of intimate partner violence against women in different life stages. *PLoS ONE*, *14*(10), e0221049.
Sapkota, M., & Dahal, K. (2022). Gender and politics: a feminist critique of the state. *Journal of Political Science*, *22*(1), 75–91.
Saravanan, S. (2000). *Violence against women in India: A literature review*. Institute of Social Studies Trust. http://www.academia.edu/2359534/Violence_against_women_in_India_A_literature_review
Saunders, K. (1990). Women's history in Australia: the decade reviewed. *Hecate*, *16*(1/2), 171–185.

Schofield-Georgeson, E., & Rawling, M. (2020). Industrial legislation in Australia in 2019. *Journal of Industrial Relations*, *62*(3), 425–445.

Scutt, J. A. (1983). *Even in the best of homes: violence in the family*. Penguin Books.

Sedman, D. (2024). *Revisiting the 'shadow pandemic': Sustainable Development Goal No. 5, gender equality and COVID-19*. In *Law and sustainable development after COVID-19* (1st ed., pp. 16).

Sen, A. K. (2003). Missing women – revisited. *BMJ*, *327*(7427), 1297–1298.

Sereno, M., Catagnus, R., Griffith, A., & Eilers, H. (2024). A systematic review of empirical studies measuring training effects on biases evidenced by professionals toward intimate partner violence. *Trauma, Violence, & Abuse*, *25*(2), 1053–1072.

Shastri, A. (2022). Importance of education in women's empowerment. *International Journal of Research Culture Society*, *6*(4), 213–216.

Shaw, N., & Pettinger, C. (2024). Gastrointestinal symptoms in the peri- and post-menopause: A protocol for a scoping review. *Pearl, School of Health Professions, Faculty of Health*. University of Plymouth.

Singhal, N. (2015). Conceptualising Domestic Violence within the Scope of United Nations Convention Against Torture. *Journal of National Law University*, Delhi, *3*(1), 183–191.

Skuster, P., Menzel, J., Ghorashi, A. R., & Perkins, M. (2022). Policy surveillance for a global analysis of national abortion laws. *Sexual and Reproductive Health Matters*, *30*(1), 2064208.

Smith, L. (2020). Menopause can lead to discrimination. *NSW Teachers Federation*. https://www.nswtf.org.au/?s=menopause

Söderlund, T., & Madison, G. (2017). Objectivity and realms of explanation in academic journal articles concerning sex/gender: a comparison of Gender studies and the other social sciences. *Scientometrics*, *112*(2), 1093–1109.

Spigelman, A. D., & Rendalls, S. (2015). Clinical governance in Australia. Clinical Governance: *An International Journal*, *20*(2), 56–73.

Stavrou, A. (2024, August 16). "It's not like you were beaten": The horrifying misogyny vulnerable women face from the judge's bench. *The Independent*. https://www.independent.co.uk/news/uk/home-news/family-court-judges-misogyny-domestic-abuse-b2595125.html

SteelFisher, G. K., Findling, M. G., Bleich, S. N., Casey, L. S., Blendon, R. J., Benson, J. M., Sayde, J. M., & Miller, C. (2019). Gender discrimination in the United States: Experiences of women. *Health Services Research*, *54*(S2), 1442–1453.

Steinem, G. (n.d..). The best thing about self-defense is knowing there is a self worth defending. *QuoteFancy*. https://quotefancy.com/quote/3032152/Gloria-Steinem-The-best-thing-about-self-defense-is-knowing-there-is-a-self-worth

Stevens, J. E. (1994). The biology of violence. *BioScience*, *44*(5), 291–294.

Stewart, S., & Arnull, E. (2023). Mothers, domestic violence, and child protection: The UK response. *Violence Against Women*, *29*(3–4), 626–647.

Stoever, J. K. (2019). Access to safety and justice: Service of process in domestic violence cases. *Washington Law Review*, *94*(1), 333–400.

Strasser, J., Ouedraogo, R., Baird, S., & Coast, E. (2024). Global workforce implications of Dobbs v Jackson Women's Health Organization. *The Lancet*, *403*(June), 2669–2671.

Stromquist, N. P. (2015). Women's empowerment and education: Linking knowledge to transformative action. *European Journal of Education*, *50*(3), 307–324.

Tahmindjis, P. (2005). Sexuality and international human rights law. International Bar Association Journal, *48*(3–4), 9–29.

Takala, T., & Häyry, M. (2023). Physicians Controlling Women's Reproductive Choices: The Slow Liberalization of Abortion Laws in Finland. *Cambridge Quarterly of Healthcare Ethics*, *32*(3), 391–396.

Tannenbaum, C., Schwarz, J. M., Clayton, J. A., Vries, G. J. D.., & Sullivan, C. (2016). Evaluating sex as a biological variable in preclinical research: the devil in the details. *Biology of Sex Differences*, *7*(13), 1–4.

The Global Statistics. (2024). *India Population Statistics 2024*. https://www.theglobalstatistics.com

The Menopause Society. (2023, October 10). *What's in your gut could be aggravating your menopause symptoms: New study suggests that stress and some gastrointestinal factors are associated with severity of menopause symptoms*. EurekAlert. AAAS. https://www.eurekalert.org/news-releases/1004199

Tidmarsh, P., & Hamilton, G. (2020). Misconceptions of sexual crimes against adult victims: Barriers to justice. *Trends and Issues in Crime and Criminal Justice*, *611*, 1–18.

Turk, K. (2023). On Account of Sex: Ruth Bader Ginsburg and the Making of Gender Equality Law by Philippa Strum. *Political Science Quarterly*, *138*(2), 307–308.

UN Women. (2020). Global norms and standards: ending violence against women. https://www.unwomen.org/en/what-we-do/ending-violence-against-women/global-norms-and-standards

UN Women. (2024, November 25). Five essential facts to know about femicide. UN. https://www.unwomen.org/en/articles/explainer/five-essential-facts-to-know-about-femicide

United Nations. (1979). *Convention on the Elimination of All Forms of Discrimination Against Women*. United Nations Treaty Series, *1249*, 13. https://www.un.org/womenwatch/daw/cedaw/cedaw.htm

United Nations. (2010). *Keeping the promise: united to achieve the Millennium Development Goals*. Outcome document of the High-level Plenary Meeting of the General Assembly, A/RES/65/1. UN https://undocs.org/A/RES/65/1

United Nations. (2018). *The Sustainable Development Goals report*. https://www.un.org/sustainabledevelopment/progress-report/

United Nations. (n.d.). *What is domestic abuse?* United Nations. https://www.un.org/en/coronavirus/what-is-domestic-abuse

United Nations Office on Drugs and Crime. (2024, November 25). *One woman is killed every 10 minutes by their intimate partners or other family members*. UNODC. https://www.unodc.org/unodc/en/press/releases/2024/November/one-woman-is-killed-every-10-minutes-by-their-intimate-partners-or-other-family-members.html

Vega, Y. K. (2023). *Sex, policy and power: The Australian experience* (Doctoral thesis, unpublished). Swinburne University of Technology.

Vicard-Olagnea, M., Pereira, B., Rougé, L., Cabaillot, A., Vorilhon, P., Lazimi, G., & Laporte, C. (2021). Signs and symptoms of intimate partner violence in women attending primary care in Europe, North America and Australia: A systematic review and meta-analysis. *Family Practice*, *39*(1), 190–199.

Victorian Government, Department of Health. (n.d.). Inquiry into women's pain. https://www.health.vic.gov.au/inquiry-into-womens-pain

Wainer, Z., Carcel, C., Hickey, M., Schiebinger, L., Schmiede, A., McKenzie, B., Jenkins, C., Webster, J., Woodward, M., Hehir, A., Solomon, B., Costa, C., Lukaszyk, C., Colville, D. J., Dempsey, E., Wright, G. M., Mishra, G. D., Fisher, J. R., Kulkarni, J., … Norton, R. (2020). Sex and gender in health research: updating policy to reflect evidence. *Medical Journal of Australia*, *212*(2), 57–62.

Walker-Descartes, I., Mineo, M., Vaca Condado, L., & Agrawal, N. (2021). Domestic violence and its effects on women, children, and families. *Pediatric Clinics of North America*, *68*(3), 455–464.

Werbinski, J. (2008). American Medical Women's Association Position Paper on Sex- and Gender-Specific Medicine. *Journal of Women's Health*, *17*(10), 1557–1557.

Westwood, S. (2024). A bloody mess? UK regulation of menopause discrimination and the need for reform. *Journal of Law and Society*, *51*(1), 104–129.

Wikipedia. (n.d.). *Louann Brizendine*. https://en.wikipedia.org/wiki/Louann_Brizendine

Women on Web. (n.d.). *Women on Web: Who we are*. https://www.womenonweb.org/en/

Women's Health East. (2020). *Creating safe and inclusive public spaces for women*. WHE. *(Updated September 2021)*.

Wood, E. J. (2018). Rape as a practice of war: Toward a typology of political violence. *Politics & Society*, *46*(4), 513–537.

Wood, W., & Eagly, A. H. (2015). Two traditions of research on gender identity. *Sex Roles*, 461–473.

World Health Organization. (2019). *World health statistics 2019: monitoring health for the Sustainable Development Goals*. WHO https://www.who.int/publications/i/item/9789241565707

World Health Organization. (2024, March 25). Violence against women. World Health Organization. https://www.who.int/news-room/fact-sheets/detail/violence-against-women

World Population Review. (2024). *World population 2024*. World Population Review. https://worldpopulationreview.com

Young, K., Fisher, J., & Kirkman, M. (2019). "Do mad people get endo or does endo make you mad?" Clinicians' discursive constructions of medicine and women with endometriosis. *Feminism & Psychology*, *29*(3), 337–356.

Chapter 5

Aapola, S., Gonick, M., & Harris, A. (2005). *Young femininity: girlhood, power and social change*. Palgrave Macmillan.

Agyapong, B., Obuobi-Donkor, G., Burback, L., & Wei, Y. (2022). Stress, burnout, anxiety and depression among teachers: A scoping review. *International Journal of Environmental Research and Public Health*, *19*(17), 10706.

Akbari, F., & True, J. (2022). One year on from the Taliban takeover of Afghanistan: re-instituting gender apartheid. *Australian Journal of International Affairs*, *76*(6), 624–633.

Anderson, J., & Boyle, C. (2015). Inclusive education in Australia: rhetoric, reality and the road ahead. *Support for Learning*, *30*(1), 5–22.

Andrews, R. J. (2004). *Birth of the chess queen: A history*. HarperCollins.

Aragonés-González, M., Rosser-Limiñana, A., & Gil-González, D. (2020). Coeducation and gender equality in education systems: A scoping review. *Children and Youth Services Review*, *111*, 104837.

Barker, R. (2020). It is not inevitable: the future funding of faith-based schools after Ruddock. *Australasian Catholic Record*, *97*(2), 144–155.

Bettella, P. (2018). Women and the Academies in Seventeenth-Century Italy: Elena Lucrezia Cornaro Piscopia's Role in Literary Academies. *Italian Culture*, *36*(2), 100–119.

Black, A. L., & Garvis, S. (Eds.). (2018). Lived experiences of women in academia: Metaphors, manifesto and memoir. Routledge, Taylor & Francis Group.

Blok, H., Merry, M. S., Karsten, S., & Gaither, M. (2021). The Legal Situation of Home Education in Europe. In M. Gaither (Ed.), *The Wiley Handbook of Home Education* (pp. 395–421). John Wiley & Sons, Inc.

Bounds, C., & Jenkins, L. N. (2018). Teacher-directed violence and stress: The role of school setting. *California School Psychologist*, *22*(4), 435–442.

Braeunig, M., Pfeifer, R., Schaarschmidt, U., Lahmann, C., & Bauer, J. (2018). Factors influencing mental health improvements in school teachers. *Plos One*, *13*(10), e0206412. https://doi.org/10.1371/journal.pone.0206412

Braun, S. (2021). *Monarchs who shaped history: Queen Isabella I.* ACIS.

Brekhus, W. H., Lombardo, C., & Sabetta, L. (2024). Sociocultural Defaults at Rest and in Motion: Cognitive Sociologies of the Unmarked. In C. Lombardo and L. Sabetta (Eds.), *Against the Background of Social Reality* (1st ed., pp. 45–65). Routledge.

Britannica Kids. (n.d.). *Maybanke Anderson.* Encyclopædia Britannica. https://kids.britannica.com/kids/article/Maybanke-Anderson/489906

British Council. (2024, March 7). *India releases updated higher education statistics.* Opportunities Insight. https://opportunities-insight.britishcouncil.org/short-articles/news/india-releases-updated-higher-education-statistics

Brown, N. M. (2015). *Ivory Vikings: The mystery of the most famous chessmen in the world and the woman who made them.* St. Martin's Press.

Buchmann, C., & DiPrete, T. A. (2006). The Growing Female Advantage in College Completion: The Role of Family Background and Academic Achievement. *American Sociology Review*, *71*(4), 515–541.

Burns, K., Egan, S., Hayes, H., & Rawlings, V. (2024). *Teach us consent: Digital feminist activism and the limits of school-based consent pedagogies.* In L. James-Hawkins & R. Ryan-Flood (Eds.), *Consent* (1st ed., pp. 265–278). Routledge.

Bush, S. S. (2011). International politics and the spread of quotas for women in legislatures. *International Organization Journal*, *65*(01), 103–137.

Caro García, C., & Monreal Gimeno, M. C. (2017). Creencias del amor romántico y violencia de género. *INFAD*, *2*(1), 47–56.

Carole, H. (2021). Single-sex versus coeducational schooling in 19th-century Victorian public schools. *History of Education Review*, *50*(2), 258–271.

Cassidy, C. (2023a, April 12). *Australian university reforms to incentivise STEM degrees over arts have 'dismally failed', peak bodies say.* The Guardian. https://www.theguardian.com/australia-news/2023/apr/12/australian-university-reforms-to-incentivise-stem-degrees-over-arts-have-dismally-failed-peak-bodies-say

Cassidy, C. (2023b, November 26). "We haven't looked back": Homeschooling in Australia seeing post-lockdown boom; Number of children learning at home has doubled since the pandemic—with parents saying the mainstream education system isn't working. The Guardian. https://www.theguardian.com

Charbonneau, S., Journault, A.-A., Cernik, R., Longpré, C., Wan, N., Giguère, C.-É., & Lupien, S. (2022). Anxiety in the Classroom: Only Girls' Anxiety Is Related to Same-Sex Peers' Anxiety. *International Journal of Environmental Research and Public Health*, *20*(1), 84.

Chzhen, Y., Rees, G., Gromada, A., Cuesta, J., & Bruckauf, Z. (2018). *An unfair start: inequality in children's education in rich countries.* UNICEF Office of Research Innocenti.

Contos, C. (2021, March 15). *'Do they even know they did this to us?': Why I launched the school sexual assault petition. The Guardian.* https://www.theguardian.com/commentisfree/2021/mar/15/do-they-even-know-they-did-this-to-us-why-i-launched-the-school-sexual-assault-petition

Convention on the Elimination of All Forms of Discrimination Against Women. (1979). CEDAW. https://treaties.un.org/Pages/ViewDetails.aspx?src=TREATY&mtdsg_no=IV-8&chapter=4&clang=_en

Convention on the Elimination of All Forms of Discrimination Against Women. (2018). CEDAW *Concluding observations on the eighth periodic report of Australia.* https://www.ohchr.org/en/documents/concluding-observations/concluding-observations-eighth-periodic-report-australia

Coren, S. A., & Luthar, S. S. (2014). Pursuing perfection: distress and interpersonal functioning among adolescent boys in single-sex and co-educational independent schools. *Psychology in the Schools*, *51*(9), 931–946.

Crocker, R. (2006). 'Some aggressive work': The Emma Willard Association and educated womanhood, 1891–1898. In *Mrs. Russell Sage* (pp. 189–199). Indiana University Press.

de las Cuevas, P., García-Arenas, M., & Rico, N. (2022). Why Not STEM? A Study Case on the Influence of Gender Factors on Students' Higher Education Choice. *Mathematics (Basel)*, *10*(2), 239.

Department of Education, 2022. *Consent and respectful relationships education (CRRE)*. Australian Government. https://www.education.gov.au/consent-and-respectful-relationships-education-crre

Department of Industry, Science and Resources. (2020). *Advancing women in STEM strategy: 2020 action plan*. Australian Government. DISR. https://www.industry.gov.au/publications/advancing-women-stem-strategy/2020-action-plan

Department of Industry, Science and Resources. (2022). *Second national data report on girls and women in STEM*. Australian Government. DISR. https://www.industry.gov.au/news/second-national-data-report-girls-and-women-stem#:~:text=The%20 2021%20Monitor%20shows%20some,increased%20by%202%252

Department of Industry, Science and Resources. (2024, August 2). *The state of STEM gender equity in 2024*. Australian Government, DISR. https://www.industry.gov.au/news/state-stem-gender-equity-2024

Diamant, J. (2022, March 15). *In India and many other countries, there is little gap between men and women in attitudes on gender issues*. Pew Research Center. https://www.pewresearch.org/short-reads/2022/03/15/in-india-and-many-other-countries-there-is-little-gap-between-men-and-women-in-attitudes-on-gender-issues/

Divekar, R., Chopra, K., Dange, P., & Mehendale, S. (2025). *Securing the Future Through Sustainability, Health, Education, and Technology*. (1st ed.). Taylor & Francis Group.

Drayton, M. (2022). The Saboteur at Work: How the Unconscious Mind Can Sabotage Ourselves, Our Organisations and Society Routledge.

Drury, K., Bukowski, W. M., Velásquez, A. M., & Stella-Lopez, L. (2013). Victimization and Gender Identity in Single-Sex and Mixed-Sex Schools: Examining Contextual Variations in Pressure to Conform to Gender Norms. *Sex Roles*, *69*(7–8), 442–454.

Dunne, M., Humphreys, S., & Leach, F. (2006). Gender violence in schools in the developing world. *Gender and Education*, *18*(1), 75–98.

Eden, L., & Wagstaff, M. F. (2020). Evidence-based policymaking and the wicked problem of SDG 5 gender equality. *Journal of International Business Policy*, *4*(1), 28–57.

Edwards, C., Bolton, R., Salazar, M., Vives-Cases, C., & Daoud, N. (2024). Young people's constructions of gender norms and attitudes towards violence against women: A critical review of qualitative empirical literature. *Journal of Gender Studies*, *33*(1), 100–111.

Emmett, K. (2018). The Social and Political Philosophy of Mary Wollstonecraft, edited by Sandrine Bergès and Alan Coffee, *Australasian Journal of Philosophy*, *96*(4), 835–836.

Encyclopaedia Britannica. (n.d.). *Isabella I, queen of Spain*. https://www.britannica.com/biography/Isabella-I-queen-of-Spain

European Parliament. (2016). *Knowledge and know-how: The role of self-defense in the prevention of violence against women*. European Union. https://www.europarl.europa.eu/thinktank/en/document/IPOL_STU(2016)571385

Fejzić-Čengić, Fahira (2020). "Fatima Al-Fihri Founder of the First World University." *Studies in Media and Communication* *8*(2), 14

Feniger, Y. (2011). The Gender Gap in Advanced Math and Science Course Taking: Does Same-Sex Education Make A Difference? *Sex Roles*, *65*(9–10), 670–679.

Ferguson, S. (1999). The radical ideas of Mary Wollstonecraft. *Canadian Journal of Political Science / Revue canadienne de science politique*, *32*(3), 427–450.

Fisher, C. R., Thompson, C. D., & Brookes, R. H. (2020). Gender differences in the Australian undergraduate STEM student experience: A systematic review. *Higher Education Research & Development, 39*(6), 1155–1168.
Foucault, M. (1982). The subject and power. *The University of Chicago Press Journals, 8*(4), 777–795.
Foucault, M. (1990). *The history of sexuality* (R. Hurley, Trans.). Penguin. (*Histoire de la sexualité*, tome 1: *Lavolonté de savoir*. Gallimard, 1976).
Foucault, M. (1991). Truth and power. In P. Rabinow (Ed.), *The Foucault Reader* (pp. 51–75). Penguin.
Friedrich, J., & Shanks, R. (2023). 'The Prison of the Body': School Uniforms between Discipline and Governmentality. *Discourse (Abingdon, England) 44*(1), 16–29.
Frontczak, S. M. (2023). Marie Curie—Lifelong Teacher. *The Physics Teacher, 61*(7), 549–552.
Gillani, N., Eynon, R., Chiabaut, C., & Finkel, K. (2023). Unpacking the "Black Box" of AI in Education. *Educational Technology & Society, 26*(1), 99–111.
GIRLS, GIRLS, GIRLS Magazine. (n.d.). *Be a lady they said* [Video]. YouTube. https://www.youtube.com/watch?v=zPQcWNyGZKA
Gray, A. (2017, February 27). *These countries have the most doctoral graduates.* World Economic Forum. https://www.weforum.org/stories/2017/02/countries-with-most-doctoral-graduates/
Gromada, A., Rees, G., Chzhen, Y., Cuesta, J., & Bruckhauf, Z. (2018). *Measuring inequality in children's education in rich countries.* Office of Research-Innocenti, United Nations Children's Fund (UNICEF).
Gukurume, S., & Shoko, M. (2023). Policing toxic masculinities and dealing with sexual violence on Zimbabwean University campuses. *Hervormde Teologiese Studies, 79*(3), 1–8.
Hána, D., & Kostelecká, Y. (2022). A comparison of home education legislation in Europe from the perspective of geography of education. *Research Papers in Education, 37*(5), 603–632.
Harry, A., & Sayudin. (2023). Role of AI in education. *Injuruty: Interdisciplinary Journal and Humanity, 2*(3), 260–268.
Hjörne, E. (2016). The narrative of special education in Sweden: History and trends in policy and practice. *Discourse: Studies in the Cultural Politics of Education, 37*(4), 540–552.
Hollander, J. A. (2014). Does self-defense training prevent sexual violence against women? *Violence Against Women, 20*(3), 252–269.
Holowchak, M. A. (2018). A system of education, not just a university: Thomas Jefferson's Philosophy of Education. *History of Education, 47*(4), 488–503.
Hsiao, H.-S., Chen, J.-H., Chang, T.-L., Li, P.-H., & Chung, G.-H. (2024). A study on the effects of using the 6E model and a robot teaching assistant on junior high school students' STEM knowledge, learning motivation, and hands-on performance. *Journal of Science Education and Technology. 33*(5), 759–778.
Hudson, V., Leidl, P., & Hunt, S. (2015). *The Hillary doctrine: Sex and American foreign policy.* Columbia University Press.
Independent Schools Council. (2023). *UK school census 2023: Key statistics and analysis. ISC.* https://www.isc.co.uk/media/9316/isc_census_2023_final.pdf
India Today Education Desk. (2024, April 22). *Online STEM education sees 12% surge in female enrollment in 2023–24: Study.* India Today. https://www.indiatoday.in/education-today/latest-studies/story/online-stem-education-sees-12-surge-in-female-enrollment-in-2023-24-study-2530134-2024-04-22
Institute for Women's Policy Research. (2015). *The status of women in the states: 2015 poverty and opportunity.* Institute for Women's Policy Research.

Jackson, R. M. (2010). *Destined for equality: the inevitable rise of women's status.* Harvard University Press.

Jackson, R. M. (2012). *Why is gender equality elusive? [Review of Framed by gender: how gender inequality persist in the modern world by C.L Ridgeway]. Contemporary Sociology, 41*(6), 787–790. SAGE Publications, Inc.

Jones, C., & Mahony, P. (1989). *Learning our lines: Sexuality and social control in education.* London: The Women's Press.

Jordan, J., & Mossman, E. (2019). "Get out of my home and don't come back!" Empowering women through self-defense. *Violence Against Women, 25*(3), 313–336.

Kalnická, Z. (2021). First Woman Philosopher with a Doctorate: Elena Cornaro Piscopia. *Studia z Historii Filozofii, 12*(3), 97–121.

Kelly, M. L., Yeigh, T., Hudson, S., Willis, R., & Lee, M. (2023). Secondary teachers' perceptions of the importance of pedagogical approaches to support students' behavioural, emotional and cognitive engagement. *Australian Educational Researcher, 50*(4), 1025–1047.

Kennedy, M. M. (2016) How Does Professional Development Improve Teaching? *Review of Educational Research 86*, (4), 945–980.

Khurshid, A. (2017). Does education empower women? The regulated empowerment of *Parhi Likhi* women in Pakistan. *Anthropology & Education Quarterly, 48*(3), 252–268.

Kim, S.-K., & Kim, Y.-C. (2024). Single-sex vs. Coeducational schooling: an empirical study on the mental health outcomes of middle school students. *Applied Economics, 56*(14), 1689–1704.

Kim, Y.-J., Baek, S.-H., Park, J.-B., Choi, S.-H., Lee, J.-D., & Nam, S.-S. (2021). The psychosocial effects of Taekwondo training: A meta-analysis. *International Journal of Environmental Research and Public Health, 18*(21), 11427.

Koniewski, M., & Hawrot, A. (2022). Are single-sex schools more effective than the coed ones? The effect of single-sex schooling on achievement among female adolescents in Catholic schools. *Research Papers in Education, 37*(6), 907–928.

Kraftl, P. (2013). Towards geographies of "alternative" education: a case study of UK home schooling families. *Transactions - Institute of British Geographers (1965), 38*(3), 436–450.

Latif, F. (2022). A study indicating the hormonal changes in teenagers and their impact on mental health. *Revista de Psiquiatria Clínica, 49*(3), 92.

Liss, P. (2008). Isabel la Católica: Topics and Topicality. *Bulletin of Hispanic Studies (Liverpool: Liverpool University Press: 1996), 85*(3), 259–284.

MacKinnon, C. A. (2017). Introduction to symposium on Toward a feminist theory of the state. Law and Inequality: A Journal of Theory and Practice, *35*(2), 255–264.

Mason, A. (2006). *Levelling the playing field: the idea of equal opportunity and its place in egalitarian thought.* Oxford University Press.

McCall, S. D. (2019). *Girls, Single-Sex Schools, and Postfeminist Fantasies.* Routledge.

McDonough, K. (2022, February 18). We did it: Major step forward for consent education in Australia. *Law Society Journal (LSJ Online).* https://lsj.com.au/articles/we-did-it-major-step-forward-for-consent-education/

McGregor, K. (2020). Material flows: Patriarchal structures and the menstruating teacher. *Gender and Education, 32*(3), 382–394.

Mondal, A., & Baugh, A. (2024). Girls' education in colonial India: A critique on the trajectory of Savitribai Phule in the twenty-first century India. *Education 3–13*, 1–21.

Mortimer, R. (2018, March 8). *Fatima al-Fihri*: Founder of the World's First University. Manchester University Press. https://manchesteruniversitypress.co.uk/blog/2018/03/08/fatima-al-fihri-founder-worlds-first-university/.

Munoz Boudet, A. M., Rodriguez Chamussy, L., Chiarella, C., & Oral Savonitto, I. (2021). *Women and STEM in Europe and Central Asia*. Report No: AUS0002179. *In World Bank*. World Bank Publications. https://files.eric.ed.gov/fulltext/ED612413.pdf

Murnen, S. K., & Smolak, L. (2000). The experience of sexual harassment among grade-school students: Early socialization of female subordination? *Sex Roles*, *43*(1/2), 1–17.

Muscari, E., Littleton, H., & Cunnane, L. (2023). Emerging adults' perceptions of school-based sex education on consent, sexual assault, and intimate partner violence. *Sex Education: Sexuality, Society and Learning*, *23*(6), 692–708.

Musielak, D. (2020). *Sophie Germain: Revolutionary Mathematician* (2nd ed., 2020.). Springer International Publishing.

Narusyte, J., Ropponen, A., Alexanderson, K., & Svedberg, P. (2017). Internalizing and externalizing problems in childhood and adolescence as predictors of work incapacity in young adulthood. *Social Psychiatry and Psychiatric Epidemiology*, *52*(9), 1159–1168.

Narwana, K., & Rathee, S. (2017). Gender dynamics in co-education schools: a comparative study of two schools in india. *Cahiers d'outre-Mer*, *70*(276), 31–49.

Narwana, K., & Rathee, S. (2019). Gender Dynamics in Schooling: A Comparative Study of Co-educational Practices in Two Socio-cultural Milieux. *Indian Journal of Gender Studies*, *26*(3), 288–308.

Nelson, M. R. (1987). Emma Willard: Pioneer in social studies education. *Theory and Research in Social Education*, *15*(4), 245–256.

Nobel Prize Outreach. (n.d.). *Marie Curie – Biographical*. NobelPrize.org. First published in *Physics 1901–1921*. Elsevier Publishing Company, Amsterdam, 1967. https://www.nobelprize.org/prizes/physics/1903/marie-curie/biographical/

Norwegian Nobel Institute. (2014). The Nobel Peace Prize 2014 - Press Release. https://www.nobelprize.org/prizes/peace/2014/press-release/

O'Keefe, R. (2021, September 15). My school is shaming girls' bodies. *ACLU*. https://www.aclu.org/news/womens-rights/my-school-is-shaming-girls-bodies/

Office for National Statistics. (2024, October 29). *Gender pay gap in the UK: 2024*. https://www.ons.gov.uk/employmentandlabourmarket/peopleinwork/earningsandworkinghours/bulletins/genderpaygapintheuk/2024

Orchard, T., & Sangaraganesan, D. M. (2023). Exploring the links between slang and sexual and gender-based violence among university students in a Canadian city. *Sex Education*, *23*(6), 677–691.

Organization for Economic Co-operation and Development (OECD). (2020). *Education at a glance 2020: OECD indicators*. OECD Publishing. https://www.oecd.org/en/publications/2020/09/education-at-a-glance-2020_19b01e87.html

Organization for Economic Co-operation and Development (OECD). (2023). *STEM 2020 Action Plan*. OECD Publishing. https://stip.oecd.org/stip/interactive-dashboards/policy-initiatives/2023%2Fdata%2FpolicyInitiatives%2F99992259

Organization for Economic Co-operation and Development (OECD). (2024). *Education at a glance 2024*: OECD indicators. OECD Publishing. https://doi.org/10.1787/c00cad36-en

Orhani, S. (2023). *Robots assist or replace teachers in the classroom. Journal of Elementary and Secondary School*, *1*(1), 1–40.

Pahlke, E., & Hyde, J. S. (2016). The Debate Over Single-Sex Schooling. *Child Development Perspectives*, *10*(2), 81–86.

Peterson, A. (2016). The contested place of religion in the Australian civics and citizenship curriculum: exploring the secular in a multi-faith society. *British Journal of Religious Education*, *39*(2), 207–222.

Pina, D., Marín-Talón, M. C., Pagán-Escribano, M., Cormos, L. S., Ruiz-Hernández, J. A., & Godoy, C. (2022). Perception of sex in the attitude-behavior relationship in school violence: A qualitative study. *Children and Youth Services Review, 139*, 106559.

Pranevičienė, B., & Pūraitė, A. (2010). Right to education in international legal documents. *Jurisprudencija/Jurisprudence, 3*(121), 133–156.

Progressive Schooling. (n.d.). *Homeschool laws in Europe by countries.* https://progressiveschooling.com/homeschool-laws-in-europe-by-countries/

Pyrmont History. (2025). *Anderson, Maybanke Susannah.* https://pyrmonthistory.net.au/anderson-maybanke-susannah

Rafferty, Y. (2013). International dimensions of discrimination and violence against girls: a human rights perspective. *Journal of International Women's Studies, 14*(1), 1–24.

Rajiva, M. (2023). A comparative analysis of White and Indigenous girls' perspectives on sexual violence, toxic masculinity and rape culture. *International Journal of Qualitative Studies in Education, 36*(6), 1139–1154.

Ramesh, V. P., & Makeshwari, M. (2023). A Note on Generalized Sophie Germain Primes: In the Direction of Legendre's Extended Sophie Germain Primes. *Resonance, 28*(6), 923–928.

Rawat, C., & Singh, R. (2016). A Study of Emotional Maturity of Adolescents with Respect to their Educational Settings. *Journal of Social Sciences (Delhi, India), 49*(3), 345.

Reddy, L. A., Espelage, D., McMahon, S. D., Anderman, E. M., Lane, K. L., Brown, V. E., Reynolds, C. R., Jones, A., & Kanrich, J. (2013). Violence against teachers: Case studies from the APA task force. *International Journal of School & Educational Psychology, 1*(4), 231–245.

Reidy, J. (2021). Reviewing school uniform through a public health lens: Evidence about the impacts of school uniform on education and health. *Public Health Reviews, 42*, Article 1604212.

Rincker, M., Henderson, M., Vidigal, R., & Delgado, D. (2019). Evaluating the representation and responsiveness of the United Nations Commission on the Status of Women (CSW) to diverse women populations worldwide. *Frontiers in Sociology, 4*, 1–15.

Riordan, C. H. (2015). *Single-sex schools: A place to learn.* Rowman & Littlefield Publishers.

Ro, H. K., Ramon, E., & Fernandez, F. (Eds.). (2022). *Gender equity in STEM in higher education: International perspectives on policy, institutional culture, and individual choice.* Taylor & Francis.

Roberts, J., & Oppenheimer, M. (1996). Maybanke Anderson: sex, suffrage & social reform [Review of *Maybanke Anderson: sex, suffrage & social reform*]. *Australian Historical Studies, 27*(106), 179–181.

Robinson, K. H. (2005). Reinforcing hegemonic masculinities through sexual harassment: Issues of identity, power, and popularity in secondary schools. *Gender and Education, 17*(1), 19–37.

Royal Collection Trust. (n.d.). *Queen Isabella I of Spain, Queen of Castille (1451–1504).* https://www.rct.uk/collection/403445/queen-isabella-i-of-spain-queen-of-castille-1451-1504

Sabic-El-Rayess, A., Mansur, N. N., Batkhuyag, B., & Otgonlkhagva, S. (2020). "School Uniform Policy's Adverse Impact on Equity and Access to Schooling." *Compare 50*(8), 1122–1139.

Sah, S. (2022). Patriarchy and the identity of women in Indian society. *Journal of Emerging Technologies and Innovative Research (JETIR), 9*(8), 596–603.

Sahni, R., & Shankar, V. K. (2012). Girls' higher education in India on the road to inclusiveness: On track but heading where? *Higher Education*, *63*(2), 237–256.

Scarduzio, J. A., Carlyle, K. E., Harris, K. L., & Savage, M. W. (2017). "Maybe she was provoked": Exploring gender stereotypes about male and female perpetrators of intimate partner violence. *Violence Against Women*, *23*(1), 89–113.

Schiff, D. (2022). Education for AI, not AI for Education: The Role of Education and Ethics in National AI Policy Strategies. *International Journal of Artificial Intelligence in Education*, *32*(3), 527–563.

Selwyn, N. (2024). On the Limits of Artificial Intelligence (AI) in Education. *Nordisk tidsskrift for pedagogikk & kritikk*, *10*(1), 3–14.

Sikora, J. (2014). Gender gap in school science: are single-sex schools important? *Sex Roles*, *70*(9–10), 400–415.

Sina, A. (2016, October 17). *Queen Isabella of Castile: A precursor to women's empowerment*. HuffPost. https://www.huffpost.com/entry/queen-isabella-of-castile-a-precursor-to-womens-empowerment_b_58057713e4b021af3477611f?timestamp=1476753384460

Smith, G., & Watson, A. R. (2024, June 10). *New U.S. Census Bureau Data Confirm Growth in Homeschooling Amid Pandemic. Education Next.* https://www.educationnext.org/new-u-s-census-bureau-data-confirm-growth-in-homeschooling-amid-pandemic/

Spain.info. (n.d.). *Santa Cruz College in Valladolid*. https://www.spain.info/en/places-of-interest/santa-cruz-college/

Stone, K. J., Schnake, K., & Moreland, A. D. (2023). Adverse childhood experiences among early childhood educators and improving teacher health and well-being: Changes in teacher affect. *Early Childhood Research Quarterly*, *65*, 195–204.

Talk Education. (2024, January 24). *Single-sex vs co-educational schools: Which is best? Talk Education.* https://www.talkeducation.com/news/single-sex-vs-co-educational-schools-which-is-best

Tanenbaum, L. (2022, January 18). The one good thing about school dress codes. *Ms. Magazine*. https://msmagazine.com/2022/01/18/school-dress-codes-riley-okeefe-florida-high-school-yearbook-photos/

The Press Association. (2014). Female GPs outnumber male counterparts. https://www.proquest.com/trade-journals/female-gps-outnumber-male-counterparts/docview/1510626890/se-2

Thompson, M. E. (2014). Empowering self-defense training. *Violence Against Women*, *20*(3), 351–359.

Thorell, L. B., Skoglund, C., Giménez de la Peña, A., Baeyens, D., Fuermaier, A. B. M., Groom, M. J., Mammarella, I. C., van der Oord, S., van den Hoofdakker, B. J., Luman, M., Marques de Miranda, D., Siu, A. F. Y., Steinmayr, R., Idrees, I., Soares, L. S., Sörlin, M., Luque, J. L., Moscardino, U. M., Roch, M., … Christiansen, H. (2022). Parental experiences of homeschooling during the COVID-19 pandemic: Differences between seven European countries and between children with and without mental health conditions. *European Child & Adolescent Psychiatry*, *31*(4), 649–661.

Tribune India. (2025). *Education is the key to unlocking the world: A passport to freedom – Oprah Winfrey*. (23 August 2024) https://www.tribuneindia.com/thoughtfortheday/education-is-the-key-to-unlocking-the-world-a-passport-to-freedom-oprah-winfrey/

U.S. Census Bureau. (2024, December 19). Household Pulse Survey: Measuring emergent social and economic matters facing U.S. households. U.S. Department of Commerce. https://www.census.gov/data/experimental-data-products/household-pulse-survey.html

UN Women. (2024). *Progress on the Sustainable Development Goals: The gender snapshot 2024*. UN. https://www.unwomen.org/sites/default/files/2024-09/progress-on-the-sustainable-development-goals-the-gender-snapshot-2024-en.pdf
United Nations. (2017). *17 Goals to transform our world*. UN. http://www.un.org/sustainabledevelopment
United Nations. (n.d.). *Sustainable Development Goals*. UN. https://sdgs.un.org/goals
United Nations Educational, Scientific and Cultural Organization (UNESCO). (2023). Progress on girls' access to education: What the new UNESCO data reveals. https://www.unesco.org/en/articles/progress-girls-access-education-what-new-unesco-data-reveals
United Nations Educational, Scientific and Cultural Organization (UNESCO). (2025, 8 April). *Global report on teachers: What you need to know*. UNESCO. https://www.unesco.org/en/articles/global-report-teachers-what-you-need-know
United Nations Educational, Scientific and Cultural Organization. (UNESCO) (2017). *School Violence and Bullying: Global Status Report*. https://doi.org/10.54675/POIV1573
Unterhalter, E. (2019). The Many Meanings of Quality Education: Politics of Targets and Indicators in SDG4. *Global Policy*, *10*(S1), 39–51.
Vann, R. T. (2024, May 3). Historiography. *Encyclopedia Britannica*. https://www.britannica.com/topic/historiography
Victorian Government. (n.d.). *Maybanke Anderson*. Published by the Victorian Government, Australia. (Last viewed June 2025): https://www.vic.gov.au/maybanke-anderson
Washington Post. (2013, December 5). *One of the most famous quotes of the revered Nelson Mandela is about education: Education is the most powerful weapon which you can use to change the world*. The Washington Post. https://www.washingtonpost.com/news/2013/12/05
Watson, M. C. (2024). *Women in Academia: Achieving our potential*. Troubador Publishing Ltd.
Weaver-Hightower, M. B. (2010). Where the guys are: males in higher education. *Change: The Magazine of Higher Learning*, *42*(3), 29–35.
Whiting, K. (2018, October 15). *More women than men earned PhDs in the US last year*. World Economic Forum. https://www.weforum.org/stories/2018/10/chart-of-the-day-more-women-than-men-earned-phds-in-the-us-last-year/
Wikipedia. (n.d.-a). *Maybanke Anderson*. Wikipedia. https://en.wikipedia.org/wiki/Maybanke_Anderson
Wikipedia. (n.d.-b). *Sophie Germain*. Wikipedia, The Free Encyclopedia. https://en.wikipedia.org/wiki/Sophie_Germain
Wilson, R., Sellman, E., & Joseph, S. (2024). Still surviving, rather than thriving - the need to reimagine post-pandemic wellbeing according to secondary school teachers. *Pastoral Care in Education*, *42*(4), 513–533.
Wollstonecraft, M. (1792). *A vindication of the rights of woman: With strictures on political and moral subjects*. Auckland: The Floating Press.
Women in STEM. (n.d.-a). *Women in STEM: Statistics, progress and challenges (UK)*. https://www.stemwomen.com/women-in-stem-statistics-progress-and-challenges
Women in STEM. (n.d.-b). *Women in STEM USA Statistics*. https://www.stemwomen.com/women-in-stem-usa-statistics
World Bank. (2023). School enrollment, tertiary (% gross) - European Union. The World Bank Group. https://data.worldbank.org/indicator/SE.TER.ENRR?locations=EU
World Economic Forum. (2017). *The global gender gap report 2017*. WEF https://www.weforum.org/reports/the-global-gender-gap-report-2017/

World Economic Forum. (2020a). *The global gender gap report 2020.* WEF https://www3.weforum.org/docs/WEF_GGGR_2020.pdf
World Economic Forum. (2020b). *The global risk report 2020.* WEF https://www.weforum.org/reports/the-global-risks-report-2020/
World Economic Forum. (2024a). *The global gender gap report 2024.* https://www.weforum.org/publications/global-gender-gap-report-2024/
World Economic Forum. (2024b). *Shaping the future of learning: The role of AI in Education 4.0.* WEF. https://www3.weforum.org/docs/WEF_Shaping_the_Future_of_Learning_2024.pdf
World History Encyclopedia. (n.d.). *Isabella I of Castile.* https://www.worldhistory.org/Isabella_I_of_Castile/
World Population Review. (2024). *PhD percentage by country / Number of doctorate degrees per country 2024.* WPR. https://worldpopulationreview.com/country-rankings/phd-percentage-by-country
Yousafzai, M., & Lamb, C. (2013). I am Malala: The girl who stood up for education and was shot by the Taliban. Weidenfeld & Nicolson.
Yunus, R. (2021). Theorising gendered childhoods and girls' schooling: Poverty, patriarchy and girls' education in urban India. *Childhood (Copenhagen, Denmark)*, *28*(2), 279–293.
Zorrilla, N. (2022). The exclusion of early modern women philosophers from the canon: Causes and counteractive strategies from the digital humanities. *Hypatia*, *37*(1), 177–186.

Chapter 6

Abalkhail, J. M. (2020). Unmasking the career impacts of Queen Bee syndrome within organizational hierarchies: Insights from Saudi Arabia on female management relationships. *Human Resource Management International Digest*, *29*(2), 23–25.
Adamson, E., & Brennan, D. (2017). Return of the nanny: Public policy towards in-home childcare in the UK, Canada and Australia. *Social Policy & Administration*, *51*(7), 1386–1405.
Agence France-Presse. (2024, March 15). *France's lower house votes to limit 'excesses' of fast fashion with environmental surcharge.* The Guardian. https://www.theguardian.com/world/2024/mar/15/france-fast-fashion-law-environmental-surcharge-lower-house-votes
Akarsu, M. Z. (2023). Unequal Society: A Detailed Investigation of Wage and Income Inequality in the United States. *Journal of the Knowledge Economy*, *14*(4), 3771–3798.
Allsopp, J., (2012). *State feminism: co-opting women's voices.* OpenDemocracy. https://www.opendemocracy.net/en/5050/state-feminism-co-opting-womens-voices/
Arpino, B., & Luppi, F. (2020). Childcare arrangements and working mothers' satisfaction with work–family balance. *Demographic Research*, *42*(19), 549–588.
Australia Institute. (2024, May 29). Australians revealed as world's biggest fashion consumers, fuelling waste crisis [Media release]. https://australiainstitute.org.au/post/australians-revealed-as-worlds-biggest-fashion-consumers-fuelling-waste-crisis/
Australia Institute. (2020, October 8). *Coalition's tax cuts favour men over women* [Media release]. https://australiainstitute.org.au/post/coalitions-tax-cuts-favour-men-over-women/
Australian Broadcasting Corporation (2010, December 1). *Yoko gives Aussies a chance at peace.* ABC News. https://www.abc.net.au/news/2010-12-01/yoko-gives-aussies-a-chance-at-peace/2357936
Australian Bureau of Statistics. (2024a). *Employee earnings and hours, Australia, May 2023.* Australian Government. https://www.abs.gov.au/

Australian Bureau of Statistics. (2024b). *Labour force, Australia: Headline estimates of employment, unemployment, underemployment, participation and hours worked from the monthly Labour Force Survey, December 2024.* ABS. https://www.abs.gov.au/statistics/labour/employment-and-unemployment/labour-force-australia/latest-release?utm_source=chatgpt.com

Australian Institute of Family Studies. (2023). *Costs and affordability of child care.* https://aifs.gov.au/research/research-snapshots/costs-and-affordability-child-care

Australian Women Against Violence Alliance. (2020). *2020–2021 Federal Budget: Budget measure to address violence against women and their children.* Australian Women Against Violence Alliance. https://awava.org.au/

Bahl, A., De La Garza, H., Lam, C., & Vashi, N. A. (2022). The lipstick effect during COVID-19 lockdown. *Clinics in Dermatology*, *40*(4), 299–302.

Balchandani, A., Rölkens, F., D'Auria, G., Barrelet, D., González Méndez, P., & Amed, I. (2024). *The State of Fashion 2025: Challenges at every turn.* McKinsey & Company. https://www.mckinsey.com/industries/retail/our-insights/state-of-fashion

Bargain, O., Doorley, K., & Van Kerm, P. (2019). Minimum Wages and the Gender Gap in Pay: New Evidence from the United Kingdom and Ireland. *Review of Income and Wealth*, *65*(3), 514–539.

Bashevkin, S. (2014). Numerical and policy representation on the international stage: Women foreign policy leaders in western industrialised systems. *International Political Science Review*, *35*(4), 409–429.

Bassok, D., Fitzpatrick, M., Loeb, S., & Paglayan, A. S. (2013). The Early Childhood Care and Education Workforce from 1990 through 2010: Changing Dynamics and Persistent Concerns. *Education Finance and Policy*, *8*(4), 581–601.

Bennett, H. B., Balestrieri, L., & Moeladi, Y. (2022). *Are you team Cheugy or team Zoom? Decoding the new visual and verbal language of Gen Z and Millennials.* Kantar.

Bhowmik, N., & Anand, N. (2023). From models to mannequins: The oxymoronic equation of international labor law standards in the world of fashion. *Cleveland State Law Review*, *71*(3), 811–852.

Bolle, P. (2013). The International Labour Review and the ILO: milestones in a shared history. *International Labour Review*, *152* (S1), 1–12.

Bordone, V., Evandrou, M., & Vlachantoni, A. (2020). Ethnicity and grandparental child care in the United Kingdom. *Ageing and Society*, *40*(4), 713–734.

Broom, F. (2024, June 12). *France has snubbed ultra-fast fashion and people are calling for Australia to follow suit.* ABC News. https://www.abc.net.au/news/2024-06-12/calls-for-australia-to-follow-france-tax-ultra-fast-fashion/103965144

Bucher-Koenen, T., Lusardi, A., Alessie, R., & van Rooij, M. (2017). How financially literate are women? An overview and new insights. *The Journal of Consumer Affairs*, *51*(2), 255–283.

Budlender, D., Elson, D., Hewitt, G., & Mukhopadhyay, T. (2002). Gender budgets make cents: understanding gender responsive budgets. *WIN News*, *28*(2), 51–52.

Campbell, M. (2018). *Women, Poverty, Equality: The Role of CEDAW.* Bloomsbury Publishing.

Carbone, P. M. (2024, November 21). *Fast fashion may seem cheap, but it's taking a costly toll on the planet and on millions of young customers.* The Conversation. https://theconversation.com/fast-fashion-may-seem-cheap-but-its-taking-a-costly-toll-on-the-planet-and-on-millions-of-young-customers-238158

Cardona, N. (2024, December 23). *Environmental impact of fast fashion statistics (2025).* UniformMarket. https://www.uniformmarket.com/statistics/fast-fashion-statistics

Chappell, L. (2002). The 'femocrat' strategy: expanding the repertoire of feminist activists. *Parliamentary Affairs*, *55*(1), 85–98.

Coleman, M. (2019). *Gender lens on the Budget 2018–2019*. National Foundation for Australian Women. https://nfaw.org/

Coombe, J., Loxton, D., Tooth, L., & Byles, J. (2019). "I can be a mum or a professional, but not both": What women say about their experiences of juggling paid employment with motherhood. *Australian Journal of Social Issues*, *54*(3), 305–322.

Compton, J., & Pollak, R. A. (2014). Family proximity, childcare, and women's labor force attachment. *Journal of Urban Economics*, *79*, 72–90.

Cooper, E. B. (2019). The appearance of professionalism. *Florida Law Review*, *71*(1), 1–64.

Craig, L., & Jenkins, B. (2016). Grandparental childcare in Australia: Gender differences in the correlates of providing regular grandparental care while parents work. *Community, Work & Family*, *19*(3), 281–301.

Crenshaw, K. (1989). Demarginalizing the intersection of race and sex: A black feminist critique of antidiscrimination doctrine, feminist theory and antiracist politics. *University of Chicago Legal Forum*, *1989*(1), 139–167.

Crowley, J. E. (2023). The life of the party: Entrepreneurial labor, sexual harassment, and the fashion industry. *Women's Studies International Forum*, *101*, 102825.

Cumming, T., Sumsion, J., & Wong, S. (2015). Rethinking early childhood workforce sustainability in the context of Australia's early childhood education and care reforms. *International Journal of Child Care and Education Policy*, *9*(2), 1–15.

DeLaney, T. (2023, June 7). *Dressing-up professionalism: How legal professionalism reinforces social power structures through attire and how civility could help us change. University of Cincinnati Law Review Blog*. https://uclawreview.org/2023/06/07/how-legal-professionalism-reinforces-social-power-structures-through-attire/

Denniss, R., Grudnoff, M., & Scott, A. (2021). Life and taxes—international comparison of tax rates, economic performance and social well-being. In A. Scott & R. Campbell (Eds.), *The Nordic edge: policy possibilities for Australia* (pp. 36–49). Melbourne University Publishing.

Department of Industry, Science and Resources. (2022). *Second national data report on girls and women in STEM*. Australian Government. DISR. https://www.industry.gov.au/news/second-national-data-report-girls-and-women-stem#:~:text=The%202021%20Monitor%20shows%20some,increased%20by%202%252

Department of Industry, Science and Resources. (2024, August 2). *The state of STEM gender equity in 2024*. Australian Government DISR. https://www.industry.gov.au/news/state-stem-gender-equity-2024

Derks, B., Van Laar, C., & Ellemers, N. (2016). The queen bee phenomenon: Why women leaders distance themselves from junior women. *Leadership Quarterly*, *27*(3), 456.

Descouens, M., & Gerbault, V. (2021). *Generation Y's attitude towards femvertising in cosmetics: Women empowerment or purplewashing?* [Master's thesis, Umeå University].

Dhaliwal, A., Singh, D. P., & Paul, J. (2020). The consumer behavior of luxury goods: a review and research agenda. *Journal of Strategic Marketing*, *33*(1), 66–92.

Di Gessa, G., Glaser, K., Price, D., Ribe, E., & Tinker, A. (2016). What Drives National Differences in Intensive Grandparental Childcare in Europe? *The Journals of Gerontology. Series B, Psychological Sciences and Social Sciences*, *71*(1), 141–153.

Dimock, M. (2019, January 17). *Defining generations: Where Millennials end and Generation Z begins*. Pew Research Center.

Djafarova, E., & Rushworth, C. (2017). Exploring the credibility of online celebrities' Instagram profiles in influencing the purchase decisions of young female users. *Computers in Human Behavior*, *68*, 1–7.

Edwards, T. (2020). Living dolls? The role of clothing and fashion in 'sexualisation'. *Sexualities*, *23*(5–6), 702–716.

Edwards, M., & Stewart, M. (2017). Pathways and processes towards a gender equality policy. In M. Stewart (Ed.), *Tax, social policy and gender* (pp. 325–348). ANU Press.

Elson, D. (2006). Budgeting for womens rights: Monitoring Government Budgets for Compliance with CEDAW. United Nations Development Fund for Women (UNIFEM). https://gender-financing.unwomen.org/en/resources/b/u/d/budgeting-for-womens-rights-monitoring-government-budgets-for-compliance-with-cedaw

Elson, D. (1998). Integrating gender issues into national budgetary policies and procedures: some policy options. *Journal of International Development*, *10*(7), 929–941.

Escriva, A., Bermúdez Figueroa, E., & Minguela, M. Á. (2024). Dual-career Spanish couples in Europe: Work-family balance in childcare. *International Migration*, *62*(4), 160–172.

European Commission. (2018). *Gender pay gap in EU countries based on SES (2014)*. Publications Office of the European Union. doi:10.2838/978935

European Commission. (2022). *The gender pay gap situation in the EU*. https://ec.europa.eu/

Feng, Y., Chen, H., & Kong, Q. (2021). An expert with whom I can identify: the role of narratives in influencer marketing. *International Journal of Advertising*, *40*(7), 972–993.

Fitz-Gibbon, K., Segrave, M., Maher, J., & Meyer, S. (2020, October 8). *Federal budget 2020 fails women on all fronts*. Monash Lens. https://lens.monash.edu/@politics-society/2020/10/08/1381494/federal-budget-2020-a-funding-fail-for-women-on-all-fronts

Fitz-Gibbon, K., True, J., & Pfitzner, N. (2021). *More help required: The crisis in family violence during the Corona virus pandemic*. The Conversation. https://theconversation.com/more-help-required-the-crisis-in-family-violence-during-the-coronavirus-pandemic-144126

Foley, M. (2023, October 5). *Gendered discrimination and disrespect 'all too common' in legal profession*. The University of Sydney.

Fraga, L. M. (2018). *The U.S. and the high cost of child care 2018: A review of prices and proposed solutions for a broken system*. Child Care Aware of America. https://www.childcareaware.org/costofcare/

García-Sanjuán, S., Gutiérrez-García, A. I., Cabañero-Martínez, M. J., Fernández-Alcántara, M., Rocamora-Rodriguez, M. D. C., & Escribano, S. (2024). Lived experience of being a grandparent in one region of Spain: a qualitative study. *Frontiers in Public Health*, *12*, 1419207.

Gasulla Tortajada, E., Moreira, A. C., Duarte, P., & Silva, S. C. (2024). Circular Economy and Sustainability in Luxury Fashion Consumer Behavior: A Review and Research Agenda. *International Journal of Consumer Studies*, *48*(5), e13089.

Gates, M. (2016, April 13). *Unlocking the potential of women and girls*. Bill & Melinda Gates Foundation. https://www.gatesfoundation.org/ideas/speeches/2016/04/melinda-gates-unlocking-the-potential-of-women-and-girls

Geczy, A., & Karaminas, V. (2024). Power and fashion: A Foucauldian analysis of power dressing. *Foucault Studies*, *36*, 201–226.

Gomes, V. B. (2015). The economic empowerment of women—the United Nations Human Rights Council Expert Working Group on Discrimination Against Women. *Human Rights Defender*, *24*(3), 5–8.

Groza, M. P., Groza, M. D., & Barral, L. M. (2020). Women backing women: The role of crowdfunding in empowering female consumer-investors and entrepreneurs. *Journal of Business Research*, *117*, 432–442.

Guest, R. (2018). The real gender pay gap. *Policy*, *34*(2), 3–7.

Guriev, S., & Treisman, D. (2019). Informational Autocrats. *The Journal of Economic Perspectives*, *33*(4), 100–127.

Haan, K., & Reilly, K. (2024, March 1). *Gender pay gap statistics in 2025*. Forbes. https://www.forbes.com/advisor/business/gender-pay-gap-statistics/

Hall, N. L. (2021). From "period poverty" to "period parity" to meet menstrual health needs. *Med (New York, N.Y. : Online)*, *2*(5), 469–472. https://doi.org/10.1016/j.medj.2021.03.001

Hartley, R. P., Mattingly, M. J., Waldfogel, J., & Wimer, C. (2022). Paying for Childcare to Work? Evaluating the Role of Policy in Affordable Care and Child Poverty. *The Social Service Review (Chicago)*, *96*(1), 34–72.

Herbst, C. M. (2023). Child Care in the United States: Markets, Policy, and Evidence. *Journal of Policy Analysis and Management*, *42*(1), 255–304.

Hill, J. (2023). Keeping up appearances: Slow-to-evolve dress codes burden female and minority lawyers more. *ABA Journal*, *109*(5), 42–49. American Bar Association.

Hill, S. E., Rodeheffer, C. D., Griskevicius, V., Durante, K., & White, A. E. (2012). Boosting beauty in an economic decline: Mating, spending, and the lipstick effect. *Journal of Personality and Social Psychology*, *103*(2), 275–291.

Hodgson, H. (2022, October 26). *Women's budget headed in the right direction, but more needed*. The Conversation. https://theconversation.com/womens-budget-headed-in-the-right-direction-but-more-needed-193100

House of Commons Library. (2023). *The gender pay gap*. https://commonslibrary.parliament.uk/

House of Commons Library. (2024, March 4). *Women and the UK economy* [Research briefing]. https://commonslibrary.parliament.uk/research-briefings/sn06838/

IBEF. (2025, January 17). *India's internet users to exceed 900 million in 2025, driven by Indic languages*. India Brand Equity Foundation. https://www.ibef.org/news/india-s-internet-users-to-exceed-900-million-in-2025-driven-by-indic-languages#:~:text=The%20'Internet%20in%20India%20Report,of%20the%20total%20internet%20population

International Labour Organization. (2022). *The state of the apparel and footwear industry: Employment, automation and their gender dimensions*. https://www.ilo.org/sites/default/files/wcmsp5/groups/public/%40ed_emp/documents/publication/wcms_835423.pdf

International Labour Organization. (n.d.). *The fight for women's rights in the workplace – an ILO history*. https://www.ilo.org/resource/fight-womens-rights-workplace-ilo-history

Jain, N., & Chaudhri, S. (2009). History of cosmetics. *Asian Journal of Pharmaceutics*, *3*(3), 164

Joy, A., Sherry, J. F., Venkatesh, A., Wang, J., & Chan, R. (2012). Fast Fashion, Sustainability, and the Ethical Appeal of Luxury Brands. *Fashion Theory*, *16*(3), 273–295.

Jun, W., Waheed, J., & Hussain, H. (2021). Do Working Women Contribute to Higher Consumption Expenditures? *Ekonomický Časopis*, *69*(4), 379–404.

Kindy, K., & Slodysko, B. (2025, February 11). *How Elon Musk's anti-government crusade could benefit Tesla and his other businesses*. Time. https://time.com/7217291/tesla-benefits-elon-musk-trump-doge-regulations-investigations/

Kochhar, R. (2023, March 1). *The enduring grip of the gender pay gap*. Pew Research Center. https://www.pewresearch.org/social-trends/2023/03/01/the-enduring-grip-of-the-gender-pay-gap/

Kriner, M. (2025, February 4). *Musk's inauguration salute is not the only apparent fascist signal from Trump's administration*. The Conversation. https://theconversation.com/musks-inauguration-salute-is-not-the-only-apparent-fascist-signal-from-trumps-administration-248517

Kulkarni, N., & Havaldar, P. P. (2024). From Rupees to Rights: India's Struggle and Progress toward Gender Pay Parity. *Journal of Applied Sciences and Clinical Practice*, *5*(1), 1–5.

Landivar, L. C., Ruppanner, L., & Scarborough, W. J. (2021). Are States Created Equal? Moving to a State With More Expensive Childcare Reduces Mothers' Odds of Employment. *Demography*, *58*(2), 451–470.

Lansbury, N., & King, M. (2024, May 21). *The budget pledged $12.5 million for free menstrual products in Indigenous communities — Here's why it's needed.* The Conversation. https://theconversation.com/the-budget-pledged-12-5-million-for-free-menstrual-products-in-indigenous-communities-heres-why-its-needed-230118

Laughlin, L. (2013). *Who's minding the kids? Child care arrangements: Spring 2011* [Current Population Reports, P70-135]. U.S. Census Bureau. https://www.census.gov/library/publications/2013/demo/p70-135.html

Leung, F. F., Gu, F. F., & Palmatier, R. W. (2022). Online influencer marketing. *Journal of the Academy of Marketing Science*, *50*(2), 226–251.

Lombardo, E., & Alonso, A. (2020). Gender regime change in decentralized states: the case of Spain. *Social Politics: International Studies in Gender, State & Society*, *27*(3), 449–466.

Lyonette, C., Kaufman, G., & Crompton, R. (2011). "We both need to work": maternal employment, childcare and health care in Britain and the USA. *Work, Employment and Society*, *25*(1), 34–50.

Macdonald, F., & Charlesworth, S. (2013). Equal pay under the *Fair Work Act 2009*: mainstreamed or marginalised? *University of New South Wales Law Journal*, *36*(2), 563–587.

MacKinnon, C. A. (2005). *Women's lives, men's laws* (2007 paperback ed). Harvard University Press.

Martínez-López, F. J., Anaya-Sánchez, R., Fernández Giordano, M., & Lopez-Lopez, D. (2020). Behind influencer marketing: key marketing decisions and their effects on followers' responses. *Journal of Marketing Management*, *36* (7-8), 579–607.

McConnell, A. (2016). A public policy approach to understanding the nature and causes of foreign policy failure. *Journal of European Public Policy*, *23*(5), 667–684.

McIntosh, K. (2023). Patching up childcare. *Community Practitioner: The Journal of Unite CPHVA*, *96*(2), 8–10.

McKinsey & Company. (2024). *The State of Fashion 2024.* https://cd.businessoffashion.com/reports/The_State_of_Fashion_2024.pdf

McLeana, C., Naumann, I., & Koslowski, A. (2017). Access to childcare in Europe: Parents' logistical challenges in cross-national perspective. *Social Policy & Administration*, *51*(7), 1367–1385.

Meara, K., Pastore, F., & Webster, A. (2020). The gender pay gap in the USA: a matching study. *Journal of Population Economics*, *33*(1), 271–305.

Ministry of Labour & Employment. (2024, November 28). *Significant increase in women participation in workforce.* Press Information Bureau. https://pib.gov.in/PressReleasePage.aspx?PRID=2078530

Monash Vale Early Learning Centre. (2024). *Average childcare costs in Australia in 2024.* https://monashvaleelc.com.au/how-much-is-childcare-per-day/

Motwani, A. (2024). Fathers and childcare: Are gender social norms in India changing? *Sociology Compass*, *18*(1).

Mufti, R., Moazzam, A., & Basit, A. (2021). Queen Bee Syndrome a Part of Sexual Politics or another Gendered Stereotype. *Journal of Business and Social Review in Emerging Economies*, *7*(4), 835–846.

Mumford, K., Parera-Nicolau, A., & Pena-Boquete, Y. (2020). Labour supply and childcare: Allowing both parents to choose. *Oxford Bulletin of Economics and Statistics*, *82*(3), 577–611.

Mun, E. (2016). Negative compliance as an organizational response to legal pressures: the case of Japanese equal employment opportunity law. *Social Forces*, *94*(4), 1409–1437.

Muñoz Boudet, A. M., Buitrago, P., Leroy de la Briere, B., Newhouse, D., Rubiano Matulevich, E., Scott, K., & Suarez-Becerra, P. (2018). *Gender differences in poverty and household composition through the life-cycle: A global perspective*. Poverty and Equity Global Practice & Gender Global Theme, World Bank.

Munsch, A. (2021). Millennial and generation Z digital marketing communication and advertising effectiveness: A qualitative exploration. *Journal of Global Scholars of Marketing Science*, *31*(1), 10–29.

Murray, C. (2024, November 14). *What to know about Alexandre Arnault—Possible LVMH successor with close celebrity ties*. Forbes. https://www.forbes.com/sites/conormurray/2024/11/14/what-to-know-about-alexandre-arnault-possible-lvmh-successor-with-close-celebrity-ties/

NielsenIQ. (2024, April 4). *Women's Spending Power Grows as Values Shift*. NielsenIQ. https://nielseniq.com/global/en/insights/analysis/2024/shaping-success-a-deep-dive-into-womens-impact-on-the-cpg-landscape/#:~:text=Women's%20Spending%20Power%20Grows%20as%20Values%20Shift&text=As%20of%202024%2C%20women%20control,in%20the%20next%205%20years

Office for National Statistics. (2023). *Gender pay gap in the UK*. https://www.ons.gov.uk/

Organization for Economic Co-operation and Development. (2024a). *Education at a glance 2024*: OECD indicators. OECD Publishing. https://doi.org/10.1787/c00cad36-en

Organization for Economic Co-operation and Development. (2024b). *Gender wage gap*. OECD https://www.oecd.org/en/data/indicators/gender-wage-gap.html

Organization for Economic Co-operation and Development. (2019). *Gender Wage Gap in India*. OECD https://www.oecd.org/

Organisation for Economic Co-operation and Development. (2002). *Towards Sustainable Household Consumption? Trends and Policies in OECD Countries*. OECD Publishing. https://www.oecd.org/en/publications/towards-sustainable-household-consumption_9789264175068-en.html

Oxley, L. (2020, October 8). *Gender lens on the 2020 Budget paints grim outlook for women*. University of Technology Sydney. https://www.uts.edu.au/partners-and-community/initiatives/social-justice-uts/news/gender-lens-2020-budget-paints-grim-outlook-women

Palriwala, R., & Neetha, N. (2011). Stratified familialism: The care regime in India through the lens of childcare. *Development and Change*, *42*(4), 1049–1078.

Peetz, D., Colley, L., & Nolan, R. (2020). The shock doctrine and industrial relations. *Journal of Australian Political Economy*, *85*, 138–146.

Pew Research Center. (2023). *The enduring grip of the gender pay gap*. PRC. https://www.pewresearch.org/

Phadke, V. K., Gromer, D. J., Rebolledo, P. A., Graciaa, D. S., Wiley, Z., Sherman, A. C., Scherer, E. M., Leary, M., Girmay, T., McCullough, M. P., Min, J.-Y., Capone, S., Sommella, A., Vitelli, A., Retallick, J., Seetahal, J., Koller, M., Tsong, R., Neill-Gubitz, H., … Rouphael, N. G. (2024). Safety and immunogenicity of a ChAd155-vectored rabies vaccine compared with inactivated, purified chick embryo cell rabies vaccine in healthy adults. *Vaccine*, *42*(26), 126441.

Pilarz, A. R., Sandstrom, H., & Henly, J. R. (2022). Making Sense of Childcare Instability Among Families with Low Incomes: (Un) desired and (Un) planned reasons for changing childcare arrangements. *RSF: Russell Sage Foundation Journal of the Social Sciences*, *8*(5), 120–142.

Pradhan, D., Kuanr, A., Anupurba Pahi, S., & Akram, M. S. (2023). Influencer marketing: When and why gen Z consumers avoid influencers and endorsed brands. *Psychology & Marketing*, *40*(1), 27–47.

Pradhan, D., Israel, D., & Jena, A. K. (2018). Materialism and compulsive buying behaviour: The role of consumer credit card use and impulse buying. *Asia Pacific Journal of Marketing and Logistics*, *30*(5), 1239–1258.

PTI. (2025, January 16). *Internet users in India set to cross 900 mn in 2025, fuelled by surge in Indic language adoption*. Deccan Herald. https://www.deccanherald.com/india/internet-users-in-india-set-to-cross-900-mn-in-2025-fuelled-by-surge-in-indic-language-adoption-3358307?utm_source=chatgpt.com

Ramalho, R., & Trumbic, T. (2020, January 14). *Women business and the law 2020: how does the law affect women's economic opportunity?* World Bank Group.

Raman, P. (2019). Understanding female consumers' intention to shop online: The role of trust, convenience and customer service. *Asia Pacific Journal of Marketing and Logistics*, *31*(4), 1138–1160.

Rehman, F. U., Bin Md Yusoff, R., Bin Mohamed Zabri, S., & Binti Ismail, F. (2017). Determinants of personal factors in influencing the buying behavior of consumers in sales promotion: A case of the fashion industry. *Young Consumers*, *18*(4), 408–424.

Ramati-Ziber, L., Shnabel, N., & Glick, P. (2020). The beauty myth: Prescriptive beauty norms for women reflect hierarchy-enhancing motivations leading to discriminatory employment practices. *Journal of Personality and Social Psychology: Interpersonal Relations and Group Processes*, *119*(2), 317–343.

Rathi, S. K., & D'Souza, P. (2018). Abuse of topical corticosteroid as cosmetic cream: A social background of steroid dermatitis. In K. Lahiri (Ed.), *A Treatise on Topical Corticosteroids in Dermatology* (pp. 129–137). Springer Nature Singapore.

Reilly, L. (2025, February 7). *Time magazine's provocative cover puts Elon Musk behind Trump's desk*. CNN. https://www.cnn.com/2025/02/07/media/time-magazine-elon-musk-cover-trump/index.html

RMIT Communications. (2024, June 13). *France is banning ultra-fast fashion advertising – should Australia do the same?* Society and Environment. https://www.rmit.edu.au/news/media-releases-and-expert-comments/2024/june/france-fast-fashion-ban#:~:text=France's%20lower%20house%20of%20parliament,every%20garment%2C%20paid%20by%20industry

Rubin, M. M., & Bartle, J. R. (2023). Gender-responsive budgeting: A budget reform to address gender inequity. *Public Administration*, *101*(2), 391–405.

Rutigliano, R. (2020). Counting on Potential Grandparents? Adult Children's Entry Into Parenthood Across European Countries. *Demography*, *57*(4), 1393–1414.

Sanchez-Sabate, R., & Sabaté, J. (2019). Consumer Attitudes Towards Environmental Concerns of Meat Consumption: A Systematic Review. *International Journal of Environmental Research and Public Health*, *16*(7), 1220–.

Sapkota, M., & Dahal, K. (2022). Gender and politics: a feminist critique of the state. *Journal of Political Science*, *22*(1), 75–91.

Sarraf, F. (2003). *Gender-Responsive Government Budgeting*. International Monetary Fund.

Sawer, M. (2007). Australia: the fall of the femocrat. In J. Outshoorn & J. Kantola (Eds.), *Changing state feminism* (pp. 20–40). Palgrave Macmillan, UK & USA.

Sawer, M. (2016). Femocrat. In N. A. Naples, Ed. *The Wiley Blackwell encyclopedia of gender and sexuality studies* (pp. 1–2). Wiley-Blackwell.

Sawer, M. (2017). Misogyny and misrepresentation: women in Australian parliaments. *Political Science*, *65*(1), 105–117.

Sawer, M., Jenkins, F., & Downing, K. (2020). *How Gender Can Transform the Social Sciences: Innovation and Impact* (1st Edition 2020). Springer International Publishing.

Schultz, A. (2020, October 8). *'Paltry, tokenistic': women left behind in the budget.* Crikey, Private Media. https://www.crikey.com.au/2020/10/08/2020-budget-women-left-behind/

Sengupta, P., & Puri, R. (2022). Gender Pay Gap in India: A Reality and the Way Forward—An Empirical Approach Using Quantile Regression Technique. *Studies in Microeconomics, 10*(1), 50–81.

Sharp, R., & Broomhill, R. (2013). *A case study of gender responsive budgeting in Australia.* The Commonwealth. https://www.parliament.vic.gov.au/495e7d/contentassets/c413b9a8570a4f7ba7a0772795c4785e/attachment-documents/07a.-gender-equity-victoria_appx.1.pdf

Sharp, R., & Broomhill, R. (2002). Budgeting for equality: the Australian experience. *Feminist Economics, 8*(1), 25–47.

Sheen, V. (2017). The implications of Australian women's precarious employment for the later pension age. *The Economic and Labour Relations Review, 28*(1), 3–19.

Shuster, S., & Bennett, B. (2025, February 7). *Inside Elon Musk's War on Washington.* Time. https://time.com/7213409/elon-musk-us-government-trump/

Siampani, A. (2024, August 20). *Bernard Arnault surpasses Mark Zuckerberg as world's third-richest person amid LVMH share surge.* CEOWORLD Magazine. https://ceoworld.biz/2024/08/20/bernard-arnault-surpasses-mark-zuckerberg-as-worlds-third-richest-person-amid-lvmh-share-surge/

Simmons, M. E. (2020). *Human rights in the fashion industry: Discovering the origins of exploitation along the supply chain (Master's thesis).* Glasgow Caledonian New York College.

Sommerlad, H. (2016). "A pit to put women in": professionalism, work intensification, sexualisation and work-life balance in the legal profession in England and Wales. *International Journal of the Legal Profession, 23*(1), 61–82.

Statista. (n.d.-a). *Cosmetics - Worldwide.* https://www.statista.com/outlook/emo/beauty-personal-care/cosmetics/worldwide

Statista. (n.d.-b). *Fashion – Worldwide.* https://www.statista.com/outlook/emo/fashion/worldwide

Statista. (2023). *Luxury fashion—Worldwide.* https://www.statista.com/outlook/cmo/luxury-goods/luxury-fashion/worldwide

Statista. (2025). *Fashion - Worldwide.* https://www.statista.com/outlook/emo/fashion/worldwide

Sutton, J. (2004). Queen Bee Syndrome? *Psychologist (London, England: 1988), 17* (10), 593–

Szelewa, D., & Polakowski, M. (2023). Who Cares, Too? Degenderization of Childcare Policies in Europe: A Dynamic Fuzzy-Set Analysis. *Feminist Economics, 29*(3), 153–177.

The Treasury. (2022). *About Treasury.* Australian Government. https://treasury.gov.au/the-department/about-treasury

Townsend, D. C. (2019). *Foundations of Stage Makeup.* Routledge.

United Nations. (2017). *17 Goals to transform our world.* UN. http://www.un.org/sustainabledevelopment

United Nations. (2018). *The Sustainable Development Goals report.* https://www.un.org/sustainabledevelopment/progress-report/

United States Agency for International Development. (2025). *USAID: From the American people.* U.S. Government. https://www.usaid.gov/

US Census Bureau. (2022). *What is the gender wage gap in your state?* https://www.census.gov/

US Department of Labor. (2024, May 3). *Statement by Acting Secretary of Labor Su on April jobs report.* https://www.dol.gov/newsroom/releases/osec/osec20240503

Vega, Y. (2023). *Sex, Policy, and Power: The Australian Experience* (Unpublished doctoral dissertation). Swinburne University of Technology, Melbourne, Australia.
Viitanen, T. K. (2005). Cost of Childcare and Female Employment in the UK. *Labour (Rome, Italy), 19* (s1), 149–170.
Vijeyarasa, R. (2021). Gender equality in Australia: looking for the silver bullets in the short and long term. *Australian Journal of Human Rights, 27*(1), 170–177.
Vrontis, D., Makrides, A., Christofi, M., & Thrassou, A. (2021). Social media influencer marketing: A systematic review, integrative framework and future research agenda. *International Journal of Consumer Studies, 45*, 617–644.
Waghmare, A. (2025). *Access to phones and the internet.* https://www.dataforindia.com/comm-tech/
Wahyuddin, M., Setyawan, A. A., & Nugroho, S. P. (2017). Shopping Behavior Among Urban Women. *Mediterranean Journal of Social Sciences, 8*(1), 306–311.
Waqar, A., Jamil, M., AL-Hazmi, N. M., & Amir, A. (2024). Unveiling femvertising: examining gratitude, consumers attitude towards femvertising and personality traits. *Cogent Business & Management, 11*(1), 40.
Watson, M. C. (2024). *Women in Academia: Achieving our potential.* Troubador Publishing Ltd.
White, M. (2017). "There's nothing makeup cannot do": Women Beauty Vloggers' Self-Representations, Transformations, and #thepowerofmakeup. *Screen Bodies, 2*(1), 1–21.
Wikipedia. (n.d.). *The Devil Wears Prada (film).* Wikipedia, The Free Encyclopedia. https://en.wikipedia.org/wiki/The_Devil_Wears_Prada_(film)
Women in STEM. (n.d.). Women in STEM: Statistics, progress and challenges (UK). https://www.stemwomen.com/women-in-stem-statistics-progress-and-challenges
Wood, J., Neels, K., & Maes, J. (2023). A closer look at demand-side explanations for the Matthew effect in formal childcare uptake in Europe and Australia. *Journal of European Social Policy, 33*(4), 451–468.
World Bank. (2020). *Women, business and the law 2020.* https://openknowledge.worldbank.org/server/api/core/bitstreams/6c2b5974-9a3b-5249-995b-2b22e5fd7909/content
World Bank. (2024). *Gender strategy 2024–2030: Accelerate gender equality to end poverty on a livable planet.* World Bank. World Bank. (2023). *Women's economic impact on global GDP.*
World Economic Forum. (2021). The global gender gap report 2021. WEF. https://www.weforum.org/publications/global-gender-gap-report-2021/
World Economic Forum. (2024). Global Gender Gap Insight Report, 2024. WEF. https://www.weforum.org/publications/global-gender-gap-report-2024/
World Population Review. (2024). *Single-parent rates by country.* https://worldpopulationreview.com/country-rankings/single-parent-rates-by-country
Workplace Gender Equality Agency. (2024a). *Australia's gender equality scorecard: Key findings from the WGEA's dataset.* https://www.wgea.gov.au/publications/australias-gender-equality-scorecard
Workplace Gender Equality Agency. (2024b). *Employers named as noncompliant under the Workplace Gender Equality Act for 2022–23: Gender equality reporting.* Australian Government. WGEA. https://www.wgea.gov.au/what-we-do/compliance-reporting/non-compliant-list
Zheng, Y., Yang, X., Liu, Q., Chu, X., Huang, Q., & Zhou, Z. (2020). Perceived stress and online compulsive buying among women: A moderated mediation model. *Computers in Human Behavior, 103*, 13–20. https://doi.org/10.1016/j.chb.2019.09.012

Chapter 7

ABC News. (2006, July 20). Bush's 'hands-on' diplomacy with German chancellor raises eyebrows. ABC News. https://abcnews.go.com/GMA/story?id=2214892

ABC News. (2013, June 11). Germaine: The PM's appearance. Q&A. https://www.abc.net.au/qanda/germaine-the-pms-appearance/10660556

ABC Radio National. (2025, January 21). The fight to protect abortion in the United States — with Dr Angel Foster. In Natasha Mitchell, *Big Ideas*. Australian Broadcasting Corporation. https://www.abc.net.au/listen/programs/bigideas/abortion-united-states-dr-angel-foster/104470644

Acheampong, A. O., Opoku, E. E. O., & Rustagi, N. (2024). *Gender quota, women in politics, and gender parity in education*. Economics & Politics.

Agius, C., Rosamond, A. B., & Kinnvall, C. (2021). Populism, ontological insecurity and gendered nationalism: masculinity, climate denial and Covid-19. *Politics, Religion & Ideology*, *21*(4), 432–450.

Akhtar, S., & Morrison, C. M. (2019). The prevalence and impact of online trolling of UK members of Parliament. *Computers in Human Behavior*, *99*, 322–327.

Al Jazeera. (2024, March 12). UK Conservatives' top donor Frank Hester spoke of hating 'all Black women'. Al Jazeera. https://www.aljazeera.com/news/2024/3/12/uk-conservatives-top-donor-frank-hester-spoke-of-hating-all-black-women

Alexandre-Collier, A., & Drolet, M. (2022). Women and the Politics of Incivility and Discrimination: Introduction. *The Political Quarterly (London. 1930)*, *93*(1), 8–16.

Arat, Z. F. K. (2015). Feminisms, women's rights, and the UN: would achieving gender equality empower women? American Political Science Review, *109*(4), 674–689.

Australian Human Rights Commission. (2021). Set the standard: Report on the independent review into Commonwealth parliamentary workplaces. AHRC. https://humanrights.gov.au/

Bachrach, P., & Baratz, M. S. (1962). Two faces of power. *The American Political Science Review*, *56*(4), 947–952.

Bader-Zaar, B. (2011). Gender and suffrage politics: new approaches to the history of women's political emancipation. Journal of Women's History, *23*(2), 208–218.

Bailliet, C. M. (2016). A Nordic approach to promoting women's rights within international law: internal v. external perspectives. *Nordic Journal of International Law*, *85*(4), 368–394.

Ballington, J., & Borovsky, G. (2023). A normative foundation for ending violence against women in politics. In E. Bjarnegård & P. Zetterberg (Eds.), *Gender and violence against political actors* (1st ed., pp. 191–200). Temple University Press.

Ballotpedia. (2024). Election results, 2024: Analysis of voter turnout in the 2024 general election. https://ballotpedia.org/Election_results%2C_2024%3A_Analysis_of_voter_turnout_in_the_2024_general_election

Barlow, K. (2025, January 25). *Lefty Meltdown*. The Saturday Paper. https://www.thesaturdaypaper.com.au/news/politics/2025/01/25/theyre-excited-trump-duttons-inclusion-strategy

Bar-Siman-Tov, I. (2021). *Comparative Multidisciplinary Perspectives on Omnibus Legislation (1st Edition 2021*, Vol. 8). Springer International Publishing AG.

Bashevkin, S. (2014). Numerical and policy representation on the international stage: Women foreign policy leaders in western industrialised systems. *International Political Science Review*, *35*(4), 409–429.

BBC News. (2016, November 14). *Labour MP Jo Cox 'murdered for political cause'*. BBC News. https://www.bbc.com/news/uk-37978582

Beazley, J. (2024, December 18). Alan Jones: New sexual assault charges, to plead not guilty. The Guardian. https://www.theguardian.com/media/2024/dec/18/alan-jones-new-sexual-assault-charges-to-plead-not-guilty-ntwnfb
Birch, S. (2009). *Full participation: A comparative study of compulsory voting.* Manchester University Press. ProQuest Ebook Central.
Birch, S. (2016). Compulsory voting and election campaigns. In S. Birch (Ed.), *Full participation* (1st ed., pp. 59–78). Manchester University Press.
Bjarnegård, E., & Zetterberg, P. (2023). *Gender and Violence Against Political Actors.* (1st ed.). Temple University Press.
Bland, A. (2023, April 4). Why did Sanna Marin lose Finland's election? Popular centre-left leader beaten on economic message amid European trend towards political splintering. The Guardian. https://www.theguardian.com/world/2023/apr/04/why-did-sanna-marin-lose-finland-election
Bonotti, M., & Strangio, P. (2021). *A century of compulsory voting in Australia: Genesis, impact and future* (1st ed.). Springer Singapore Pte. Limited.
Boysen, J. (2005). *Angela Merkel: Eine Karriere.* Ullstein.
Bustelo, M. (2016). Three decades of state feminism and gender equality policies in multi-governed Spain. *Sex Roles, 74*(1), 107–120.
Caiazza, A. (2002). Does women's representation in elected office lead to women-friendly policy? Institute for Women's Policy Research. *26*(1), 35–70.
Cambridge University Press. (n.d.-a). Law. In Cambridge English Dictionary. CUP. https://dictionary.cambridge.org/dictionary/english/law
Cambridge University Press. (n.d.-b). Legislation. In Cambridge English Dictionary. CUP. https://dictionary.cambridge.org/dictionary/english/legislation
Cambridge University Press. (n.d.-c). Policy. In Cambridge English Dictionary. CUP. https://dictionary.cambridge.org/dictionary/english/policy
Center for American Women and Politics (CAWP). (2024, December 28). Gender differences in 2024 vote choice are similar to most recent presidential elections. https://cawp.rutgers.edu/blog/gender-differences-2024-presidential-vote
Chairiyah, S. Z. (2020). Political Identity and Citizenship Participation (Representatives) in Politics by Minangkabau Women in Post-2019 Election. *Politik Indonesia (Online), 5*(1), 139–155.
Charlesworth, H., & Charlesworth, S. (2004). The Sex Discrimination Act and international law. *University of New South Wales Law Journal, 858*(3), 1–9.
Charrel, M. (2025, January 23). *Young women are increasingly progressive, while men of the same age are leaning conservative.* Le Monde. https://www.lemonde.fr/en/opinion/article/2024/04/05/young-women-are-increasingly-progressive-while-men-of-the-same-age-are-leaning-conservative_6667508_23.html
Chaudhury, P. R. (2022). The political asceticism of Mamata Banerjee: Female populist leadership in contemporary India. *Politics & Gender, 18*(4), 942–977.
CNN. (2024). 2024 election exit polls: National results – General presidential election. https://edition.cnn.com/election/2024/exit-polls/national-results/general/president/0
Collignon D.S., Hudson, J., Rüdig, W., & Campbell, R. (2017). Inappropriate behaviour: Experiences of 2017 parliamentary candidates. Evidence from the Representative Audit of Britain Study (ESRC—ES/M500410/1). Written submission.
Committee on Standards in Public Life (CSPL). (2017). Intimidation in public life: A review by the Committee on Standards in Public Life [Report]. https://assets.publishing.service.gov.uk/government/uploads/system/uploads/attachment_data/file/666927/6.3637_CO_v6_061217_Web3.1__2_.pdf
Commons Library. (2024, February 20). Female Members of Parliament. House of Commons Library. https://commonslibrary.parliament.uk/research-briefings/cbp-7529/

Commonwealth of Australia. (1984). Sex Discrimination Act 1984 (Cth). Federal Register of Legislation. https://www.legislation.gov.au/Details/C2023C00167

Congressional Research Service. (2024, December 10). Statistics on women in national governments around the world. https://sgp.fas.org/crs/misc/R45483.pdf

Cope, K. L., Creamer, C. D., & Versteeg, M. (2019). Empirical studies of human rights law. *Annual Review of Law and Social Science*, *15*(1), 155–182.

Council of Europe. (2018). *Gender Equality Strategy 2018-2023.* (COE) November 1, 2022. https://www.coe.int/en/web/genderequality/gender-equality-strategy

Cowan, J., & Brissenden, M. (2011, January 9). *US politician shot at point-blank range.* ABC News. https://www.abc.net.au/news/2011-01-09/us-politician-shot-at-point-blank-range/1899030

Crawford, E., Rothwell, D. R., Charlesworth, H., Bailey, P., Baird, R., Bartsch, R., . . . Triggs, G. (2017). *International law in Australia.* Thomson Reuters (Professional) Australia.

Crawford, L. B. (2024). The problem of complex legislation. *Legal Theory*, *30*(1), 1–21.

Crenshaw, K. (1989). Demarginalizing the intersection of race and sex: A black feminist critique of antidiscrimination doctrine, feminist theory and antiracist politics. *University of Chicago Legal Forum*, *1989*(1), 139–167.

Crewe, E. (2022, December 22). From Queen Elizabeth to Sanna Marin, young women in politics have always faced prejudice. The Conversation. https://theconversation.com/from-queen-elizabeth-to-sanna-marin-young-women-in-politics-have-always-faced-prejudice-191306

Currell, M. E. (2024). *Political Woman.* Taylor & Francis.

Dahlerup, D. (2007). Electoral gender quotas: between equality of opportunity and equality of result. *Representation (McDougall Trust)*, *43*(2), 73–92.

Davidson-Schmich, L. K. (2011). Gender, intersectionality, and the executive branch: The case of Angela Merkel. German Politics, *20*(3), 325–341.

Davies, S. E., & True, J. (2022). Follow the money: Assessing Women, Peace, and Security through financing for gender-inclusive peace. *Review of International Studies*, *48*(4), 668–688.

de Silva de Alwis, R. (2024). Holding the Taliban Accountable for Gender Persecution: The Search for New Accountability Paradigms under International Human Rights Law, International Criminal Law and Women, Peace, and Security. *German Law Journal*, *25*(2), 289–334.

Denniss, R., Grudnoff, M., & Scott, A. (2021). Life and taxes—international comparison of tax rates, economic performance and social well-being. In A. Scott & R. Campbell (Eds.), *The Nordic edge: policy possibilities for Australia* (pp. 36–49). Melbourne University Publishing.

Department of Foreign Affairs and Trade. (2020). *The Australian Treaty Series: Convention on the Elimination of All Forms of Discrimination against Women.* DFAT. Australian Government. https://www.info.dfat.gov.au/info/treaties/treaties.nsf/alldocids/333d22b9ed69b058ca256b300024f1ba

DeSilver, D. (2022, November 1). *Turnout in U.S. has soared in recent elections but by some measures still trails that of many other countries.* Pew Research Center. https://www.pewresearch.org/short-reads/2022/11/01/turnout-in-u-s-has-soared-in-|recent-elections-but-by-some-measures-still-trails-that-of-many-other-countries/

Devereux, A., & McCosker, S. (2017). *International law and Australian law.* In D. R. Rothwell & E. Crawford (Eds.), *International law in Australia* (3rd ed.). Thomson Reuters (Professional) Australia.

Dolan, J., Deckman, M. M., Swers, M. L. (2021). *Women and Politics: Paths to Power and Political Influence.* United States: Rowman & Littlefield Publishers.

Dowse, S. (2014). The prime minister's women. *Australian Feminist Studies*, *29*(82), 391–402.

Edwards, L., & Roces, M. (2004). Introduction: Orienting the global women's suffrage movement. In L. Edwards & M. Roces (Eds.), Women's suffrage in Asia: Gender, nationalism, and democracy (pp. 1–21). Routledge.

Ehrenberg, V. (1950). Origins of Democracy. *Historia: Zeitschrift Für Alte Geschichte*, *1*, 515

Eurostat. (2025, March 7). *International Women's Day 2025: Women in national parliaments*. https://ec.europa.eu/eurostat/web/products-eurostat-news/w/edn-20250307-1

Fingerhut, H. (2016, August 16). *In both parties, men and women differ over whether women still face obstacles to progress*. Pew Research Center. https://www.pewresearch.org/short-reads/2016/08/16/in-both-parties-men-and-women-differ-over-whether-women-still-face-obstacles-to-progress/

Fleming, P. (2007). Sexuality, power and resistance in the workplace. *Organization Studies*, *28*(2), 239–256.

Ford, L. (2018). *Women and politics: The pursuit of equality*. Routledge.

Forrester, J., Finlay, L., & Zimmermann, A. (2018). Finding the stream's true sources: the implied freedom of political communication and executive power. *University of Western Australia Law Review*, *43*(2), 188–254.

Foster, S., & Markham, S. A. (2024). *Feminist Foreign Policy in Theory and in Practice: An Introduction*. Routledge.

Fredman, S. (2006). Democracy: the role of equality under the Human Rights Act 1998. *The Law Quarterly Review*, *122*, 53–81.

Gangoli, G. (2016). *Indian feminisms: Law, patriarchies and violence in India*. Routledge.

GenderNet. (2016). Gender equality in the 2030 agenda. Organisation for the Economic Co-operation and Development (OECD).

Gerangelos, P. (2018). Reflections on the executive power of the Commonwealth: recent developments, interpretational methodology and constitutional symmetry. *University of Queensland Law Journal*, *37*(2), 191–235.

Giffords. (n.d.). The issue. Giffords. https://giffords.org/the-issue/

Giffords, G., Kelly, M., & Zaslow, J. (2011). *Gabby: A story of courage and hope*. Scribner.

Gillard, J. (2014). *My Story*. Random House Australia.

Gillin, J. L. (1919). The Origin of Democracy. *American Journal of Sociology*, *24*(6), 704–714.

Giorgi, C. (2024, August 13). *More than two years on, two recommendations of the Jenkins Review remain unresolved*. Foundation for Alcohol Research and Education (FARE). https://fare.org.au/recommendations-of-the-jenkins-review-remain-unresolved/

Goodall, J. (2013, February 11). Dressing the part: Women, power, fashion, and that bloody jacket. The Conversation. https://theconversation.com/dressing-the-part-women-power-fashion-and-that-bloody-jacket-13659

Greer, G. (1971). The Female Eunuch. McGraw-Hill.

Guzman, A. T. (2012). Against consent. Virginia Journal of International Law, *52*(4), 747–790.

Hart, H. L. A. (1961). *The Concept of Law*. Oxford University Press.

Henkin, L. (1990). Law and politics in international relations: state and human values. Journal of International Affairs, *44*(1), 183–208.

Hill, L., & Rutledge-Prior, S. (2016). Young people and intentional informal voting in Australia. *Australian Journal of Political Science*, *51*(3), 400–417.

History.com Editors. (2021, October 27). Indian prime minister Indira Gandhi is assassinated. HISTORY. https://www.history.com/this-day-in-history/the-prime-minister-of-india-is-assassinated

Hooghe, M., & Kern, A. (2017). The tipping point between stability and decline: Trends in voter turnout, 1950–1980–2012. *European Political Science*, *16*(4), 535–552.

Horni, P. (2023). Voter turnout and abstention pricing: quasi-experimental evidence on the effects of a marginal increase in the monetary enforcement of compulsory voting. *Journal of Elections, Public Opinion and Parties*, *33*(1), 118–136.

Hume, T. (2016, January 12). Vladimir Putin: I didn't mean to scare Angela Merkel with my dog. CNN. https://edition.cnn.com/2016/01/11/europe/putin-merkel-dog/index.html

Inter-Parliamentary Union. (2016). Sexism, harassment and violence against women parliamentarians. https://www.ipu.org/resources/publications/issue-briefs/2016-10/sexism-harassment-and-violence-against-women-parliamentarians

Inter-Parliamentary Union. (2019, March 5). *New IPU report shows well-designed quotas lead to significantly more women MPs*. https://www.ipu.org/news/press-releases/2019-03/new-ipu-report-shows-well-designed-quotas-lead-significantly-more-women-mps

Inter-Parliamentary Union. (2021). Women in Parliament in 2020. IPU. https://www.ipu.org/women-in-parliament-2020

Inter-Parliamentary Union. (2023). Women in parliament in 2023: The year in review. IPU. https://www.ipu.org/resources/publications/reports/2024-03/women-in-parliament-2023

Inter-Parliamentary Union. (n.d.). Global and regional averages of women in national parliaments. https://data.ipu.org/women-averages/?date_year=2025&date_month=04

James, D. V., Sukhwal, S., Farnham, F. R., Evans, J., Barrie, C., Taylor, A., & Wilson, S. P. (2016). Harassment and stalking of members of the United Kingdom Parliament: Associations and consequences. *Journal of Forensic Psychiatry and Psychology*, *27*(3), 309–330.

Jenkins, J. A., & Monroe, N. W. (2015). On measuring legislative agenda-setting power. *American Journal of Political Science*, *60*(1), 158–174.

Jha, M. K., & Choubey, K. N. (Eds.). (2024). *Indian politics and political processes: Ideas, institutions and practices* (1st ed.). Routledge.

Kay, J. B., & Mendes, K. (2020). Gender, Media and Protest: Changing Representations of the Suffragette Emily Wilding Davison in British Newspapers, 1913-2013. *Media History*, *26*(2), 137–152.

Kelly, J. F. (2003). The Papacy: An Encyclopedia (review). *Journal of Early Christian Studies*, *11*(4), 582–584.

Keyssar, A. (2000). *The right to vote: The contested history of democracy in the United States*. Basic Books.

Khalid, T. (2023). Parliaments free from sexism, harassment and violence against women: A case study from Pakistan. Parliamentarian, *104*(1), 70–73.

Khan, A. (2024, March 15). Black Britons fear for Diane Abbott after a millionaire's call for violence. Al Jazeera. https://www.aljazeera.com/features/2024/3/15/black-britons-fear-for-diane-abbott-after-millionaires-call-for-violence

Kosti, N., Levi-Faur, D., & Mor, G. (2019). Legislation and regulation: three analytical distinctions. *The Theory and Practice of Legislation*, *7*(3), 169–178.

Kouba, K., & Lysek, J. (2019). What affects invalid voting? A review and meta-analysis. *Government and Opposition*, *54*(4), 745–775.

Krook, M. L. (2017). Violence against women in politics. *Journal of Democracy*, *28*(1), 74–88.

Krook, M. L., & Restrepo Sanín, J. (2020). The Cost of Doing Politics? Analyzing Violence and Harassment against Female Politicians. *Perspectives on Politics*, *18*(3), 740–755.

Kumari, H. (2021, May 26). Indira Gandhi: Paradoxes of a Prime Minister | #IndianWomenInHistory. Feminism in India. https://feminisminindia.com/2021/05/26/indira-gandhi-first-woman-prime-minister-profile/

Kumari, S.S., Sohail, R., & Benagiano, G. (2024). New perspectives on fighting violence against women. *International Journal of Gynecology and Obstetrics*, *166*(3), 1014–1022.

Kusuma, Y. S., & Babu, B. V. (2017). Elimination of violence against women and girls as a global action agenda. *Journal of Injury and Violence Research*, *9*(2), 117–122.

Larsen, E., Manns, U., & Östman, A.-C. (2022). Gender-equality pioneering, or how three Nordic states celebrated 100 years of women's suffrage. *Scandinavian Journal of History*, *47*(5), 624–647.

Lindsay, J. M. (2024, December 18). The 2024 election by the numbers. Council on Foreign Relations. https://www.cfr.org/article/2024-election-numbers

MacIntyre, R. (2025, January 23). *The US intends to leave the World Health Organization. What happens next?* The Conversation. https://theconversation.com/the-us-intends-to-leave-the-world-health-organization-what-happens-next-247997

Mackay, F., Kenny, M., & Chappell, L. (2011). New institutionalism through a gender lens: towards a feminist institutionalism? International Political Science Review, *31*(5), 573–588.

MacKinnon, C. A. (2005). Women's lives, men's laws (2007 paperback ed). Harvard University Press.

MacKinnon, C. A. (2013). Creating international law: gender and leading edge. *Harvard Journal of Law & Gender*, *36*(1), 105–122.

MacKinnon, C. A. (2017). Introduction to symposium on Toward a feminist theory of the state. *Law and Inequality: A Journal of Theory and Practice*, *35*(2), 255–264.

MacKinnon, C. A. (2020). Equality. Daedalus, *149*(1), 213–221.

Macklin, R. (2022). Abortion laws in the United States: Turning the calendar back 50 years? *Indian Journal of Medical Ethics*, *7*(3), 175–178.

Malkopoulou, A. (2014). The history of compulsory voting in Europe: Democracy's duty? (1st ed.). Routledge.

Mancosu, M., & Hopmann, D. N. (2019). Political disagreement and vote volatility: the role of familism across different European countries. *European Political Science Review*, *11*(3), 301–317.

Manfield, E. (2025, May 5). *Record-breaking number of women to enter Parliament*. Australian Broadcasting Corporation (ABC). https://www.abc.net.au/news/2025-05-05/record-number-women-elected-australian-parliament/105254048

Mata, W. (2022, December 1). Prime ministers Jacinda Ardern and Sanna Marin deny meeting because they're 'both women of a similar age'. *Evening Standard*. https://www.standard.co.uk/news/world/jacinda-ardern-sanna-marin-new-zealand-finland-both-women-similar-age-b1043842.html

McCarthy, N. (2015, May 8). *The countries where voting is compulsory* [Infographic]. Statista. https://www.statista.com/chart/3466/the-countries-where-voting-is-compulsory/

McConnell, A. (2016). A public policy approach to understanding the nature and causes of foreign policy failure. *Journal of European Public Policy*, 23(5), 667–684.

McDonald, M. P. (2020). National General Election VEP Turnout Rates, 1789-Present. *United States Election Project*. http://www.electproject.org/

Medel, R. M. (2024). When do active citizens abstain from the polls? Civic associations, non-electoral participation, and voting in 21st-century democracies. *Acta Politica*, *59*(1), 220–244.

Merkel, A. (2018, November 12). *Speech by Federal Chancellor Dr Angela Merkel at the event in Berlin on 12 November 2018 to mark the centenary of women's suffrage*. The

Federal Government of Germany. https://www.bundesregierung.de/breg-en/service/archive/speech-by-federal-chancellor-dr-angela-merkel-at-the-event-in-berlin-on-12-november-2018-to-mark-the-centenary-of-women-s-suffrage-1551696

Mushaben, J. M. (2018). The reluctant feminist: Angela Merkel and the modernization of gender politics in Germany. *Femina Politica*, *27*(2), 83–95.

National Archives of Australia. (n.d.). *Julia Gillard: Before office*. https://www.naa.gov.au/explore-collection/australias-prime-ministers/julia-gillard/before-office

National Museum of Australia. (n.d.). First women in parliament: 1943 – First women elected to Australian Parliament. https://www.nma.gov.au/defining-moments/resources/first-women-in-parliament

Newman, D. (2017). Judicial power, living tree-ism, and alterations of private rights by unconstrained public law reasoning. *University of Queensland Law Journal*, *36*(2), 247–257.

Nigam, S. (2022). *Domestic violence law in India: Myth and misogyny*. Routledge.

Njiri, K. N. (2020). *Definition of law*. SSRN Electronic Journal. Electronic article posted 29 Aug 2020. https://doi.org/10.2139/ssrn.3658011

Nourse, V. (2018). Reclaiming the constitutional text from originalism: the case of executive power. California Law Review, *106*(1), 1–44.

Olson, A., & Miller, Z. (2025, January 22). *Trump administration directs all federal diversity, equity and inclusion staff be put on leave*. Associated Press. https://apnews.com/article/dei-trump-executive-order-diversity-834a241a60ee92722ef2443b62572540

Our Bodies Ourselves Today. (n.d.). Angel M. Foster. https://ourbodiesourselves.org/people/angel-foster

Ouyang, Y. (2019). Checking executive power: a simulation model of unilateral executive behavior. Congress & the Presidency, *46*(3), 351–384.

Oxford University Press. (n.d.). Democracy. Oxford English Dictionary. https://www.oed.com/search/dictionary/?scope=Entries&q=democracy

Palmieri, S., Williams, B., & Sawer, M. (2021). Parliament as a gendered workplace: Introduction to this special issue. Australasian Parliamentary Review, *36*(2), 8–19.

Patterson, C. (2022, December 1). Jacinda Ardern, New Zealand Prime Minister, fires back at reporter's misogynistic question. People. https://people.com/politics/jacinda-ardern-new-zealand-prime-minister-fires-back-at-reporters-misogynistic-question/

Paxton, P., & Hughes, M. M. (2014). Women struggle for representation: accessing positions of power. In *Women, politics, and power: a global perspective* (pp. 66–99). SAGE Publications, Inc.

Pengelly, M., & Leingang, R. (2025, January 20). *Trump issues 1,500 'unconditional' pardons over January 6 Capitol attack*. The Guardian. https://www.theguardian.com/us-news/2025/jan/20/trump-executive-orders-jan-6-pardons

Peterson, A. (2016). The contested place of religion in the Australian civics and citizenship curriculum: exploring the secular in a multi-faith society. *British Journal of Religious Education*, *39*(2), 207–222.

Purvis, J. (2013). Remembering Emily Wilding Davison (1872–1913). Women's History Review, *22*(3), 353–362. https://doi.org/10.1080/09612025.2013.781405

Ramirez, F. O., Soysal, Y., & Shanahan, S. (1997). The changing logic of political citizenship: cross-national acquisition of women's suffrage rights, 1890 to 1990. *American Sociological Review*, *62*(5), 735–745.

Restrepo Sanín, J. (2018). The Law and Violence against Women in Politics. *Politics & Gender*, *14*(4), 676–680.

Riccardi, N. (2024, November 18). Election 2024: Voter turnout sees Republicans and Trump secure victory over Harris. AP News. https://apnews.com/article/election-2024-voter-turnout-republicans-trump-harris-7ef18c115c8e1e76210820e0146bc3a5

Ripper, F. (2022, November 30). *Jacinda Ardern shuts down suggestion she met with Finnish leader because of age, gender*. ABC World Politics. https://www.abc.net.au/news/2022-11-30/jacinda-ardern-hits-back-at-comment-about-meeting-sanna-marin/101717814

Rollins, J. (2011). Political science, political sex. *Political Science & Politics*, *44*(01), 27–30.

Rubin, E. L. (1989). Law and Legislation in the Administrative State. *Columbia Law Review*, *89*(3), 369–426.

Ruud, A. E., & Heierstad, G. (Eds.). (2016). *India's Democracies*. Universiteitsforlaget.

Sari, F., Sapriya, S., Supriatna, N., Mulyadi, H., & Hasanuddin, H. (2024). Woman Creativepreneurship Based on Minangkabau Culture. Jurnal Arbitrer (Online), *11*(1), 60–71.

Saunders, G. E. (2002). A history of Brunei (New ed.). RoutledgeCurzon.

Sawer, M. (2017). Misogyny and misrepresentation: women in Australian parliaments. *Political Science*, *65*(1), 105–117.

SBS News. (2025, January 21). 'Only two genders,' stars and stripes on Mars: Key takeaways from Trump's inaugural speech. https://www.sbs.com.au/news/article/only-two-genders-stars-and-stripes-on-mars-key-takeaways-from-trumps-inaugural-speech/npvpoif3x

Shaw, E., McCormick, D., Hartmann, H., & Gault, B. (2013). *Enhancing the status of women: how engaging women in leadership creates a more inclusive democracy and improves women's lives*. Institute for Women's Policy Research.

Sherman, C. (2024a, November 7). Trump vs. Harris: How women voters shaped the 2024 election. The Guardian. https://www.theguardian.com/us-news/2024/nov/06/election-trump-harris-women-voters

Sherman, C. (2024b, August 7). *Young women are the most progressive group in American history Young men are checked out*. The Guardian. https://www.theguardian.com/us-news/ng-interactive/2024/aug/07/gen-z-voters-political-ideology-gender-gap

Shortis, E. (2024, November 7). *Why did white women and the Democratic base abandon Kamala Harris? My view from the campaign trail*. The Conversation. https://theconversation.com/why-did-white-women-and-the-democratic-base-abandon-kamala-harris-my-view-from-the-campaign-trail-243136

Silve, A. (2015). Democratic spillovers—rent-seeking elites, mobile capital, and the coevolution of political institutions. *The Journal of Economic Literature*, *53*(3), 48–103.

Šimonović, D. (2020). Violence against women in politics. *Expert Group Meeting paper, Sixty-fifth session of the Commission on the Status of Women (CSW 65)*, UN Women. https://www.unwomen.org/sites/default/files/Headquarters/Attachments/Sections/CSW/65/EGM/SRVAW_VAW%20in%20Politics_EP9_EGMCSW65.pdf

Simpson, A. W. B. (2011). *Reflections on "The Concept of Law"* (1st ed.). Oxford University Press.

Singh, S. P. (2021). Beyond turnout: How compulsory voting shapes citizens and political parties. Oxford University Press.

Sisak, M. R., Peltz, J., Tucker, E., Price, M. L., & Colvin, J. (2024, May 31). *Trump trial deliberations: Jury hears testimony before reaching verdict*. Associated Press. https://apnews.com/article/trump-trial-deliberations-jury-testimony-verdict-85558c6d08efb434d05b694364470aa0

Sluga, G., & James, C. (2016). *Women, diplomacy and international politics since 1500* (1st ed.). Routledge.

Staszewska, E. (2025, May 10). *As some Liberals hail a 'new era', is it time to lock in gender quotas?* SBS News. https://www.sbs.com.au/news/article/coalitions-quota-question-as-labor-swears-in-record-number-of-women/dgvvi54km

Stephenson, E., & Williams, B. (2025, May 26). *Labor women make history by overtaking men in cabinet. So is the job done?* The Conversation. https://theconversation.com/labor-women-make-history-by-overtaking-men-in-cabinet-so-is-the-job-done-256603

Stevenson, A. (2019). Ms. Prime Minister : Gender, Media, and Leadership [Review of *Ms. Prime Minister: Gender, Media, and Leadership*]. *The Australian Journal of Politics and Hist\= -ory*, *65*(3), 495–497. Wiley Publishing Asia Pty Ltd.

Summers, A. (2012). Her rights at work: The political persecution of Australia's first female prime minister. *The Economic and Labour Relations Review: ELRR*, *23*(4), 115–126.

Syal, R. (2024, July 15). *Yvette Cooper says 'disgraceful scenes' of election candidate abuse must end.* The Guardian. https://www.theguardian.com/politics/article/2024/jul/15/yvette-cooper-disgraceful-scenes-election-campaign-abuse-intimidation-harassment-candidates-mps

Thompson, C., & Hedman, J. (2020). *Putting finance to work for gender equality and women's empowerment – the way forward.* OECD Development Policy Paper No. 25. Organisation for Economic Co-operation and Development. https://www.oecd.org/en/publications/putting-finance-to-work-for-gender-equality-and-women-s-empowerment_f0fa4d91-en.html

Thompson, L., & Clement, R. (2024). *Advancing feminist foreign policy in the multilateral system. International Peace Institute.* https://www.ipinst.org/wp-content/uploads/2024/03/2403_Advancing-Feminist-Foreign-Policyweb.pdf

Thomson, J. (2017). Thinking globally, acting locally? The women's sector, international human rights mechanisms and politics in Northern Ireland. *Politics*, *37*(1), 82–96.

Toshkov, D., & Cretti, G. (2024). Who is afraid of more women in politics, and why? An analysis of public opinion in 28 European countries. *Journal of Women, Politics & Policy*, *45*(3), 296–314.

UK DCMS Committee. 2019. "The Online Harms White Paper" *House of Commons*, April 8, 2019. https://assets.publishing.service.gov.uk/media/605e60c6e90e07750810b439/Online_Harms_White_Paper_V2.pdf

UN Women. (2012, August 24). *Michelle Bachelet spotlights remarkable Australian women in her address to students at the Australian National University.* https://www.unwomen.org/en/news/stories/2012/8/michelle-bachelet-spotlights-remarkable-australian-women-in-her-address-to-students-at-the-australia

UN Women. (2023, October). India passes law to reserve seats for women legislators. https://www.unwomen.org/en/news-stories/feature-story/2023/10/india-passes-law-to-reserve-seats-for-women-legislators.

UN Women. (2024, December). Only five women elected in direct presidential elections in 2024. https://www.unwomen.org/en/news-stories/press-release/2024/12/only-five-women-elected-in-direct-presidential-elections-in-2024

UN Women, & International Labour Organization (ILO). (2019). *Handbook: Addressing violence and harassment against women in the world of work.* United Nations Entity for Gender Equality and the Empowerment of Women (UN Women) and International Labour Organization (ILO). https://www.unwomen.org/en/digital-library/publications/2019/03/handbook-addressing-violence-and-harassment-against-women-in-the-world-of-work

United Nations. (2017). 17 Goals to transform our world. UN. http://www.un.org/sustainabledevelopment

United Nations, Department of Economic and Social Affairs, Population Division. (2024). World population prospects 2024: UN Summary of results. UN. https://www.un.org/development/desa/pd/

Van Halsema, C. (2019). Merkel the Mutti? A linguistic analysis of domestic language in European news media coverage of Angela Merkel. *Women and Language*, *42*(1), 7–17.

Vega, Y.K. (2023). *Sex, policy, and power: The Australian experience (Unpublished doctoral dissertation)*. Swinburne University of Technology.

Wallström, M. (2021). Sweden's feminist foreign policy. In S. Andrew & R. Campbell (Eds.), *In Nordic Edge: policy possibilities for Australia*. Melbourne University Publishing.

Walsh, K.A. *The Stalking of Julia Gillard*. Crows Nest, NSW: Allen & Unwin, 2013.

Werbinski, J. (2008). American Medical Women's Association Position Paper on Sex- and Gender-Specific Medicine. *Journal of Women's Health*, *17*(10), 1557–1557.

Wikipedia. (n.d.). *Diane Abbott*. Wikipedia. https://en.wikipedia.org/wiki/Diane_Abbott

World Economic Forum. (2024). Parity for Women Remains Five Generations Away: WEF Report. Business World. https://www.proquest.com/magazines/parity-women-remains-five-generations-away-wef/docview/3068108194/se-2

World Population Review. (n.d.). Countries with mandatory voting. WPR. https://worldpopulationreview.com/country-rankings/countries-with-mandatory-voting

Wright, C. (2018). *You daughters of freedom: Australians who won the vote and inspired the world*. Text Publishing Company.

Wright, K., & Holland, J. (2014). Leadership and the media: gendered framings of Julia Gillard's "sexism and misogyny" speech. *Australian Journal of Political Science*, *49*(3), 455–468.

Zetterberg, P., Bjarnegård, E., Hughes, M. M., & Paxton, P. (2022). Democracy and the Adoption of Electoral Gender Quotas Worldwide. *Comparative Politics*, *54*(2), 327–348.

Index

For Product Safety Concerns and Information please contact our EU
representative GPSR@taylorandfrancis.com
Taylor & Francis Verlag GmbH, Kaufingerstraße 24, 80331 München, Germany

www.ingramcontent.com/pod-product-compliance
Ingram Content Group UK Ltd.
Pitfield, Milton Keynes, MK11 3LW, UK
UKHW021058011125
464590UK00009B/138